W9-CTM-607

Armchair Warriors

Armchair Warriors

Private Citizens, Popular Press, and
the Rise of American Power

by Joel R. Davidson

NAVAL INSTITUTE PRESS
Annapolis, Maryland

Naval Institute Press
291 Wood Road
Annapolis, MD 21402

Library of Congress Cataloging-in-Publication Data

Davidson, Joel R. (Joel Robert), 1959–
  Armchair warriors : private citizens, popular press, and the rise of American power / Joel R. Davidson.
    p. cm.
  Includes bibliographical references and index.
  ISBN 978-1-59114-201-0 (alk. paper)
    1. War—Press coverage—United States—History—20th century. 2. War—Press coverage—United States—History—19th century. 3. Letters to the editor—United States. I. Title.
  PN4888.W37D38 2008
  070.4'4935502—dc22

                                                                                    2008015591

Printed in the United States of America on acid-free paper ∞

14 13 12 11 10 09 08   9 8 7 6 5 4 3 2
First printing

All photos are from the National Archives and Records Administration's Army, Navy, Air Force, and Coast Guard still pictures collections.

To my daughter Natalie, with love.
May she grow to see a world
where only historians think about war.

Contents

Acknowledgments

I am indebted to a number of individuals and organizations for their assistance on this project. My research was only possible with help from the staff of the National Archives, especially archivists Wil Mahoney, Mitch Yockelson, and Barry Zerby. I am also grateful to archivists at the Harry S. Truman and Lyndon Baines Johnson presidential libraries, as well as to the staff of the Library of Congress. Several accomplished historians gave me invaluable advice and encouragement. My thanks go out to Jeff Clarke of the Army Center of Military History, Professor Alex Roland of Duke University, and Bob Schneller of the Naval Historical Center. Finally, regards to Rick Russell of the Naval Institute Press for his early and steadfast support.

Introduction

More than most nations, the United States draws strength from the free exchange of ideas and the empowerment of individual citizens. In the American ideal, free speech and an unfettered press facilitate public discourse, while allowing superior ideas to percolate up through the citizenry and gain widespread acceptance. War demands the opposite approach: free will is overborne, individuals sacrificed, and decisions—often made in secret—flow from the top down without debate.

The American public has generally experienced the nation's wars secondhand, with little direct input on their conduct. Military service has been the exception rather than the rule. Even in World War II only one in ten wore a uniform. Individuals paid taxes, worked in factories, voted, and sometimes protested or rioted, but such expressions of support or disapproval only indirectly influenced how wars were fought. For more than a century, the conduct of warfare (though not the actual fighting and dying) has remained the province of experts—professionals educated by service academies and entrusted with carrying out national military policy. Yet ordinary citizens have felt free, sometimes even compelled, to offer their advice on America's military endeavors.

Most Americans relied on the press to make sense of what war "really" was. Popular media sources shaped public perceptions regarding military issues. Articles and editorials celebrated the country's successes in war, but also explained its setbacks, as well as the perils and opportunities that lay ahead. Despite their isolation from the actual fighting of wars, many Americans took the information provided by news accounts and attempted to play an active role in guiding the nation's military efforts. Often encouraged by media outlets, these citizens formulated a wealth of proposals aimed at solving particular tactical or strategic problems, and submitted their ideas directly to policy makers. Media accounts of military challenges together with the pragmatic suggestions they inspired together constitute an unexamined national dialogue about one of the most important aspects of

U.S. history: the use of force for national survival. The articles and letters in this book are part of America's social, intellectual, and military life, reflecting an interest in the practicalities of waging war that belies images of a supine public passively following events.

The "conversations" examined herein had historical antecedents. From the earliest days of the republic, citizens felt at liberty to offer advice regarding military issues. George Washington received a suggestion during the siege of Boston that he place his artillery at the harbor mouth to prevent British ships from entering.[1] Inventors wrote Thomas Jefferson to propose that the Navy use steam pumps to throw streams of boiling water at the Barbary Pirates' ships.[2] Abraham Lincoln received numerous letters with advice on the appointment and dismissal of generals, manpower mobilization, and the treatment of Confederate sympathizers.[3]

This phenomenon continued during the sixty years or so from the emergence of the United States as a world power through the early Cold War—the period covered in this book. During these years, American military activities spanned the globe. Coupled with the accelerating pace of technological change, this created a remarkably broad set of military problems. The press brought these issues before the public, and ordinary Americans responded with innovative proposals on a wide range of topics. These suggestions reflect the key military issues as the public saw them, forming the best available snapshot of popular conceptions regarding warfare.

The suggestions from average Americans provide a unique window into the minds of patriotic citizens grappling with issues ranging from grand strategy to individual combat. These letters, laid alongside extracts from the popular press, suggest the ways that publications both informed and motivated the public to think about war. Few of the letters reveal explicit links between news articles and the ideas proffered, but the relation is clear. The issues covered were important, the press treated them as such, and these Americans believed their solutions were valuable enough to place before the authorities.

The writers themselves are representative of America. They range across the spectrum of society, from famous scientists to semiliterate laborers, from socialites and senators to prison inmates. The letters include various shades of public opinion on war, from outright imperialism to extreme pacifism. Their authors shared a high level of creativity, a willingness to devote their energies to furthering national military goals, and a belief that the man on the street could apply common sense to solve even the most intractable military problems. The press often encouraged this belief by distilling complex issues down to a level that the ordinary reader could understand and by actively encouraging private citizens to find solutions that had eluded the "experts." This anti-intellectual or antielitist approach to governance found support in the uniquely American values of equality and individualism, keys to democratic society. Thus, the same ideals the nation fought to protect also produced the wealth of ideas about how to win the fight.

Note: All letters and articles are quoted verbatim, except for minor spelling and punctuation corrections; ellipses indicate omitted sentences or paragraphs. Where words in the original were illegible, I have used braces { } to include my best guess as to the actual language; I have used brackets [ ] to insert clarifying material, where appropriate.

CHAPTER 1

To the World Stage: The Spanish War and the Philippine Insurrection

During the 1890s Spain's brutal suppression of indigenous rebellions in Cuba and the Philippines stirred American resentment. Sensational news accounts of Spanish atrocities in Cuba increased the public's anti-Spanish sentiment.[1] After the USS *Maine* exploded in Havana harbor, prointerventionist newspapers quickly pinned the blame on Spain. The United States declared war on Spain on April 25, 1898.[2]

Sea power would ultimately determine the war's outcome. Navy leaders planned to blockade Cuba to starve out the garrison, land an expeditionary force, and tempt the Spanish fleet into battle far from its bases. Smaller squadrons would support the main effort by seizing Manila, bombarding the Spanish coast, or occupying the Canary Islands.[3] The *New York Times* reported as follows:

> It is now decided that the fleet will at once move on Havana, invest it, and at the same time hold open the Florida straits for the free transportation of troops into the island. A part of the fleet will be employed for this purpose, as well as to keep open the gulf to the west of Havana for a like purpose. As soon as the army is ready, which will be within forty-eight hours, a considerable body of troops will be thrown into the Province of Pinar del Rio, in the neighborhood, probably, of Bahia Honda, and an advance upon Havana will begin at once.[4]

This writer hoped to confuse the enemy about U.S. fleet movements:

To the Secretary of the Navy
April 29, 1898

Dear Sir:
Please read and {enact} this! In order to mystify Spanish naval authorities publicly change the names—temporarily—of the vessels in the fleet to numbers or letter

and the "numbers" or "letters" to be secretly changed at irregular or hap-hazard dates. The "key" of the numbers or letters and change of date to be in the possession of only the department and the head officer of the fleet and head officer of each vessel. Names of captains changed in the same way and only to be made known publicly after an engagement or accident.

Respectfully,
T. F., Coffeyville, KS[5]

The United States possessed a larger fleet than Spain, but changes in naval technology threatened the established calculus favoring the side with more guns and armor. Even as a *Harper's Weekly* article compared the tonnage and firepower of the rival ironclads, accompanying photos showed the successful test of Holland's remarkable new submarine.[6] The submarine's principal weapon, the motor torpedo, already equipped many navies. The *New York Times* called the torpedo "a miniature battleship within itself, with magazines and a silent little gunner, who only fires at the right moment; a pilot, who gets his instructions before starting on his voyage and conducts his ship by the course laid out; an engineer force that works silently and effectively, with never a thought of the danger to be encountered, all working in unison for one common cause, none human, but all the result of man's ingenuity."[7]

Harpers' Weekly warned that torpedoes might negate America's naval advantage:

While the batteries of heavy guns and light guns are the armaments depended upon for daytime naval fighting, there yet remains the modern and supposedly powerful equipment of torpedo boats to be taken into account for night attack and foggy-weather operations and battle-smoke assault. In this regard Spain's navy greatly outranks that of this country. The report summarizes 56 torpedo boats for Spain, while it credits our own navy with but 21. Should these little monsters prove as effectual as theory would make them appear, then Spain's naval equipment much more nearly balances that of this country.[8]

This letter proposed a defense against surprise attack by torpedo boat:

Secretary of the Navy
May 17, 1898

Had better send a dispatch boat immediately from Key West informing Sampson that the Spanish fleet will make a dash for Havana harbor in the night time. Their torpedo boats will lead, in their efforts to destroy our battleships. All our ships should have a special colored light and in a certain place on their vessels in combination with other lights so as to distinguish between friend and foe, as the

Spaniards may adopt our lights and by this means get close enough to destroy our vessels. If all the cables were cut leading from Havana but one, and that one cut and connected with a dispatch boat anchored close to shore, we could regulate Spain's news and direct her battleships so as to meet ours. I have done all I can to help our dear country. You will have to govern yourself accordingly.

W. R., Washington, DC[9]

American torpedo boats could use decoys and camouflage to surprise Spanish warships, as the next two writers suggested:

Secretary of War
April 29, 1898

Dear Sir:
. . . My plan is this, that we make a vast number of barrels or on any other order best to imitate a torpedo boat and paint these green and fill with sand or any other substance of enough quantity so as enable them to float with the water and to make them up in every respect similar to that of torpedo boats so as to be unable to discriminate these from the genuine. If successfully built these mocking torpedo boats will serve for four purposes. 1st. When we put a number of these mocking torpedoes to sea they will attract the attention of the Spanish Navy and cause them to order some of their ships to sail in defense to protect the port these mocking torpedoes will appear to be sailing for, by which course we will use up some of their ships with no benefit to them. . . . On the Spaniards being unable to discriminate from these mocking torpedo boats to the genuine, and on their discovering the trick, they may overlook these "mockers" to such an extent as to leave one of our genuine torpedo boats to get right by them. . . .

Your most humble servant,
L. R., Philadelphia, PA[10]

Theodore Roosevelt, Esq.
May 5th, 1898

Dear Sir:
With apologies with the liberty I take in addressing you, I venture to ask you to give the following war idea a few moments' consideration. As the modern searchlight has proved such a valuable adjunct to marine warfare, I propose to reduce its efficiency by hiding our ships (especially torpedo scouts) behind a screen of wire gauze, roughly painted in imitation of active water. I believe this could be

so arranged as to cover the entire outline of a vessel and admit of being removed immediately to avoid interference with the action of the vessel. That this idea is practicable and valuable in recommending I am convinced, the application I leave to you as the worthy representative of the navy of my adopted country. I remain,

Dear Sir, your respectful fellow subject (formerly British),
A. S., New York, NY[11]

Once hostilities began, the Navy set its strategic plans in motion. Within days, an American squadron arrived off Havana, Cuba's largest seaport and the seat of Spain's colonial government.[12] In the Pacific, Admiral Dewey's small Asiatic Squadron sailed for the Philippines from Hong Kong. Barely a week into the war Dewey's force destroyed Spain's Philippine squadron in Manila Bay. Although Dewey had won a crushing victory, his small force would be no match for the remainder of the Spanish fleet, should it sail to Manila. The *Chicago Tribune* warned, "If Dewey is not to be reinforced then he should be ordered home. If those islands are to be left as a prize to any European power which wants them and Dewey's glorious victory is not to be utilized, then it is inexplicable why he should be left there in danger of being crushed by an overwhelming force."[13]

The shortest route from Spain to the Philippines lay through the British-controlled Suez Canal. The *Atlanta Constitution* speculated, "[T]he Spanish squadron might make a quick passage into the Pacific through the Suez Canal and attack Dewey at Manila. It is said that contrary to the common understanding, the Suez Canal is open to the warships of belligerent powers so that if the Spanish choose to take this course they would have a long start of any pursuing fleet from our side of the Atlantic."[14]

This writer proposed a covert operation to thwart a Spanish relief expedition:

Engineer-in-Chief, U.S. Navy
May 14, 1898

Dear Sir:
It seems to be pretty hard to tell what the Dagos are up to with this game of hide and seek with their fleets. Possibly there may be something in the rumor that they will send a fleet from Cadiz through the Suez Canal to try to get the better of Dewey. There are plenty of places where they could coal from colliers on the way. If they should make such a start, they could get to Manila before we could head them off. It has occurred to me that a valuable delay would be caused if some steamer should accidentally sink in the Suez Canal just ahead of the Spanish fleet. Suppose for instance that somebody should obtain a British tramp steamer (a big one), load her with coal and send her to Alexandria to wait orders. When the Spanish fleet

starts, the steamer might be ordered to go to Aden to discharge cargo, and she might time the departure so as to get into the canal a little ahead of the Dagos. . . . Now suppose that while the steamer is in one of the narrower parts of the canal, the captain should proceed to test the thermostats. And further suppose that by mistake, detonating fuses had been placed in the boxes instead of thermostats. When the captain closed the testing circuit (the switch having previously been kept under lock and key) a hole would most likely be blown in the side of the ship. If the captain should lose his head and get the steamer pointed across the canal before she sank, there would be the devil to pay. . . .

Very truly yours,
A. M., Cambridgeport, MA[15]

The Naval War Board thought little of this plan: "It appears to the Board that the method proposed for sinking this vessel in the Suez Canal is so complicated that the facts could scarcely fail to transpire, and would implicate us in a breach of neutrality of the canal affecting the commerce of the whole world; and particularly of Great Britain, who is also a large owner of canal stock, and whose good will is considered of great importance at the present time."

The *New York Times* discounted the danger to Dewey: "The dispatch of the remaining Spanish squadron would leave the coast of Spain and her possessions in the Mediterranean and the Atlantic absolutely undefended and at the mercy of an American fleet which, combined, is far more powerful than Spain's fleet on the Atlantic. Talk of an expedition to recover the Philippines has served its entire purpose when it has amused the public of Madrid."[16]

This writer argued that the threat of a transatlantic naval sortie might keep Spain's fleet at home:

The Strategy Board
May 11, 1898

Gentlemen:
I see that there is talk of the Spaniards sending a strong force against Dewey. It occurs to me that if you will have it hinted strongly in the press that in that event, a strong fleet and 20,000 men will be sent by us towards Spain, you will deter them. If they send a strong force against Dewey, you can shake them up around Spain; if they send a weak one, you can both shatter them. Every one of us here is greatly pleased at the plan of sending 10,000, or even 20,000 men to aid Dewey—as well as at the idea of putting overwhelming force in both Cuba and Puerto Rico.

Yours most respectfully,
R. H., St. Louis, MO[17]

Perhaps an actual transatlantic offensive could do more than help Dewey. The *Washington Post* believed the "Canary Islands could be easily seized, and if such a step—or the more radical policy of bombardment—would bring Spain to a realization of the futility of continuing the struggle, the end of the war might come without bloodshed in front of Havana."[18]

Secretary of Navy
May 12, 1898

Dear Countryman:
I have been greatly interested in present war and by a quiet study, I have formed a plan, both strategic, and stern. I think that if you study it over you will find it to be a great help towards exterminating the Spanish Navy. The plan will also help to capture the Canary Islands. A new squadron is to be formed without injuring Sampson's or Schley's force. The squadron which I have formed in this plan would be without any equal on the Atlantic waters. . . . According to my plan our vessels of this squadron could leave on the night of the 22nd and take a straight path for Cadiz going at a rate of 325 miles a day reaching Cadiz in 9 or 10 days and destroying the vessels there as they will be completely ignorant of this squadron. After destroying the Spanish vessels at Cadiz take a straight path for the Canary Islands, reaching Las Palmas in 4 days. Bombard the city and after reducing the city land the 12,000 soldiers to keep order. . . . I am well acquainted with the Spaniards and their tricks. They are always at cafes at night, leaving the vessels at the mercy of their crew and even they are nearly always playing cards or something else. They are generally always full of wine. Please take advantage of this plan and I will assure you that United States will profit more from this plan in 20 days than otherwise in 5 years. . . . I will not sign my name. I'll let you reap the honors of the victory.

Taylor, TX[19]

This writer proposed a preemptive invasion of the Spanish homeland:

Gen. R. A. Alger
March 16, 1898

My dear Sir:
I take the liberty of submitting for your personal consideration a suggestion in connection with a possible declaration of war with Spain; namely to organize a Brigade of Volunteers privately and quietly, including attachments from various regular Army Regiments to form the nucleus thereof; and to send the same in small detachments, going as civilians abroad on various passengers, to be united when

abroad when aboard the *Amazonas* and other war vessels which may be acquired abroad; and with the object of having the same landed quickly on the coast of Spain at some point which could be held until a large force could be sent from here. Even if unsuccessful the loss would be immaterial. And if successful the moral effect would aid in materially shortening the duration of the war; and would be in line with making the conflict short, sharp, and effective....

Yours very respectfully,
J. B., New York, NY[20]

The overstretched U.S. Navy could spare few ships to reinforce Dewey, and international laws forbade neutrals from selling military equipment to either side. These two writers proposed strengthening Dewey while observing neutrality laws:

Honorable John D. Long, Secretary of the Navy
May 17, 1898

Sir:
For a portion of the Philippine Islands Japan would rent us several of her most powerful cruisers or battleships. By this means we could resist all reinforcements from Spain that may be sent against Dewey. It would be a great dishonor to our country to allow such a brave man as Dewey to be sacrificed. I've no doubt the Japanese minister would telegraph our wants to his country if it is the will and pleasure of the United States. We would only want them for a few weeks or months. It could be arranged that the Japanese captains could be instructed by our captains so that the Japs could handle the guns in case they did not want our gunners to handle them. The Grecian Navy would be a great benefit to us if we would buy or rent it immediately. We want two heavy battleships at the Philippines, and Dewey should set secretly in the night time mines so as to destroy the Spanish ships going to him.

Respectfully,
M. R., Washington, DC[21]

Secretary Long, U.S.N.
May 17, 1898

Honorable Sir:
Having the interest of my country at heart, in the present war, and feeling that its navy in the Pacific is inadequate to cope with the situation in the event of

Spain sending a strong fleet to recapture the Philippine Islands, I beg to offer a suggestion which (If it is worth anything) you may consider. Is it not possible to furnish President Dole, of the Hawaiian Republic, sufficient funds to purchase one or more good men-of-war and then annex the Islands to the United States. I understand they have not declared neutrality and thought possibly he might be able to buy a British or other war vessels before they do so and in the event of their considering making a stand in harmony with the U.S. they might make such purchases ostensibly for their own protection. If the above is ridiculous trust you will pardon my ignorance and carry out some feasible plan to furnish our Great Hero (Admiral Dewey) such equipment as is necessary to meet any possible contingency.

Very respectfully a citizen,
H. B., Chicago, IL[22]

Dewey needed troops to seize Manila, but the Army would need months to assemble and ship units to the Philippines. This writer suggested an alternative source of manpower:

Hon. William McKinley
June 14th, 1898

Dear Mr. President:
. . . [I]t would be an easy matter to secure a large body of acclimatized Europeans along the Asiatic coast between India and Japan, who would be fearless soldiers under good officers, and would save the cost of transportation of a large body of troops from this country. . . . All English speaking soldiers and fighters who would, however, ask about $20 per month and subsistence. Captain Smith also estimates that 20 ships could be purchased along the coast at a cost of not more than a million dollars; good ships for colliers and transports. He also informs me that by shipping these men to procure coal, there would be no difficulty in afterwards bringing them to the Philippine Islands, where they would be glad to enlist. . . . Possibly these facts may interest you, as it may be necessary to substitute for the unacclimated American troops, some of these hardy veterans of the Asiatic coast, who can do the hard work in the interior and with storming parties. By telegraphing Dewey, giving him ample means, and authorizing him to organize this force under someone like Ward or Gordon, you would save many valuable lives and have men to garrison coaling stations every 2,000 miles around the world. In making these suggestions, believe me to be,

Very respectfully,
V. C., Albany, NY[23]

Many Americans feared that Spain would strike directly at the United States. According to the *Atlanta Constitution*, "[A] Spanish squadron, consisting of four ironclads and two torpedo boat destroyers, sailed for the United States yesterday. It was rumored that the squadron was to steam direct across the Atlantic and bombard northern ports of the United States."[24] Calls for protection flooded in from coastal towns, and the Navy held a "flying squadron" of fast warships in reserve to intercept a Spanish raid.

These two writers submitted plans to thwart such an attack:

Army and Navy Department
May 8, 1898

There are too many bright lights from Patchogue to Nortons Point, Coney Island. Close and shutter darken all seaward windows from shore to half [a] mile back. Permit no lights in any seaward rooms or observatories. Remove all flag poles from private houses and hotel summer resorts on range.

C. S., Wilkes-Barre, PA[25]

To the editor of the *New York Times:*
When the Cape Verde fleet disappeared from human ken for a week or more, we heard a good deal about Spanish "treachery." To those of us who know something about naval movements, the proper word should be "strategy," and in this the Spaniards have shown themselves to be better than we. While so many ideas are advanced as to the Spanish plans, I should like, also to advance one that I have not yet seen mooted. . . . For all we know, the Cadiz fleet may have left Spain several days ago; and I believe it has done so, while we are getting daily dispatches of it being prepared for Manila. What then, is its destination? My answer is, our seacoast towns, whose fortifications all the nations of the world contemn [*sic*]. . . . Our second line of defense, instead of patrolling our coast on the hundred-fathom line, should strike out 300 or 400 miles out into the Atlantic and try and reach the rendezvous with the Spanish colliers before the Cadiz fleet does. That fleet, composed of battleships like the Pelayo and Numancia, is meant for heavy work against fortifications, where they can both give and take. Deprive them of their coal, and they are helpless. . . .

Ex-Navy[26]

Spanish forces also threatened America's merchant fleet. The Navy received (and ignored) numerous requests for protection by ship owners. This writer suggested a ruse to thwart commerce raiders:

Secretary of the Navy
April 28, 1898

Dear Sir:
Would it not be practicable and effective to disguise some of our battle ships giving
them the appearance of merchantmen and using them as decoys for Spanish prize
chasers? At the proper moment the disguise could be temporarily dropped and our
guns frown upon the enemy in a menacing manner or if necessary send a projectile
or dynamite shell into them before they could recover from their astonishment.
If this suggestion is worthy the consideration of the department I shall be glad to
know it. If not, no damage is done in the sending of it.

Yours very respectfully,
O. S., Joppa, MI[27]

Both navies used coal-fired ships, so the availability of coaling stations had a major
impact on naval planning. The *Chicago Tribune* argued, "[A] steam navy is useless
beyond the range of its coaling base. As applied to the future of the American
continents this fact promises to be a most powerful ally of the Monroe doctrine. . . .
Spain must resign itself to the loss of Cuba and of everything else on this side of
the Atlantic for one imperative reason, if for no other: Steam navies cannot operate
beyond the range of their coaling base."[28] The *Los Angeles Times* reported that
economic strife in England was hampering Spanish operations: "It is impossible
for Spain to procure coal in England, because of the strike now in progress in the
mines and because the English coal dealers refuse to receive promises to pay, and
will only sell to the Madrid government for cash."[29]

This writer suggested economic warfare to reduce Spain's coal supply:

Secretary of the Navy
April 26, 1898

As a means of embarrassing Spain it occurs to me that if a secret commission was
appointed with the necessary funds to go Wales England and get in touch with the
strike leaders and with money support and prolong the present strikes in the coal
mines much good could be accomplished.

Very truly yours,
T. F., New York, NY[30]

Despite the excitement over Dewey's victory, Cuba remained the main prize. The loss of Havana, Cuba's largest port and principal garrison, would cost Spain the island. The *Chicago Tribune* asked, "The left wing [Dewey] having been so successful, why does not the right wing, which has as its objective Havana, Cuba, and the Spanish soldiers encamped there, make a forward movement also, so that Spain may be bundled out of its American possessions as it has been rushed out of those it held in the Pacific?"[31]

Spanish defenders had invested considerable resources fortifying Havana. Employing recent developments in naval technology, they supplemented their traditional fortifications with three lines of underwater mines, both electrically fired and contact types, as well as a pair of torpedo tubes supported by powerful searchlights.[32] The *Los Angeles Times* published the following:

> The dynamite cruiser *Vesuvius*, which sailed south Monday, is to clear a path into Havana harbor. Her business will be to explode the submarine mines that carpet the entrance to the inner harbor between Moro Castle and Punta Brava. At that point the channel is only about 500 feet wide. The *Vesuvius* will make a path by dropping shells filled with a thousand pounds of nitro-gelatine in the water above the mines. The shells will be timed to explode four seconds after they strike the water. That will be sufficient time for them to sink to the bottom, where the Spanish mines are planted. Then they will explode. The concussion will either explode the mines or break the connections, so that they will be rendered harmless, Each shell is expected to clear a path 100 feet wide.[33]

This writer offered an alternative method for clearing electrically fired underwater mines:

Secretary of War
May 2nd, 1898

Dear Sir:
Please allow me to suggest to the Naval Board of War a plan to blow up the mines in and around the harbors held by the Spanish—Havana—for instance. That is to have one of the swiftest and lightest draft boats to carry trailing behind attached to a strong metallic cable say 300 feet long a strong rod of steel or copper, the surface made as a rat tail file, with a heavy metallic core at the extremity to drag deeply in the mud at the bottom of the bay and heavily charged with electric current. In making a circuit across the wires connecting from the shore to the mine, this file would cut away the cover of any cable and explode the mine as soon as contact is made. A small boat could make a swift circuit most any night and almost free of

danger. The same device with some heavy hooks substituted for the core could be used to grapple and break the connecting wires of the Enemy.

Respectfully submitted,
J. B., Mexico, MO[34]

This writer proposed using high explosives to force the entrance to Havana harbor:

Honorable J. Long
May 18th, 1898

Sir:

In view of the fact that actual operations by an army in Cuba are now impossible I would like to suggest a plan by which, perhaps, Havana can be taken by the ordinary light armed vessels near there with no loss whatever. In substance it is this: Load a barge with say 100 tons of dynamite, have it towed under cover of darkness as close to Morro as the safety of the crew will permit. Point both the tug and barge straight for the entrance to the harbor, put on full steam and let both go as far as they can get toward the harbor, the crew leaving the tug at the same time in a small boat. The barge may get close up under Morro, perhaps into the channel, but wherever they get before the time fuse explodes the cargo it will do good. If several barges are sent in a few minutes apart each successive one will get further into the harbor and after the third explosion no soldier will remain in Morro or Cabanas and by the time your vessels can get to Morro there will be no gunners there, as human beings simply cannot stand such shocks, even at a considerable distance. The first would be a surprise, the second, nearer, would be unbearable and the third would finish the {game}, and the third might get as far as Cabanas. The cost would be very small compared with any army operations and Havana, next morning, would belong to the Navy. The explosions could clear out a portion of the channel and even should the small guns in Morro stop the first barge, its explosion there would leave the Morro gunners in no condition to stop the second. As no danger to life exists in this plan and it is cheap, it seems to me to be worth consideration.

Very truly,
S. H., New York, NY[35]

Spanish leaders decided to challenge the U.S. fleet off Havana, and dispatched their best remaining ships across the Atlantic with the ill-defined mission of somehow raising the blockade. For nearly a month, these ships played a cat-and-mouse game with superior American forces. Short of coal and despairing of victory, they took refuge in the port of Santiago in southeastern Cuba. American scouts soon discovered the Spanish squadron in Santiago harbor, setting the stage for the war's decisive campaign.

The guns and underwater mines covering Santiago's narrow harbor entrance were enough to deter the American fleet from attacking the port. The *Chicago Tribune* noted, "One man of war stationed on the inside of the outer channel could hold at bay the combined fleets of the world. The same advantage to a naval resistance is offered here as was offered the Greeks in the pass at Thermopylae. The ships could only enter one at a time and as they poked their noses past the granite wall at the entrance they could be blown out of the water by a well equipped sea fighter or battery."[36] When pressured to force the entrance, the U.S. commander on the scene replied that to "throw my ships to certain destruction upon mine fields would be suicidal folly."[37]

The *Washington Post* favored preserving the trapped ships: "The probability is, therefore, that the Spanish cruisers will be kept bottled up until such time as Spain surrenders to the United States, when four most excellent vessels will be transferred to the American flag without the loss of a single life. The fleet is just as helpless in Santiago harbor as though it were at the bottom of the deep blue sea, and it is much more available as part of the future assets of the United States."[38] The Americans tried to seal the harbor by sinking an old collier in the narrowest part of the entrance, but the plan failed when Spanish artillery destroyed the ship's steering controls.[39]

Army troops assembling for a landing near Havana instead prepared to seize Santiago, shifting the campaign's entire focus to this hitherto obscure port. *Harper's Weekly* opposed the change, arguing the "Spanish fleet, being trapped and amply guarded, can no longer be considered a menace. It would be wasting time and effort to land troops at Santiago, for the main issue of this campaign is the taking of Havana, and as it looks now, this war will not be over until the Cuban capital surrenders, and the war will end with the fall of that city."[40]

In mid-June, about seventeen thousand U.S. soldiers landed on the coast near Santiago. The limited scale of this campaign proved a blessing, as the Army was having difficulty making the transition from chasing Native Americans to fighting a modern war. To deal with the debilitating effects of the Caribbean climate, the Army raised regiments of "immunes," men better able to withstand heat and tropical diseases. Among these so-called immunes were African Americans serving in segregated units. Americans had mixed feelings about organizing the sons of slaves into military units. The *Chicago Tribune* commented as follows:

There seems to be a feeling in some parts of the South that to allow the negroes to fight alongside the white men would be an admission of equality, which cannot be tolerated. . . . The black men of the South, properly handled, would be excellent soldiers. Their indifference to tropical heat and their comparative immunity from certain diseases would enable them to endure some of the disagreeable features of a Cuban campaign better than white soldiers. Therefore the colored men should be given a chance to fight whenever they show any willingness to do so.[41]

This letter proposed recruiting African Americans to fulfill a special role in Cuba:

To His Excellency, William M'Kinley
April 18, 1898

. . . It is plain to see from your message that if you fail peacefully to induce Spain to allow you to pacify Cuba you will use force, in which event, judging from the movements of our army, the plan is to invade Cuba, and in that case Spain will no doubt make the effort to isolate the American force in Cuba by cutting off its supplies and retreat with its navy. I most respectfully suggest that it can at least do no harm to provide against such a contingency as much as possible. The island of Cuba, as I understand it, is practically depleted of all sustenance for an army large enough to be of effect there. For the above reasons, in connection with regulating and establishing the material industrial affairs of Cuba, it occurs to me that it would be a good idea to add to the army an agricultural branch, to be composed primarily of southern negroes mostly from lower Mississippi, Louisiana, Alabama, and Georgia; the strength of which would be about one tenth of the entire force. In other words, I assume from my experience as a southern planter that one man properly equipped for agricultural purposes will be able to produce enough in Cuba to sustain at least ten fighting men as well as himself. . . .

A. M., Philadelphia, PA[42]

American troops hoped to receive valuable assistance from Cuban rebels, whose forces under General Gómez controlled much of the countryside. Some observers hoped that the insurgents would enable the United States to fight a proxy war in Cuba. Given the small number of trained American soldiers available, the prospect of fighting Spain with American guns and Cuban lives appealed to the *New York Times*: "Gómez has said that he could put a force of 100,000 men in the field if he had rifles and ammunition for them. Army officials are of the opinion that if this country would furnish arms and ammunition it could at once raise in Cuba itself an effective force of 80,000 to 100,000 men to operate against the Spanish armies, which together with the 15,000 to 20,000 regular American troops, ought to be able to clean the Dons out of Cuba in very short order."[43]

This writer proposed a plan to recruit Cuban rebels:

General Alger
April 25, 1898

This is not intended to be an elaborate outline, but a hasty letter suggesting, rather than covering, the points. . . . I recommend that a bill be immediately passed by Congress, placing soldiers of the Cuban army on the same footing as our own, as regards pay, clothing, rations and medical attendance. The people of Cuba are hungry. When men know that plenty reigns in the camps of Gomez, that food, clothing, medicine and pay are there, he will have 100,000 men in no time at all—all the men he can handle or will want. Your business is to immediately get arms and munitions to him in boundless quantities. Every Cuban who wants a gun and a hundred cartridges should be supplied instanter and not be told to "Wait! Wait! Wait!". . . . I believe that a land blockade of Havana could be established at once. Without serious trouble, a line of entrenchments could be drawn around Havana from water to water, and the American fleet made the base of supplies—just as was done at Vicksburg and with the same victorious result. If the American fleet is beaten (which is improbable) Cuba would be so well armed that Spain could only hold Havana. If our fleet maintained its blockade, Havana would only be a trap for the Spanish army. . . .

Respectfully,
C. P., Philadelphia, PA[44]

This writer suggested another Spanish possession ripe for an American-sponsored insurrection:

Secretary of War
May 12, 1898

Sir:
I am a native of Morocco but a naturalized citizen of this country. I have the honor to inform you that I think I can be of great service in view of the present war with Spain to this my adopted land. There is a place called Mlilia [in Algeria] which is on the Riffian coast [in northern Morocco]. There was a war there in 1894 between the Riffians and Spain. The result was that the Riffians captured Mlilia and killed many officers and Spaniards. The Spanish government then asked the Sultan of Morocco to stop the Riffians, and force them to leave Mlilia. The people

are still opposed to Spanish rule, and it takes but a spark to cause them to rise and overthrow the hated Spanish rule. Once lost it would never be regained. I propose to visit the place and incite an insurrection secretly. . . . As I am an American, as soon as I should capture the town I would raise the stars and stripes and declare it under the dominion of the United States. . . . It will cause a general uprising in all the Moorish countries which are at present under Spanish control and even those not under it, perhaps the Moorish government will be enabled to seize an opportunity long expected and waited, to wrest some of her territory from Spain. . . . The capture of Mlilia would be a great loss to the Spanish government in many ways and would afford the United States a coaling station near Gibralter. If you favor the plan, You will greatly oblige me by addressing,

Your obedient servant,
H. Z., New York, NY[45]

Technological developments had radically changed land warfare since Appomattox. Smokeless gunpowder enabled troops to fire their weapons without producing a telltale white smoke cloud, and high explosive shells with sophisticated fuses exponentially increased the lethality of artillery. For the first time, a single man (or animal) could carry enough explosives to destroy important military targets, as suggested by this writer:

War Department
May 12, 1898

Honorable Sir:
An Idea has occurred to me which in the present crisis might be availed of by the War Department, Viz: That St. Bernard dogs could be trained, in a short time, to go under cover of night into the camps of the enemy and deposit a small mine or bomb there. The mine or bomb of course to have a time fuse or else a small electric battery. The battery to be set in motion by the dog pulling a small wire, after he has placed the explosive under the enemy's artillery, etc. The dog of course would carry the explosive in his mouth by a small grip or handle. Forts or bridges in the enemy's territory could by this means be easily destroyed. This idea is given you in strict confidence for the benefit of your government and in the interest of the U.S.A. and no other person has had any knowledge of the idea from me. If availed of I am sure it will prove a success. I have the honor to be Honorable Sir your obedient servant,

D. K., New York, NY[46]

This letter contained an idea for using electric lights as a weapon of war:

General Alger, Secretary of War
April 28th, 1898

Dear Sir:
As a patriot and desiring the success of the Union troops, I would suggest that the use of an Electric Search Light thrown into the faces of advancing cavalry or infantry would confuse and obstruct their advance, especially in the case of a charge. I am aware that the argument will be made that an Electric Light on the battle field would draw at once the enemy's fire. This would be the case with artillery or any object of defense. If the idea is practicable, a dynamo driven by steam engine could be self propelled or drawn on the field and the lights there thrown in the faces of the cavalry or infantry. As the Government intends soon to establish camps of instruction the experiment could be made on single horses or a detachment and then on a body of men. I trust that as is usual, as the idea is new it will not be thrown aside but carefully considered. If this matter is of interest to the Government the writer will supply further details. The writer served in the Civil War.

Yours patriotically,
G. E., Troy, NY

P.S. It does not take much to confuse horses, as they are a nervous animal, and this plan would not permanently disable them but check them and throw them into confusion.[47]

After skirmishing their way close to Santiago, U.S. troops captured the heights overlooking the harbor in the Battle of San Juan Hill. Two days later the Spanish ships tried to escape, and the waiting American fleet sank them. Santiago surrendered shortly thereafter. Although Spanish forces still held Havana, their position was hopeless. With undisputed naval superiority, U.S. forces overran Puerto Rico until a general cease-fire ended the fighting in August.[48] Few doubted that defeat would cost Spain her Caribbean possessions, but some felt that the war's moral justification would be undermined if the United States gained any material benefits. This writer believed the opposite:

May 2, 1898

Dear Governor Long:
I like to say Governor from the admiration I had for you when in that office. I cannot resist the desire to send you a word in regard to a matter which sooner or

later must come up for decision, and is of great importance. I find some editors and some clergymen speaking about an indemnity as if it were not to be thought of. I look upon it as one of the best agents in the efforts for ensuring peace. Nothing can more forcibly teach a nation its awful responsibility for causing war. I would insist upon an indemnity, not exorbitant, not at the whim of victor, not in the spirit of vengeance or retaliation, but as a great moral factor in modern civilization. The amount might be referred to some arbitration board, but it should be quite equal to the cost of the war, a reasonable sum for every life lost, for pensions, and it surely would include the entire fleet of the defeated nation, as well as the surrender of its armies. Then it would be a supreme peace measure for many years. In the interests of peace, of the best ethics and of the best Christianity, I would urge it. Your praises are on all our lips and our constant prayers for your well being.

Most truly yours,
Rev. J. D., Boston, MA[49]

Realities in the field, rather than moral abstractions, dictated the peace terms. The parties agreed on independence for Cuba, while Guam and Puerto Rico became U.S. possessions. The Philippines remained the major point of contention, as neither side really controlled the islands. Spain had no fleet left to challenge U.S. claims, so Spanish leaders reluctantly ceded her interests in the archipelago. American attempts to control these islands led to a protracted guerilla campaign unlike anything the public might have imagined before the war. Three years of campaigning revealed the darker aspects of America's imperial tendencies, proving that Old World monarchies had no monopoly on violently subjugating indigenous people.

The rebellion began in early 1899, but the seeds had been planted months earlier. Shortly after Dewey's victory U.S. officials brought rebel leader Emilio Aguinaldo back from exile to strengthen the Filipino insurgents. The American press initially lionized Aguinaldo as a patriot in the tradition of Simón Bolívar or George Washington. The *Los Angeles Times* gushed, "General Emilio Aguinaldo is the big man of the Philippines. He is the President of the republic of the islands, the leader of the insurgents, the idol of the natives and the terror of the Spanish. He is the Antonio Maceo of Spain's Asiatic colonies. Young, handsome, brave as a lion, patriotic and self-sacrificing, this native Malay is the type of the insurrectionists who, like the Cubans, have fought the tyranny of Spain through blood and death and destruction until they now seem assured of victory."[50]

A key misapprehension undercut U.S.-Filipino relations: Aguinaldo believed the Filipinos would receive independence in return for their help, while many

Americans thought the islands would welcome annexation.[51] The buildup of U.S. forces around Manila antagonized the insurgents, who responded by gathering arms from Spanish posts in anticipation of renewed violence. Americans hotly debated whether to annex the islands or leave them to be snatched up by another colonial power. Proannexation groups stressed the merits of the islands as naval bases and the benefits of bringing democracy to the Filipinos.[52] Self-proclaimed anti-imperialists argued that seizing the archipelago by force would tarnish America's democratic image, entangle the nation in Asian politics, and lead to conflict with rival colonial powers.[53]

The president supported the annexationists, and the Spanish-American peace treaty made the Philippines an American possession.[54] McKinley promised the Filipinos "benevolent assimilation." The insurgents prepared for war. As tensions rose, the American press took a dimmer view of Aguinaldo. The *New York Times* noted, "We know that he comes of a mixed race remarkable rather for the lightness and celerity of its intellectual operations than for the qualities of steadfastness, wisdom, and sound judgement. . . . Yet the ardent anti-expansionist wants to intrust the lives, fortunes, and the future of these children among the races of men to this tricky, vain, shifty, feather-headed and self-chosen leader in order that they may be spared the horrors of enslavement under that ruthless despot William McKinley."[55] In February 1899 the war began. A few days later the Senate narrowly approved the treaty that made the Philippines American and America a colonial power.[56] Despite early American successes, subduing the insurrection proved difficult. American troops could drive the Filipinos back at will, but had trouble controlling the territory they captured. Some Americans, such as the writer of this letter, supported the old imperial tactic of using auxiliary troops drawn from conquered territories:

Mr. President
March 14, 1899

Now that the army bill gives you authority to enlist 35,000 troops from amongst the Islanders, I would most respectfully suggest that, instead of adopting General Gomez suggestion by withdrawing troops from Cuba and enlisting 10,000 Cubans for service in Cuba, you enlist 35,000 troops in Cuba and send them all to the Philippine islands to fight the Filipinos. Thus you would rid Cuba of its lawless, restless, troublesome ex-rebel elements and at the same time release our volunteers from further service in the Philippines.

Your Most Obedient Servant,
W. J., New York, NY[57]

The United States had its own nonassimilated ethnic group with an image as fierce warriors. Why anyone would assume Native Americans from the plains would have excelled at jungle fighting remains unclear, but papers reported on such proposals. This writer suggested a tribe famous for its ferocity:

> To the Honorable Mr. Root
> August 7, 1899
>
> Dear Sir:
> It may seem strange to some men that a private citizen should address you on the management of the coming campaign in Luzon but I know no excuse not to offer being an American born who has traveled largely within this country, Europe, Africa, Mexico, and other semi-civilized countries. . . . By all means send the Apache against the Filipinos just as in Austria they have the troops of one section act as police in another, when they get too friendly with the people they move them to some other place. 10 Apache attached to each company would be of great value in trailing and as scouts to carry messages and etc. from one command to the other.
>
> Yours Truly,
> P. B., Fruitvale, CA[58]

Some writers argued that African American troops would provoke less resistance by the Filipinos. The *New York Times* explained, "One-third of the population of the Philippines are negroes of the same race as those in the United States. . . . The advocates of the scheme believe that in a short time there would be an assimilation between the negroes of the Philippines and their kindred from the United States, and that there would follow for the colored people opportunities to get homes and possibilities of careers they could not hope for in this country."[59]

Other Americans advocated colonizing the islands. The *New York Times* quoted one officer who claimed as follows:

> There is not less than 10 percent of the volunteers who wish to remain in these islands and make homes here and engage in agriculture, lumbering and mining. From every point of view this should be encouraged unless America means to haul down its flag and sneak home. . . . Knowing the value of the pioneer, I say, deliberately, that each of these plain soldiers—young, vigorous, and accustomed to this climate—by remaining here will be of inestimable value to our country. The only way to Americanize these islands is by the example of American pioneers engaged in making homes for themselves.[60]

Harpers Weekly agreed:

> I need not dwell upon the commercial value of the islands—that subject has been exhausted and proven to the satisfaction of the most skeptical. But we need, besides a commercial outlet, an outlet for surplus population! This country is rapidly filling up; we will soon feel the suffocating sense of being jammed together, and with that comes the loss of activity, like the Chinese, at one time the most enlightened nation of the world, but now the most degraded, the most inhuman, the most sluggish people of God's creation!—all caused by the terrible overcrowding of the country from which there was no outlet; but walled up like a vast cockroach trap—after once inside he can never escape! Like Cooper's "Lo! The poor Indian," it will soon be Lo! the poor Filipino![61]

This letter from a U.S. Senator—a leading proponent of emigration of African Americans—suggested using African American soldiers as settlers:

December 27, 1901

Dear Mr. Secretary:

If you could send negro troops to the Philippines, to occupy three or four of the islands, more or less distant from Luzon, you would soon subdue the people there; not exclusively by compulsion, but by the more agreeable (to them) means of "induction." The negroes would be easily controlled, and they would soon lead the natives. If these negro troops were offered land bounties in the Philippines, on the outlying islands, for a full term of service, the inducement would be very strong for enlistment. The bounty lands should be given and located during the term of service, but the title should be held back until the expiration of that service, and should be inalienable for, say, 20 years. This would be an auxiliary force, to be placed in suitable groups, in camps of instruction, and assigned for the military occupation of the outlying islands, so long as needed or permanently, if necessary, and officered by regular army officers. This auxiliary force would repress violence and crime in the localities of the camps of instruction and would make a most useful reserve, for its moral effect and as a military resource. . . . If we keep a regular white force in this service there will be constant agitation by their friends in Congress, while if a negro force is employed, they will not be missed in the U.S. and will not be in the way in the islands. . . .

With great respect, yours sincerely,
John T. Morgan, Washington, DC[62]

When the insurrection began, the Army was still switching from black-powder rifles to magazine weapons firing smokeless powder cartridges. Regular troops carried the Krag-Jørgensen, a modern bolt action rifle, but many volunteers used old single-shot Springfields with black powder cartridges.[63] Firing the Springfield produced a puff of smoke that obscured the shooter's view and provided a convenient aiming point for enemy marksmen.[64] Many insurgents had modern Mauser rifles captured from Spanish garrisons, so the rebels often were better armed than their "civilized" foes. The *New York Times* complained as follows:

> There has been more or less uneasiness over the fact that the volunteers on the firing line around Manila were at a decided disadvantage against the native owing to the fact that the Filipino sharpshooters, armed with Mausers, could lie out of range of the Springfields with which our volunteers were armed and pot them to an extent that was limited only by the bad marksmanship of the natives. This was not only the source of a great many casualties among our troops, but had a bad moral effect on them, since it was very trying to be continually under fire from an enemy who kept discreetly out of range.[65]

This writer notified his congressional representative:

April 1, 1899

Dear Colonel [Rep. B. F. Marsh]:
Don't dispatches of this character make your blood boil! Haven't we money enough to buy guns as good as these half civilized pirates? It's enough to make an old soldier swear, the war department or some body else is near the line of responsible for murder. The best the bravest of the land, our own boys, sent out with short ranged, old style muskets. It's all wrong if true.

Yours,
W. S., Monmouth, IL[66]

Responding to complaints, the Army adjutant general promised to send more Krags to the Philippines, as well as new smokeless cartridges for the Springfields. He noted that the .45 caliber Springfield produced better results "against a partly savage foe" because it hit harder than the smaller Krag round.[67] The notion that smaller modern bullets were ineffective against "natives" enjoyed wide acceptance. The *Washington Post* noted, "[C]ivilized beings are much more susceptible to injury than savages. As a rule, when a 'white man' is wounded, he has had enough, and is quite ready to drop out of the ranks and go to the rear, but the savage, like the tiger, is not so impressionable, and will go on fighting even when desperately wounded."[68] Despite the supposed advantages of Springfields, American troops soon replaced them. "Civilize them with a Krag" became a slogan of the campaign.

As American troops advanced across Luzon, press reports predicted imminent victory. The *Chicago Tribune* crowed, "The splendid work of General MacArthur at the fall of Calumpit appears to have broken the back of the Filipino insurrection. General Luna, Aguinaldo's chief in command, has sent officers under a flag of truce to sue for peace in the name of his superior. The insurgents have offered to suspend hostilities pending negotiations for peace. The authorities at Washington believe this means that the fighting in Luzon has ended. This is the crowning triumph of American arms."[69] A single offensive could not defeat a popular insurgency, however, as U.S. troops soon discovered:

Adjutant General Corbin
U.S. Army
April 14, 1899

My Dear General:
With the most kind regard for you personally, I am constrained to say that the American people, judging from the expressions of our Baltimore businessmen, are much displeased with the conduct of the war in the Philippines; our soldiers are being killed in detail in skirmishes with no decisive battle. Why not call a halt—delay strengthens us and weakens the Rebels—until Gen'l Otis can have at least 75,000 troops and a large corps of engineers and constructionists to build [railroads] as our Army advances to keep a full supply of ammunition and provisions. Nothing will make that savage and ignorant race acknowledge the sovereignty of the U.S. but the cannon and the sword, and that should be given them most freely; the more of them who are killed, the better for humanity.

Yours very truly,
H. B., Baltimore, MD[70]

American reinforcements poured into the islands, and in late 1899 a large offensive completely scattered Aguinaldo's army.[71] The American commander duly announced, "[O]rganized rebellion no longer exists, and our troops are actively pursuing robber bands."[72] Once again, papers announced victory over the rebels. The *Los Angeles Times* cheered, "It appears clear that the bandits are so demoralized that campaigning is in the nature of an excursion, which indicates how cleverly our troops will be able to disperse the bands of marauders when Aguinaldo's so-called army has been broken up and what is left of it has resolved itself into guerrilla commands. The end of the fighting is practically at hand."[73]

The collapse of Aguinaldo's army did not bring peace, as essayist Ambrose Bierce commented: "It is a trifle too soon to go glorying over the suppression of the Filipino insurrection. . . . In Luzon we have encountered only one phase of the insurrection, and we have altered its character from field-fighting to bush-whacking, and that is all."[74] Bierce's words proved prophetic: the war entered a new stage, where guerilla tactics replaced large battles. American soldiers faced foes who melted into the jungle when attacked. The following two letters suggested methods to prevent insurgents from escaping death or capture:

Honorable Elihu Root
September 30, 1899

Dear Sir:
I see in today's papers that the affair at Porac, in the Philippines, was neatly done, but that the "blackbirds" took alarm and flew away so our troops didn't get enough for even a "pie" according to Mother Goose. Well, this move serves to point out what else is necessary to make a "bagging" expedition successful. A five-mile radius seems to be too short, as a runner can report every movement, at the center, in an hour or so. If 10, 15, or 20-mile radii could be employed, along which each column would move toward the rebel center simultaneously, each halting and "extending" and forming junction with the next whenever fired on from the center, but never replying till after completion of the investing line, a fairly good "haul" of prisoners might be made, at least in most instances. It is incomprehensible how there could be any firing when the enemy "escaped" or how they could possibly escape by a "mountain road" or any other, so long as we held it with an unbroken investing line. Evidently the investing line was more or less a gauzy one, and the truth is that we didn't have troops enough in the move to make success either possible or probable under the circumstances! If such was the case, all will no doubt be remedied and provided for in the next move. Suggestions: (1) Greater radii of action from rebel center; (2) More troops; (3) No reply fire till line of investment is complete and impregnable; (4) Use all possible means to prevent premature alarm and flight, even falling back short distances to make the enemy believe he has effected a repulse if he can thereby be induced to remain till investment is complete. And thereafter the subject is not interesting. As soon as we have from 20,000 to 30,000 of those "blackbirds" caged on an island, the war will collapse of its own weight, most likely. . . .

Sincerely yours,
G. J., San Francisco, CA[75]

Honorable Elihu Root
December 11, 1900

Dear Sir:
I trust you will excuse a 3 score year and 10 making any suggestions, I simply desire what is to hinder in the Philippine Islands in order to crush out the rebellion there and in future elsewhere [quickly] and before the return of troops from China and others from Philippines before close of enlistment; instead of scattering them over the hills, to take one at a time, stretch a line or lines from either end when desirable and sufficient men to do so, and not to add if any reliable natives to be had enlist them to march in line with our own sweeping isle after isle in arms, destroy ammunition and etc. that cannot be utilized, capture such who will not swear allegiance and place them on an island to be held as prisoners but on which [they] could by little aid maintain themselves until peace and order is fully restored. . . .

Respectfully,
A. D., Philadelphia, PA[76]

Not only did insurgents disperse when attacked, but individual guerillas blended in with the populace to avoid identification and capture. The *San Francisco Chronicle* reported, "The problem of suppressing this guerilla warfare is anything but easy of solution. Some American officers think it worse than fighting Indians, owing to the difficulties of the country and the trouble in locating the enemy, who resort when hard pressed to the 'amigo' dodge and hide their guns."[77] The Army usually released suspected insurgents. The *New York Times* reported, "No prisoners except officers and civil leaders are retained by the Americans. Their policy is to release all others almost immediately."[78]

This writer wanted to ensure that released prisoners did not rejoin the rebels:

The Honorable Elihu Root
October 16, 1899

Dear Sir:
I wonder if it has occurred to your department to brand or tattoo the Filipinos captured to prevent their claiming that they are amigos. This course I am informed has been pursued in India.

Yours Respectfully,
L. S., Buffalo, NY[79]

The insurgents hoped to hold out until Americans tired of the war. The presidential election of 1900 represented their best opportunity to influence voters to repudiate the administration's Philippine policy. The *Washington Post* noted that the rebels were "divided into small bands, which have been instructed by Aguinaldo to hold out in small parties, harass the Americans, and carry on a bushwhacking warfare until after the fall election, when they expect their friend Bryan to be elected. Bryan's name is as well known to them as the name of Aguinaldo."[80]

McKinley's reelection dealt a major blow to insurgent morale, while the additional American troops garrisoned towns, protecting pro-U.S. elements and isolating the rebels from their supporters.[81] U.S. forces increased military operations, funded civic improvements, and created pro-American local governments, all parts of the "pacification" process. The guerillas resorted to terror to prevent other Filipinos from collaborating. After American troops captured Aguinaldo at his hideout in early 1901, he appealed to his followers to surrender, a call that many heeded. The war-weary American public hoped that the ordeal had ended, but local rebels continued to fight. Punitive expeditions in late 1901 involved such brutality that Congress held hearings on atrocities committed by American troops. In 1902 President Roosevelt finally declared the insurrection over.[82] Scattered resistance continued for several years, but the prospect of the Filipinos winning independence through military resistance had vanished.

CHAPTER 2

Gun Bases, Pancho Villa, and Hyphenated Americans: Prelude to Armageddon

The European war created unprecedented tensions between ethnic groups in America who identified with different combatants. In 1910 approximately one in twelve Americans was of German extraction, and German-born residents were the largest group of first-generation immigrants in the country.[1] Language and culture made these "hyphenated" Americans different; sheer numbers made them potentially dangerous. German diplomats encouraged their former countrymen to publicize the fatherland's cause and to use their influence in support of American neutrality. Their efforts produced a negative reaction in the press, creating an atmosphere of distrust where seemingly innocent activities took on a sinister tone.[2] Even the *New York Times* questioned whether "German bands" performing as street musicians constituted "an organized effort among Germans to arouse a pro-German sentiment by having these itinerant musicians play such airs as the *Watch on the Rhine*."[3]

This writer warned of further subversive activities:

Secretary of War
June 9, 1915

Honorable Sir:
If you have a list of arsenals, manufacturers of powder and ammunition of any description, makers of automobiles, motor trucks, or any materials essential to war, mail all of them to guard their premises to the limits, or some German will blow them up. Discharge from the Navy every German. Mail steamship companies to inspect baggage of every German, no matter how innocent looking the package. There are Germans so fired by fatalism that they would sacrifice their lives to sink

ships. In Army or navy trust no Germans. How do you know but that Germany have submarines already in our waters? Mr. Charles Schwab says he can build them to travel to Europe—don't you think the Germans can do the same? Guard every harbor now. Germany relies on traitors in this country to accomplish much. . . . If you have Germans about you, discharge them. We will soon be at war with Germany.

Yours Respectfully,
W. R.[4]

Some citizens feared that German Americans, many of whom had already served in the Kaiser's army, had secretly formed military units that would spring into action if war came. Under the circumstances, armed German Americans were likely to raise suspicions:

Adjutant General
U.S. Army
March 10, 1917

Dear Sir:
I have the honor to respectfully state that I have my suspicions as to the patriotic and loyal intent of the Englewood Rifle Club. Although I was the organizer of the club over a year ago, a radical change has taken place since. Last January a few Germans contrived at the election of officers of the club which now are in the majority and lately seem to make special effort increasing the membership of the same nationality, this may be all good and well but as I have heard some of them make unpatriotic remarks, and are now making large requisition for arms and ammunition from the Arsenal, they also have been buying reloading tools, etc. which in my opinion as an ex-sergeant of the U.S. Army is in excess of ordinary needs. Since I have openly proclaimed myself to be American throughout and that I stood for Americanism and American rights, I note that I am no longer taken into full confidence. I therefore as a precautionary measure submit this information for a cautious investigation.

I am Sir, very respectfully,
M. D., Chicago, IL[5]

One of the more persistent if bizarre ideas regarding German Americans involved the construction of concrete platforms for heavy siege artillery. In 1914 the Germans employed huge siege guns to attack Belgian fortresses. These super-heavy cannons wrecked the concrete and steel defenses and forced surrender of the forts in a battle that lasted just a few days.[6] This battle received widespread news coverage, as did the heavy guns. *Collier's* proclaimed, "The day of the fortress has passed; the new siege gun is responsible for the passing."[7] Somehow the idea took hold that siege guns required reinforced concrete firing platforms. Reputable publications repeated this fable: *Scientific American* explained that these guns required "the construction of a massive circular concrete base in which are embedded holding-down bolts. Upon this is placed and firmly bolted down the lower ring, or race, of a turntable upon which, by means of a rack and pinion, the gun is traversed."[8] Papers reported the discovery of concrete gun bases along the German invasion routes into Belgium. The *New York Times* suggested, "[T]he Germans bought or rented certain stretches of land years before the war and then got exact measurements of the ranges, which is the reason their artillery fire was so accurate."[9]

Worried Americans reasoned that an invading German army might use concrete gun platforms prepared in advance by German Americans. Such traitors might be quite literally laying the foundations for a German victory in their own backyards. One article reported, "The last two or three days have seen the development of several sensational rumors involving three prominent and well-to-do businessmen, one of German birth and the others of German descent, who are American citizens. According to a report around Washington, it was found that the principal man concerned had built concrete foundations for German siege guns on his country estate outside the city, placed to enable them to demolish the Capitol and disguised as fish ponds or similar landscape gardening."[10] The *Los Angeles Times* warned of "the presence in the western part of the city of a peculiar concrete foundation—one such as were secretly built as bases for the giant German guns that later demolished the forts in Belgium. The foundation is on a site overlooking the city. . . . The owner of the site is an ardent German sympathizer."[11] This writer suggested a plan to uncover secret gun platforms:

The Adjutant General of the Army
January 29, 1916

Sir:
It is respectfully suggested that a secret board of engineer officers appointed to work in conjunction with secret service agents might produce an instructive report, especially if assigned to the further duty of ascertaining what concrete foundations for heavy siege artillery are to be found concealed in the vicinity of U.S. fortifications and other strategic points, under the guise of foundations for heavy machinery, factories, buildings, cemetery mausoleums, monuments, and the

like. It is but the work of a moment to blow off all encumbrances and expose such foundations ready to serve their intended purpose.

Very respectfully,
W. J., 1st Lt., USA (Ret.), Pasadena, CA[12]

Not every writer took the gun-base threat seriously:

War Department
August 29, 1915

Dear Sir:
I can't understand why a neutral government should give out such a foolish report as the enclosed. It seems to me that such as that would be beneath the dignity of the war office to even as much as allow "thought" to be given to such rot as "constructing concrete foundations for big guns in tennis courts." Must be pro-allied agents at work here. They got out the same kind of reports of concrete foundations being built by the Germans in Belgium and France before the war. Just as tho an army knows just where they will be able to "plant" their heavy guns years ahead. I see where they are hammering [hell] out of the Russian forts; I presume the Germans must have built concrete foundations there before the war also. Nobody but a demented being would give such reports even as much as a passing thought. Furthermore, how would the Germans get their army and big guns over here when they would have to reckon first with the English fleet. . . . Germany wants to be let alone, and as Uncle Sam will never seek a war with Germany there therefore will not be any such a war.

Yours truly,
H. B., Dallas, TX[13]

When the United States declared war in April 1917 German Americans found themselves the objects of suspicion by the authorities and, in some cases, abuse at the hands of "patriotic" vigilante groups. Wartime news reports stirred up further public distrust. In a single issue of the *Philadelphia Inquirer* in late 1917 readers could find at least three headlines about German American disloyalty: "Former U.S. Arsenal Worker Held for Plot—Naturalized German Accused of Ruining Shells Being Manufactured for Government"; "Fire Destroys Cherry Street Pier Building; Suspect Enemy Aliens"; and "German Woman Charged with Spitting on Flag."[14] The *Literary Digest* proclaimed that American war facilities were "menaced by furtive, un-uniformed armies whose weapons are spying, sabotage, bomb-planting, incendiarism, murder, and a hundred forms of insidious propaganda."[15]

This writer brought a potential sabotage target to official attention:

September 9, 1917

Dear Sir:

Walking along Riverside Drive [in New York City] here with half dozen war vessels in sight and only short distance, broadside from either shore. It occurred to me that enemys [*sic*] could easily torpedo at no hazard from the shore. Suppose two men had a small portable torpedo, in sections say, so they could carry it and in the dark locate at convenient point on bank at Riverside Park. It seems as tho it would be easy to sink such vessel and make their getaway. Six such pairs of men each pair having a torpedo could plan to discharge them simultaneously with deadly effect, or a string of mines could easily be arranged on a motor boat which studying the tides could be set overboard at such time and place that it would inevitably float down on and envelop the bow of the war vessel. This may be merely a scare on my part and the authorities may have anticipated and provided against any such attacks.

W. S.[16]

Another writer advocated collective punishment for all German Americans, to discourage treason:

To the Editor,
September 1917

We continually see fresh evidences of what German money and German trickery are doing to assist the barbarous Kaiser to victory. We saw that the Germans of this country duly notified the U-boats when to look for the squadron that [brought] our troops to France. We know that if it had not been for our preparation and bravery every one of those troops would have been in the bottom of the ocean. It is high time that we made the Germans and the German Americans of this country responsible for damages by sea and land. In the case of the sea make the Germans pay for every ship destroyed, every cargo lost, every life taken and every man disabled. Make both the Germans and the German Americans responsible. We have seen too many samples of how even the German American works for the "faderland." If any claim perfect loyalty let them pay their assessment all the same and call it their patriotic offering. It is time that a sure thing must be made of it.

If the rich Germans and German Americans knew that they were to be assessed for all of the war damages, they might get busy keeping quiet themselves and in dissuading their lesser fellows from deviltry in general. . . . There is nothing cruel or barbarous in the idea, nor would anybody be made bankrupt—it would be merely "pay as you go" where "fun" is lively and money is plentiful.

F. L., West Friendship, MD[17]

In December 1917 the Canadian port of Halifax was devastated and thousands killed when a ship packed with high explosives caught fire and blew up in the harbor.[18] This writer proposed a plan to prevent saboteurs from creating a similar disaster in America. (The "Hobson" mentioned by the writer had commanded the explosive-laden ship that tried to block the entrance to Santiago Harbor.)

Secretary Daniels
U.S. Navy
December 18, 1917

Dear Sir:
I made a suggestion today to United States Marshal Mitchell of Boston which he greatly appreciated, namely that he have all kinds of craft searched from ten to twenty miles out of [sic] sea before entering into any harbor thereby saving another Halifax disaster. There are plenty of our enemies who might play the Hobson trick and do great damage. There are plenty of chances to do same, as I see conditions at present. You will pardon me, but I feel it my duty as an American citizen to call your attention to this matter.

Yours respectfully,
H. H., East Weymouth, MA[19]

This letter warned of unusual coded messages posted in a particular community:

Bureau of Secret Service
October 23, 1915

Gentlemen:
During the latter part of September I was visiting in Evans, Pa., and while there noticed some rather queer looking patterns or designs painted on some of the barns in the surrounding country. These designs may contain some hidden meaning or they may just be an odd decoration; nevertheless as they aroused a certain amount of curiosity in myself I thought it best to acquaint you with them. On one barn

some of the windows had a semi-circle painted above them. Still farther on (along the road between Evans and Allentown) another barn had one or two of the following designs painted on it [segmented circle]. Another barn had the following design painted on it [another segmented circle]. The point that struck me as being odd was that one circle was divided into six segments while the other was divided into five. On still another barn I noticed the picture of a cow painted; the front and hind quarters being entirely painted black and the entire central portion of the animal painted white. As only some of the barns have designs painted on them and as I understand that a great proportion of the farmers in that section are of staunch German descent, and as that locality borders a state pike road, I believe, and is also near Bethlehem as well as Allentown (the former city our great steel center); I thought that the "decorations of the barns" might stand an investigation. I am an American citizen, having been born and raised in Wyoming, Pa.

J. K., Waukesha, WI[20]

The recent invention of radio raised new possibilities for transmission of stolen secrets. This letter suggested a primitive system for "jamming" nocturnal transmissions:

Secretary of United States Navy
September 20, 1917

Dear Sir:
After many hours of serious thought, I have come to a decision concerning the possible source of the German's means of information, or rather the transmitting of the information. I believe it is accomplished by a sort of wireless relay. For example—a German living in Oklahoma City raises a wireless outfit out of the top of his chimney at midnight, and then sends his information during the night to the same kind of the outfit in Fort Worth, Texas, then to Galveston and from there to a submarine two or three hundred miles out to sea—and thence from sub to sub across the sea to Germany. The submarines, of course submerge at day-break. As a block the allied nations of the world could co-operate, instructing every wireless station to commence at a given time after dark, making a dot or E (Morse Code) every three seconds during the night, thus tying up wireless communication at night. Germany could use her wireless at home during the day but would be unable to communicate with the outside world. . . .

I am,
Very much at your services,
[Unsigned], Oklahoma City, OK[21]

This writer warned that enemy spies might use less traditional modes of communication:

Secretary of War
September 9, 1915

Dear Sir:
My attention has just been called to a German spy in the person of a Mrs. D. of Oyster Bay, NY. A close friend of the Roosevelts and near neighbor. Her husband is said to be related to the Crown Prince of Germany by a previous incarnation his son. The woman is a practicing theosophist and they say has written to the Crown Prince personally and told all about our coast defenses and other secrets she gets by going out in a way theosophists have in the aura. They say she is the present incarnation of Lady Jane Grey of England. I am a theosophist and a psychic a practicing one. I do not know whether a layman can read this with understanding but if you have any theosophist friends they can assist you. . . . They say she takes her information to the Crown Prince himself by mail and by visits in trances as a theosophist can show you. Any good theosophist knows how it is done. She has written they say and sent plans of our coast defenses on the Atlantic front. Am told to refer you to H. D. Le Valley, Kankakee, Ill. for assistance and verification.

Respectfully,
N. L., Silver Lake, OR[22]

In 1917 most transoceanic messages traveled over submerged cables. These provided the best means to communicate with the nation's new allies, and with the rapidly growing U.S. armies in France. German spies might consider cable traffic as a source of information:

Navy Department
May 28, 1917

Gentlemen:
The question of how Germany obtains information relative to our country's war plans etc. is a serious matter and causing grave concern, suspecting a general spy system, etc. At the beginning of this great war England immediately cut all of Germany's cables and sought to isolate Germany from the rest of the world. To a certain extent this was successful but did Germany retaliate and if not why didn't she do likewise? In my opinion the source that gives England information is the source from which Germany derives all her knowledge of our ship movements, etc. It seems to me it is a question of cable tapping. Is it not possible with Germany's

submarines to at one time or other have raised the ocean cable attached some {fine} instruments thereto or made some cable connection and diverted it to some submarine base or to Germany direct? This does not seem to me to have been impossible and the Germans have shown themselves to be able to resort to every trick possible. . . . If in doubt send some fake cable messages. Trusting this suggestion will help to solve some of the mysteries which are perplexing all good Americans.

I am very humbly,
H. K., Fellows, CA[23]

In 1918 the Germans sent a submarine to American waters to cut the transatlantic cable. Arriving off Massachusetts the submarine failed to snag the cable but caused a minor panic by shelling coastal shipping.[24] At about the same time another U-boat cut two undersea cables off New York harbor.[25] Although these incidents had little strategic impact, they highlighted the danger of attack from the sea. The coast defense issue received considerable media coverage. In 1915 the *Boston Globe* ran a lurid ten-part serial entitled, "The Invasion of America," styled as "A Narrative Fact Story Based Authoritatively on the Inexorable Mathematics of War."[26] In the series, unnamed enemy powers occupy New England against pitifully unprepared defenses and extort huge war reparations from a prostrate America. This Bostonian urged authorities to take the invasion threat seriously:

Secretary of the Navy of the United States
May 25, 1918

Sir:
We believe our greatest peril to be a German armada, an invasion which might seriously cripple us and our Allies if the Huns should take it into their heads, which they may most any time, to dispatch 100,000 or more seasoned, well armed soldiers with munitions and equipments to our side. They have the ships and are building more every day in anticipation of capturing the commerce of the world after the war. Their Navy is practically intact. What would prevent them from making a dash across to our side, destroy our largest seaport cities, invade New England and the Eastern States and make us pay an enormous indemnity to get them out? No reply to this inquiry is expected, merely acknowledge receipt.

Very truly yours,
R. S., Boston, MA[27]

A coastal fortification program begun in the 1890s had established forts around major seaports, with heavy guns protected by concrete and steel.[28] By 1917, however, advances in naval armament during the intervening years had rendered these forts obsolete.[29] The *New York Times* noted that, without the U.S. fleet, Gotham would be at the mercy of any warships mounting guns larger than the 12-inch cannons of the city's defenses: "A hostile war vessel mounting 14 or 15 inch guns, if unmolested, could lie ten miles off Rockaway Beach, due south of Edgemore and about twelve miles from the Sandy Hook forts, and drop shells into any part of Manhattan Island as far north as Columbus Circle."[30]

This writer suggested a plan for improving New York's defenses:

The Honorable Woodrow Wilson
March 10, 1915

Honorable Sir:
Of late, throughout the country, I may venture to say, there is considerable talk about our coast defenses. These discussions naturally are the result of conditions in Europe at the present time. Here in New York City the line of talk that is most common around the bulletin boards, would make an uninformed outsider think that New York's fortifications are among the weakest in the world. However true or untrue this statement may be, I would like to offer for your approval one suggestion which if adopted, I think would make New York City the best fortified city in the world. My suggestion is this: to have Congress pass a bill the object of which will be to enforce all owners of N.Y. skyscrapers to make the roofs of said skyscrapers strong enough in every way to sustain such a heavy gun as the German 42 cm. Gun. With our skyscrapers equipped with such guns, our imaginary enemy would certainly have to go some to get in touch with our Port. The above suggestion is offered to you because I really think, from the bottom of my heart, that it can be put to excellent advantage, and because, as an American citizen, I consider it my duty to make any suggestion that would benefit the people of the United States of America.

Yours very respectfully,
A. O., New York, NY[31]

These two writers warned that German U-boats could attack U.S. cities, either by conventional bombardment or by more insidious means:

Secretary of the Navy
June 7, 1918

Dear Sir:

Drawing conclusions from what has happened upon the English coast is it not to
be inferred that some bright morning a submarine may appear off the Jersey coast
and shell the civilian population. Would it not be advisable to mount a 5-inch gun
on the old steel pier and Young's Atlantic City steel pier, to meet such a contingency.
It would be cause for much rejoicing in Berlin to have a sub pull off such a stunt
and get away unharmed.

Yours for the cause,
L. G., Scranton, PA[32]

Secretary of the Navy,
June 4, 1918

Dear Sir:

Just a word to suggest that our Atlantic coast cities be on guard against a gas attack
from the "U-boats." During the night time they may be able to release sufficient
gas by means of small floats or tanks to inflict great injury to sleeping inhabitants
of coast cities. Possibly they may find this the easiest and most fiendish method
against us.

Respectfully yours,
J. S., New Haven, CT[33]

Germany began air raids on London in 1915, signaling that it considered Allied
cities legitimate military targets. The *New York Times* issued this warning:

> The Germans intend to settle this war with the airplane. What is more, they intend
> to carry the war right to our doors with a fleet of huge hydroplanes, which will be
> able to travel from 100 to 200 miles per hour. It is time here that people knew the
> truth about these things. Thus far the western line and the British fleet have stood
> between America and the fate of Belgium. But airplanes that can rise to the height
> of 20,000 feet and travel from 100 to 200 miles an hour will overcome even those
> barriers, and America, unless she is awake, unless she is prepared, is from that
> moment at Germany's mercy.[34]

One article entitled, "Can the Germans Bomb New York From the Air?" reported that submarine-borne seaplanes posed an immediate risk: "Although a bombing pilot's attack would probably end in capture or death, who can deny that New York may be thus bombarded? Lives and machines are not reckoned in waging war. Because an enterprise is suicidal, it is not impossible."[35]

This letter described a possible attack by aircraft-carrying submarines:

Chief of Staff
August 8, 1917

Sir:
The possible attack on our seaboard described may already have been taken into consideration in the Government's plans for the defense of Washington, Boston, New York, and other places of importance within the radius of aeroplane flight from the coast. It is better, however, that your attention be directed to the danger a number of times [than] the danger of such an attack be overlooked. Possible German Attack on New York: (1) Cargo carrying submarines such as the Deutschland would be outfitted as a base in Germany as follows: (a) Stores and provisions necessary for a voyage to the United States and return, and maintenance for a month in American waters, (b) Cargo to consist of sea-going aeroplanes, with pontoons, and all other necessary equipment, H. E. aerial bombs such [as] are used in the raids on England, etc., (c) In addition to her crew the submarines would carry as passengers expert airmen. (2) Submarines would make the voyage without difficulty to a point say 50 miles off New York. They would there wait for favorable weather conditions and an opportunity under cover of darkness to launch the aeroplanes. (3) All conditions favorable, the aeroplanes would be rapidly assembled on the decks of the submarines, aerial bombs placed in them, launched, and sent away toward New York. (4) The raid on New York would probably be made at 10,000 to 20,000 feet altitude, too high for the airmen to make sure of hitting marks aimed at. (5) By means of signal lights seen only from above the submarines could direct the airmen back to their floating base. Time required for the attack, from departure of airmen from submarine until return thereto need not exceed 90 minutes. As a further suggestion, I beg to submit that such an attack as herein described could be directed by our navy against German coast defenses and submarine bases. Trusting that the attack as explained above will be of value to you, I beg to remain,

Respectfully yours,
C. D., Chicago, IL[36]

New York authorities took the air raid threat seriously, and held drills in which house lights and electric signs were extinguished.[37] With both sides bombing cities, national leaders were likely targets in an attempt to "decapitate" America at a critical moment:

Secretary of War and Secretary of the Navy
March 29, 1917

My Dear Mr. Secretaries:
As the subject matter of this communication pertains to both your great departments effecting the nation's safety, and having the honor of your acquaintance, I beg to submit what the press would willingly print and pay for, but my loyalty to you both, and to my country, bids me send this to you personally. In addition to my suggestions to Secretary Baker, under date of March 7th, that all flying machines within the United States should be placed under strict Government registry from now on, till peace is declared and that no flying machine of any description can be used except by personal permit from the Government, so as to prevent the Germans from flying over the White House and attempting to destroy the same, or the Capitol, as could be done from machines within our land, or from Mexico or Cuba. This precaution means safety assured. Also I suggest that on top of the Army and Navy buildings and treasury, there be stationed the most effective and far reaching guns in the United States and efficient gunners who would shoot down aeroplanes. . . .

C. M., New York, NY[38]

While Americans anxiously watched the European bloodbath, trouble boiled over south of the border. Mexico had been wracked with civil war for years, and the United States had already briefly occupied the city of Veracruz in 1914. That confrontation ended when a government led by Venustiano Carranza took power and U.S. forces withdrew.[39] The relative peace proved short lived, and a new civil war soon broke out. Disorder in Mexico—banditry and stray gunfire—threatened Americans living near the border. President Wilson eventually recognized Carranza's faction as the legitimate government of Mexico and provided military aid.[40]

These actions angered Carranza's foe Pancho Villa, whose forces operated in northern Mexico. In March 1916 Villa retaliated by attacking Columbus, New Mexico. The raid made front-page news, alongside accounts of the slaughter at Verdun-sur-Meuse (France), and Germany's all-out submarine campaign. As the

Boston Globe noted, "Villa has directed our attention toward the South. We had forgotten Mexico for a time because of the terrible conflict in the Old World, but Villa has made us remember the problem of poor Mexico to the exclusion of less imperative though more important matters. We can now cool off concerning submarines and blockaders. Northern Mexico is on the screen."[41]

President Wilson decided to send troops into northern Mexico to capture Villa, despite Carranza's refusal to condone such action. Less than a week after the Columbus raid, Gen. John Pershing and nearly five thousand American soldiers crossed the border in pursuit of Villa's forces. Given the poor state of relations, many expected Carranza's troops to violently resist any American incursion, even one in pursuit of their enemy. The *Chicago Tribune* warned, "If Carranza should make trouble the United States will find itself at war with the de facto government as well as the Villistas. In that event it will be necessary for the president to employ not only the entire regular army in continental United States, numbering 35,000 men, but a volunteer army of from 250,000 to 500,000 men raised under the specific authorization of Congress."[42]

Some Americans saw General Pershing's force as the vanguard of an all-out invasion that might again lead to U.S. annexation of parts of Mexico. The *Boston Globe* reported as follows:

> [T]he Administration has in hand a plan to purchase the north half of Mexico, to organize the country under our methods of government, and establish peace in all that part of the present republic in which Americans are most interested. The transaction would cut off the possibility of such border troubles in Texas, New Mexico, and Arizona as have occurred in the last few years and it would enable Carranza, through a large money payment, to create stability in the remainder of the country. . . . Such a plan is perfectly natural to President Wilson because of his abhorrence of war and ruffianism, and the American people would no doubt approve of it. They would be glad to see it demonstrated that the dollar is mightier than the sword and more beneficent in its operation.[43]

This writer proposed using the threat of annexation to achieve American goals:

Secretary of War
March 16, 1916

Dear Sir:
. . . The Public, naturally, wishes to see peace restored in Mexico, and we want Americans protected there, and we want Carranza's goodwill, and the good will of his army, and we want them to assist our soldiers in bringing about peace—and

the newspapers apparently want the same, and yet in the same papers in other columns, they stoutly maintain that we ought, by all means, to take Mexico, or at least certain choice portions of it, just as we did at other times—and then these same newspapers speculate on why Carranza's army, or part of it, is mutinying, and why we do not receive their hearty cooperation! Any one, with the slight intelligence of the Mexicans even, would revolt at the thought of an army coming to take part of his country. . . . Such articles have been getting through to Mexico, doubtless, through agents of Villa and his men. I cannot imagine anything that would arouse his half-starved men to action sooner than to be told such a thing—even though it is only the sentiment of certain newspapers. But, had the newspapers put such suggestions in the form of a threat, and said that the U.S. Government would not take one acre of Mexican territory, provided Villa is captured say within one week from a specified date; his men laying down their arms and agreeing to peace terms for a specified number of years at least; Carranza to assume charge of the Mexican Government; all factions to agree to peace, etc., etc.,—but failing to agree to this, that the United States would at the expiration of say two weeks take over a certain section of Mexico for their own for a certain period of years, work it and take the proceeds, for a period of say fifty years, and so on, taking each month or semi-month another section under these conditions, but promising if they lay down their arms within a given time, no territory shall be taken, and the United States Government will assist them to build up certain sections of Mexico; and back it up with our army and navy being stationed there for a few months. . . . [T]his would put an entirely different face on the situation in the eyes of the Mexicans and the world in general. . . .

Yours for all success and skillful diplomacy,
C. L., Chicago, IL[44]

The *Chicago Tribune* ridiculed opponents of annexation:

The United States intervenes in Cuba, Haiti, Nicaragua, Panama, etc. and accomplishes things. It makes life better for the people who live in those places. It relieves intolerable conditions. It protects its own security. . . . But if it be proposed that the United States shall extend a similar benevolent supervision over Mexico, make Mexico endurable to the Mexicans and safe for foreigners, and block the possibility that some debt collecting nation will start trouble right on the flank of the United States, outraged opinion declares that this is a cowardly picking on a little fellow.[45]

The *Washington Post* published a virtual catalog of the cultural treasures and natural resources the United States might gain from a war: "If Mexico is annexed we will have—31 new states and territories, 15,000,000 new Americans and 767,290 square miles of picturesque, historic and rich lumber, agricultural, and mineral lands."[46]

This letter proposed the forming of a puppet Mexican government to help restore order:

War Department
June 28, 1916

Sirs:

In addition to Springfield Daily News enclosure, let me observe that your Administration under President Woodrow Wilson, Commander-in-Chief of our Army and Navy, gets a lot of newspaper advice about "going in with our troops and cleaning up all Mexico." Let me, a G.A.R. [Grand Army of the Republic, i.e., Union Army] veteran's son born in 1858, indelibly remembering our Civil War, and serving in the escort to our gallant boys of the 2nd Regiment here on their departure a week ago, now say that your worthy tactics will be to cut a cleavage right through Mexico from Pershing's advance base and from Vera Cruz to a junction at Mexico City, forcing the Mexicans to meet us along that line and let our border securely alone; then set up young Diaz as the provisional Governor in temporary alliance with us (see Washington's Farewell Address: "Alliances") and let Diaz organize his native troops to clean up Mexico. While the people of the United States who have made our line of Mexico's cleavage along the main railroad lines, proceed to put them in running order, get a stream of our United States civilization flowing along this line and thence out through Mexico, making that naturally rich country worth while as an asset to its own people and to the world. And incidentally, take Lower California as a prompt measure of war exigency; hold it forevermore, count this taking as an indemnity to our nation and to our people who have suffered in property and life in Mexico: and pay individual indemnity to those sufferers or heirs as their cases are proven.

Yours faithfully,
A. C., Springfield, MA[47]

Could the United States really overrun Mexico? Pershing's force was too weak to achieve anything decisive, yet the Army had few additional troops available. Preparations for a wider war highlighted America's weakness, as the *Washington Post* noted: "The fact is, that the army of the United States is the same in regard to this country as a fly would appear to you looking through the wrong end of a telescope. The cold fact is that the American army of today is the most pathetic thing any nation ever knew or contemplated, and other nations know it very well, I assure you."[48] This weakness prompted the *Chicago Tribune* to urge rapid rearmament:

> If we have war with Mexico there is one end to seek and that is the complete military defeat of the Mexicans. This would take a force of not less than 200,000 to 250,000 men if it is to be done expeditiously and with the minimum loss to ourselves. . . . As we have only 32,000 mobile regulars in the country and only 129,000 national guard, who are but partly trained troops and who cannot be used outside the United States until they have been converted into volunteers, it is self-evident that we are in no way prepared immediately to strike should war come.[49]

These two letters offered ideas for increasing the Army:

Honored Sec. Baker
March 20, 1916

As I see the United States is going to take some decided action in capturing the Bandit Villa I propose to you to have a few regiments of boy scouts in towns bordering the international boundary line between Mexico and the United States, so as to render first aid to the wounded civilians in case of attack of Villa's soldiers upon an American town. In this case the United States soldiers would probably fire or give chase and would have no time to give aid to the wounded people; they could also help the hospital corps in carrying severely injured persons to the hospital camps. The person writing this letter is an American boy 15 years of age and a student in the De Witt Clinton High School of New York City. If this plan suits you kindly let me know. I remain a faithful citizen of the USA.

A. G., New York, NY

P.S. They could also be of use in quieting the fears of the people who think an attack is going to be made on that town.[50]

Secy War
[June 1916]

Dear Sir:
Allow me to suggest that you have some one to organize all the baseball teams in the United States into regiments for the Mexican campaign. I can see no reason why you should not get in this way one hundred thousand men who will make

as fine soldiers as ever shouldered a gun. They will make fine grenade throwers, if they have any of this to do.

[Respectfully],
C. O., Athens, GA[51]

Scientific American argued America could win without an all-out invasion through "[T]he occupation of the coast cities having railroad termini, and of the main routes of travel. This places in the hands of the forces occupying these points and routes all the commerce and practically all the resources of the country. . . . Nothing would remain for the Mexicans except a guerilla warfare, more injurious, probably, to their own nationals, who would be exploited for the control of the several bands, than to the occupying army."[52]

This writer suggested a similar scheme:

Woodrow Wilson
March 24, 1916

Sir:
As a believer in and supporter of your Mexican Policy from the beginning, would you allow me to suggest that in case the present movement for the capture of Villa results in intervention and war you send naval vessels with sufficient Marines to take and hold all principal seaport cities on both coasts, and put a strong line of troops along the inland border. In other words, "bottle them up" taking export and import duties to remunerate the cost in part, and so hold them until satisfactory conditions prevail, that policy would save thousands of lives and keep our men where they could be cared for and kept in health. In case Carranza troops join Villa and a strong resistance to our expedition to capture him develops withdraw all our troops to the border and await developments, would not that policy tend to allay suspicions in So. America?

Yours Very Respectfully,
W. C., Allegass, MI[53]

This writer stressed the advantages of an all-out invasion:

The President
June 23, 1916

Sir:
Of course I know you have had no advice at all on the Mexican situation. I only want to offer an idea, no advice. The condition there is that of a mob. The Mexicans

are a mob. If there was a mob in a City, the Mayor would not send two policemen to scatter the mob; he would send all his Police, and at the sight of the big squad the mob would lose their nerve and go home without a blow being struck. If the Mayor had sent two only, they would in all probability have been torn to pieces. If you will send one million men to the border and just let them spread out and start to Mexico City, you won't have to kill a single "Greaser." They will simply go home. If you send a small number, you will have to kill every one in sight, and get many an American boy slain. I greatly admire your cool patience in the unfortunate affair. Don't let the "Jingoes" harass you into declaring war. America doesn't want a war with Mexico. No glory in it. Ten able bodied men might just as well get into a fight with a few half grown boys. Just start a million soldiers across the continent with their faces towards City of Mexico and you will never have to fire a gun.

Loyally Yours,
H. J., Denver, CO[54]

Once Villa eluded Pershing's initial thrust, U.S. soldiers settled in for a prolonged stay. Their presence enraged most Mexicans, who viewed them as an occupying force. U.S. officials attempted to calm matters by publicizing America's good intentions. The *Washington Post* reported, "By cable, telegraph, radio and mail full statements of all that has transpired since the raid upon Columbus and of the attitude of the United States government and its reciprocal agreement with the Carranza government went forward to consuls and State Department agents throughout the southern republic. . . . In effect, the United States has established a publicity bureau in Mexico to make clear its peaceful purposes toward every resident of Mexico with the exception of Villa and the bandits who raided Columbus."[55]

These two writers tendered ideas for winning over ordinary Mexicans:

President of the United States
March 20, 1916

Dear Honorable Sir:
Kindly permit me to make a suggestion to you in regard to the Mexicans, which I think might prove of some value, and that is, if in some way the troops now in Mexico and those on the way, and also those on the border, could have a small Mexican flag to give to the natives, one that could be worn on the breast, and with it a little feeling of friendship. I think it would go a long way towards making a better feeling with the United States, and also start a better feeling towards their own country. I don't suppose many of them know just what such a thing is, like we do here. Let the troops wave them and also give them to the children as well,

for it would teach them to love their country the same way it does here in the United States.

Yours very truly,
F. M., Boston, MA[56]

Secretary of War
June 28, 1916

Dear Sir:
As an old Spanish war veteran let me advance a suggestion which may perhaps be useful. In 1898 the Cubans did not want us in Cuba. Today they would be distressed if the American population should leave, because their country is so immensely prosperous. If we are going to have trouble in Mexico, why not circulate newspapers among the poorer classes in so far as it can be done, publishing articles signed by prominent Cubans, telling the Mexicans how much better off they will be after citizens of the United States can settle there in force, because of the immense amounts of money that will be spent. This idea could be enlarged upon possibly to a point where it would be of immense benefit. It is Mexican ignorance that must be overcome. In all the territory that we conquer we could spread bulletins of this kind, and the news would soon sweep the country, making our task less difficult. Please think it over.

Sincerely yours,
M. M., Chicago, IL[57]

These two writers believed music would dissipate anti-American feelings in Mexico:

To the Honorable The Secretary of War
July 11, 1916

Sir:
If press reports at the time spoke true, Gen. Pershing's force went into Mexico with camping and fighting equipment only. Brass bands suppressed, and a scant allowance of bugles. Will you pardon a civilian with nothing of Mexico, but with twelve years in Greek and Latin Europe to his credit, if he voices an impression that the contrary habit of allowing your friendly expedition, and any expedition to a non-Anglo-Saxon country, an abundance of schooled players, should commend

itself. An offer to play on a town square or promenade is of happier augury and effect with any southern population than utilitarian demands. . . . Italian bandmasters would doubtless cajole Latin ears better than others. But applications are of executive domain. I am, Sir,

Yours very truly,
A. E., Ithaca, NY[58]

Secretary of War
March 26, 1916

Dear Sir:
If suggestions are not annoying to you will you read this in the spirit of friendship. To overcome the irritation across the Rio Grande we want the friendly feeling of every Mexican who is not simply a bloodletting idler. The big appeal to the Mexican must be thru sentiment. Find some one who will write a song, praising the Mexican man and woman, their country. Put it into the atmosphere of the Country fit it to a tune suggestive of a popular Mexican air. Have a squad of our soldiers learn the song, teach it to the troops in Mexico and have the troops sing it whenever near Mexican persons. In Mexican Spanish or native dialect. No Mexican appreciates our way of fighting or operating business. It is doubtful if any evidence of force will convert them to our way of thinking. Make this friendly appeal in the language and manner they understand and we will not have to fight long.

Sincerely yours,
W. B., Cleveland, OH[59]

General Pershing's force operated in a twilight zone between the traditions of the Old West and the new realities of mass warfare. The cavalry still galloped into town, only to be met by barbed wire and entrenched machine guns. Motor trucks replaced pack mules, and Army scouts included both pilots in airplanes and Apache horsemen. The Army's use of airplanes raised expectations that Villa would be easily located from the air. The *Atlanta Journal* noted, "[T]he task in hand and the crystal air of northern Mexico present unusual opportunities to test this auxiliary of the army service. In such a situation one skilled aviator could do more and better scouting than a troop of cavalry; at least, he could cooperate with the cavalry and render its work more certain and safe."[60] The Army's primitive airplanes proved underpowered and extremely fragile. Within a month of joining Pershing the few survivors recrossed the border after accomplishing almost nothing.[61] In contrast, the Apaches proved expert trackers well-suited to chasing Villa's fighters.[62]

This writer suggesting using airships to bombard Villa:

Adjutant Generals Office
March 20, 1916

Right now is when air ships could be doing inestimable service in Mexico. 50 air ships supplied with an unlimited quantity of 1 to 2 oz cheap cast iron shot could do more service in demolishing every band of outlaws or opponents of the government than 50,000 soldiers with comparatively little loss of life. This would bring certain and lasting peace in Mexico as no other method can accomplish. Their refuge in the inaccessible rough sections would be little or no protection from air craft raids. Bombs are expensive and unreliable, but millions of small shot poured on mobilized troops will find almost every man on his horse.

Respectfully,
W. R., veteran of the Civil War, Sawtelle, CA[63]

Because America supplied Carranza's forces with weapons, U.S. troops might face enemies armed with the same rifles they carried:

Secretary of War
June 26, 1916

As the U.S. Gov't has permitted the shipment of arms and ammunition to Mexico for a long time past, which will now be used against our troops, can you not protect them by issuing to the troops for use in rifles and machine guns cartridges having a carrying power of say one-eighth mile greater than that of the ammunition now in the hands of the Mexican troops? Is this not your duty!!—as it would enable our fire to be effective before they could reach us, resulting in a panic in their troops and flight or surrender? Kindly give this immediate consideration as I believe it is the duty of the Government to protect our men in the field from our past mistakes. As I presume our rifles can be used with "irregular" or "extra long" cartridges I believe the foregoing suggestion practicable and necessary.

Sincerely yours,
E. P., Philadelphia, PA

P.S. Of course this should be done secretly![64]

This writer advocated using local resources to create a frontier version of European gas warfare:

March 27, 1916

I would suggest that you consider the use of Chile Copenias in war fare that are many times hotter than red pepper one atom in each eye would render the soldier helpless for two or three hours but would not cause permanent injury—if it could be got in trenches I don't think they could be used any more and if these border towns was fixed to use it we could cause the bandits to become blind—a bullet seldom hits but one man while a good chard of Chile Copenias would fill the air for several feet they would have to be finely ground and one atom in each eye would capture him as well as a bullet—we are in six mi of the border and we don't feel any too safe we know the nature of the Mexican so well—don't turn this down as a joke the more you study it the more you will see in it.

E. C., Sommertown, AZ[65]

Many Americans feared that if war broke out, Mexicans in the United States would revolt. The *Chicago Tribune* warned, "Hundreds of Mexicans have been arriving at San Antonio and many other Texas towns during the last three weeks. Many of them purchased arms and ammunition, which they secreted in their homes and boarding houses. . . . The plan at San Antonio, as outlined to the sheriff and the chief of police, is for the Mexicans to attack the water works, electric light plant, city hall, courthouse, banks, and other public buildings."[66]

This writer warned that an uprising would have foreign backing:

Honorable Secretary of War
June 24, 1916

Dear Sir:
. . . I wish to suggest that the government should at once ship arms to Arizona, New Mexico and California and in sufficient amount to arm the citizens so they can protect themselves. We should have 150,000 small arms in this state and same number in Arizona and New Mexico. I think you will find that the Mexicans in the south west are all prepared with arms etc. to carry out a plot to burn the cities destroy the railroads and murder all the white population in that section of the United States included in Arizona, New Mexico & {southern} part of California. They will incite the Negro to do likewise. The Japs will no doubt join them inside of a short period of time. The Japs can take all the Pacific coast cities inside of 48 hours. Our troops in Mexico will find terrible surprises awaiting them I fear as it

is reported that the Japs have been landing ship load after ship load of munitions of war on the coast of southern California. There is about 40,000 Japs in our state here that are soldiers and all they need is the equipment. . . . When the towns are burning and men, women and children are being murdered by the thousands in the sections I refer to and Mexican soldiers have swept our troops aside you will then realize the horrible condition that has been brought about by some unknown cause.

Yours Very Respectfully,
E. B., San Francisco, CA[67]

Some saw Villa's attack as part of a German plot to divert the United States from supporting France and Great Britain. Germany took an active interest in Mexico, and the infamous "Zimmerman Telegram" offering a military alliance against the United States helped propel America into the War in 1917. Did the expedition to capture Villa play into the Kaiser's hands?

U.S. War Department
[June 1916]

Notwithstanding I am not yet citizen of the U.S. I am friendly inclined to this country and therefore I am writing this letter to day. When you will look at the secret service department you will find that I wrote already an anonymous letter regarding the German attaches 6 months before their activities were discovered. Therefore I hope also these informations will find your attention because they are written by an honest friend of the country. I want to warn you to start a fight with Mexico at the present time. These provocations are doubtless started with German money in order to tie up the American horse and ammunition exports. Then the German rulers suppose that this country will soon be so tied up with Mexico that the German submarine outrages can be started new again. Besides this the U.S. to have to consider that in case the Army will be occupied in Mexico Japan will intervene in the Philippines and probably also in Hawaii and Alaska. . . . Therefore I hope earnestly that the U.S. will not start a fight when this country is so ridiculous unprepared and would get such a licking that the U.S. would lose their present position in the world.[68]

Unsigned

Tensions between the United States and Mexico peaked in June 1916 as the president called the national guard into service. Carranza announced that any further American advances would meet armed resistance, and war fever began to grip the

American press. The *Washington Post* published maps of probable invasion routes, and noted that one senior officer "declared that he would not go into Mexico unless he had an initial army of 250,000 men and 500,000 volunteers to draw from. In order to be successful, he stated, the United States should be in force at every seaport and at every important interior town in Mexico. Practically a whole army of cavalry is needed now, this officer said, to fight guerrilla bands into which the Mexican army will break when it is defeated in a pitched battle."[69]

When Carranza demanded that all U.S. forces leave Mexico immediately, President Wilson refused. The *Los Angeles Times* noted, "If war with Mexico shall be forced upon us—and it looks now as if war is almost inevitable—it will not be the fault of the United States. We have done all that honorable men can do to avoid it. No gory locks can be shaken at us. We cannot now, without incurring the contempt of the civilized world, repudiate our duty to protect the lives and property of American citizens from the assaults of a nation of bandits."[70] At this crucial juncture, part of Pershing's force clashed with Carranza's troops. Several Americans were killed, and others were captured. The war, it seemed, had begun. Incendiary articles detailed the treachery of the Mexicans and the ill treatment of U.S. prisoners, while others noted the massing of troops on either side of the border.

Facing the specter of an all-out war, both sides pulled back. General Pershing restrained his natural impulse to retaliate, while President Wilson ignored public calls for an immediate invasion. Carranza released the prisoners and called for talks. War fever began to subside, and Americans soon turned their attention to the more menacing events across the Atlantic. Pershing's men idled away the summer and autumn as Carranza's forces took over the hunt for Villa and an American-Mexican high commission wrangled over the details of border security. In February 1917 the expedition recrossed the border, its original mission all but forgotten. Two months later the United States entered the Great War, and Americans turned their full attention to the struggle for Europe.

CHAPTER 3

A New Type of Pirate: World War I at Sea

Although World War I is remembered for its bloody trench battles, America's initial contribution came at sea. During the months needed to train U.S. troops and transport them overseas, America did what it could to bolster the naval efforts of its allies. By April 1917 the Entente's surface navies dominated the seas, so the U.S. Navy focused on fighting U-boats. At this point Germany was close to winning the submarine campaign, sinking Allied ships at a rate that could destroy England's ability to survive.[1] Finally freed from restraints imposed in deference to American public opinion, the Germans began an all-out effort against Allied merchant fleets. To keep Britain in the fight and protect American troops at sea, the Entente would need to find an antidote to the U-boat.

Submarine operations received ample press coverage, and the lack of military precedents encouraged ordinary citizens to propose ideas for combating the threat. The results overwhelmed officials. In 1916 the Navy created the Naval Consulting Board to examine inventions that might prove useful in the war. Headed by Thomas A. Edison, the board examined suggestions and inventions for the Navy, handling up to three thousand letters a week. Altogether it considered more than sixty-five thousand submissions.[2] The publishers of *Scientific American* announced they, too, would screen ideas to defeat German submarines. The magazine ran a series of articles on U-boat capabilities and tactics, which were specifically intended to provide readers with the necessary background for working on antisubmarine ideas. The editors explained, "[I]t may well happen that the effective answer to the submarine will come from some citizen who has never had anything to do with the sea or ships and who, looking upon the problem with a mind absolutely free from prejudice and untrammeled by any of the conventions of the technically-trained man, hits upon some line of attack which will prove to be thoroughly effective."[3]

Scientific American noted that the Naval Consulting Board was swamped with submissions, mostly related to U-boats, and that "99.999 percent of suggested ideas are either (1) old and already adopted, (2) old and discarded, (3) mechanically or scientifically impossible, (4) possible but inexpedient, or (5) defeating one aim in achieving another. . . . [T]he purposes of efficient prosecution of the war are much better served if all such vague and tentative ideas are kept from taking time and effort on the part of government scientists, committees, and boards."[4] *Scientific American* promised to screen antisubmarine ideas proposed by inventive citizens and publish the best of them.

The U-boats' greatest asset was their ability to strike without warning, diving to escape pursuit. Many antisubmarine suggestions involved tricking submarines into revealing their presence. The next letter described a scheme already in use. In 1915 the British began using decoy vessels, called "Q-ships." Disguised as ordinary merchantmen, they carried heavy armament hidden under hatches or behind false cargo piles. These seemingly helpless ships attempted to lure U-boats to the surface at close range and then sink them with gunfire.[5] Anticipating that they might be torpedoed, they carried empty drums or other buoyant materials in their holds. Q-ships enjoyed some successes, but once U-boat commanders discovered the ruse, their days were numbered.

Hon. Josephus Daniels
June 11, 1917

Dear Mr. Daniels:
Realizing fully the danger of suggestions from a layman, but feeling that some stray thought may "hit the mark," I take the liberty of suggesting a plan for a "decoy ship" for fighting submarines. If the plan is not founded on a fallacy, a "decoy ship" would seem to have the following advantages: (1) unsinkable, (2) easily repaired, (3) immediately available, (4) disconcerting to the enemy, (5) a dependable fighting machine. *Details:* A. Take any standard merchant ship, say from 5,000 to 10,000 tons displacement, and fill the cargo space with empty air tight casks, these to be held firmly in place by stanchions, so that they would act as a great number of sealed compartments in event of the ship being partly filled with water. B. Equip the ship with the best submarine fighting devices, in such a way as not to be easily detected. C. Use water ballast in bringing the ship down to the load line, by filling in between the casks, the ship to appear to be carrying a heavy cargo. D. Have the "decoy ship" follow a route previously agreed upon, and accompanied at a distance as great as possible in order to avoid the appearance of a convoy, by submarine chasers. E. Upon attack from submarine the ship to act in

every way like a poorly defended merchantman, until the effective devices could be used to the greatest advantage. . . . If this plan could be used its value would be dependant upon secrecy.

Very truly yours,
H. M., Wilmington, NC[6]

Some Q-ships worked in tandem with British submarines linked to them by a cable. The British submarine would remain submerged until a U-boat surfaced, then torpedo it. This combination claimed a few victims.[7] The U.S. Navy adopted a similar scheme in 1918, pairing an unarmed schooner with two submarines in the vain hope of ambushing a U-boat off the eastern coast of North America.[8] This writer proposed a variation on the submarine–Q-ship combination:

Commander Horne
August 3, 1917

Sir:
Prompted by the desire to help, I hereby submit for your consideration the following of an antidote for the "submarine peril." I think it is practicable and capable of at least demoralizing the activities of the subs. I suggest to transform a number of merchant ships into "decoy" steamers having two watertight compartments with doors hinged and opening under the surface. Two "Baby" submarines built as small in size as practicable to answer the purpose, made of standardized parts and manned by two or three men to be carried by the mother ship in the compartments mentioned. Nearing the danger zone the "Babies" can be released and taken in tow by the "Mother" or have the compartments partly filled and the crews ready for action, and as soon as the presence of the enemy is discovered, the doors can be dropped (by suitable arrangement) and the "Babies" pushed out ready to launch their torpedoes or train their guns at the foe. . . . Any steamer could be converted for the purpose in a very short time and little expense. A limited number shall be required, for, by making a few changes with the stack, masts, etc. they can be made to appear as different ships every time, and the "Babies" could be built fast enough (standardized) and cheap enough to make the undertaking the less costly of them all, provided the scheme is practicable. Trusting you appreciate the spirit these lines are written in, and will pardon me for interfering with your valuable time. I remain, Sir,

Respectfully Yours,
N. C., Balboa, CZ [Panama Canal Zone][9]

Q-ships operated individually, hoping to pick off an unwary U-boat here and there. These two writers submitted ideas for tricking large numbers of submarines into revealing themselves:

Naval Consulting Board
July 6, 1917

Gentlemen:
I am taking the liberty to propose for your consideration the following strategy to be employed in fighting the submarines. A number of dummy transports, preferably made "non-sinkable" by means of vertical compartments, can be escorted by destroyers as though they were the actual transports. If war practice permits, a "leak" as to the time of sailing of our "transports" and the port of destination could reach the enemy at the proper time. The submarines in large numbers would attack, and on account of the imagined great prize would expose themselves to greater than ordinary risks. Our destroyers could sink large numbers of them if prepared for such a contest. By a succession of such sailings we could at least confuse the enemy and our actual transports might reach port with comparative safety. Our destroyers would also acquire valuable experience which would be of service when protecting the actual transports. Strict secrecy of the method, of course, would be required.

Yours very respectfully,
A. Z., MN[10]

Hon. Secretary of the Navy
June 30, 1917

Dear Sir:
I would suggest that when the Allies have the maximum of submarine chasers within the war zone that all movement of shipping be withheld for a limited period, keeping the matter secret. With aeroplanes and chasers fulling covering the ground they ought to locate quite a number of them. The submarines would be puzzled and undoubtedly would come up frequently. . . .

Yours truly,
M. D., Washington, DC

Supplemental to my first communication, I would also suggest that as soon as the limitation of shipping goes into effect that the machinery of all chasers should be stopped. The only machinery working would be that of the submarines. With listening devices they could detect their presence.[11]

Other decoys might distract U-boats from attacking more important targets:

Secretary of the Navy
[ca. August 1917]

Dear Sir:
Herewith I give you [a] sketch, etc. of a "dummy ship" to be put into operation as a target for submarines, and for the purpose of wasting the enemy's torpedoes. It is to be a flat bottom ship large enough to make it seem worth while to the enemy to shoot torpedoes at. It can be built with a raft bottom, with the sides of a good sized ship, at each end of the dummy ship is to be a steel beam extending down into the water for approximately thirty feet, the lower end of the steel beam to be much larger than the upper end—this to give the dummy ship stability, and in case it should be tipped over in a heavy or rough sea the heavy steel beam would cause it to turn back right side up. The ship does not need to be water tight, and there will be no insides to the ship except a gasoline or steam engine to give it some speed to move it about. Somewhere on the dummy ship will be placed one or two five inch guns for the purpose of sinking submarines when possible. The object of the flat bottom is that as torpedoes are fired to go to a depth of five or ten feet below the water the torpedo will pass under the ship, and in this way a submarine may exhaust all of its supply of torpedoes. . . . One or two could be started immediately to learn its merits and advantages, and practicability. They could be built right on the surface of the water anywhere desired, and not in a ship yard, just near some lumber yard. The dummy ship should be painted and imitate the genuine as much as possible. Please acknowledge receipt.

Respectfully,
V. H., Chicago, IL[12]

The Secretary for the Navy
August 1, 1917

Sir:
A simple and inexpensive way of puzzling enemy submarine boats and causing them to waste much time in fruitless journeys occurs to me. It is that all merchant and warships crossing the Atlantic should drop overboard at intervals contrivances

timed by clockwork and to give off (some hours afterwards) clouds of smoke resembling that from a passing steamer. On perceiving the smoke an enemy would proceed toward it, and if the contrivance was so made as only to act for a short time and then sink he would be puzzled, and then seeing more smoke further on could probably be led on a long chase. The use could be varied at night by having the thing emit sparks at intervals as steamers do when stoked. Of course, it is to be [realized] that sooner or later the trick will be discovered, but even then the enemy would be unable to decide, on seeing smoke, whether it came from a ship or not. I have sent a copy of this letter to the Board of Inventions London, but as we are nationally somewhat unresponsive to ideas I thought it well to write also to you in case it may appear to you that the idea may be of use.

Yours faithfully,
E. H., Lauranga, New Zealand[13]

Deception schemes could only affect a few U-boats. America needed some reliable means for locating submerged submarines. These writers believed that lights or special vision devices might provide the answer:

Navy Department
May 28, 1917

Subject: Use of principle of glass-bottomed boat for submarine hunting. Suggestion is made of the possibility of using the same idea now in use at Catalina Island, in Bermuda, and in the Bahamas in sponge fishing, in what are known as glass bottomed boats, for the purpose of detecting by vision the presence of submarine boats. The suggestion is particularly made as applicable to light patrol boats and submarine chasers, where an inset section of clear glass, heavy enough to withstand the ordinary water pressure, may be placed at the bottom of a water tight well, or truncated pyramidal form, carried to above the water line level, where a light-tight eyepiece, such as is used on the Graflex camera for focusing, will adapt the apparatus for use. If the well is placed in a light-tight room the eyepiece will be unnecessary. When the water is not turbid, with the sun at any considerable altitude, bottom depths of 75 to 100 feet may be easily distinguished, and it is believed that the idea suggested might be used for daylight detection of submarines resting on the bottom in the shallow waters of the east English, Belgian, and Dutch coasts, as well as certain parts of the Mediterranean. The possible development of a submarine light projector for use in this connection is further suggested.

R. C., Asst. Eng., USN (Ret.)
Philadelphia, PA[14]

Council of National Defense
May 25, 1917

Gentlemen:
I take pleasure in sending you herewith a brief description of two anti submarine
theories which I have been working on for some weeks. I hope on investigation
that these ideas may be found to be of some value in combating the submarine
problem.

Very Respectfully yours,
T. G., Norwood, OH . . .

My theory is to continually keep the submarine exposed in certain sections by means
of powerful electric lights inserted in the water thereby rendering the submarine
exposed to attack, as the water is lighted to a depth of thirty or more feet. . . . A
lighted "dead line" might be established whereby submarines could not come out
or go in without showing themselves and consequently the observer could sink
the submarine with spear pointed bombs. A lighted lane might also be established
where freight and passenger ships could travel with comparative safety.[15]

After screening suggestions for spotting submerged U-boats, *Scientific American*
reported that visibility underwater using a viewing glass was no more than one
hundred feet, and that even a concentrated beam from a powerful searchlight
would penetrate no more than two hundred feet. Thus, neither method would
work in any but the most restricted waters.[16] Sound detectors held more promise.
The Entente deployed underwater listening devices called hydrophones, but only
two U-boats were definitely sunk using sound detection.[17] Hydrophones worked
best in narrow harbor entrances when combined with controlled mine fields. Such
a combination guarded the British fleet's main anchorage, sinking the last German
U-boat destroyed during the war.[18] *Scientific American* proposed a string of floating
observation posts equipped with nets and sound-detecting gear to guard harbor
entrances. These posts would establish the submarine's location and call in mobile
units to attack.[19] This letter suggested sea-floor listening stations:

American Minister
La Paz, Bolivia
August 30, 1917

Dear Sir:
Since you are probably less bothered with useless information than is the National
Defense Board, I am writing to you to describe an idea about submarines which

is probably in use now, but which seems worth telling, because I am not sure. It is well known that the submarine carries a form of water telephone receiver, by which it can detect the nearness of passing ships, by listening to the churn of the propellers, and that other ships can hear a submarine in the same way, when it can be distinguished from other shipping in the neighborhood. Would it not be possible to use this same apparatus in connection with the telephone, to determine the passing position, speed and direction of submarines through a narrow channel, such as the English channel, Gibraltar, the North Sea, or even across a badly infected area at sea. Suppose that the effective range of one of these receiving stations be five hundred yards, and that they be placed in a straight line across a channel and five hundred yards apart, each connected by its private wire to an ear piece in a listening station on the shore. . . . Now suppose that there were a second line of listening stations parallel to and a thousand yards from the first. Then by noting the time and position of the passage of the submarine across each line of listening stations, the position, bearing and rate of travel of the submarine could be quickly determined. With this information in hand, the air service working in connection with the listening stations, could be readily made to sail, or in the air over the line and in wireless connection with the land stations. Then being informed of the passage of the submarine across the first line, the aeroplane could come to the station designated, which could be located by the floating number, and when the position, bearing, and speed of the submarine were given, as shown by its crossing the second line, the air man would have a very good chance of finding the submarine, provided that the water conditions were such as to allow underwater observation from the air. . . .

B. B., La Paz, Bolivia[20]

Aircraft provided the Entente with another potential antisubmarine weapon. Britain used them for antisubmarine patrols, but their short range limited land-based planes to coastal waters. This writer proposed basing patrol planes at sea:

Council of National Defense
May 4, 1917

Gentlemen:
I am submitting to you herewith a plan for controlling submarine activities of our enemy and at the same time aiding our allies in every way we see fit. . . . The plan is this: Equip a certain number of our ships, either 25 or 50, with facilities for taking care of hydro-airplanes, machinery to repair them, means for launching, picking up out of the water, and storing the airplanes. If the hydro-airplanes are used exclusively the special preparation needs would be small. In that case it would be well for the mother ship to have oil enough to insure safe landing of her airplanes

in stormy weather. The distance across to England is 2500 to 3000 miles. Start the airplane ships for England so that they will cross the ocean 200 miles apart. When they arrive there have them start back on a path 200 miles from their former path. It will then be seen that there is a zone of safety between the two lines of battleships thru which it will be practically perfectly safe for ships to pass. . . . This plan will enable us to destroy and render harmless the enemy's submarine campaign in the shortest time, at the least expenditure of men and money, and will at the same time enable us to give the allies the support they need, at once.

R. M., Hunter, ND[21]

Seaplanes available in 1917 lacked the engine power to carry a useful bomb load and had difficulty landing and taking off in the open sea, preventing them from escorting ships in mid-ocean.[22] *Scientific American* suggested building aircraft-carrying merchantmen, complete with a flight deck and folding smokestack: "With from one to three aeroplanes covering a wide stretch of water ahead of the ship, it would be practically impossible for a submarine to get within torpedo range unobserved."[23] Even in areas covered by air patrols, U-boats could remain submerged by day, surfacing at night to recharge batteries. This writer suggested an aid to nocturnal operations by antisubmarine aircraft:

The Board of National Defense
September 2, 1917

Gentlemen:
I beg to refer you to blue print and letter descriptive of my device for the destruction of submarines sent you some 6 or 8 days ago and submit an additional idea in connection therewith, as follows. Could there be a flyer equipped with strong light which would enable [the] commander of [an] airplane to see a U boat at close distance at night; the airplane to carry destructive bombs and drop them when over a U boat. The U boats, I am told, are on the surface at night. In order that airplane can keep in touch with the mother ship, the latter could occasionally flash with her search light, and when the airplane wished to return it could signal the mother ship with its light. . . .

I am Sir, Very Respectfully,
A. P., National Soldiers Home, [No city given], CA[24]

The next writer described a primitive version of the depth charge launchers and hedgehog mortars of World War II:

To the Editor of the *Scientific American:*

Merchantmen and "chasers" are equipped with cannon to fight U-boats, from 3 to 6-inch calibre. The press accounts seem to indicate that unless they can make a direct hit on the periscope, when it only shows, the shot is wasted and no harm results. I read that a U-boat is somewhat fragile and a shock of some violence would injure or destroy them. Some years ago I read of the installation of mortars in pits in a fort near New York. It stated they could be fired in the air with such accuracy that the ball would descend on the deck of a vessel miles distant. The U-boat when using torpedoes is seldom over a mile distant. In addition to cannon, why not have our merchant ships armed with short mortars of huge calibre, throwing a round ball of large size, loaded with high explosive, set to explode at 20 feet depth. Since the target would be close the mortars could be short, not rifled, quickly aimed and fired. It should be an easy matter to come within 20, 50, or 100 feet of the target, and the explosion would either destroy the U-boat or put it out of action for a while. On war vessels they might have half a dozen mortars and fire a volley, and one would be certain to come near enough [to] the boat to destroy it. This idea is so obvious and so simple that it surely must be in use, or there must be some reason unknown to me, why it is not utilized. But I know mankind often overlooks the simple to adopt the complicated. If through some miracle of stupidity or mental strabismus it has not been thought of won't you call attention of the proper authorities to it?

A. P., Philadelphia, PA[25]

The next writer anticipated the hunter-killer submarines of the Cold War:

To the Editor of the *Scientific American:*

What I recommend is feasible and practical, and will grow from the smallest unit to the covering of the seas with *Entente* U-boats which will ultimately make the presence of a German U-boat so infrequent as to be a negligible factor in the progress of this war. It means the replacement of the German U-boats by those of the *Entente* allies, and the work can be put under way at once with the factors now at hand. Wherever a German U-boat may be, it is possible for an *Entente* Scout U-boat to operate in the following manner to detect the presence of the former. The probable location of the German U-boat having been given through the reports of freighters, steamers, destroyers or any other agency, one or more Scout *Entente* U-boats is assigned to that locality, to which they proceed quietly, secretly and remain submerged as much as possible, depending on the periscopes; taking advantage of the morning and evening twilights, and lighter nights to observe the unsuspecting German U-boat rise to the surface. (The *Entente* craft lying quiescent will prevent the German sound detectors from being aware of her presence.) The location of the enemies' U-boats here and there, throughout the great field of their operation, will enable an extensive chart to be provided that will show at a glance their general location and enable the commander of the *Entente* flotilla to take advantage of such information.

G. F., Chicago, IL[26]

A number of ideas emerged for using seagulls to spot submarines:

Chief of Naval Operations
October 15, 1917

Detecting the presence of enemy U-boats. Respectfully submitted: Let all Allied submarines while cruising throw out food (refuse) plentifully to seagulls. Give them the kind of food they crave. These birds will soon find U-boats well worth following up. Have the submarine submerge while feeding the gulls so that they will learn to detect and follow the boats while under the surface. The Allied submarines seem not to be playing an important part in this war, and they can easily make themselves known to Allied destroyers. Of course the German U-boat dares not. It is believed that when an enemy U-boat enters Allied waters it will be picked up by these clever and keen-eyed birds and that they will hang over its trail, expecting food. Sighting a moving flock of gulls hovering over the surface of the water might indicate to destroyers the presence of an enemy U-boat, even far out at sea.

Yours very respectfully,
A. B., New York, NY[27]

One magazine reported that an inventor had developed a device for disgorging gull food from a submerged submarine, and the National Audubon Society offered to provide gulls for a training program.[28] Navy officials rejected the idea, however:

Commander Submarine Force to Chief of Naval Operations
March 8, 1918

Subject: Seagulls as submarine trailers. 1. Returned. 2. The use of sea gulls as submarine trailers was suggested some time ago as a joke. Evidently it was repeated so many times as to be taken seriously. 3. The nature of sea gulls is such that they will follow any ship entering or leaving port, that throws overboard garbage. As for sea gulls following submarines, the Force Commander is quite positive that such is not the case. There is quite a large number of gulls around New London and they have never followed any operating submarine. 4. During the war, several ships having livestock on board have been sunk by German submarines. Naturally thousands of sea gulls would be attracted by the carcasses of dead animals. Surface vessels seeing the sea gulls have, quite correctly, deduced the conclusion that a ship had been sunk, and that a submarine was somewhere within twenty or thirty miles of the vicinity. 5. Other than the above, the Force Commander considers that sea gulls never have been and never will be of any use.[29]

These two writers suggested means for blinding U-boats as they tried to attack:

Commandant, Brooklyn Navy Yard
April 28, 1917

Dear Sir:
I have the following suggestion to offer: I am advised that when a submarine emerges from the water, the view from the periscope is blurred and dimmed until the lens becomes dry, therefore any condition which delays the clearing of the lens is of vital importance. My suggestion is that the lane laid out by the Admiralty be oiled with crude oil in sufficient quantity to create an oil film on the water. By experiment I have ascertained that on an ordinary lens a very small proportion of oil suffices to effectually blur it for a considerable period of time, and the use of crude oil would undoubtedly make it necessary for the submarine to come to the surface in order to clean her lenses. This suggestion is respectfully submitted in the hope that some solution for the defense against submarines may be evolved.

Respectfully yours,
J. C.[30]

Council of National Defense
May 8, 1917

Gentlemen:
The following suggestions may contain some germ of merit and I offer them for what they are worth. "A." On the assumption that transports carrying troops will be convoyed by destroyers stationed at proper intervals about the transports would it not be possible to equip each destroyer with a powerful instrument of the nature of a heliograph. One or more strong beams of light thrown upon the object glass of the periscope should effectively blind a submarine. Possibly the same result could be obtained by means of powerful searchlights should the sky be overcast.

The purpose being to delay action by the submarine crew and perhaps make it impossible to properly discharge a torpedo. . . . I offer suggestion "A" as practicable for it would seem that to blind a submarine even for a brief interval of time would give a gun pointer a decided advantage with his target brilliantly illuminated as well. I am acting wholly from a sense of duty in offering these suggestions. Anything that might promote the science of offensive action against the submarine should be at once communicated to proper authorities.

Sincerely yours,
F. N., Roslyn Heights, NY[31]

Although hunting and destroying U-boats fit the American public's aggressive approach to the war, sinking submarines was not strictly necessary. Each Allied merchantman arriving safely in Britain represented a victory, so writers submitted ideas for protecting ships against torpedoes. Many involved schemes for hanging nets or steel plates alongside the ships:

Secretary of the Navy
May 3, 1917

Having in mind the fact that the Navy Department considers all suggestions made to it, with a view to selecting such as may have some value, I am submitting herewith a scheme which appears to me to be practicable and possibly a help towards protection against submarine attacks. I propose that a column of cylindrical floats suspending iron shields in 50 or 75 foot sections, more or less, be hooked up in tandem and towed on both sides of ship covering same from flank attack from bow to stern. From each float I propose to suspend an iron plate which will extend longitudinally beyond the ends of each float to overlap well the one preceding and the one following, and to extend downwards a sufficient depth to catch the deepest traveling torpedo, and I am told that this distance is about 14 feet. These two columns of floats would be held at such distance from the vessel as would protect it from effect of explosion when contact takes place. The difficulty of maintaining the columns of floats at a necessary distance from the ship is appreciated but it is thought that a rudder could be arranged on the leading section which would require the columns to move parallel to the sides of the ship. . . .

E. C., Eagle Pass, TX[32]

Scientific American pointed out the fault with all such schemes—in this case, maintaining the nets or plates against the power of the ocean. In order to protect the ship against a torpedo, the shields would have to be positioned thirty feet from the hull, presumably with some combination of booms and chains. Ships crossing the Atlantic might encounter waves fifteen to thirty feet high: "Such a sea meeting a ship end on and striking the booms which hold the nets or plates in position, would snap them as if they had no more strength than so many pipe stems."[33] *Illustrated World* put it bluntly: "It is doubtful that any sort of false hull, double bottom, extended torpedo net or other barrier between torpedo and hull of victim is likely to be the answer, and those who propose new methods of net making, screen hanging, or double bottom fashioning can save time and postage, not to say effort, by leaving the obvious alone."[34]

The best way for ships to avoid attack was to avoid U-boats. If U-boats hid underwater, could not merchantmen use similar tactics to run the submarine gauntlet? *Scientific American* backed the idea of submersible cargo ships, arguing, "[I]t is folly to expect successfully to fight submarine craft with craft on the surface, or successfully to send a surface merchant ship through waters that are swarming with these invisible sharks of the sea. Just as aerial navies must be fought with aerial navies, so the menace of the invisible sub-surface craft must be met and neutralized by setting afloat an invisible merchant navy."[35]

This letter suggested building cargo submarines that could be converted to fighting vessels:

Secretary of the Navy
February 26, 1917

The Navy Department should build merchant submarines of the "Deutschland" type instead of war submarines as it is now doing. They should be so constructed that they could be converted into war craft by the addition of torpedo tubes; guns could be carried both as war craft and as merchantmen. In case of war with the Teutonic Alliance there would be comparatively little demand for the war submarine in our Navy so long as present conditions prevail; should these conditions change and we have a fleet of merchant submarines, these could readily be converted into war craft. In the meantime much more valuable service could be rendered by the merchant submarine in the carrying of freight to and from Europe as they would be practically immune to enemy attack. . . . Naturally many obstacles would be encountered in putting of such a plan into operation but its practical value is obvious.

Respectfully yours,
F. M., New York, NY[36]

As the Germans had already discovered, cargo submarines proved impractical for moving large quantities of goods. High construction costs and the need for specially trained crews, coupled with relatively small cargo capacity, made them uneconomical for anything but the most critical loads. *Scientific American* therefore proposed a simple submersible cargo ship that could be easily mass-produced: a low-tech submarine that would transit danger zones awash and submerge only when an enemy was nearby.[37] This writer sent in another method for moving cargo underwater:

Secretary of the Navy
June 1, 1917

Dear Sir:
Is it not practical to make very large containers of several thicknesses of canvas, lined with suitable substance of a flexible nature to make it available as a submersible bladder container of large dimensions to carry oil across the sea. Such containers having a separate bottom for having [heavier-than-oil] cargo (which would be desirable) to carry [heavier-than-oil] cargo to keep the gravity at a point where the whole canvas container would be under water quite a depth supported on the surface by air bags. Thus making it possible to be taken into tow and relieve shipping to a great extent and ensure delivery against submarines. Such bladder once filled with oil could be used to carry under sea all cargoes in quantity sufficient to supply oversea needs if there were enough of them made and put into use, the idea being not only to make use of the means of [transporting] oil but taking advantage of its gravity to transport other commodities under water as a good means of protection against submarines.

Very truly yours,
J. R., Lovelock, NV[38]

Moving cargo to Europe by air would avoid submarines altogether:

To the Editor of the *Scientific American:*
I have read with interest various methods proposed by readers of your interesting journal for breaking the so-called German submarine blockade. My idea may not be practicable just at present, but in case an effective device is not invented to protect our and our Allies' merchant men within the near future (which I sincerely hope will not be the case), we will have to search for another means of transporting the necessary food, equipment, etc. for our and the Allies' armies. I suggest we look into the matter of utilising super-aircraft similar to Zepplins or the large aeroplanes reported soon to be in use on the Western front, on which twenty to thirty

passengers may ride, for transporting the necessary supplies across the Atlantic. Of course there will have to be new inventions and improvements installed but the scheme is possible. Haven't we read of long distant Zepplin raids over England, aircraft coming from Chicago to New York, etc.? . . . . America has the brains and ability, the raw materials and the men successfully to master problems which would arise if the foregoing or some similar scheme were carried out. So even if the Germans do cripple our merchant sea-service, they can never beat us over the water.

J. S., Newark, NJ[39]

Ships could also sail around submarine-infested waters. This writer suggested an alternative route to Europe:

July 27, 1917

Dear Sir:
Copies of this letter are being sent to the leading newspapers of the United States, Great Britian and France. If you agree with me, put all your influence behind it. . . . Block the Straits of Gibralter with a net. The distance is 10 miles. Block the Straits of Otranto, the heel of Italy. The distance is 40 miles. Block the Dardenelles. By doing this we will make the Mediterranean as safe as Lake Michigan. Turn every pound of freight westward to the Pacific coast. Send all Allied ships through the canal to the ports of San Diego, Los Angeles, San Francisco, Oakland, Portland, Tacoma, Seattle, and Vancouver. . . . Make provision for coaling at Nagasaki, Singapore, Colombo and Aden. Yes, the distance is longer but the U-boat has proven to us that the longest way around is the shortest way home. The consumer pays the freight. England will object, but not if she reasons this method will save her from possible hunger and defeat. Japan will naturally furnish her great merchant marine, and with no future losses our steel plants can turn their attention to munitions and guns. Freight can be landed in France and transshipped across country to Calais, thence to Dover. Is it not wiser to be absolutely sure that you are going to deliver food to England in 90 days than to have it sunk? Don't let the influence of Eastern docking and lighterage interests stand in the way of this plan. Discount the wild reports of German submarines capable of operation in the Indian Ocean. Sixty miles of net, which can be placed in ninety days, will win the war.

W. V., New York, NY[40]

German U-boats had to pass through the English Channel or the narrow sea between Scotland and Norway to reach the Atlantic. The Entente heavily patrolled the Channel, employing listening buoys and electrically detonated mines.[41] The larger North Sea passage remained open, however. *Scientific American* proposed spanning the North Sea with a mesh curtain two hundred feet deep embedded with thousands of small mines, closing off the entire two hundred and fifty–mile gap between Great Britain and Norway: "If the approaches to the North Sea were protected by successive lines of aeroplanes, scouts, destroyers and patrol boats, and finally by an impassable wall of bombs, it is safe to say that the Atlantic routes would be rid, once and for all, of the submarine pest, and America would be free to send over food, munitions and troops without fear of molestation."[42]

These two writers suggested variations on a North Sea barrier:

Secretary of State for the Navy
November 23, 1917

Dear Mr. Secretary:
I enclose a statement drawn up by the staff of engineers who are working with me which covers the various points relating to the building of a concrete barrier across the North Sea. . . . The barrier proposed is composed of units five hundred feet long, eighty feet base and one hundred twenty feet high. This design may be varied to conform to the particular spot to be blocked. The distance from Elamborough Head, England across the Dogger Bank to Horns Reef, Denmark is three hundred miles. The average depth is fifteen fathoms. . . . The completed structure will require three thousand units. The plan is to provide thirty batteries or complete building plants. Each battery would require four months to be ready for operation and at each battery twenty-five units could be under construction at one time and be completed in seventy days. In other words, the proposed organization will turn out seven hundred fifty complete units every seventy days and the entire number of three thousand in two hundred eighty days. . . . If all of the material, except the sand and gravel, is taken from the United States, it will require one million tons of shipping to maintain the supplies of material during the time of construction, on the basis of two months time for return trips of cargo boats.

G. M., New York, NY[43]

Chief of Bureau, Naval Inventions
August 20, 1917

This plan for preventing U-boats from entering or departing from their bases via the North Sea, the only route now open to them, contemplates the employment of 3,700 patrol boats, one-half of which would be kept moving in a continuous procession from a point off the Shetland Islands to the shoal indicated in the diagram off the coast of Norway and outside of Norway's three mile limit. The other half of the patrol fleet would act as relief vessels, taking their place in line as others drop out for fuel and supplies. Each patrol vessel would trail over her stern a long, heavy pliant wire to which would be fitted a sufficient number of contact bombs of explosive strength sufficient to destroy any submarine with which they come in contact. . . . Formed in double column with each line indented, 1,850 vessels would allow for one at every 400-yard interval in each line, the interval in the double line being 200 yards. The idea of the indented formation is to narrow the space between the lines of trailed bombs, this formation also minimizing the danger of injuring the next vessel astern when the bombs of the leader are set off by contact with a submarine. . . . As submarines cannot operate for a longer period than thirty days, it is obvious that those that are at sea at the time this barrier is stretched across the North Sea must essay the forlorn hope of breaking through it, else come up and surrender, or perish. Thus in a short time the seas would be cleared of U-boats and the barrier would prevent others from going out. . . .

Plan suggested by
W. M., Naval Editor, *New York World,* New York, NY[44]

In 1918 the Entente began mining the North Sea gap, using a new type of antenna mine that covered as much sea space as four ordinary mines.[45] This North Sea mine barrage eventually included more than seventy thousand mines, the vast majority of them American.[46] The war ended before the barrier could be fully tested, but the mines sank several U-boats and demonstrated America's determination to commit vast resources to the antisubmarine campaign.

Most Americans viewed submarine operations as a barbaric form of naval piracy. Torpedo attacks on unarmed ships, often resulting in great loss of life, inflamed U.S. public opinion and boosted support for war with Germany. Paradoxically, increased antisubmarine efforts encouraged surprise attacks, for any U-boat that surfaced to warn its intended victim risked being sunk itself. Thus, the percentage of ships sunk without warning rose from 1915 to 1917, adding to the perception of U-boat men as cold-blooded killers.[47] Some Americans considered U-boats beyond the pale, and offered proposals that ignored traditional constraints on military action. This writer submitted one of the more questionable schemes, which would have made all lifeboats legitimate military targets. Fortunately for sailors on both sides, the Navy declared the idea impractical:

Secretary of the Navy
June 22, 1917

Sir:

In an article which appeared in today's *New York Sun*, clipping enclosed herewith, it was stated by a member of the crew of the ship which was torpedoed, one James A. Powers of Nangatuck, Conn., that all those alive after the explosion got away in four boats but no submarine was seen until the boat containing Powers and his companions was forty yards from the sinking ship when a submarine appeared alongside and her crew crawled out of the conning tower. The commander of the submarine asked for the name of the ship and when this was given the submarine crew laughed and jeered and made off. Why would it not be a good scheme to have a certain number of life boats on merchant vessels equipped with automatic machine guns which could easily be concealed, and when opportunities like the one in question offer, some well directed shots would prevent members of the submarine crews from laughing and jeering in the future and possibly cause other conditions which would curtail Mr. Submarine's activities for a time at least.

Respectfully Submitted,
T. M., New York, NY[48]

This writer warned that the U-boats might have sinister motives for approaching survivors:

The War Department
June 10, 1918

Gentlemen:

Upon reading reports of submarine activities off the New England coast, an idea passed through my mind that looks dangerous. The paper states that the enemy are saving passengers and crews of some ships, also that those rescued are landed at New York. This practice of the Huns is out of the ordinary for them, do you think it probable that they would innoculate those rescued with some fatal disease that may spread among our people, should not those rescued be interned for a period to determine this. . . .

F. P., Sacramento, CA[49]

This letter contained another antisubmarine scheme remarkable for its ruthlessness:

President of the United States
Nov. 20, 1917

Dear Sir:
I respectfully wish to suggest the following as a possible solution of the U-Boat menace: On and after a specified date to be announced by proclamation, the holds of all ships sailing to and from this country to European ports be made to contain a number of German prisoners, 50 to 500 or even more if necessary, depending on the size of the vessel and the importance of its cargo. The exact number of prisoners thus contained on each boat should be given the widest possible publicity, and streamers or signs on the boats should likewise convey the information. In my opinion, the German Government with full knowledge that their men would be killed by the explosion of the torpedo or drowned by the sinking of the boat would voluntarily discontinue their present practice, or if not they would be compelled to by the public demand of their subjects. . . .

H. H., New York, NY[50]

The Navy rejected this idea as both ineffective and dangerous:

It is anticipated that in its present temper and frame of mind the Imperial German Government would interpret the presence of Teutonic prisoners of war on board of merchant ships of the Allies voyaging in Teutonic-prohibited waters as very much, or entirely, in the same category with the deliberate exposure of war prisoners on land in dangerous proximity to the firing line so as to cause the enemy to withhold fire and therefore as an illegal method of warfare justifying retaliation. There are no apparent convincing arguments supporting the idea that the German Government will, by reason of the knowledge that Germans are on board of merchant vessels of the Allies as hostages for immunity from submarine attack, be deterred in any degree whatever from the desperate and irrevocable policy of attacking every vessel non-Teutonic in character. It is believed that for every Teutonic prisoner of war so hazarded, and from the German standpoint, so sacrificed, a prisoner of war of Allied nationality will be summarily executed. Thus the extent of retaliation and counter-retaliation will be limitless.[51]

The Entente ultimately defeated the U-boats by organizing merchantmen into convoys. This reduced the number of targets and ensured that submarines lucky enough to spot a ship dared not surface to use their guns. Together with coastal air patrols and extensive mining, the convoy system frustrated German submarine strategy, and by mid-1918 the crisis had passed.

While U-boats stalked Allied merchantmen, outnumbered German battleships sought refuge in port. The island of Helgoland off the northwest coast of Germany formed a natural outpost guarding their bases. The Germans had heavily fortified Helgoland and mined the surrounding waters to deter Allied raids.[52] As long as German battleships sheltered behind Helgoland, the British and Americans had to keep their own navies on constant watch for a possible sortie. Allied admirals refused to risk their ships in an attack against German ports. *Scientific American* conceded, "[A] naval attack by capital ships against the naval bases would not only fail to make any serious impression, but, because of the shoals, sandbars, and narrow channels of the German coast and the enormous strength of the heavy guns and mortars of the German fortifications, any such attack would mean the loss and disablement of the flower of the Allied dreadnought fleet."[53]

The *Forum* proposed an air strike using Whitehead torpedoes against the German fleet as it lay at anchor: "It requires no stretch of the imagination to picture what would happen if a squadron of these 'planes ever got into action at Wilhelmshaven or Kiel. One large Whitehead would serve more effectively to disturb the Sabbath calm reputed to exist in those safe harbors than anything else one could imagine. There would not be much chance for its escaping damaging that rather closely-packed German fleet."[54]

A number of writers submitted schemes to breach German harbor defenses by neutralizing Helgoland with fire or a Halifax-like detonation:

August 5, 1917

A scheme for prosecuting an attack on the German naval base at Helgoland. 10,000,000 gallons of crude oil will cover an area 60 miles by 1 and 1/4 miles by 1/16" deep. It is desired to tow crude oil in steel tanks, running awash, by (preferably) oil fired obsolete warships, using as many ships as may be necessary in order to attain a towing speed of at least two miles per hour. It is desired to string such a series of vessels and their tows in a line as long as possible and under control of a small crew on each vessel until what ought to be considered a critically dangerous line is reached, when the ships are abandoned by the crews taking to a destroyer detailed to each towing ship. The expectation being that they (all ships and tows) could continue on their way until a time device on each tank explodes the tank and fires the contents. The result depends upon a suitable steady wind towards Helgoland. Defense of Dover Strait against mines for the ships would probably be necessary; further it might be desirable to have some device for wrecking and firing tanks if mines or submarines struck them. The result (if conditions can be made right) would be a wall of flame and dense smoke which would blind and destroy and act as a screen and barrier for the attacking fleet. Guns on Helgoland, if the attack can be brought close enough, could not operate, as the heat would sizzle it, airplanes would be of little use. It might be that the time for attack provided by such an oil screen would not be long enough and that it would have to be followed at once by a second dose directed almost entirely at Helgoland and at a much closer range. If the first attack can possibly be executed, the second would be a simple matter.

Respectfully,
F. C., Cleveland, OH[55]

Council of National Defense
December 8, 1917

Gentlemen:
The explosion at Halifax caused great disaster for miles around. The German navy is behind land defenses and will not come out and we can not get in to them with out great risk. Load a boat with high explosive, go with it to the nearest point of safety to Wilhelmshaven, lash the steering apparatus with boat under full steam going towards the German harbor, all hands desert the boat, leave electric wire attached to set off explosion, smudge boxes working or fog. If they shoot into it the worst could only be an explosion a little premature. Follow this boat with another one same kind and from a layman's point of view it would seem that about the third or fourth boat explosion would be pretty close to their fountain head. This would blast the way for entrance by the Allied fleet, if there was anything for them to do after a few explosions.

Yours truly,
G. W., Kansas City, MO[56]

These two writers suggested using submarines as Trojan horses:

Navy Department
September, 1917

Dear Sir:
Why not use a bit of "camouflage" in the Navy along the following line:—Take for each submarine base a captured German submarine, batter off their periscope and

put a safe snap lock inside each hatch that it becomes necessary to use dynamite to open them. Fill each submarine with a hundred tons or more of the most powerful explosive. Then take them out and set adrift just outside the mine fields just one off each base. They may be loaded so as to list a bit and given the appearance of being disabled. The natural thing for the Germans will be to tow each in to the harbor. In addition to having a battery attached to each hatch have time batteries set to explode her when you may deem it best. A destroyer or two could chase each in about dawn. Not in the history of this war has so much high explosive been placed in an absolutely air and water tight steel encasement, where the force generated would wreck all shipping in any of the coast town harbors, also it would dangerously affect Heligoland [sic]. Would it not be possible to use it as a starter for a general attack? I made this suggestion to the Navy Department August 3rd, but doubt it got beyond the clerical force. Myself as well as a few engineering friends with some idea of psychology have considerable faith that such a plan would work out as designed. It should be good enough for one try out and if successful a second would not be necessary.

Very truly yours,
D. F., New York, NY[57]

Assistant Secretary of the Navy Roosevelt
November 11, 1917

Sir:
I hope that when [you] receive and read this letter, that you will not consider me a crank or crazy, but a good American who was in the Spanish American War, and can not pass physical examination to get into this one, so I have been studying and planned the following hard and desperate chance. I fully understand that there is only one chance in a thousand of full success and if successful that there is only one chance in a million of escaping, but would willingly take the chance. . . .

C. S., Passaic, NJ

PLAN: This is to have England turn over a captured German submarine and equip it with torpedoes and a volunteer crew and enter the naval harbor of Wilhemshaven under the German flag just about dark, and as submerging to pull the German flag down and let the American flag wave, start to torpedo the German fleet of course our depending in this case is nerve and surprise, a lone submarine is best as everything is an enemy and no danger of destroying a friend. The notice asking for volunteers is to say that there are one in a million of coming out alive, and describe the different kind of men needed. Then if successful to try some way of getting to the rest of their navy.[58]

Expendable ships or manned torpedoes might clear the minefields protecting these bases:

Secretary of the Navy
August 31, 1917

. . . If the British Admiralty would adopt the methods so successfully employed by Admiral Farragut in our civil war, it would soon end German submarine operations. . . . As is well known, one of the most formidable obstacles to be overcome in attacking the German naval bases are the mine fields and lines of torpedoes. If an average of twenty English merchant vessels are to be sunk every week by the enemy, why not let the English take about ten of their large merchantmen, fully equipped with drag nets and grappling irons, and place four of these merchantmen in a diagonal single file so as to completely sweep a channel two hundred feet wide. If one of them strikes a mine or torpedo and sinks, one of the six reserve merchantmen will immediately take its place. These merchantmen should be loaded down with ballast so as to draw more water that the heaviest war craft following them. An attacking fleet following immediately behind this vanguard of "sacrifice ships" would have a channel two hundred feet wide, absolutely free from mines or torpedoes. . . . With a vanguard of "sacrifice merchantmen" properly equipped with drag-nets and grappling irons, an attacking fleet could safely pass through any body of water, no matter how thickly strewn with mines or torpedoes. Suppose a few of the "sacrifice ships" are lost? If they have cleared the channel of dangerous explosives, have they not performed a valuable military service. Is this not better than to have an average of twenty merchantmen (laden with men, women and children passengers, with valuable cargoes and with the crew dependent on small boats far out at sea for their preservation) sunk every week? Farragut and Dewey demonstrated that the most effectual way to fight an enemy was to strike him directly at his headquarters. German submarine operations never will be completely checked until the nests in which these pests are hatched are destroyed. A submarine cannot operate for any considerable period of time without a home base. Capture their home bases and you will speedily put an end to submarine activities.

E. M., Washington, DC[59]

I wish to suggest a possible means of striking at submarine bases by means of submarines. Since submarines leave these bases, other submarines can approach them if they can find their way though the mine fields and net systems which constitute the protection of the bases against submarine attack. There would seem to be a possibility that a diver who could move about freely, and who carried with him a search light of moderate intensity might be able to pick his way through the defenses and guide a submarine through them. My plan for giving the driver the necessary mobility would be to seat him in the cockpit of a one-man submarine of suitable type. The type I have in mind consists of a body substantially like that of a Whitehead torpedo. . . . A suitable search light should be mounted on the scout. No doubt care would have to be taken to avoid using this in such a way as to reveal to watchers on the surface the presence of the hostile force. . . .

Respectfully submitted,
E. M., Austin, MN
No remuneration desired.[60]

Although German defenses deterred a direct assault, the British raided several harbors in an unsuccessful effort to block them with sunken ships. This writer suggested obstructing the shallow waters off German ports:

Council for National Defense
July 26, 1917

Gentlemen:
As the submarine problem is a serious one, it seems to me that the easiest way to solve it is to block them in their bases. I have been informed that the west coast of Europe is very much like our own Gulf coast. If this is the case, it strikes me that it would be easy to block Zeebrugge by the use of sand dredges by pumping sand into the channel. This will be difficult to accomplish but it can be done. It can be done by having the outlet pipe from the dredge well bolted together and extending out in front of it for five to seven miles, supported from place to place by means of gigantic floats. It will be necessary to protect the dredge and pipe from submarines by means of nets. Torpedo boats must act as a patrol. Having this arrangement ready, the dredges will move into position, using submarines to guide the outlet pipe into place, and pump sand into the channel. To do this rapidly it may be necessary to use hundreds of dredges, but once the channel is blocked, a small number can keep them filled by continually working at it and pumping in. It is necessary that torpedo boats guard the dredges and it is necessary that big ships keep counter dredging operations down. . . .

Yours truly,
M. T., Dover, NJ[61]

Finally, from the fertile mind of the nation's greatest inventor:

The Secretary of the Navy
July 26, 1917

My Dear Mr. Daniels:
Only a suggestion. If the Allies desire to mine the harbor of Zeebrugge, I suggest flat bottom row boats, 15 feet long, 4 feet wide, like the country-boy uses, but covered over water tight. In this boat is a gyrostat run by a 2 H.P. motor and a storage battery smaller than used in an electric vehicle. Fastened to the bottom of the boat is a standard mine with chain. In addition, there is also a pole connected to the bottom extending down about 26 feet, which is the depth of water just off Zeebrugge breakwater. When the pole strikes the bottom it releases the mine and chain and sinks the boat. The pole in question can be set for any depth. These boats which only appear six inches above the sea, having a circular top, are very difficult to see with any searchlight at night, hence, cannot be shot at. The speed of the boat is about 2-1/2 miles per hour. The scheme is that in favorable nights a lot of small vessels approach within say 15 miles of Zeebrugge, each boat being provided with 1/2 dozen of these skiffs. Knowing the direction of the searchlights, tide, and drift, they can set the gyrostatic rudder and aim the boats for the harbor, inner or outer, and they can do this at all kinds of times. The boats are very cheap.

Thomas A. Edison
Orange, NJ[62]

The Allied strategy of containing the German fleet eventually succeeded. Penned in by superior British and American forces, the Kaiser's navy sat while crew morale steadily declined. Ordered to sea for a last-ditch sortie in October 1918, the sailors mutinied rather than face almost certain death.[63] The mutineers seized the bases their enemies had never dared attack, raised the banner of revolution, and helped force Germany out of the war.

CHAPTER 4

Over There: The Campaign in Europe

I n April 1917 the United States joined one of two great coalitions striving for world dominance. Suddenly, events unfolding in strange lands thousands of miles away became vitally important to ordinary Americans. The *Independent* (a magazine published in New York City from 1848 to 1923) published tips for citizens seeking to better understand the fighting. It suggested procuring terrain maps, a compass for distances, and a subscription to a newspaper that carried the largest number of war communiqués: "[T]he amateur who altogether lacks training and presumably native genius has the advantage of not being burdened by responsibility or limited by time and he will find the solution of the strategical problems presented by the current news often easy and always fascinating."[1]

The strategic balance sheet in April 1917 contained both promise and peril. America's growing Army needed time to train and equip, while its leaders learned to operate within an alliance that had been fighting for nearly three years. Although U.S. entry seemed to give the Entente a decisive advantage, two of America's strongest allies soon faced disaster. In Russia, a series of upheavals created chaos that destroyed the czar's army and eventually degenerated into a bloody civil war. In Italy, an enemy offensive routed the Italian army and threatened to knock that nation out of the war. Many Americans justifiably feared that their alliance might suffer fatal losses before U.S. power could make itself felt.

Russia remained an enigma to foreigners, as an enormous empire with seemingly limitless resources that floundered in a miasma of technological backwardness, social unrest, and military ineptitude. Despite its problems, Russia's sheer size and huge population convinced many Americans that it would play a key role in any Allied victory. *Scientific American* predicted, "[T]wo years from now, when the vast Russian hordes, fully drilled and equipped, move forward, it is believed that the final and decisive phase of the great war will have been reached."[2] Others had less faith in Russia's "hordes." The *Washington Post* concluded, "Russia, in spite of her inexhaustible human material, is weakening far faster than Germany and Austria-Hungary, and than her own allies, because she cannot produce competent officers quickly enough and will never be able to organize her resources sufficiently. The exhaustion of the manpower of Russia is out of the question, but the breakdown of the colossus will surely come as soon as England and France are no longer able to furnish the enormous sums of money needed by the Czar."[3] Some Americans urged the dispatch of U.S. troops to bolster Russia:

Harry S. New
U.S. Senate
[April 1917]

Out of justice to the plan herein unfolded, I would ask that you hold in mind the fact that, sometimes the ideas, inventions etc., that sound so simple are the ones that prove of the most value, because of their very simplicity. . . . The plan would be without virtue as an open move, and its greatest value lies in its being developed and executed in absolute secret. It is the one move that the Imperial German government would least expect, and would be almost devoid of any danger from attack by said Imperial German Government. I refer to an expedition or expeditions to be started from the western coast of our country or Canada, preferably from the port of Victoria, B.C. or Seattle, Washington, U.S.A., the supplies, munitions, arms, artillery equipment and men to be drawn from the heretofore most inactive and far-removed section of our land, the western states, and if a joint expedition with Canada, they could also utilize the western part of their country in drawing upon its resources. This expedition or expeditions to make Russia their destination, as the Russians are, without question, the one section of the Allied Armies most in need of assistance, both moral and material. With the assistance we could give them, they would probably prove to be the strongest force in the war. We could take arms, munitions, and food. If deemed necessary, we could even send some troops, giving the Russian Army new impetus and a new spirit that would without question shorten the war by several months. A big drive from the East front into the German army would trap the forces of the Kaiser between the French and English on the west and the Russian on the east, totally crushing them in the center, until surrender would be absolutely necessary. This plan would divide the enemy's force, in that they would have to face both ways, guarding their east as well as their west. . . .

E. C.[4]

Although Russia and Japan had fought each other a decade earlier, they now found themselves on the same side. Japanese troops were close enough to help their erstwhile enemies:

> To the Editor of the *New York Times*
> May 1, 1917
>
> . . . No doubt the active participation of the Japanese land forces in the great struggle has been a matter of consideration in the allied camp during the last two years and a half, but no decision has apparently been reached. . . . Along that eastern front are a half score points at which a large, well-found Japanese army would give the coup de grace to the war. The Entente lines barely hold there. Russia today is only safe in her endless, engulfing immensity that eats up enemies as it ate up the greatest soldier of the age. . . . As to transport, I feel sure that American railroad skill joined to Russian experience could forward with surprising speed an immense army with all its belongings over the Siberian roads that landed the Russians in Manchuria thirteen years ago. If the sea route were necessary for some of the army or supplies, it must be noted that the Red Sea route would bring them to the Saloniki front weeks before they could be placed in northern France. . . .
>
> J. C., New York, NY[5]

Russia's real weakness was not military but moral. The *Washington Post* suggested the following:

> Russian-born citizens of the United States should be urged to return to Russia on a mission of fraternity, to explain to their old neighbors the real nature and purpose of America. The Russian-speaking Americans, if sent to Russia, could perform an invaluable service for all the nations that are arrayed against Germany. . . . Such men could reach the minds and hearts of their former countrymen. Their missionary efforts could be followed by visible evidence of American helpfulness in the shape of farm tractors, railroad material, electric equipment, flour mills, mining and industrial machinery, and for the time being foodstuffs, if necessary, pending the reestablishment of railroad operations.[6]

This writer suggested a mission to strengthen the moral fabric of Russian society:

> Secretary of War
> September 11, 1917
>
> In 1914 at the outbreak of the war, three women held a conference over the question of preparedness and the conditions of the women of America as physically being

able to defend themselves, in case of invasion. It was then decided to organize a league whereby women could be developed physically, along military lines, realizing that if it were good for man to learn the manual of arms and military discipline, it would also be good for the woman and so the American Woman's League for Self-Defense was formed and incorporated under the New York laws. . . . We are the only woman's military organization drilling in different armories in New York, New Jersey, Ohio, and Illinois. The work has proven clearly that women can make fine soldiers and be of great value to our government, and I believe that a National Woman's Army can be organized among the better class of Russian women in our country, they to be sent to Russia to teach American ideals and democracy to the Russian women, and it is by reaching the masses through its women, can the refining influences within man be brought about and harmony restored in Russia. . . .

Respectfully yours,
N. B., New York, NY[7]

Like Russia, Italy found itself in desperate trouble by late 1917, avoiding a complete rout only with British and French help. Once Russia collapsed, the Entente could not afford to lose another member. The *Boston Globe* argued, "Italy must be saved. And she who saved Europe once may not be able to save herself now. After enduring such an experience, the Italian armies and the Italian people hardly can be expected to gather themselves together at once and stand alone against the onrush of a victorious pursuer."[8] An American show of goodwill might bolster Italian morale:

March 8, 1918

If word, but a little less than official, received from Italy is to be relied upon, that country, her people and soldiery are in sore need of a helping hand from the Government and people of the United States. Because as a race they are sensitive proud spirited and however needy yet reluctant to appeal for help, the extremity of their need has not been brought to the attention of the American people. . . . Italy asks that America speak through her flag borne, if only by a single troop of her soldiers, through the principal streets of the principal Northern or other populous cities, and carried before her own troops at the front, to the trenches where they shall ultimately take their stand and fight side by side with the flag and the men of Italy for the same cause of humanity for which she is offering and pouring out her life blood. The effect of such a visible recognition of Italy by the United States would be such that the 3,000,000 men in the ranks of Italy's army would so fight with renewed assurance, quickened faith and gladdening hope that they would become as 5,000,000 and make impossible the way of the Hun through northern

Italy and southern France to Paris and a German stipulated peace. Let the response of America to Italy's mute appeal be so swift and helpful that such a calamity shall not befall her and our own cause.

S. W., Boston, MA[9]

With Russia gone and Italy stabilized, Americans focused again on the Western Front. Repeated offensives there by both sides had produced huge losses for little gain. Many Americans believed that adding their Army to this meat grinder would only increase the casualty lists without bringing victory. The *Yale Review* argued against an American offensive: "Henceforth, we must be satisfied, on the Western front, with not letting our line be pierced. . . . [T]he belligerents would be compelled to direct their efforts, first to aerial warfare and submarine attacks, and, secondly, to all that contributes to material life, continuing meanwhile the manu-facture of engines of war and munitions, and not neglecting the aid of diplomacy. Thus shall we win, but not otherwise."[10]

Other writers suggested alternatives to a Western Front strategy. Austria-Hungary seemed ripe for revolution. The *Washington Post* suggested that the Entente should do to the Hapsburgs what the Central Powers had done to the czar:

> Tens of thousands of men in the Austrian army would mutiny if they had reason to believe they would be aided in their efforts to shake off the Hapsburg chains. They remain in chains merely because they are not organized and because they are prevented from hearing the call of the trumpet that will never sound retreat. What are the allied governments thinking of, that they do not strike down Austria, as Germany struck down Russia. . . . When will the allies take a leaf from Germany's book. When will they strike at the enemy's vulnerable spot, instead of closing their eyes to his weakness?[11]

These two writers proposed attacking Germany's weakened allies:

Mr. T. J. Rock
Houston, Texas
June 23, 1917

Dear Sir:
As per our conversation at the noon day lunch with reference to the present condition of the present European war and as to the fortified position of Germany on the Western Front, it is preposterous for even the combined armies of the world

to break the German line, for the reason that those lines are made in three tiers deep, extending from France through Belgium back to the German line proper; then you reach the German line on the Rhine, she having the largest rivers and largest mountains in Europe and all strategical points fortified by the best of engineering skill, in my opinion, the male population of both hemispheres will be destroyed without accomplishing its purpose. On the east through a mammoth island Heligoland, which the combined fleets of the world cannot reduce, and with all waters mined at the mouths of these rivers, where the German seaports exist, it seems to me to be suicidal to flank Germany by way of water. But in my opinion, the one weak point, and it is a well known fact that no nation the size of Germany can be conquered without being flanked, and in order to flank her, in my opinion, the invasion should start from Greece, retake and conquer the Balkan States, capture the Baghdad railway, invade Austria and reduce her, then Germany can be invaded from the Austrian line on the east. In the mean time I would hold the French and English line and conduct the battle in Austria. This being done will more quickly bring Germany to her knees with a much less loss of men, for the battles conducted there will be more on the order of the war fifty or sixty years ago. . . .

Yours very truly,
A. S., Chenango, TX[12]

Secretary of War
November 12, 1917

Dear Sir:
Again pleading the friendship of Mr. Vance C. McCormick, I beg you not to despise the word of an obscure rail-splitter. Since the battle of the Marne our allies have done only one thing that could be classed as in any degree sensational and effective. On the contrary they have done scores of things ill-timed, shortsighted and wretchedly unwise. They have many magnificent leaders, but apparently not one with vision. . . . The one thing our allies have done that approaches the sensational and effective is the movement in the far southeastern theatre of war, the movement up the Tigris, up from Egypt, and down from the north along the southeastern coast of the Black Sea. This is some strategy. The world watches it with intense interest and hopefulness while it looks and has looked at every other front with a feeling approaching disgust and dismay. There has been one evidently wise course—which Germany has followed frequently: While holding the enemy on all fronts, break in through the back door. We should have a vast army in

Palestine and Mesopotamia, with a view to nipping the whole Teutonic scheme of conquest in the bud, concentrating on Asia Minor, putting the Turkish Empire out of commission, and thereby speedily terminating this frightful onslaught on civilization. When Germany sees that the hope of her gains is gone, she will go to pieces and quit. This is by all odds the one wise thing to do. Therefore, I venture to say, it will not be done, but we will continue to sacrifice our men by the millions and our money by the billions, to little or no purpose, on ineffective offensives along other fronts.

Very truly yours,
H. B., Philadelphia, PA[13]

While the Balkans and the Middle East offered strategic opportunities, northern Europe also tempted strategists. The Scandinavian nations and Holland remained neutral, effectively shielding Germany's northern flank. While newspapers speculated on the possibility of these neutrals joining the Entente, the *Washington Post* pointed out a major problem: "The allies have never been able to save a single small state that has come in on their side. Belgium, Serbia, and Roumania have each been crushed before the allies could move a finger to help them. If Holland, Denmark, Sweden, Norway or Switzerland should join the allies tomorrow, what guarantee have they that they would not share the fate of the other small states?"[14]

This writer proposed opening a Scandinavian front:

To the Staff of the War College
December 6, 1917

I beg to respectfully submit to your honorable body the following plan. The three Scandinavian countries are chiefly controlled by Sweden. That is, she is so much the larger that they count for little with the allies on account of Sweden's pro-German leanings. If Norway can be induced to join the Allies what will result? Perhaps war with Sweden. But if the Allies England and America will guarantee to place an armed force with the Norwegian army a different result is apparent. It would act as a deterrent or else prevent Sweden from fighting on the side of Germany and might even bring her over to the side of the allies. In case of this being the consequence of the protecting of Norway it would be a great advantage as then even if she were coerced into joining the allied side, it would give us two great advantages—a base for the air attack on Berlin—and it would open up the way to Finland and to aid Russia. I had forgotten the submarine base it might open up for the Allies and the crushing of the German subs now holding the Baltic. Please believe I am writing this with due knowledge of how little I know about such things and the belief that it has all been thought out before. I simply send it as it is very easy to throw it aside if not worth anything. Denmark would be overrun and perhaps be forced to the side of Germany. This is a chance. Norway occupied as a drill ground for English and American soldiers would give a strong outpost for the winning of Sweden—this is most evident I think. I believe this is the keystone to the arch, the heel of Achilles. With best wishes, very respectfully,

H. S., Washington, DC[15]

American leaders shunned indirect approaches to concentrate U.S. efforts in France, hoping that the "Doughs" could break the stalemate there. Most observers expected the Germans to try to break the Allied line before American troops arrived in force. The *Washington Post* warned that the Entente could expect "an unprecedented effort by Germany to force decisive action upon her European enemies before the United States is fully in the field."[16] This writer warned of a possible tactic in the impending German attack:

February 18, 1918

It is over three years since the Germans were entrenched on the West front, and in some places they have not been moved. What is to hinder them from tunneling from their side, many miles to the rear of the allied lines, then letting loose hordes of men dressed in British and French uniforms, taken from prisoners, and attacking the rear lines? Von Hindenberg says he will be in Paris in April. Can it be that a tunnel route will supply the surprise and enable them to break through? They have carried on warfare in every conceivable manner, on, under and above the seas, on, under and above the land, and have employed methods devilish in their cruelty and resourcefulness. Can they tunnel? This may seem like madness to you, but is it not a possibility, if not a probability?

D. F., Kenosha, WI[17]

Any offensive on the Western Front would involve aircraft in unprecedented numbers. Although neither side proved able to employ air power decisively, visionaries suggested various ways that airplanes could end the stalemate in the trenches. The *Boston Globe* rhapsodized, "In that boundless, trenchless field, is the one clear space for a war of maneuver. There are no ditches, no mines, no barbed wire in the sky. Up there alone the old decisive warfare that the world knew from Alexander to Napoleon is waiting for us, waiting only for our imagination to free itself from the earth and to take wings like our machines."[18]

Scientific American explained the benefits of air superiority in this way:

[I]f our aeroplane strength were suddenly doubled, we could hold the aerial forces of Germany so far back of the front that it would be possible to concentrate an army of 500,000 men at a selected point, without the Germans having the slightest inkling of what was going on. . . . with his men in constant terror of aeroplanes dropping out of the skies and flying less than 100 feet above the earth, pouring streams of accurate machine-gun fire into their ranks; with relieving troops attacked with machine-gun fire before they even reached the trenches—indeed, just as they were leaving the troop trains; with his communications, both rail and road, utterly disorganized by continuous bombing and bursts of machine-gun fire and accurate shelling; and with his utter lack of knowledge of what his enemy was preparing for him back of his own lines, the German commander on any given sector would be in a perilous, hopeless position.[19]

This writer suggested using planes to carry what were later known as airmobile forces:

To the Secretary of War
March 8, 1918

Kindly allow me to suggest the possibility of equipping the army in France with sufficient air transportation to transport a half million or more men over the German lines far into Germany where they can alight upon a defenseless city, bomb it and burn it, then rise into the air and drop down into another, thus devastating the country. They could return for supplies or supplies could be carried to them by flying squadrons. Flyers could also distribute vegetable parasites to damage the crop production.

F. B., Fort Dodge, FL[20]

Both sides used aircraft to bomb and strafe along the trenches, but this writer suggested an alternative to the usual high explosives:

Thomas Edison
[1917]

Dear Mr. Edison:
I have been thinking and working for some time on war inventions and I do not see why we—the U.S. I mean—could not with the aid of aeroplanes sprinkle the German army just the same as we do the potato bug. By using an acid diluted with

water it would cause the clothes to fall apart and be of no use to the soldier and if this can be done between now and fall cold weather would drive the soldiers out of the trenches and home, and I think you could do more damage than with powder [and] ball, and if you think there is any merit in this scheme please answer. . . .

Yours truly an American citizen,
C. A., Dollar Bay, MI[21]

If planes could cross the lines and destroy the enemy's communications, they might prevent the Germans from sustaining their troops at the front:

Third Assistant Secretary of War
July 26, 1918

Dear Mr. Keppel:
You no doubt have to listen to many schemes for "winning the war" and have probably become expert in judging their value. I am therefore taking the liberty of sending you a few thoughts on the subject, which if they meet with your approval, you may think worth while forwarding to the proper authorities. Some years ago while traveling on the Continent I had occasion to examine most of the railroad bridges across the Rhine, and since reading about the Handley-Page machines, I have become obsessed with the idea that if these bridges could be kept out of commission by air attacks it would stop all railroad traffic across the Rhine, and the German armies would be forced to retreat to that river for lack of necessary supplies. . . . There are probably not over thirty railroad bridges across the Rhine at this time, and my idea would be to place the work of damaging all of these bridges and keeping them continuously out of commission in the hands of some one authority which would have first call on the use of all of the heavy long distance bombing machines of all of the Allies. . . .

Sincerely yours,
C. T., Philadelphia, PA[22]

Nations on both sides directed their total productive capacity into the war effort, making the home front more important than ever before. The availability of long-range bombers gave rise to strategic bombing against the production centers that supported troops at the front. The *Boston Globe* noted the following:

An ammunition dump blown up means destroying perhaps a day's or a week's or even a month's output from a munition factory. But let us go into Germany and destroy the factory itself and we destroy the output for three months at least. . . . Bomb the workshops and mines and furnaces and you throw the workers out of work. If they are out of work they will collect together and talk, which they are too busy to do at present, and they will then wonder why they endure being bombed for the sake of a war which will not do them any good, and for which they are already suffering the greatest privations. And from such enforced idleness will spring the real peace movement in Germany.[23]

This writer suggested air raids on petroleum supplies:

[Secretary of War]
July 27, 1917

My dear Mr. Baker:
I enclose a suggestion sent me that, if it reaches your eye, will be given the consideration necessary, I am sure.

Very truly yours,
E. W., Pittsburgh, PA

One of the most significant things about Germany's attack on Rumania does not seem to have been recognized—Germany's need for petroleum for her U-boats. It is true alcohol could be used, but not in any large amount in these times of scarcity of grain, potatoes, sugar, and other foodstuffs from which alcohol can be made. The shortage of this petroleum fuel, rather than any lack of shipbuilding capacity, or of crews, or of torpedoes, is probably limiting the number of U-boats Germany can send out—perhaps limiting even more than the mines and other war measures of Great Britain, France, and Italy. If that supply can be cut down by airplanes passing over the Rumanian and Austrian oil fields and firing incendiary bullets or dropping incendiary bombs on oil tanks and refineries, it would seem to be one of the best methods of attack on the U-boat, and worth almost anything it might cost in airplanes lost.[24]

Army leaders seriously considered bombing German food supplies, noting "action should be taken immediately toward the propagation and planting of insect pests in Germany by means of airplanes for the devastation of crops, especially of potatoes." The judge advocate general reviewed the legality of this scheme and advised that, while "under ordinary conditions of warfare the propriety of such a move would be seriously questioned because of its effect on the civil population," Germany "has totally disregarded any and every provision of international law and has attempted repeatedly the particular act which is the subject of this paper." Thus, the plan passed legal muster as an act of retaliation.[25]

This writer proposed one method of destroying food crops:

The Honorable Secretary of War
April 30, 1917

Dear Sir:
As I am convinced that the American people are now in the dire throes of the most disastrous crisis of the world's history, I know that it is the imperative duty of each and every American citizen to exert to the maximum extent of his or her ability to assist in every way possible in successfully conquering the nations now at war against the civilized world; and to that end I wish to suggest the following scheme which, if at all practicable, will deal a death blow to Prussian militarism, viz: The use of cellulose such as wood, fiber, cotton, hemp, flax or anything that is light and combustible, pressed into separate small masses, say of 1/4 lb. weight each, and then an aggregation of these fiber-masses (balls, cubes, or whatever form is most suitable) compressed into convenient form (cube, globe, etc.) and provided with a central charge of some suitable explosive to be fired by fuse or by percussion cap. The small fiber masses can be treated with a small quantity of petroleum which in a short time, will permeate the entire aggregation by capillary attraction, rendering the whole mass highly inflammable. The pressing of the fiber into small masses and then compressing any number of these together into a larger mass in convenient form will insure a complete separation and complete dispersion of the small bodies when the explosion occurs, and, at the same time, the whole collection will be ignited. If this scheme can be effectually applied, as contemplated and designed, the cereal crops of the central warring nations can be devastated to such an extent, between the present time and the time of harvest, that actual starvation will bring our enemies to the attitude of miserable supplicants before the close of A.D. 1917. . . .

N. C., Fredericktown, MO[26]

The next letter proposed bombing enemy cities, reasoning that, however barbaric this tactic might seem, it ultimately saved lives by breaking enemy morale and shortening the war. The tactics described, save the use of poison, foreshadowed methods employed over Berlin a generation later:

Secretary of the Navy
July 5, 1917

My Dear Sir:
. . . Why should we sacrifice the flower of our country in Europe in a long war? Why not fight the battle to gain the victory, and do it now? Some one will say that

this is inhuman, but we were forced to it. Our foes have violated all international laws; we cried for peace and our cries were unheard. We pleaded for mercy, and no mercy was given. So now our interest is in America, our country, our homes, and our flag is at stake. So it means to murder or be murdered. If fight they will and fight they must, let us meet them like loyal sons of America, in the same spirit. And with such means as will thicken space with the gray twilight, and cause nature to pull down the curtain of night as we deal to the Germans both hell and death by putting the following plans into execution. 1st. Manufacture 100,000 airplanes, equip each with a machine gun to sweep out German aircraft. Supply each airplane with ten, twenty, or twenty five bombs made in the most destructive manner possible, after which cover this bomb with an extra shell or jacket, and fill space with poison liquid. And those who escape the shots and shells will be destroyed by the poison liquid. After this 100,000 airplanes are completed and men well trained, set apart 50,000 for Berlin, and 50,000 for the Krupp manufactories. Start 50,000 to Berlin, line them up 100 abreast. That will give us 500 lines. Or if necessary to cover the city, place 200 abreast. That would give us 250 lines. Let one line follow the other about 100 yards apart, till the 250 lines pass over Berlin. Each line of airplanes will drop 2000 to 5000 explosive and poisoned bombs, and where will Berlin be? Have 49,000 of these airplanes equipped as above mentioned, but have the last 1000 in the rear loaded with ignitible [sic] bombs made in a way that will produce the greatest flames when ignited. The foremost lines will destroy every living human, and pile up the wreckage. The latter will set the wreckage on fire, and there will be no one or means to quench the flames, and Berlin will be in sixty minutes a desolated plain. . . . Is it not a fact that we will lose fewer lives, and spend less money by taking Germany by storm with airplanes using shot, shell, and poison liquid than in any other manner? Let every son of America use all of the God-given brain that he possesses to save our country, our home, and our flag, and after victory to bring back the brave from over the sea, is my prayer. I am yours patriotically and sincerely,

R. S., Waldron, AR[27]

A number of writers submitted ideas for remote-controlled or pilotless bombing airplanes:

War Department
May 22, 1917

Gentlemen:
Beg to submit the following plan machine for your consideration. "Flying torpedo" to put propeller and wings with a time steering apparatus, traveling along at a rate

of 120–30 miles per hour could be sent a distance of 150 to 200 miles loaded with gas, explosives, or anything else. No enemy could approach it in the air, and when it hit would destroy itself, so no German could imitate it, and cause a destruction for a large distance around it. The enemy is absolutely helpless as there is no defense against it in any way. A fleet of these could be sent from France and also from Russia into Germany, could be steered toward Berlin and the Krupp works. Submitting this for your approval if I can be of any assistance. I am

Yours very truly,
R. F., South Bend, IN[28]

The westerly winds prevailing over Europe gave the Entente an advantage for balloon warfare:

The Adjutant General
June 24, 1917

Dear Sir:
Will try to explain to you on paper in the best way I can my scheme or idea to terrorize Germany. This scheme would depend upon the wind the same way as gas or fire attacks, this consists of three things now in use, Balloons, Time Fuzes or Clock Arrangements, and Bombs or Shrapnel. Balloons—any kind that will carry a little weight say 100 lbs or more. Time Fuze or Clock Arrangement—to release bombs as you may set your clock to release bombs. If you wanted the balloon to drop bombs 100 miles from our line and the wind was blowing 100 miles an hour, then you would set your clock to drop the bombs in 1 hour's time from start. You could have 25 to 50 bombs on a big balloon and have it so arranged that after the first bomb dropped, one would drop off every five minutes, and also have it so that the last bomb to be released should destroy the balloon so that it would not get in the enemy's hands. If this stunt is used it should be used on a very big scale, say send up from 100 to 500 in a single night and terrorize Germany just as they have done to France and England with their Zepplins and aeroplanes. . . .

Yours very truly,
J. C., Chicago, IL[29]

One writer suggested using aircraft as the modern equivalent of battle flags, proposing the "use of high flying airplanes to carry in front of Allied troops, floating [in the] air, ghost-like figures of Joan of Arc in front of French troops, Washington in front of American troops, and the Duke of Wellington in front of

English troops, as having [a] demoralizing effect on enemy and stimulating effect on Allied troops."[30]

Despite the hopes of air enthusiasts, aircraft of 1917–18 lacked the range, payload, and reliability to have a major impact on the millions of men struggling in the trenches below. Victory would come only through land combat across the trench lines of France. Army leaders hoped to break the deadlock with aggressive attacks, an approach certain to produce heavy losses. The *Washington Post* even announced that U.S. commanders planned to mount frontal assaults "Like Pickett at Gettysburg."[31] Dense barbed wire barriers screened most trenches, and attackers used artillery bombardments to batter these prior to an assault. Both sides soon found that shelling rarely eliminated wire defenses. These two letters proposed special ordnance to deal with entanglements:

To the Editor of *Scientific American:*
I have it on the authority of two well-known officers of the French artillery, that the Allied armies depend more upon high explosive shells for the destruction of barb-wire entanglements, than on any other single means. This means that, unless a shell bursts sufficiently close to a support so that its location is included in the ensuing crater, the chance of the dislocation of the support is small indeed. The breakage of the wire must be accomplished, generally speaking, by fragments of the shell, or by detritus sufficiently hard and heavy to withstand the impact. Of course, if circumstances favor the explosion of the shell, the mere concussion may flatten the entanglement, but is it not probable that little is accomplished in this way? I have wondered continually, since all former methods of fighting have been superseded as desired or found necessary, why some modern adaptation of the old chain shot could not be used to good advantage. True, this is not allowed by international law, but just what is international law, in the light of daily events? For instance, suppose a shell were made in two or four sections, connected by light chains of good material, and these sections were banded together lightly for loading and firing, the bands being so proportioned that their disruption would be a certainty. . . . When fired, the projectile would open up, assume its gyratory motion about the junction of the chains as a center, roughly speaking. The effect of such a projectile on entanglements can readily be imagined, and if made heavy enough, would easily shear itself through several strands of wire. No support could withstand the impact of the chain, let alone the section of the shell. . . .

R. P., Chicago, IL[32]

Hon. Duncan Fletcher
U.S. Senate
February 22, 1918

I can see the underground trenches, with subway connections and their best and largest guns commanding the hills; and standing between these and the Allies' line of battle there is the protective barrier against infantry charges; the barbed wire entanglements. Here is a method of getting rid of this wire that I would like to see tried out. Prepare an anchor shaped hook, with 3 flukes, about 3 1/2 feet long; let the body in which the flukes are set be the size of the bore of the mortar or gun, and to the body attach a 5/8" wire cable of proper length (a mile and a half if necessary), other end of the cable attached to a drum operated by a donkey engine. Then shoot this hook over the entanglements and set the engine in operation, drawing the cable in; the hooks will catch the wire and drag them down. . . . [I]f it does what I believe it will do, the German trenches can be taken one after another.

E. D., Tallahassee, FL[33]

Scientific American described a "land torpedo," which consisted of an explosive charge mounted on a motorized carriage and controlled remotely through cables: "The idea is to launch such torpedoes against the enemy's trenches and barbed-wire entanglements and to blow up the charges at the propitious moment, in this way preparing a breach for the infantry assault."[34] This writer suggested a subterranean variant:

War Department
February 27, 1917

Sir:
For some time I have been working out plans for a land torpedo which I am certain would be more effective than anything known at this time, for trench warfare. It is especially designed for that purpose, and does away entirely with the expense of heavy bombardments preceding infantry attacks. To use this appliance it is only necessary to get the direction of the nearest enemy trench, set the torpedoes about 50 yards apart, or less, as desired and turn them loose. They are set off about four feet from the surface, in our trench, and drill their way through to the enemy. They can be fired at will, simultaneously or singly, or in groups, either by wireless or by a wire connected with the tail end of same, as it is run by electricity. It is easy enough to picture the result of one of these torpedoes, measuring 24" in diameter and 5 to 10 feet in length, charged with high explosives, being fired just as it enters

an enemy trench, filled with soldiers. You can easily see what would happen to the trenches, and, coming without warning, as does the submarine torpedo, I think it would prove more effective in places than the heaviest artillery. . . .

Yours sincerely,
U. D., Jacksonville, FL[35]

Newspapers reported that in some cases the Germans had run electricity through their barbed wire. This letter suggested a method determining whether the enemy wire was "hot":

To Chief of Staff
February 27, 1918

I submit the following, trusting it may be useful in military. During a recent night raid, over there, our boys crawled under the enemy wires, and were nearly trapped by live wires. Why not have a few soldiers in each unit equipped with fine steel stranded wire, of high electrical resistance qualities, and where wire barriers are encountered which are in doubt, this fine wire tossed into the enemy wire. If the latter is heavily charged with electricity [it] will seek outlet through the fine wire and due to its high resistance a decided heat and red glow will be almost immediately apparent. This naturally would be a danger signal. Any competent signal officer could work out proper sizes & etc.

A. B., San Francisco, CA[36]

Electrified wires might also serve as an offensive weapon:

To the General Staff
January 19, 1918

. . . Suppose the Germans were coming out of their trenches for a charge or preceding an attack by our men, would it be possible to throw an entangling mass of live wires among them from a series of trench mortars, similar to the manner in which the Coast guards throw a line to a storm-beaten ship? It seems to me that if it were feasible it would have been attempted before now at least by the Germans, if they had thought of it and could put it into practice. Could the wires be thrown across barbed wire to burn through them? A different conductor than copper might do it. The dynamo could be mounted as they are in track welding outfits for electric railways or on motor trucks. Surely the transportation could not be more

cumbersome than that of large caliber guns or tanks. The current, of course, to be off when our men go in to finish what the deadly wires have begun. . . .
Thanking you in advance for considering this communication, I am

W. N.[37]

Defenders protected by trenches and bunkers had a significant advantage over troops in the open, so prying the Germans out of their fortifications became a prime American objective. These two writers proposed using water to penetrate enemy defenses:

Chief of Staff, Washington, DC
October 15, 1917

Dear Sir:
. . . From my rather inadequate maps of Europe, I find that the head waters of the Aisne, the Meuse, and the Moselle [rivers] might be controlled in such a way that enormous damage might possibly be inflicted on the enemy. Would it not be practicable to work out a plan along the following lines? 1. Build a series of dams at the head waters of all streams flowing into the enemy lines. 2. Constantly guard these operations with extra troops and large forces of air planes. 3. Equip several hundred heavily armed boats and several thousand small launches with men and supplies. Place these boats on skid-ways just above the point to be reached by the crest of the flood from the lower ponds. 4. Order certain boat crews to endeavor to reach certain points and let the men land and dig in. 5. On a given night, during a rainy spell, divert the attention of the enemy by landing heavy attacks at points in his line farthest removed from the river entrances. 6. At a given signal, turn the waters loose and let all the boats be launched just behind the first rush of the flood. 7. Keep up as steady a flow of water as possible by regulating gates in the secondary dams. 8. Seize all possible points of advantage on both sides of the rivers and try to cut off all enemy lines of supplies. 9. Keep the small boats plying back and forth with reinforcements and supplies. If this plan seems reasonable and if I can be of any service in carrying it through, I am yours to command.

Very respectfully,
G. A., Gainesville, FL[38]

War Department
May 21, 1917

Gentlemen:
As a suggestion for a feature of offensive trench warfare. In the vicinity of a large amount of water, for instance where a river runs through both ours and enemy trenches at right angles, install many large centrifugal pumps (running by motor) and pump directly into pipe lines up to our trenches. A dozen or so hydraulic giants played toward the enemy trenches if the ground were level or has some slope toward the enemy trench would very rapidly bring every one out of the dugouts by water and mud and fill the trench full of earth and water. In this way they would be suddenly exposed to fire. If this is feasible consult some big machine house about centrifugal pumps and some mining men about hydraulic mining to know what water will do. Ask about the La Grange mine in Trinity County California.

Yours very truly,
H. B., San Francisco, CA[39]

Army officials rejected proposals for using high-pressure water as a weapon. One memo noted the force needed "to throw a 12" stream 1500' would require a pressure of 325 lbs per square inch and a flow of 78,000 gallons per minute, which is equivalent to 222 second feet. This quantity is half the water supply of the City of Los Angeles."[40]

In lieu of wonder weapons, U.S. forces would rely on infantry attacks to clear the way. Press reports suggested that cold steel often decided the issue in trench combat. The *Atlanta Constitution* noted the following point: "Only a few years ago the wise men of all armies predicted that because of high-power, long-range artillery and rifles, and automatic and machine guns, troops would never come to actual grips. The complete reorganization of the whole infantry service outlined in the new tables, however, is based on the proven fact that the battle will be decided by the foot soldiers, fighting breast to breast with bombs, bayonets and knives."[41] *Illustrated World* made another suggestion:

[Might it] be possible to make Fritz fearful as well as surprised? There is no doubt that if loosed at such a time fear would at least give the attackers the "drop" and a chance to hurl their bombs and bring their revolvers into play with deadly effect. Disregarding the possibility of bringing this about through a noise of any kind, let us consider something that can be seen, something diabolical and ghastly that will arouse fear. What is more effective than a horrible face? . . . But something more awe-inspiring than the self-scarred, livid faces of Attila's Huns, or the paint-daubed visages of American Indians must be devised. A mask has been suggested. A mask made to look like nothing earthly, but still having the features of a living creature. Made of steel, these head pieces would serve as a shield against rifle and machine gun bullets and hand grenades; worn by a raiding party they would serve not only as a protection but as a weapon.[42]

These three writers proposed specialized weapons for trench fighting. While fright masks, bows, spears and shields might seem anachronistic, it is worth noting that Allied soldiers used catapults and giant slingshots to throw grenades into enemy lines.[43]

Honorable Secretary of War
February 17, 1917

Dear Sir:
Would our Government be interested in a rapid-fire gun that will fire 1,000 shots, in every direction, in 10 seconds? It being a one-man gun, using a special cartridge, and is worn as a belt, being about two and a half inches thick all the way around, having 1,000 or more small barrels, 1 1/2" long, each charged with powder and ball, the rear of each barrel connecting a fuse passage, said passage being filled with fuse powder, and ignited at several places at once by a current from a tungsten battery, which will start it peppering in every direction. It would be very effective in trench raiding, a man would jump in a trench, throw up his hands, close the circuit and clean up a large space in a few seconds. The gun will not be noticeable on a man with a long coat, so it will also be good for spies and scouts, as if the scout got cornered or in with a lot of the enemy soldiers or officers he could mow down a good many. As there is no moving parts it is absolutely safe and can only be fired by the battery current. It can be cheaply and easily made in any machine shop. If you are interested I will furnish blue-prints.

Very Truly Yours,
E. C., St. Elizabeth, NJ[44]

Chief of Staff, War College Division, War Department
September 27, 1917

Sir:
I do not apologize for my presumption in making the following suggestion, as out of a million ideas, one may prove valuable, and we need that one. I therefore

suggest the arming of platoons for close fighting, as follows: All should have a small steel shield strapped to the chest, and a V-shaped one (like a Coolie's belt) across the abdomen. The abdominal shield should have holsters for two automatics pointing toward the groin. Half the platoon should carry no rifles, but instead should carry automatic shot guns carrying large-shot shells. In addition, and most important, they should carry in brackets (fastened with springs so as to be readily jerked free) on breast shield and pointing over left shoulder, a stout 8-foot spear with 12" head similar to a bayonet. This spear is much lighter than a rifle and bayonet, and has greater reach. (It is, aside from superior effectiveness, much cheaper and more quickly produced.) . . . It would seem that the spear would be far more advantageous than the short, heavy rifle and bayonet. I have the honor to be,

Very respectfully yours,
C. J., Los Angeles, CA[45]

Assistant Secretary of War
October 8, 1917

Dear Mr. Ingraham:
For trench fighting, in the place of hand grenades or trench mortars, or rather supplementing these methods of offense, permit me to offer the following suggestion, which may or may not be feasible. Employ what is know as an Indian "hunting bow" with arrows tipped on the end with a glass phial of nitroglycerine, or other powerful explosive that would be detonated upon impact with the earth, or any solid object. Containers of celluloid might perhaps be better than glass. A man can shoot one of these arrows with its explosive charge a great deal farther than he can throw a bomb, and they have the advantage of making no noise in their discharge, of being almost if not fully as destructive in effect as an explosive shell, and give the men a wider range of action. They could reach the Boches with an arrow where the Boches could not throw a bomb. I believe that the idea could be worked out intelligently by some of your army experts, and either proved a valuable weapon in modern warfare as conducted today, or else just as speedily and surely found to be inefficient. At any rate, there's the idea for what it may be worth.

Respectfully submitted,
D. L., Philadelphia, PA[46]

This writer advocated using Native Americans for trench raids:

Mr. Woodrow Wilson
Nov. 5, 1917

My Dear Mr. Wilson:
Another thought, by whom would night scout work be best performed, by none better than our own Native Indians, for stealth and disguise (from what we have read) they could not be excelled. True it will bring their primal instincts to the fore once more, but then, we are skating on pretty thin ice when we talk about civilization these days. Another thing, we understand that the scouts black their faces when doing this work, would it help any if they wore uniforms to match the ground they crawl over. At last we get to copy the little animals that take on the hue of their surroundings to escape their enemies. Wonderful, ain't it.

Yours very truly,
J. W., Reading, PA[47]

Americans viewed poison gas as another example of German barbarity, but its counteruse by the allies seemed justified. The *Chicago Tribune* reasoned, "Finally the decision was made in favor of putting our fighting men on a par in this respect with the enemy, and late reports are that unprecedented quantities and a new form of very deadly gas are to be provided for our troops. We devoutly hope so and that it can be provided soon."

This letter proposed using poison shrapnel:

Secretary of War
May 18, 1917

Dear Sir:
Now that we are in this great war, and I feel it is every person's duty to help in whatever way he can, and all [moderating] warfare has been violated, I have this offer to make if it is of any value to our government. [It] is an explosive projectile filled with old wire drilling cable. This cable is as poison as a rattlesnake bite wherever it marks the flesh. This I know from personal experience from more than a score of people being just scratched with it. In nearly every case it results in blood poison. Think this over, as there [are] old wire cables to be gotten in nearly every oil field in the world for projectiles. . . .

Yours very truly,
T. G., Tulsa, OK[48]

Ultimately, the Entente found an antidote for trenches and barbed wire through an inspired combination of armor, engines, and caterpillar tracks. The introduction of tanks heralded a revolution in warfare, though few realized how great an impact they would have. *Scientific American* predicted that if early tanks proved successful, "Germany is certain to come back with something of the same kind; and, if so, we may see squadrons of these mechanical armadillos maneuvering against each other in the open field—truly a sight for the gods."[49] *Illustrated World* concluded that tanks would reduce casualties: "The usual custom has been for the soldier in hot fighting to be nothing more or less than a free target for the enemy's fire. In case he came upon a detachment of the enemy, he was almost certain to be killed. The tank or armed fort is to change this, however."[50]

The *Boston Globe* predicted that America's auto industry would give the Allies a decisive edge: "The tanks are fairly starting to breed. America is their great stock farm. Automobile factories are making cars that will give our boys joy rides 'nacht Berlin.' Thus far Germany has hit back but feebly. Perhaps Germany is hard put to it for raw materials and manufacturing capacity. Anyway, the tanks they have shown are few and clumsy. The offensive of 1919 will see American-made and American-manned tanks swarming toward the Rhine as flivvers swarm toward the beach on a 30th of May."[51] Inevitably, the antagonists would try to field superior tanks:

Secretary of the Navy or Army
December 3, 1917

Dear Sir:
Consider this. Begin at once building "tanks," the first twice as large as any now known with all of its abilities doubled. When this is approaching completion start another again double the last, &c &c till nothing known can resist them. This kind of thing is now showing its effectiveness and will at once become the effective tool of the army that puts in service the heavier machine.

Yours truly,
E. J., Dobbs Ferry, NY[52]

All wars disrupt the social fabric, but World War I shook Western civilization to its core. Many felt that the combatants had lost any sense of restraint in their pursuit of victory. They saw the war as a watershed where centuries of progress might be swept away, and beyond which the world faced a new dark age. These two writers were moved to suggest ways to mitigate the war's physical and moral damage:

Mr. President
March 24, 1917

Dear Sir:
Has the following plan of obtaining a victory in war ever been tried by any nation
at any time? The first nation retreats leaving behind it three fourths of a circle
of electrically controllable underground mines, over which neither man nor beast
can pass when the current is on. The circle is then completed with mines over
which anything except steel or iron can pass. They are naturally pursued by their
opponents who find themselves in the open space inside the ring at which time they
are notified that they may leave their war machines behind them and march out
through the last quarter of the circle, which might be reduced to a mere roadway
in place of a full quarter. This plan is so simple of arrangement that it has doubtless
been worked out before. But in case you are interested I will supply you with my
idea of the electrical and mechanical arrangements.

Yours for bloodless victories,
R. R., Coolidge, KS[53]

Secretary of War
July 3, 1917

Dear Sir:
I have been reading of late how the U.S. was going to exterminate the German
people with high explosives and other means of destruction and death. Some
months ago the German War Lords conceived the idea of visiting the coast of
England and drop explosives upon innocent men, women and children and the
papers of this country had much to say about the barbarous methods pursued
and well they should condemn such acts. It seems to me that the dropping of
high explosives on men women and children is little short of murder and a most
heinous method for an enlightened nation to pursue; to murder them just because
they are subjects of an enemy at war is wrong. To me it is a cheap war system and
more revenge than even common sense and I herewith offer my condemnation
to such a course and appeal to the better sense of those who may be in power to
adopt a more humane method. In connection therewith I am desirous of saying
that I have invented a plan of explosives which if properly used, will go far in
bringing the war crazed German people to their right senses and by its use will
relieve the death to a minimum, which I believe will be acceptable to all parties
concerned. . . . To drop explosives in large quantities is murder, but to drop it in

proper arranged small quantities is "Good War" and will cause but a small death
rate and will cripple the whole German army. As an example, shoot a roman candle
against a brick wall and observe the splatter, then if you can, imagine what that
same kind of a device would mean and the effect it would exert if all of those small
splatters were small missiles splattering in all directions in a German trench and
guess if you please, how many would get out without a scratch and how few would
actually be killed in the undertaking . . . to the cause of bringing this great war hell
to a close. I am,

Very truly yours,
I. M., Los Angeles, CA[54]

The "great war hell" eventually ended through the application of new technologies
like the tank, and the expenditure of munitions and lives on an unimaginable
scale. The old system had crumbled, and the United States emerged as the first
among equals with its exhausted allies. More than ever before, Americans had a
stake in preserving the new order that rose from the debris, and in discovering ways
to prevent future cataclysms.

CHAPTER 5

Disarmament and Depression: The Great War's Aftermath

When World War I ended, Americans found themselves players in the power struggles that had governed world diplomacy for centuries. Diplomats hoped to prevent a repeat of the conflict that had so nearly wrecked civilization. A second world war, featuring fiendish new devices conjured up by the best scientific minds of the day, was sure to be even worse. Proposals to prevent war, or at least ameliorate its effects, therefore received an enthusiastic response in the United States. As the world's richest nation, U.S. participation was crucial if the victors were to replace the international system that had signally failed to prevent catastrophe in 1914. Although America refused to join the League of Nations, it participated in negotiations aimed at reducing international tensions by regulating armaments.

In 1921 the United States hosted an international conference to limit the world's navies. Germany's defeat left America and Britain as the world's dominant sea powers. Britain had the strongest fleet, but a massive U.S. building program threatened to overtake the Royal Navy by the mid-1920s.[1] *Scientific American* noted that if the United States, Britain, and Japan forged ahead with their ship-building plans, within three years America would have the largest and the newest fleet afloat.[2] American leaders hoped to avoid a naval race with Britain similar to Germany's race with Britain that helped spark World War I. At home, politicians faced pressure to cut defense spending and popular agitation, spurred in part by the press, to achieve international naval disarmament.[3] Before the conference convened, press articles, including one in the *New Republic*, proposed setting fixed ratios of relative fleet strengths:

> The safest ground America can occupy is to have a navy larger than Japan's, but not so as to menace Japan, smaller than Britain's, but not so small that the British navy is a menace to us. That is exactly what we have now. Why not maintain this

status by an agreement with both Britain and Japan not to disturb the existing ratio? The ratio, not absolute size, is what counts. If Japan, America and Britain are as 2:4:6 it is just as safe, and a sight less costly and provocative, than as if they are as 10:20:30. . . . Now the only ratio that does not lead to interminable debate is the ratio of existing strength. Therefore the thing to do (whether by world conference or by the leading naval Powers does not matter) is to have a neutral commission of non-naval Powers determine what the existing numerical ratio is at a given date.[4]

Although the notion limiting fleet strength through treaties had broad appeal, others urged more radical steps:

Secretary of War
November 8, 1921

My dear Mr. Secretary:
I am forwarding you a suggestion, thinking possibly it might prove a means to the end sought for. If you do not think so, consign it to the waste-basket. Why not organize a world corporation to be called, "The League of Naval Equipment"? Charter 10 years; privilege of increasing to 50 years. Authorize 13 directors, hold 2 directorships open. 1. Great Britain to control 4 Directors. 2. United States to control 3 Directors. 3. Japan to control 3 Directors. . . . [Then] divide present, up-to-date naval equipment as follows: Class A. For Aggressive Service. Ships of Line, up-to-date auxiliaries, capable of quickly overcoming any nation or combination of nations; to be stationed around the world, but acting in concert and fully prepared, i.e. a combination of sufficient strength to enforce peace when authorized by supreme judicial power (Hague). Placement of officers and crews left to discretion of Board of Directors. Expense of maintenance and upkeep to be divided proportionally among the nations enjoying the benefits of assured peace. . . .

Respectfully submitted,
E. F.[5]

Not all Americans favored a naval disarmament pact that gave up America's advantages of overwhelming wealth and industrial capacity:

[Secretary of the Navy] Edward Denby
November 29, 1921

My Dear Mr. Denby:
The reading of this letter will appear very much exaggerated to you. I beg, therefore, to submit the following argument. The American navy, which would very soon have

become the most powerful in the world, was built for the protection of our coasts and not for conquest. The British navy is now the first upon the seas; but England is in financial difficulties of so serious a nature that she must, in any case, almost entirely cease to build capital ships, from sheer lack of money. For this reason, the command of the seas would have fallen to the United States in a very few years automatically, and without an effort. We should have become absolutely safe from foreign attack. Under these circumstances to reduce our navy, to actually destroy a number of powerful war ships, built for own defense would be self destruction; it would be suicide for the benefit of our enemies, actual and potential.

Very sincerely yours,
B. S., Boston, MA[6]

This writer worried that rivals would use a treaty to secretly gain a military advantage:

Secretary of the United States Navy
July 7, 1921

Dear Sir:
. . . "Disarmament" is only preachers' talk. Let them go deeper into the bible and seek some thing worth while to preach. Remember that this disarmament talk has a tendency to discourage inventors in this country working along different lines for the country's defense, and opens a new field for inventors in other countries. . . . England can not junk her ships. How can she protect her colonies nearly all over the world if disarmament takes place, she will want to be allowed so many ships per colony, to protect them if anything should arise in these colonies. This will outnumber our quota and a new Germany will arise within the Royal Kingdom. Therefore we must keep our eyes open and study a little more about the outside world, we are young and willing to learn. England will overpower us with her merchant marine and America will notice that she will build ships and more ships. These ships will be so constructed as to withstand the most powerful gun that can be thrusted upon a battleship. Big guns will be stored away ready to be mounted on her "merchant ships." This is where she will mobilize her inventive power to conquer the United States and other valuable spots in different parts of the world.

Yours for a big navy. I remain,
Yours truly,
A. T., Fairhaven, MA[7]

The United States, Britain, and Japan, along with France and Italy, met in
Washington in late 1921 to negotiate naval reductions. The Washington
Conference focused on the relative number of dreadnoughts each nation would
be permitted. The resulting treaty set a ratio for battleships of 5:5:3 for the United
States, Britain, and Japan; Italy and France were restricted to lower ratios.[8] In order
to reach treaty limits, the parties agreed to destroy existing or partially completed
ships. This involved sinking or scrapping a number of older American battleships,
along with cancelling or converting several vessels under construction.[9] Naturally,
some Americans opposed demolishing ships built at great expense and still fit for
decades of service. The president proposed ceremonial sinking of the excess ships
as an object lesson to the world, but many objected to such an extravagant waste
of resources. Inventive writers proposed a number of alternative uses for these
doomed ships. *Scientific American* described one possibility:

> It was inevitable that the proposal of the Conference to scrap our six battle
> cruisers should suggest the thought that they might profitably be completed as
> ocean liners. Were that done, their great length of 875 feet and their beam of
> over 100 feet would put them in the class of the largest ocean liners. . . . The best
> point in favor of such reconstructed vessels would be their safety against loss by
> collision. . . . The underwater projecting ledge of an iceberg that ripped open five
> forward compartments of the *Titanic* and sent her to the bottom, would scarcely
> affect the stability of one of these ships, and the amount of flooding that ensued
> could be quickly controlled by the ship's pumps.[10]

These two letters contained schemes for recycling unwanted dreadnoughts:

Senator Joseph E. Randall
December 19, 1921

My dear Senator
. . . In the wrecking of these splendid old battleships, such as the "Maine" and
the others that are on the program, would it be possible for you to recommend
to the Navy Department that say two of these ships be brought to Washington,
with full complement; and have say one of the ships brought in close to the end of
the seawall on the island, and there used as a municipal club-house and pleasure
resort for those using the park and the municipal golf links and pleasure grounds.
I believe an arrangement could be made for another of the ships to be turned
into a yacht club by the Capital Yacht Club and one or two other yacht clubs in
Washington. . . .

Sincerely yours,
E. S., Shreveport, LA[11]

The Secretary of the Navy
January 16, 1922

Sir:

May I trespass upon your time to lay before you the following suggestion. Much has been appearing in the public prints of late regarding the scrapping of obsolete war vessels, and of such vessels as may possibly be put out of use by the international agreements now under discussion. . . . My suggestion is that instead of disposing of the ships in this manner, that they should be used in the construction of harbors. At various places along our coasts there are long stretches where no natural harbor exists, or where such harbors as there are have no proper depth of water. To make an artificial harbor of any reasonable size is generally a matter of enormous expense—an expense often quite incommensurate with the benefits to be obtained. . . . [T]here are many places where harbors would be most desirable, where within reasonable harbor limits, a depth of say 40 to 60 feet would be as great as would have to be reckoned with. Therefore, if at such places as it might be decided that harbor facilities would be of real value, suitable ships, both as to length and draught could be towed to such places, and sunk in such positions as would best suit the conditions. . . .

Very Respectfully,
J. C., New York, NY[12]

In keeping with the aims of the naval treaty, some citizens wanted the excess ships used to serve humanity, as *Illustrated World* reported:

It has been proposed therefore, that the government take obsolete or obsolescent warships, which would otherwise be used for targets, and convert them to this scientific and humanitarian use. They could be stripped of all equipment except wireless and other utilities needed by a small crew of six or eight men; could be towed to some suitable small land-locked harbors previously picked out in the desired localities; run aground permanently, so that they could be considered as scrapped, there to remain as commodious, substantial, well-equipped and warm meteorological stations, impervious to storms and practically to time.[13]

The *Washington Post* noted an ambitious scheme that would use the ships to alter the weather:

Battleships as ice barriers to block the Straits of Labrador, better known as "Belle Isle," and thus stop the flow of ice down our coasts from the arctic region is one of the unique and practical uses suggested for the disposal of the 17 old warships doomed to be scrapped by the naval treaty. . . . [T]he suggestion of a gentleman from Maine, while lacking somewhat in practicability, has a potent appeal to the imagination. His is the scheme to block the straits of Labrador and thus divert the masses of ice from our shores so that in the future the "Cold New Englander" will be nothing but a memory. . . . The hulks of the dismantled warship would comprise splendid material for this purpose of dumping in the Labrador straits for the purpose mentioned.[14]

The next two letters contained proposals for using excess warships for the public good:

Representative Benjamin Fairchild
December 17, 1921

My Dear Mr. Fairchild:
Knowing you are always on the job in public matters it has occurred to me that a suggestion might be interesting to you. There is all this talk of scrapping these American war vessels, and did it ever occur to you what a desirable thing it would be to have these vessels anchored in the different ports along the Atlantic Coast and used as hospitals for the poor of the district. It seems to me that this would be a very desirable thing to take up because wherever these vessels anchored I am certain the physicians and surgeons of that locality would offer their services free. Think it over and let me know what you think of it. . . .
Yours faithfully,
E. L., New York, NY[15]

[January 1922]

My Dear Mr. Harding:
. . . The thought of such a waste of valuable materials and time suggests a use probably a great example of economy and monumental example of putting labor and materials to a better use than for war purposes. Why not haul each ship out on land and after dismantling convert each one into a school building, cutting openings for windows, etc., machinery already in place for light heat and power—New York, Philadelphia, Baltimore, Boston, etc. will all gladly accept the donation. . . .

Yours Very Sincerely,
C. B., [New York, NY?][16]

Although nations still measured sea power by counting battleships, the Washington Conference addressed the increasing sophistication and lethality of submarines and aircraft. Submarines created a dilemma. While the participants publicly condemned their use, their navies all included submarines. A British proposal to ban them entirely received widespread support in America, where U-boat atrocities had provoked the declaration of war in 1917. Some Americans saw an opportunity to reverse the slide toward naval barbarism that unrestricted submarine warfare represented. The *New York Times* asked the following question:

> Why should not the submarine be proscribed and outlawed altogether? As a defensive machine or weapon the swift bombing airplane is far more effective in warfare. . . . If the conference were to agree to scrap all the submarines in commission and building, the whole world would applaud, in such abhorrence is submarine warfare held. There is no time like the present for such action, no place like the conference at Washington. If the United States, Great Britain, Japan, France and Italy condemned the submarine, what other nation would dare to include the monster in its navy?[17]

Instead of banning submarines, the Conference instead pronounced rules (which were subsequently ignored in World War II) prohibiting surprise torpedo attacks on merchant ships. This writer proposed a humane restriction on submarine operations:

Secretary of the Navy
December 29, 1921

Sir:
I have been reading in the morning papers Mr. Root's rules for submarines in future wars, but he makes no reference whatever to bonding. . . . One hundred years ago there was a system of ship bonding which had some vogue as late as our civil war. If a vessel was captured the captain could give a bond to his captor and his owner would pay an amount agreed upon, if he was allowed to continue his voyage. . . . It might be possible to revive this bonding plan in principle for submarines, the vessel being pledged also to go to the nearest neutral port or to be accompanied there by the submarine. The vessel to remain in port during the war. The enemy would thus be weakened but the ship and cargo and the crew and passengers would be saved for the general benefit of mankind. I still think that something might be made of this idea.

Very respectfully,
F. B., New York, NY[18]

Because submarines did not fight each other, the ratio approach for limitations made no sense. This letter set out a more logical alternative:

> Secretary of U.S. Navy
> January 2, 1922
>
> Dear Sir:
> The Armament Conference appears to want to have submarines controlled. Why not make it as follows: allotments of submarines per naval power should be governed according to coast line mileage of the homeland. This coastline mileage should be measured at a distance of 600 feet out from the low water mark. No more than one submarine should be allowed for each 10 nautical miles of such coastline. Submarine protection for outlying possessions to be withdrawn from the home allowance. . . .
>
> Yours very truly,
> J. B., Brooklyn, NY[19]

Some Americans wanted the Navy to keep its submarines. One editorial noted as follows:

> The submarine has no equal or substitute as a weapon for coast defense for the United States. We could build and keep in a state of high efficiency a fleet of a thousand submarines and never feel the cost. And with even 1,000 submarines we could guard our two coasts against any possible attack. We could defeat any nations making a war of aggression against us by the simple process of destroying their merchant marines and reducing their home populations to helplessness through lack of food and materials. Ourselves immune to blockade because our vast land produces everything we should need to keep on making war indefinitely, all the submarines in the world could not reduce us to helplessness or even make serious attacks against our thousands of miles of sea coast. And, on the other hand, with the submarine navy we could easily build and keep in commission we could and would strike fatal blows at any naval power attacking us.[20]

This letter described a submarine defense system:

> Honorable [Rep.] Ira Copley
> [December 1921]
>
> . . . I have a scheme or idea whereby we can junk our navy and cut out that terrible expense on the people and then the world would laugh at us and all join hands with

their navies combined. Oh no we could still whip the world. My idea is as follows and where I am showing Uncle Sam how to save millions of money in Expenses I wish to be rewarded for my idea etc. My idea is simply as follows by building towers along the coast with powerful electric colored lights for signaling in code to instruct submarines to assemble at a given point to rush at full speed say to N.Y. harbor we could have 100 submarines assembled in a few hours. We would have to have an outer guard as it were composed of the swiftest boats obtainable equipped with wireless and could be manned by just a few men to patrol our coast all the time to notify headquarters of the approach of the enemy at a moments notice. Then these men stationed in these towers to commence relaying their messages to submarines stationed all along our coast to rush to a certain point at once. . . .

Respect,

E. H., Chicago, IL[21]

Several months before the Conference, American general Billy Mitchell had proven in tests that aircraft bombs could sink a battleship. This cast doubt on whether dreadnoughts were still the ultimate measure of naval power. The *New York Times* wrote the following:

There are naval officers in England and America who think with Admiral Sir Percy Scott and Brig. General Mitchell that submarines and aircraft have rendered the capital ship obsolete. If so, a nation that spent its millions chiefly on aviation and maintained a fleet of swift carriers would be a more terrible enemy than a power that placed its dependence upon capital surface ships and neglected aviation. Granting that surface ships are necessary to a navy for police duty in time of peace and for offense and defense in war, it would be judicious not to have too much faith in them.[22]

Naturally, battleships had their defenders, including *Scientific American:*

Notwithstanding all the hysteria concerning the passing of the capital ship as a type, it must be remembered that the cheapest and most powerful unit weapon is the gun. It hurls explosives in large quantities at enormous velocity. The battleship is the type developed to use it at sea. And, the battleship or some other type developed to carry this weapon, with protection inherent in itself, or in supporting types, against the menace from the air and subsurface, will always control the sea and be the dominating factor in naval warfare as long as commerce moves in surface ships.[23]

New technologies might arise to restore the battleship's dominance:

Secretary of the Navy
[ca. December 1921]

Dear Sir:
Enclosed is a cutting stating that the battleship is obsolete with Adm. Sims as
authority. Presumably so on account of aerial bombs sinking that man-of-war last
summer. . . . But is it, is the battleship obsolete? Some day some inventor will
construct a gun that will lay a barrage in the path of the oncoming torpedo and
explode it. Another inventor will construct a gun that will throw a barrage of deep
sea bombs and sink the submarine or the onrushing destroyer. Another inventor
will construct a high angle gun that throws an aerial barrage and explodes the
dropped bomb in midair. Another man will construct some means of defense so
that a bomb dropped when the battleship is unaware of the bomber's presence or
has run short of aerial defense projectiles, the bomb will not land on the battleship
nor close enough to do harm to the battleship. And then there is battling planes
to down the bombing planes and other means of defense. Furthermore in a war of
attrition, a war to the bitter end, [the] United States is not likely to give up [until]
the last ditch is taken. Before that stage of operation is reached the adversary is
liable to run short of motor fuel for the aeroplanes, run short of aeroplanes, run
short of mechanics to keep the aeroplanes fit for flight, run short of fliers to man
the aeroplanes. And when that stage is reached the battleship will not be obsolete,
but will be a very lively corpse in the naval warfare. All these patent medicine
doctrines for elimination of war and war's horrors reminds me of those Englishmen
who stopped breeding horses after Stephanson had built the first railroad, because
they thought there would be no demand for horses. Their conclusion was all right
except for the fact that the theory was wrong. So it is with the battleship today.
More will be needed in the future. . . .

Yours very truly,
W. S.[24]

Battleship enthusiasts argued that in a real attack the planes would encounter interceptors, smoke screens, and defensive fire from rapidly moving targets:

Chief of Naval Operations
February 5, 1921

My Dear Admiral Coontz:
Referring to the question of aircraft versus battleships, it will be conceded that in
order to hit a ship, save by chance, the crew of the aircraft must see her. Chemistry

today can accomplish almost anything in reason, and is it not practicable to use smoke screens in what may be termed a horizontal plane against aircraft as we have used them in what may be termed a vertical plane against destroyer attack? Roughly, my idea would be that a screen of scouts, destroyers or other fast vessels could be liberally provided with means of discharging smoke bombs, the vapors of which would rise rather than hang on the surface and produce, to the windward of course, a cloud hard to dissipate and that would have a specific gravity which would prevent too rapid rising. . . . Moreover, it would seem possible to discharge highly inflammable gases that might be ignited by the aeromotor exhausts or by electric sparking, say, as from radio equipment. I have witnessed two volcanic eruptions and in both cases have observed that masses of gases would ignite hundreds and perhaps thousands of feet in the air above the volcano's cone. I have seen the same phenomena at several very large oil tank fires, notably at Long Island City about two years ago. In other words, I do not think that we have given sufficient consideration to what my be termed smoke and gas defenses above ships. . . .

Yours very faithfully,
W. C., New York, NY[25]

Scientific American pointed out that attacking aircraft could themselves use smoke screens: "Two or three fast and small airplanes may drop from a formation that is approaching or has not yet come in sight of the battleships, and circle the targets with smoke screens or curtains. Their speed of about 200 miles an hour would provide a hummingbird sort of a target to anti-aircraft gunners. The bombers following up could sweep down behind the screen, break through at an unexpected point, drop the bombs upon their targets and disappear behind the smoke screen on the other side."[26] In response to the aircraft threat, design changes could make battleships more bomb-resistant. This writer proposed a scheme to bomb-proof these powerful yet increasingly vulnerable vessels:

United States Navy Dept.
December 29, 1925

Gentlemen:
The writer wishes to offer the following suggestion. Would it not be possible as well as practical to design a steel roof over our best and largest battleships having a given angle. For an aeroplane operated by only one or two men at a high altitude could very easily drop a shell or a bomb (only a trifling cost) which in a twinkling would destroy several millions in property and hundreds of lives impossible to replace. By given angle we mean to construct a steel roof overhead, so should a shell strike and explode it would be some distance from the deck without causing any serious

injury, or this protection would deflect it into the ocean, at the same time the side armor would withstand this shock. The bow and stern could be left open for use of anti-air guns, as no doubt the center of the battleship would be the objective point where the greatest damage could be accomplished. Trusting this may have your consideration, we beg to remain,

Yours truly,
G. W., Dayton, OH[27]

The Washington Conference raised hopes that the great powers would work together to reduce international tensions. Some saw the naval treaty as the opening act in a broader effort to limit armaments and perhaps ultimately to renounce war. The *American Mercury* hailed the naval treaty:

> [It is a victory] of common sense over exaggerated fear, of logic over hysteria. . . . Peace has never been secure in modern times when any nation showed a desire to pass England in naval strength; and on paper we had already passed England. . . . I do not claim that the Arms Conference has ended war. It has, however, removed all the causes for war that were showing their ugly heads in 1921. If war comes, there will have to be found a new *casus belli*. The Conference made all the old ones ridiculous.[28]

The *Washington Star* proposed a formula for limiting armies:

> Let it be one soldier for each 1,000 inhabitants. The people of America are willing to conform to that basis, and the peoples of Europe ought to welcome it eagerly as the one sure way out of their almost intolerable difficulties. There is not, in fact, a nation in the world which could not afford to conform to it. One soldier for to each 1,000 of inhabitants would give every nation all the force needed to maintain order and police its own domain. It would not give any nation an army sufficiently large to constitute a menace to its neighbor, nor would it give any nation an army so large that its maintenance would be a crushing burden. And it would end competition in land armament, more important to Europe even than that competition in naval armament should be ended. . . . [T]he war-made deficit in manpower and production would largely and soon be overcome, national budgets would be brought nearer to balancing, and out of this greatest of sanities would come sanity in other things.[29]

USS *Olympia*, flagship of Dewey's Asiatic Squadron.

German heavy siege artillery in firing position—without a gun base.

From friend to foe: Philippine insurgent leader Emilio Aguinaldo.

The German U-boat that sank the *Lusitania* and helped bring America into World War I.

American sailors laying mines—important weapons in the antisubmarine campaign.

German barbed wire on the Western Front, a major obstacle for American troops.

Delegates to the 1921 Washington Conference on naval limitations.

An Apache scout in Mexico with Pershing's punitive expedition.

Two keys to U.S. sea power: an American battleship passes through the Panama Canal locks.

The former USS *Foote,* one of fifty old destroyers transferred to Great Britain in 1940.

A torpedoed tanker and its cargo burn within sight of the Virginia coast, 1942.

A Japanese suicide rocket plane captured on Okinawa.

A blasted Japanese bunker on Tarawa Atoll.

The YB-40, failed heavy fighter conversion of the B-17 Flying Fortress.

American soldiers wade ashore from a landing craft at a Normandy beach on D-day.

Communist prisoners of war ready for repatriation at the end of the Korean conflict.

Tethered goats await the atomic blast aboard a target ship in Bikini lagoon.

The Norden bombsight enabled U.S. airmen to achieve remarkable accuracy—in theory.

Others, such as this letter to the *New York Times*, were less optimistic:

[To the *New York Times*:]
No one has yet given a thought to the possibilities that lie in devising new and more terrible machines of destruction without in the least violating an agreement that considers only tonnage and masses and not fighting efficiency. . . . Who knows but that the limitation of armaments may result simply in directing the course of military and naval invention into new channels? . . . An inventor with bloodthirsty inclinations has a more brilliant opportunity now than ever before. Our fighting machinery has cost us much money in the past—so much that mere financial consideration prevented the adoption of devices that needed expensive engineering development before they could be introduced. If armaments are to be reduced, more money becomes available for research which may result in the perfection of inventions that are still in an embryonic stage. . . .

W. K., New York, NY[30]

The achievements of the Washington Conference soon lost their luster, though, because they never led to general disarmament. The participants quickly found ways to compete in weapons not covered by treaty, and conspicuously failed to agree on additional limitations even for navies. Americans soon found that potential rivals were exploiting gaps in the treaty to gain military advantages. Just months after the conference, the *New York Times* warned that Japan was threatening America's naval superiority by building large numbers of smaller warships: "[N]aval officers are convinced that Japan is gaining an advantage over the United States with respect to light cruisers and submarines. Japan has an unassailable right to do that, if she can. The remedy would be to build more ships of those types to fly the American flag."[31] The *Los Angeles Times* reported that improved foreign dreadnoughts outranged and outclassed American units: "Opposed to the modernized British fleet today, navy officers have stated, the bulk of the American fleet would face the necessity of closing in five miles under salvo fire before they could bring their own guns to bear. As the British ships are also slightly faster, it is said, the possibility of bringing the entire fleet into action would be negligible."[32]

A follow-up conference in Geneva failed to limit smaller warships, leading to new building programs and strained relations between the naval powers.[33] Reviewing the renewed arms race, the *New Republic* concluded, "[The] Washington Conference did little for the cause to which it was supposedly devoted. It was not a disarmament conference; it limited one type of vessel, a type which is of dwindling importance and is believed by many naval experts to be altogether obsolete. . . . Since then, there has been absolutely no movement in the direction of limitation."[34]

One writer suggested a symbolic means to encourage progress at any future conferences:

Honorable Charles Frances Adams
June 29, 1929

Honorable Sir:
It occurs to me that it would be most fitting and proper, when the next conference on naval reduction and disarmament is called, to have the governments that are to participate at the conference, especially the governments of the United States and the British Empire, extend an invitation to all the nations of the world, inviting them to send one or more of their representative youths to attend the conference, say between the ages of eighteen and thirty years, in order that they may have the privilege of discussing the issues with their seniors. For it is the youth who must fight all wars and bear the years of burdensome taxes which wars entail. It is also the younger generation upon whom in future years the Government of their respective countries will rest. Sincerely appreciating your consideration, I am

Yours very truly,
W. H., Oglethorpe, GA[35]

In a last-ditch attempt to avoid a new naval race, another conference convened in London in 1930. The *New Republic* proposed a dramatic move to spur negotiations:

It is not enough to arrange parity and to limit building. This conference can dissipate the Old World reasoning about the balance of power only by a great renunciation of power itself. In plain words, it must be by a bold reduction in naval armaments that we prepare the new era in which war is outlawed. . . . The trend, then, alike of the political and of the technical argument, carries us to the bold conclusion that the battleship ought to be abolished. By this one means, either a ruthless and simultaneous scrapping of every ship over 10,000 tons, or else an agreement (adjusted equitably among the three fleets) not to replace existing ships when their normal term of life expires. The former would be incomparably the more satisfactory solution, for it would be difficult to exaggerate its value as a proof that we were all sincere in our renunciation of war.[36]

The London Conference achieved no such breakthroughs, although the powers agreed on ratios for smaller surface units and submarines.[37] By 1930, few believed that legalistic formulas would lead to true disarmament. The *Christian Science*

Monitor put it this way: "Indeed, it seems almost a hopeless task. But hope should not be lost. There is enough righteousness and intelligence and brotherly love in the world to overcome 'the powers of darkness,' ignorance, hatred and confusion. . . . However, it will be well to drop illusions, to face the fact that 'disarmament' needs to be disarmed of its false hopes. Today it usually means limitation of arms, and except for the three navies bound by the London Naval Treaty, it does not even mean that."[38]

Repeated failures to build on the achievements of the Washington Conference undermined public faith in arms limitations. The *Washington Post* scoffed at the proceedings of another Geneva conference:

> There will be no agreement upon the reduction of armaments, and all the delegates know it. They are deliberately maintaining a mockery conference for the purpose of misleading the peoples. If the delegates had the courage to join in a statement of the blunt truth they would say: "None of the nations wishes to disarm. Each makes proposals which it knows the others will reject. Each is trying to make it appear that the other fellow is responsible for the refusal to disarm. All are equally guilty. We refuse to participate in the fraud any longer, and this conference is hereby adjourned."[39]

As the hopes inspired by the Washington Conference faded, Americans wondered whether all segments of society shared their abhorrence of war. The *New Republic* identified some of the groups blocking disarmament:

> Among the actual and potential fomenters of war are the following: First, manufacturers of armaments and munitions. Under the modern conditions of war, munitions include most of the products of agriculture and industry. Second, militarists. Although they often profess themselves humanitarian ("the best pacifists are in the army"), they are bound to seek a field of action worthy of their special talents. Third, domestic bankers, involved potentially or actually in the manufacture of munitions. . . . These are, in the main, the same forces that got us into the last war.[40]

Pacifist organizations tried to rally support against the supposed warmongers, reminding readers of the costs of war:

> 17,000,000 dead—17,000,000 soldiers and sailors killed in the last war! Who are they? Statesmen? Politicians? Big-navy advocates? Munitions manufacturers? Business leaders whose factories hummed during wartimes? Editors whose papers

love to stir up international bad feeling, because it helps circulation? No—not one!
Just average citizens. Young men with their lives before them. They were told it
was glory, and look what they got. Look what all of us got! Back-breaking taxes.
Economic disorders that have not yet been righted. A bitter defeat for one side, a
bitter victory for the other. Yet the world is drifting toward another war right now.
And those who profit by war will encourage that drift unless we who suffer by war
fight them![41]

During the 1920s and 1930s various groups floated proposals to "take the profit out
of war," thereby thwarting the merchants of death and equalizing war's burdens on
all sections of society. Such proposals garnered popular support after congressional
investigations found that arms makers had formed close and mutually beneficial
ties with the military. In the mid-1930s the Senate's Nye Committee identified the
nascent outlines of what later became known as the military-industrial complex,
and suggested that arms makers had colluded with military leaders to block disarmament.[42] This inspired ideas for making war less appealing to those who might
otherwise see little harm in sending others off to die:

Honorable George H. Dern
[ca. October 1935]

Dear Sir:
In view of the present world crisis, and the possibility of the United States being
involved in what may be one of the most destructive and chaotic wars of modern
civilization . . . I offer a plan which I consider war-proof. . . . It has been often stated
that "wars are started and made by old men and fought out by the young men," in
view of this I'd say that one man out of fifteen from the ages of 31 to 55 be drafted
for service in case of war. And also one out of four men whose income is $100,000,
one out of three men out of the ranks of those who possess one million dollars, and
one out of two from the ranks of those who have more than one million dollars,
and finally, in case of war, twenty percent of the members of both the House of
Representatives and the Senate be drafted for active service. This is not meant to
[be] a means of punishment, but rather a privilege. It is they who cast the dice.

Yours truly,
J. F., Milwaukee, WI[43]

These two writers offered ideas for changing popular perceptions about war at home and abroad:

President of the United States
May 9, 1935

Dear Mr. President:
At the risk of being classed with that large army of people who send you wild ideas that are impossible of use, I submit the following with the hope that it may contain some germ of an idea that may be of some help in the prevention of war. My idea may be compared to the medical theory of inoculating a patient with the dead germs of a disease in order to immune him from further attacks of that disease. I respectfully suggest that this country donate all of its naval and army equipment that is to be scrapped to a commission whose sole aim is the advertising of the horrors of war and searching out the friction between nations and advertising these causes of war. This discarded equipment to be sold to the highest bidder for scrapping purposes only. Why should not these derelicts of a vicious system of wholesale murder be used to start a train of thought that may in time outlaw war and divert vast sums of money into channels that would make the world a better place to live and give the average man a better chance in his pursuit of happiness. This I think is a new approach to a question sadly in need of same, and one that might be the means of approaching other nations to work out an agreement on a world advertising peace plan. If there is anything in this letter that will help you in your efforts, I am glad, if not I am still wishing you luck.

Yours Respectfully,
G. F., Roanoke, VA[44]

Honorable Franklin Roosevelt
March 29, 1933

Dear Mr. President:
Nothing less than a matter of the first importance could justify any man in adding the burden of one letter to your correspondence and to your heavy cares. . . . In view of the fact that the Kellogg (or Paris) Pact, fathered by our nation, and signed with us by more than forty of the governments of the world, has literally outlawed war, we respectfully suggest and urge that the word "war" in "war department," "ministry of war," "secretary of war" and the like in the frame work of our government, be changed to the word "peace," etc. May I add only this? 1. That beyond all controversy amongst pacifists and jingoes, war has ceased to be the

nation's objective and chief expectation as it was in the beginning, and peace has become its goal in spirit and (now) in law. 2. That, while such a verbal change as above suggested might be regarded as no more than a gesture, yet—What a gesture! . . .

Most respectfully and sincerely yours,
C. W., Bolivar, TN[45]

By the 1930s most Americans had more pressing worries than disarmament. The Great Depression devastated businesses across the country and created a vast pool of jobless men. These men placed a significant burden on society, and some Americans believed the military should provide food, shelter, work, and training for the army of unemployed. The *Los Angeles Times* suggested that "[d]iscipline is as necessary to them right now as food. A generation of young people is growing up without ambition, without hope and without definite aim. Whatever else you may say about the army, its officers leave West Point with high standards of honor and idealism; with the habit of direct and purposeful thought. They have more to give boys at a formative age than grub."[46]

This letter proposed using the military to solve the unemployment problem:

July 5, 1934

Dear Sir:
A solution of the difficulties confronting the stability of the United States to day suggests itself to me. It is simply this: Let all the unemployed become members of the Army or the Navy. To be subject to regulation as to age, wealth, family and other conditions. Families can be taken care of by establishing camps in each state and allowing the families of the enlisted men to reside nearby. The government to regulate the pay of [*sic*] so as to provide for the families also. That the government produce better men and women by establishing schools for the families and the enlisted and that an opportunity be afforded to acquire industrial educations in aviation, electricity, engineering, merchandising, motor machines, garages, gas stations, business, accounting, banking, and almost anything excepting the professions—let them be taken care of by individual effort. The government might select its employees from the army and navy ranks. This plan it seems to me would end the cry of unemployment. As the world demanded more men they could be discharged to accept positions or engage in business. Detachments could be used in making improvements, repairs, building roads and on other projects, if used not to the detriment of local industry and unemployment. This plan could be worked out splendidly it seems to me.

J. M., Hancock, MD[47]

The Depression reduced tax revenues, and the costs of social welfare programs cut deeply into military spending. These two writers submitted plans to provide trained personnel in an era of tight military budgets:

Secretary of War
October 18, 1932

Dear Sir:

In training the choruses under my supervision, including the Roxyettes at the Roxy Theater in New York, it has come to my attention that these highly trained and finely developed units would be of great use to the nation as elements in the national defense. You will remember that during the World War the Russian Government made effective use of a corps of women soldiers known as "The Corps of Death." This organization was rapidly trained in a period of emergency. Choruses are constantly in a state of intensive training as highly coordinated and well-drilled units that are kept in perfect physical condition and often engage in semi-military maneuvers that are perfected by frequent repetition. The only thing that these women lack to make them effective soldiers available at a moment's call is a knowledge of the use of the rifle and bayonet. This one deficiency could be remedied by placing at their disposal the indoor rifle ranges of the National Guard with competent instructors in rifle and bayonet drill. In the matter of esprit de corps, military precision, the habit of obeying and carrying out orders with celerity, these choruses have already reached the acme of perfection. The girls are selected in accordance with strict physical standards that make them the very flower of American womanhood and they obey rules of health and are constantly subject to a regimen that keeps them always in perfect trim. Consider therefore, how favorably they compare with a conscripted army of men torn from office desks whose daily activity is limited and whose attention to health and strength is a minor matter in their daily lives. When it comes to actual physical conflict, I would match any Roxyette against a man who ordinarily leads a sedentary or semi-sedentary life, provided that both were armed with bayonets and had received equal instruction in their use. In my opinion the highly trained chorus girls of America are splendidly equipped to form the nucleus of a women's corps, and if some of them were trained in military tactics and commissioned as reserve officers they would form a basis for an organization of athletic young women that could be put into the field as a highly drilled and effective army in a very short space of time.

Respectfully yours,
R. M., New York, NY[48]

[Secretary of the Navy]
July 1, 1929

Dear Mr. Secretary:
I have a suggestion to give to the Navy Department which perhaps may already have been acted upon. It has been my idea that a great deal of interest might be roused in naval matters by approaching the yacht clubs and enlisting the interest of their members in using their power craft to learn something about naval tactics and strategy. I was very much interested the other day to see the South Boston Yacht club go by my house here, the flotilla of boats consisting of small launches, most of them under forty feet. These launches, while on the cruise which they were making, carried out very nicely the various tactical maneuvers of a battle fleet in action—line abreast, column formation etc. It seems to me that this general idea could be carried further with much interest to the various yachtsmen of America. The Navy, it seems to me, could afford to detail some junior officers for a few summer months, to some of the leading yacht clubs. Squadrons would be formed of power boats. Tactical drills could be held, and the whole season might end up with sham battles and various conditions depicting actual warfare. This certainly would be more interesting than the average afternoon jaunt of the average power boat owner. It would give him an incentive to use his boat in an intelligent way and to educate himself. The boats could be divided for their different speeds into a destroyer division, cruiser division, and battle ships. There being a thorough classification of boats available, it would not be difficult to plan for the creation of these small fleets. The experience given to the younger officers at the same time would be useful, and in fact the war games would constitute a simple form of game board. The games could be more and more elaborate as the personnel was better trained; proper rules could be drawn up, and the scheme developed into a real sport. At the same time, it would be very beneficial propaganda for the Navy. This is only a suggestion, but I am sending it to you for what it is worth. With best wishes, I am,

Sincerely,
J. H., Gloucester, MA[49]

Similar innovations might create a pool of trained pilots without the concomitant expense of maintaining a large air force:

Secretary of War
May 11, 1933

Hon. Secretary:
Suppose we were being invaded by a foreign enemy, and a hostile fleet much greater than ours was lying off our western or eastern coast, and we were being raided in

our west and east cities by hostile air bombers. . . . Should we have a sufficient number of combat planes, and trained pilots to meet and conquer the enemy, if so I suggest this plan to you. Have Congress to reduce the airmail postage rate to five cents an ounce or fraction thereof. Let the post office department enlarge its airmail service as follows: Put in operation a drop pouch service, similar to the one used by the fast railroad trains, and known as a catcher pouch service. The planes used in air mail service would be equipped the same as our present bombing planes. In peace times they would drop air-mail bags, but in case of war or an invasion, they could be used to drop explosive bombs without any alterations. . . . My plan is this—at all the important towns along our present air routes, have the post office department erect small rope nets about the size of a small building. Have the larger terminals offices make up pouches for these smaller towns they could be equipped with markers and the towns having this service would donate the space gladly. Then our airmail pilot could dive down, drop his pouch on this net and continue on his flight. . . . [T]his plan would enable all our mail pilots to become expert marksmen while at the same time practically double the speed of our airmail service. This would give you a large reserve of combat planes and pilots over and above the number allotted to you by our present treaties with foreign countries. If you would be interested in my plan, would be glad to discuss it with you in detail.

Very [Respectfully] Yours,
C. M., Lexington, MO[50]

President of the United States
August 15, 1935

My Dear President:
May I offer a suggestion. . . . My idea is for a huge privately owned air force, a force of probably a hundred thousand planes to be built and maintained at practically no cost to the United States. And a personnel of a hundred thousand of the best flyers in the world. My plan is as follows, and presumes that Federal plants, with an order for 75,000 to 100,000 planes, could produce a machine for a fraction of the present cost of small production. There are several hundred thousand young men of a high type in this country who are employed at fair salaries, and who would make strenuous efforts to own a machine of their own. The United States would build these planes comparatively cheaply on a very large scale and would sell them to the most desirable type of young men at cost, taking a payment of say $500.00 down and extending the balance over four or five years. . . . The owner-flyer would be trained by U.S. Army flyers at little additional expense to the government and would become a member of an organization similar to the National Guard. Each member would be subject to immediate call in case of war.

Each year there would be a period of training at army air fields, in war tactics and military formations. The more a member used his plane for pleasure, meanwhile, the more proficient a flyer he would become and the more valuable in time of war. Small, swift two-seaters, that could quickly be converted into combat or pursuit planes, could be purchased by a single man. A larger plane, readily convertible into a bomber, could be purchased by those in better financial circumstances. There are a hundred thousand young men who would be glad to have machines offered to them on terms of say $500.00 a year, and the investment would be almost entirely returned to the United States. . . .

Your faithful servant,
W. M., Bayview, ID[51]

As the Great Depression spread across the world, governments and individuals alike concentrated on their own survival. The humanistic hopes sparked by the disarmament treaties faded away. By the end of 1936 even the naval limits agreed to in Washington had lapsed, as nations bolstered their defenses in hopes of either preserving or upsetting the balance of power. In America a concerned citizenry looked abroad and discovered that the danger of "war" in the abstract had been replaced by the threat of militant regimes willing and able to use force to attain political ends. The long slide toward a second global conflagration had begun.

CHAPTER 6
Vulnerable Giant: Defending the Homeland

As the international order established after World War I began to collapse, authoritarian regimes in Germany, Italy, and Japan flaunted their growing power. Japanese aggressiveness troubled Americans most. When Japan refused to observe the naval treaty limits beyond 1936, the *Washington Post* concluded "students of sea power view Japan's action as a determination on her part to build a navy second to none so that under its protection she can proceed at will with her program of expansion in the Far East and ultimately declare a Japanese Monroe Doctrine for the Pacific."[1] News photos of Japanese atrocities in China hardened American sentiment, while U.S. support for China irritated Japan. Many Americans concluded that war with Japan was inevitable.

The *New York Times* argued that Japan's expansionist policies reflected a need for more living space: "The pressure of population in Japan (almost 1,000,000 a year increase, with a 70,000,000 population) and need for raw materials were Japan's stock reason for her establishment of the puppet state of Manchukuo, carved out of the Chinese provinces of Manchuria and Jehol."[2] Such reports prompted the following suggestion:

Secretary of the Navy
July 20, 1938

Dear Sir:
The navy of course is seeking all the latest and best weapons, but there is one weapon of war which I never heard of anyone using which I would like to call to your attention, and that is to flood the enemy country with birth control literature and contraceptives. Wars are largely caused by population pressure. The present one between China and Japan is one of that nature. Just now the U.S. seems to fear Japan more than any other nation. The price of one battleship could almost flood Japan with birth control literature and contraceptives. Nationalities [*sic*] do not

have large families except where birth control information is denied them. Did you ever stop to think that if each family would have only one child, in one generation's time [it] would reduce the population of a nation by half and make double the wealth for each individual? What do you think of this weapon of war?

Yours truly,
B. R., Rockwell City, IA[3]

Control of Pacific islands would be crucial in any war with Japan. The *New York Times* explained the situation: "[The Pacific Ocean], some 9,000 miles in length, with 4,900 miles of blue water between Seattle and Yokohama, is too vast to be dominated from the four great continents and the two frozen land masses that border it. The key to its conquest has been for ages past, is now and will continue to be, at least in the immediate future, the atolls and myriad island that are sprinkled here and there, over its 68,000,000 square miles."[4]

The United States already held Guam and the Philippines, but could America defend these far-flung bases if war broke out? The *Los Angeles Times* published this account:

If the United States elects to renounce her long-established commercial "stake" in China and the Philippines, she can withdraw to her own "inland sea" described by the triangle Alaska-Hawaii-Panama, and no power on earth can dislodge her therefrom. But is it conceivable that the national pride of the American people would consent to such surrender of world prestige? The only alternative left to the United States is to build a second Pearl Harbor on Manila and Subic bays, station there a battle force powerful enough to block Japan's summary seizure of the Philippines, and then to embark on a naval building policy for the inevitable conflict with Japan's "Asia for the Asiatics" policy.[5]

These two letters took different views on holding the island outposts:

To the Editor of the *New York Times*
April 13, 1936:

. . . A reasonable American national defense policy would be one that provides for control of the seas in the vicinity of our country as well as for the protection of our own borders and coasts. In the Pacific, it would, of course, include the permanent defense of Hawaii and the Panama Canal. It would not include the permanent defense of the Philippines and Guam. . . . Students generally agree that for the permanent defense of Guam and the Philippines we would require in the Pacific a fleet three times the size of the fleet of any other Pacific power. We would need also a large army in the islands, with a vast amount of war impedimenta. Not only would there be needed an increase in the navy beyond the greatest limits ever yet considered, but the regular army would have to be increased to a total above that ever heretofore thought of by the American people. All this would entail for our people an ever-growing expenditure.

W C. R., Maj. Gen, USA Ret.
New York, NY[6]

Secretary of the Navy
December 28, 1937

Dear Sir:
In a recent news dispatch, I read that the military (Army) was in favor of a line of defense on our West coast from Alaska to Hawaii, to [the] Panama Canal. Also, that the Navy was in favor of a line to [the] Philippine Islands. Personally, I believe with the Navy. First of all, American blood was shed in the gaining of the islands. They may cost us more than what we actually get from them in raw material and consumption of American made goods. But we need a foothold in the Orient, not only as a brake for present and future purposes. But to insure commerce an inlet to China. . . . Japan I believe, is at the back of all internal strife and revolts among the people of the Philippines. . . . I believe it won't be but a short time after they gain their independence, but that the stars and stripes will be replaced by the Rising Sun. Personally, I believe we should hold the Philippines at all cost. If we start giving up, we will give the Hawaiian [islands] next, then a strip of the West coast, possibly Alaska. . . .

Yours for a larger first line of defense, and "preparedness."
Very truly yours,
J. B., Tacoma, WA[7]

This letter advocated seizing Pacific islands as nature created them:

President of the U.S.
April 12, 1935

Dear Sir:
Feeling that it is of the utmost importance that the United States control all the possible land bases and airplane landing places in the Pacific I take the liberty, at the risk of being thought visionary, to point out to you the advisability of having

government aviators instructed and ready at a moment's notice to fly out over the Pacific and claim in the name of the United States any new islands or continents which may be raised above that ocean by the distinctive and unusual seismological disturbances which are promised for that region in the perhaps not distant future by observers who seem to know whereof they speak. Lest you think this is not likely to occur, let me assure you that Japan, a country that knows far more of earthquakes than we do and is even more anxious for Pacific strongholds, will not be found lacking in preparedness for any such eventuality. The simplicity of the necessary formalities could at least justify attention to this matter, so slight in the doing, but so far-reaching in its possible effect.

Respectfully,
A. M., Somerville, MA[8]

The next writer proposed strengthening Alaska's defenses:

Secretary of War
February 17, 1935

Sirs:
May I take the liberty to make the following suggestions for the defense of our country in case of an armed conflict between this and the Japanese nation. You may take these as being made with the best of intentions, as to their being logical and prudent, I will leave that to your engineers. First: We will presume that we maintain our now friendly relationship with Russia. We have Alaska, rich in resources; of which any nation may well be jealous of, there are very few motor roads into the heart of Alaska now as I understand it; let our Government build military roads through Alaska and to the Bering Strait; come to some understanding with Russia that she will do the same by Siberia, to the Strait, then with our obsolete ships and what obsolete ships Russia has, build a pontoon bridge across the strait. Should there not be enough of the old ships, build some extremely large battleships, which could be used as 'plane hangars and carriers, to fill out the pontoon for our half. Russia will do the same for her half. This will form part of the longest military road in the world; can be used for peace time and war, either and a toll charged (as the Panama Canal) to help carry the burden of expense. Should our country and Russia form a duet, every country in the world will have to applaud when we sing, whether they like the tune and song or not. We Ex-veterans [sic] would like to see some action taken and not so much talk, for the protection of Alaska. With the kindest personal regards, I am,

Yours sincerely,
A. H., Ruidoso, NM[9]

As relations with Japan soured, press reports noted potential threats to the West Coast. The *San Francisco Examiner* ran a full-page map depicting a hypothetical Japanese invasion of California. The map highlighted the aqueducts, power lines, and mountain passes that the invaders would bomb or occupy to cut off California from the rest of the country. It also identified undefended stretches of coastline where the Japanese could conduct landings to gain a foothold on American soil.[10] Some citizens expressed shock that an American newspaper would print a detailed map of potential invasion targets:

Chief of War Department
November 8, 1937

Find enclosed a war map of the U.S. which looks like it was made for the War Department of Japan, as it shows all the vulnerable spots of the Pacific Coast. . . . Anybody who has not put in about 6 hours on hot desert without water don't know what real thirst is. You will notice the maker of this map is very particular to show the yellow boners [*sic*] just how to ruin the water supply of L. A. There is never anything but sewer water in the L. A. River and a little muddy water in the rainy season. I have been around here about 7 years and never saw a creek or a spring if the water supply is ever ruined there won't be any kind of water in the river bed and there will be no beer or soft drinks as it takes water to make. It's dollars to doughnuts there is thousands of these maps in the mail right now probably not to Japan's War Department but to friends in Japan with instructions to turn them over to the high mucky mucks. Ask Farley if he noticed any increase in the mail to Japan.

Old Snagpuller

P.S. If you find a letter to Japan that weighs almost exactly as much as this letter and envelope there is probably a map enclosed.[11]

Other articles downplayed the danger of a Japanese attack, attributing invasion warnings to militarists attempting to justify a large Navy. *The Nation* argued that the Pacific's vastness made such an attack virtually impossible:

[Such an attack is] about as feasible as military combat between Switzerland and Paraguay. How, for example, could either of them succeed in placing landing parties on the soil of the other? . . . It is said that there are Japanese aviators who are pledged to undertake one-way trips against an enemy, striking for an objective which would exhaust the small supply of fuel they would be able to carry along with a load of aerial torpedoes. Such patriotic heroism might be effective in operations against the strategic centers of Far Eastern Siberia, but the gasoline load required for even a one-way trip from any Japanese air base or venturesome aircraft carrier to the nearest vital center of the United States, Pearl Harbor, would still be so large as to preclude the carrying of bombs large enough to cause serious damage.[12]

Responding to the invasion threat, the government began to modernize America's coastal defense system in the late 1930s.[13] These two writers submitted suggestions about Pacific coast defenses:

Chief Field Supervisor, C.W.A.
April 15, 1934

1. For any nation or nations of the Eastern Hemisphere to successfully carry on a war against us they would first have to have naval supremacy. With such naval supremacy they could form bases on our islands such as the Catalina or Santa Barbara groups. After they had established the necessary anti-aircraft defense artillery they could emplace long range guns such as were used against Paris and with a minimum expenditure of personnel and materiel cause the greatest destruction to coastal cities of So. California. 2. Our fortification of these islands would not only prevent an enemy from establishing long range gun and air bases on these islands but would also give defended areas from which our fleet could operate without the chance of being bottled up. . . . Long range guns such as used in Paris if located on San Clemente Island with a 100 mile range, would cover the area from Ventura to the Mexican border including San Diego, San Bernardino, L. A., Pasadena and other foothill cities, and be entirely out of range of any guns we now have. . . .

J. K., Sierra Madre, CA[14]

Chief of Staff
January 8, 1938

Sir:
. . . The plan is simply as follows—Excavate, erect, cement and make ready torpedo tube emplacements at every river and harbor entrance, and at every extensive landing place or potential troop landing place all along the coast. Cement can be had cheap, digging could be done with WPA labor (Thousands of good men here are ready and willing to work), the cement placements could be gotten ready now

and the actual placing of the tubes and torpedoes could be made when things start, or the placing of the tubes, air chambers & air machines could be done now and the actual loaded torpedoes could be stored when [sic] wanted. Unloaded torpedoes could be stored at each place in sufficient number to defend the place, in each case, for a week and then things would be ready. I'll bet I could place a dozen tubes on each side of the Golden Gate at San Francisco, some under water, and I could keep the whole United States Navy and the British Navy too, out of the Bay, if I had sufficient torpedoes on hand. . . . At several of the river entrances emplacements should be included in the docks and sea walls. No one would even notice what they were if they were made when the sea wall was first made, especially if they were put under water levels and connected with land under water levels. Even pleasure fishing docks could be extended out at lots of places and chambers from which to launch torpedoes could be included and no one the wiser if the thing was done right.

Respectfully,
C. E., Portland, OR[15]

Advances in amphibious warfare made almost any strip of shoreline a potential target, and these two letters proposed ambitious plans for defenses covering the entire coast:

President Roosevelt
[ca. January 1935]

Dear Sir:
I take the liberty of writing you to send you the enclosed plan for the defense of the Pacific Coast, which is, as you doubtless know, badly needed. . . . Dig, excavate or tunnel a sunken railway grade from Cape Flattery, State of Washington, to the Mexican boundary line, wherever it is an engineering possibility, close to the shore line. The grade to be ten or twelve feet below the surrounding land surface, and wide enough to hold say four separate tracks of rails. On these tracks could be operated heavy electric engines, which would haul heavy guns, capable of firing large shells out to sea at least five miles or more. The guns would have to be disappearing so that they could be raised up above the edge of the cut, to fire and then drop back out of sight. Powerful searchlights could be used at night to locate enemy ships.

G. B., Olympia, WA[16]

Mrs. Franklin D. Roosevelt
February 5, 1934

Dear Madam:
I want to submit this idea to you and if you think it is good you can pass it on to the President for his consideration and action. That the shore line of all our coasts be made into a park, primarily for military defense purposes. See United States Code, title 50 Sections 171 to 179, which gives the Secretary of War authority to take over private lands for the defense of the country. Actually this strip would be used as a recreation park for all the people of the U.S., except in the infrequent times of war. My idea would be to take over every foot of coastline and then lease back to cities, railroads, warehouse and wharf companies the lands that they need and have in beneficial use. All private clubs, residence, oil derricks etc. to be abolished from the Park. The Code gives the Secretary of War authority to accept donations of lands for the purpose mentioned and it is possible that a large percent of these lands would be donated free. A marker or tablet could be set up on each donated tract, giving the donor's name, etc. That would appeal to many owners. I suggest a width of 660 feet, and this might make a total of 2,600,000 acres, more or less, in the entire tract. . . . This park would be a permanent improvement, built for a thousand years, for the good of all of the people all the time. In building this park much useful labor and jobs will be created, and it might be arranged to give these jobs to the elder men who need them, rather than to give them a pension or a dole. There is much talk of wars and rumors of wars these days and I think that now is a very favorable time to get this park established and provided for. A word to say that we are proud of our President and what he is doing for the benefit of the people and we wish him all the success in the world.

Yours Truly,
G. F., Los Angeles, CA[17]

This writer advocated using the nation's vast petroleum and gas resources to create anti-invasion barriers:

Hon. [Rep.] Overton T. Brooks
December 24, 1937

Dear Mr. Brooks:
I believe that crude oil and natural gas can be used as the most effective weapons of defensive warfare in the world today. Troops could be prevented from landing on our shores by covering the water with oil, and setting the oil on fire. The supply of oil could be made continuous by means of underwater pipes. This method might even prove successful in preventing battleships from entering our rivers and

harbors. One has but to view a burning gas well to realize what a barrier thousands of miniature burning wells would offer to an invading army. Tanks might be able to go through the flames, but they could not clear the way for troops. If this method did not stop the enemy, the gas could then be used in a number of ways as an offensive weapon. For instance, trenches and dugouts could be prepared with gas outlets concealed in them. When the enemy occupied these positions, the gas could be turned on and exploded. . . . There are many other ways these natural resources could be used to completely demoralize and destroy an invading army, but I believe that these examples will convince you of their possibilities. I do not know much about the supply of natural gas in other parts of our nation, but I do know that there is enough gas being wasted each day within one hundred miles of Barsksdale Field to destroy all the armies of the world. And there are oil fields near enough all our water boundaries to literally surround our country with a wall of fire. . . .

Respectfully yours,
A. R., Saline, LA[18]

The Army replied that the lower forty-eight states had more than twelve thousand miles of coastline, two-thirds of which was suitable for an amphibious landing. Thus, the "enormous expense that would be incurred by an endeavor to adopt [this] proposal" made the scheme impractical.[19] If the invaders came ashore in strength, only a major counterattack could drive them off. This strategy required reliable communications so that scattered American units could respond quickly to the danger area.

This writer proposed the construction of military highways:

President of the United States
April 27, 1934

Dear President Roosevelt:
Permit me to submit for your consideration a proposal which I have had in my mind for a number of years. Four years of service in the United States Navy have given me an excellent idea of our land and sea protection. Unfortunately, our coast lines are inadequately protected and we are wide open to attack. The protection on the Pacific Coast is especially weak and entirely dependent on the naval force in cases of emergency. The plan I have in mind is one for the construction of highways skirting all of the boundaries of the United States and additional cross country roads, all for the movement of heavy equipment in time of war. At present the highways are absolutely unfit for automotive transportation of wartime supplies, freight and ammunition. The system of roads should be constructed

wide enough to accommodate all classes of traffic and with grades light enough to speed up tremendously every type of motor movement, thereby insuring speed greater than produced by the railroads. . . . The construction of emergency landing fields situated every 50 to 100 miles near the coast should also assist thousands in quest of employment. Please let me hear from you in connection with these several proposals and accept my very best wishes for continued success in your great work.

Faithfully yours,
C. M., San Francisco, CA[20]

Given the vast distances between Japanese bases and U.S. targets, any attack on the West Coast would include carrier-borne aircraft. Thus, the activities of Japan's carriers might provide warning of an attack:

Chief of Operations
The Navy Department
November 20, 1938

Dear Sir:
Hirohito really is a Navy man and will do as the Navy desires. I offer the following suggestion: That in view of the certainty that some time it will be necessary to have a set policy based on what shall be done when Japan's Navy gets ready to strike, a unit of the intelligence service be made responsible for sure knowledge at all times and under all circumstances of the location of Japan's airplane carriers. If she decides to fight, our first warnings would be the appearance of carriers off our coast, prepared to attack our fleet's vital units. They will not wait, but hit first, as Japan has done in all cases. Togo's maxims will never be forgotten by Japan. Secondly, a force able to care for Japan's carriers shall be always [ready] to meet such a threat and to hit first, with success. We must first put out the eyes of the Dragons before we can feel safe.

G. G., Port Dickinson, NY[21]

Japan didn't have enough carriers to support an invasion, so some considered that she might seek to launch air attacks from alternative bases:

February 6, 1933

Dear Sir:
I take the privilege of writing you this letter. I have read in the "Daily News Paper" of our fleet that is now on the Pacific Coast. The Japanese attitude, the bad feeling

against the United States. In case war should be declared between United States and Japan, territories of Mexico is very large and they can very easily have airplane parts shipped into Mexico. By such a maneuver the Japanese could very easily put those parts together in a very short time and attack our fleet from this side of the ocean. This may not happen. It would be well for our intelligence department to check up on activities of airplane construction in Mexico in case there is such a thing happening and prevent a surprise attack on this side of the water we least expected it from. This is my suggestion that might happen. I thought it my duty to write to you and explain my thoughts to you in this matter. If Japan makes such a move, it will be well for us to know it.

Sincerely,

F. J.[22]

Chief of Staff
July 30, 1939

Dear General Marshall:
. . . I happen to know that at least two nations have been not only toying, but making real calculations, for operations from an entirely different standpoint. It is quite clear that a country could build enough airplane carriers to stage a massed attack from floating bases, of say 2,000 planes, but that would be an extremely expensive proposition as the speed and limitations of aircraft carriers are governing factors. In a few words, here is what two nations have been figuring on for distant air attacks, and to illustrate it, I will assume that the Pelleu Islands have concluded to secure a land base [in] the area of Washington, Oregon, and California. Large steel barges, with numerous compartments, decked over, and capable of accommodating the largest type planes, would be constructed in sufficient numbers to carry, say 1,500 planes, and keeping out of shipping lanes would be towed leisurely (no rush whatever) to a position off the western coast, these decked barges connected together for ample runways for the largest planes with heavy loads. As the declaration of war has gone out of style, it is perfectly legitimate to start military operations without official notice, so when everything was ready, the attack staged by these 1,500 planes could be pulled off, and if this number of planes could not establish a land base to cover a troop landing, after isolating this coast strip by bombing bridges, snow sheds, etc. in the mountain passes, they should be sent back to the kindergarten. . . .

Yours very truly,
J. C., Cortland, NY[23]

Growing U.S.-Japanese tensions focused public attention on persons of Japanese ancestry living in the United States. Their numbers were fairly small, according to the 1940 census, but more than seven-eighths of the total lived in the three West Coast states.[24] Concerns over the loyalty of Japanese Americans, and over their rising economic status, fostered resentment and suspicion among their neighbors. In a well-publicized speech, a California congressman issued this warning:

> [Japanese-owned fishing boats on the West Coast are] subsidized and paid for by the Japanese government. They are built in such a way that you can, within a very short space of time, erect a small cannon or machine gun on them. Some of them carry a pressure tank sufficient to contain pressure sufficient to launch torpedoes off those boats. Those are the kind of boats that leave Los Angeles harbor for several weeks of a stretch, ostensibly to fish, and then they appear on the scene at Panama. . . . [O]f all the Japanese on the Pacific coast, there is a reserve army of 25,000 that could be under arms immediately if there was any disturbance.[25]

The popular press stoked these fears. *Liberty Magazine* suggested that Hawaii was particularly at risk:

> Out of a population of some 368,000 there are nearly 140,000 Japanese living on these islands. If there were an uprising concurrent with the declaration of war, there would be at least 30,000 Japanese of military age available to participate in it. The remainder of the population is largely composed of races sympathetic to the Japanese. The only real resistance in such event would be offered by the regular troops and they would be greatly outnumbered. The Japanese in the Hawaiian Islands do not attempt to conceal their loyalty to their homeland, and many of the men have served in the Japanese army.[26]

This writer suggested using African American settlers in Hawaii to strengthen U.S. control:

> Chief of Staff
> March 10, 1935
>
> Dear Sir:
> As an American, I am interested in National Defense, therefore I am writing you. I understand the Hawaiian Islands have more resident Japanese than Americans. This would weaken our defense of the Islands, should we ever become involved in war with Japan. My idea is, that the Army Intelligence Service devise some way, that American Negroes be immigrated to the Islands, thru C.C.C. work, P.W.A.

or some other agency. They would easily become acclimated and could do much of the work now done by the Japanese. I also have an idea for use by infantry in an attack, that I would like to divulge to some responsible officer in the New York Corps Area.

Very truly yours,
F. H., Brooklyn, NY[27]

Some Americans worried that Japanese farmers in California threatened the nation's food supply. This letter suggested solving both security and employment problems in one stroke:

Office of the Secretary of War
December 18, 1934

Dear Mr. Dern:
Am taking the liberty of making a few suggestions that may or may not have been considered as seriously as I often thought they should be. The food supply for our fighting force on the west coast particularly, is a serious problem considering the many poisons, germs and ova of microbes that may find its way into such foods as fresh vegetables and fruits causing considerable serious afflictions among the men. . . . Considering the large proportion of our truck gardens, groves and markets are controlled and in a sense dependent on the Japanese race and the rate they are taking over such responsibilities, it would seem possible the whole set up on the west coast or even in westerly states, would be demoralized in the event the Japanese should become unfriendly. Of course many of these people are citizens of this country but they could not be criticized if they felt they had been discriminated against, causing them to feel justified in remaining loyal to their own fatherland. I took the liberty of calling Mr. Hopkins' attention to the thought of starting colonies for truck gardeners selected from the more reliable families of the unemployed out here in the western states to guard against any such contingencies or even providing food for the fighting forces in peace time. . . .

Respectfully,
T. S., Van Nuys, CA[28]

The prospect of a surprise attack made the threat of Japanese American sabotage even greater, because fifth columnists might synchronize their strikes with the start of an undeclared war. These two writers warned of sneak attacks against Navy units:

Office of Naval Intelligence
January 29, 1934

Dear Sir:
. . . We have in various parts of the country, Japanese importers and perhaps even chemical manufacturers, who may be secretly connected with the military party in Japan and who may, if occasion arises help to strike a sudden blow upon outbreak of conflict. We can expect a blow to be struck without warning, supposing the military party of Japan should recklessly decide on a war against the U.S. With the proper high explosives on hand and with men on hand willing to sacrifice their lives, a destructive blow against the U.S. naval or other military establishments could be delivered in various ways, such as for instance: small craft in harbors or inland waterways could be loaded with a heavy charge of explosives and run into a dry dock, a canal lock or even into a ship tied up at a dock and do great damage. Of course the Japanese-U.S. war talk may be just so much hot air, let loose by irresponsible persons. It does not seem reasonable that any sensible Jap should for a moment think that Japan could gain anything in a war with the U.S.

Very Truly Yours,
J. R., Seattle, WA[29]

Director of Naval Intelligence
May 11, 1939

Dear Sir:
It is presumed, of course, that security of the fleet includes a thorough and continued study of possible avenues of attack; and that comprehensive precautions are taken against all conceived contingencies. In the hope, however, that I shall not appear a nuisance, I should like briefly to outline a situation in which it seems possible the fleet may be to some degree vulnerable to seriously damaging attack. The undersigned has observed that when the fleet lies in San Francisco harbor, there are a few moments, shortly following each turning of the tide, when the ships, pivoting about their anchors, present an almost unbroken target to the approaches from the Golden Gate. Now, would it be possible for, let us say, some old "tub" of a freighter, familiar to the coastwise trade, to reach the "range" and be prepared to fire at a carefully calculated moment,—i.e., when the fleet would present its broadside as a target? It would not seem impracticable to fit out such a ship with a number of torpedo tubes on its starboard, so that it should be able to fire a large number of torpedoes within the space of a couple of minutes. The thought in the back of my mind is that he ship would be the "double" of a boat perhaps carrying lumber between San Francisco Bay and some point on the north coast. If necessary,

the lumber carrier could, I suppose, be circuitously acquired and so managed as to assure its helpful conduct. This is just an idea, which probably has long since occurred to someone in the Navy; if so, just file it in the wastebasket. Please do not trouble yourself to write a reply.

Respectfully,
B. M., Palo Alto, CA[30]

These two writers argued that saboteurs were already at work in America:

Secretary of War
November 30, 1936

Dear Sir:
I read some of your recommendations for bolstering defense in the air service and other army units and it has prompted me to write you about some of my observations and to tell you what I think of them. I have no faith in the pacifists' claim that we are geographically secure from the attack of foreign countries in case of war; in fact I think we are already a target of the warring nations. So many transport airline planes and fast trains being wrecked, and so many fires of unknown origin leads me to believe it is the results of planned espionage probably emanating from foreign countries. All this could be passed up as merely coincidental, but is seems to me that the laws of average is exceeded, and especially so in destruction of property that is so potential in the event of a declaration of war. . . . There could be a double motive in destroying property by fire—one to weaken this country and the other to put more scrap steel on the market. Scrap steel of this nature—burned machinery—is what the other countries want—it can be reconditioned cheaply and easily by a mere tempering process. . . . I think there is a well planned course including espionage, vandalism and incendiarism throughout all the threatening countries classed as democracies by the Press-Scimitar editorial.

Respectfully,
C. W., Memphis, TN[31]

Federal Bureau of Investigation
June 19, 1939

Dear Mr. Hoover:
I am a little afraid you will feel that abnormal psychology has finally gone to my head when you read this. . . . You probably recall the details of the experiment by

Rowland in the January issue of the *Journal of Abnormal and Social Psychology*. Startling sort of thing wherein, using invisible glass, he demonstrated that the subject would reach for an angry rattle snake or would throw sulphuric acid in the experimenter's face. Evidently an uncontrolled impulse which he simply cannot resist. Frankly I would not have thought it possible had not an experimenter of Rowland's ability obtained such results. Now for a little melodrama. An American, a British, and a French submarine have all come to grief in the last two months. From the purely experimental point of view I see no reason why a high grade hypnotic subject, acting on the basis of a post-hypnotic suggestion, might not have tampered with some of the very delicate contrivances necessary to the proper functioning of the submarine. To be sure, he would have killed himself in the process, but Rowland's subject was perfectly willing to reach for that rattlesnake. Please don't think that I take this subject too seriously, but, if there could be any basis of fact in it, and I see no reason why it is impossible, then obviously the further implications are pretty serious. If a man could do this with a submarine, he might do the same with a battleship.

Cordially yours,
G. E., Hamilton, NY[32]

In the event of war with Japan, the Panama Canal would enable the U.S. Navy to quickly shift forces between the Atlantic and Pacific. This made the canal a tempting target for any potential foe, as the *Washington Post* noted:

> The Panama Canal stands out more than ever as the most vital—and vulnerable—spot in our armament. . . . Today the safety of our coasts demands that our navy be able to operate in either the Atlantic or the Pacific on short notice. It is equally important that it be kept open as a great trade route—for the Panama Canal is now one of the two chief points of concentration of world shipping, the other being the Suez Canal. The defense of the Panama Canal thus outshadows all other defensive problems in importance. . . . [T]here are already on this side of the Atlantic a substantial number of large foreign-owned commercial air liners that can quickly and easily be transformed into heavy bombers. Such an eventuality cannot be ignored in a world in which undeclared wars have become common, and in which hostilities are begun without warning.[33]

Although fortifications guarded both ends of the canal, its vital locks remained vulnerable to air attack, as the *Boston Herald* cautioned:

Just think: a single bomb, dropping on a ship passing through a lock of the Canal, at the moment of the declaration of war, with the United States fleet in Atlantic waters, would be an enormous disaster. The United States fleet would have to steam the whole way around South America. . . . The problem is not only to hold the canal but also to keep it open. A plane can reach it today in two hours from a dozen points, both from the mainland and from islands, and in three or four hours from innumerable points. With speedier aviation, the distances become shorter every day. Surely a clever enemy would find the means for hiding a few planes somewhere within striking distance, just to have them ready. A jungle, a deserted island, who knows? . . . What is to prevent a pilot who is willing to sacrifice his own life to slip out from behind a cloud, in full sunshine if you wish, turn on full gas, and dive down with his ton or two of high explosives at a speed of say 500 miles an hour at some ship or lock?[34]

The Army increased air defenses around the canal, but the threat demanded more radical measures. Two options made sense: adding bomb-resistant locks, or constructing a second canal across Nicaragua. The *Los Angeles Times* argued that both plans simply created more targets:

At their farthest point the new series of locks will be less than a mile from the existing ones and . . . all three sets could be destroyed during one bombing flight of hostile airplanes almost as readily as one. This is perhaps true, but it does not follow that a new canal in Nicaragua would necessarily insure us, in such a contingency, against interruption of water communication between the oceans. The site of the proposed Nicaragua ditch is only about 500 miles from that in Panama and easily within the range of a single attack expedition.[35]

The next two letters proposed alternative schemes:

December 5, 1938

To the Editor of the *New York Times:*
The President and many others believe that we should have a navy large enough to give us ample protection on either coast, even should the Panama Canal be blocked. The possibility, or even probability, that the canal would be blocked should any nation plan to attack us, or any part of this hemisphere which our policy requires us to protect, cannot be ignored. Should our fleet be in the Pacific, and a European power or powers want to keep it there, it is almost certain that they could succeed by acting before taking any other warlike measures. Heavily laden ships could be sunk in locks and gate hinges could easily be destroyed by

powerful explosives, taken to the vulnerable points under the guise of innocent cargo; or possibly attacks by bombing planes might do the trick. . . . The canal could still be changed to a sea level by excavating for a distance of about thirty-one miles alongside the present high level of the canal. . . . Should the canal be changed to sea level, it would be impossible to block it with anything like the effectiveness or for anything like the time which would be possible in the case of a lock canal. Even should a ship be sunk across the waterway, its demolition and removal would be much simpler than if this were done in locks. . . . We would thus have the enormous advantage of a route between the two coasts which could not be blocked for any serious period, with resultant far greater flexibility for our navy.

S. K., Englewood, NJ[36]

Secretary of War
January 30, 1937

Dear Mr. Secretary:
I have just returned from the Panama Canal and was impressed with the necessity, for national defense, of a motor road across the Isthmus and a protection of the locks against bombing; my idea of the latter is a net, placed high enough to permit the largest vessels to pass under, made of rust proof steel or steel cable, in strips say 150 feet to 200 feet wide running across all locks, including the new one which will eventually be built for such vessels as the "Queen Mary" and air plane carriers, each strip to have independent supports and to be say, 3 feet higher or lower than the adjoining strips, and overlap them, so that damage by bombs or hurricane would not destroy the whole structure. By having the strips of uniform size a few duplicates could be kept on hand at each set of locks, together with machines (also protected) to replace damaged sections so that repairs could be made in a few hours; to make it more effective auxiliary nets could be strung from the same supports at a lower level. . . .

Respectfully submitted,
C. C., Bedford Hills, NY[37]

The canal's dual nature made it especially vulnerable. Transit fees from merchant vessels kept the canal economically viable, but the presence of foreign ships opened up new possibilities for sneak attacks:

President Franklin D. Roosevelt
April 27, 1934

Sir:
Kindly draw the attention of the War Department to my letter, at the same time
excuse the liberty I am taking in drawing the matter to your attention. Reading in
the papers the precautions which were taken in guarding the war ships through the
Panama Canal, it struck me that apparently no precaution is taken for guarding
the Canal itself, except by planes and Marines. The Canal can be blown up by an
unfriendly nation, especially now that our fleet is in eastern waters, and by the
time our fleet comes around the Horn, she can have taken the Hawaiian Islands,
destroyed several of our Coast cities and landed enough troops to hold them. They
simply have to load about fifty tons of dynamite in the bottom of one of her
freighters, connect firing wires, run them through the holds and connect them
to a switch on the bridge or other convenient place, fill up the hold with general
merchandise, and who can tell what is in the hold below, underneath the cargo.
Its destination New York or some other place on the Eastern coast. My suggestion
would be that all merchant ships before going through the Canal must stop all
electric apparatus, have the throttle valves of all the generating engines locked and
an adequate guard placed in the engine room, until the ships are clear of the Canal.
Also captain's quarters, bridge, officers' and engineer's quarters and wireless room
and quarters searched for storage batteries. . . .

Very respectfully,
H. L., Los Gatos, CA[38]

The interwar years witnessed astounding progress in aircraft technology, which
sparked worries that any future war would feature mass bombing raids on cities.
The public grew especially concerned that such raids might involve one notorious
product of the Great War: poison gas. Partly due to sensationalistic media coverage,
gas bombing became the great terror of the 1920s and 1930s. The *New Republic*
described an apocalyptic gas-bomb attack on England:

Say that war is declared. Nay, war is only threatened, for he who speaks first, speaks
last. In Bremen or Calais a thousand men climb into the cockpits of a thousand
aircraft, and to each is given a bomb which the pressure of a finger will release,
together with instructions as to where, precisely, and at what altitude, that pressure
is to be applied. A starting signal, an hour or two of flight, a little veering, dropping,
and dodging as the defense planes rise, a casualty or two as the radium atomite of
anti-aircraft guns tries vainly to fill a space one hundred miles square and four miles

deep, one muffled roar after another as the bombs are dropped per schedule, and so, to all intents and purposes, the civilization founded by William the Conqueror, which gave Bacon, Newton, and Watt to the world, comes, in something like half an hour, to a close. London, Liverpool, Manchester, Bristol, Birmingham, Leeds—each has had its appointed place on the code of instructions, and each now vanishes from the list of habitable places on the planet. Not even a rat, not even an ant, not even a roach can survive. . . . There is at least one good thing to be said about the next war: it will not keep us long on edge."[39]

Nor would such horrors necessarily be confined to Europe, as the *Chicago Tribune* warned: "Giant airplanes now being perfected could swoop down on the United States from either Europe or the orient and level great cities like Chicago or New York in a few minutes. . . . It wouldn't just be bombs, unfortunately, but more probably poison gas which would wipe out the population of Manhattan and the adjacent centers."[40] The *Washington Post* noted that fear of gas would only increase the devastation: "The effects of chemicals will be far more important than that of merely piling up the dead. They will cause panic and a breakdown of the country's resistance. The blaze seldom takes as many lives in a theater fire as does the mad crowd."[41]

Other publications questioned these doomsday scenarios, dismissing tales of cities being obliterated as so much hyperbole. *Scientific American* criticized alarmists for "persistently dinning it in our ears that in the next war we shall witness the instantaneous wiping out of whole cities by the dropping of bombs filled with high explosives and death-dealing gasses. . . . [M]aking all allowances for the post-war development of the airship and the bomb, we can see how ridiculously exaggerated is this talk of a capital city being wiped out in a few hours' bombardment."[42] An Army spokesman suggested that cities made poor bombing targets:

> Lurid articles, with still more lurid pictorial displays, envision vast air fleets manned by robots circling over defenseless cities, dropping tons of dynamite, poison gas and germs. Huge buildings are seen crashing to earth, burying the inhabitants in a chaos of brick, stone, and twisted steel. Multitudes are death-stricken by poison gas, devastated by typhoid, cholera, glanders, and other malignant diseases. . . . A most elementary calculation of the number of bases and ships, amount of ammunition, and the flying and ground personnel required for an attempt at even a partial destruction of any American border city puts the matter outside the bounds of possibility. . . . Military and naval men realize the futility of wasting their munitions in demolishing dwellings and killing non-combatants.[43]

The *Washington Post* reported on a proposal to calm popular apprehension by bombarding a middle-sized American city with tear gas, thus "convincing the public of the effectiveness and humanity of gas warfare." The proposed attack on citizens provided with gas masks would demonstrate "how quickly a population of 10,000, for example, could protect itself from tear gas. The protection might possibly be extended to horses, although this is less important. From such experiments on a large scale we might arrange for a thoroughly tested conclusion as to the real merits of gas warfare. In the meantime the public bases its opinion upon prejudice and unreasoning fears."[44] These two writers suggested defenses against gas raids:

President, the United States of America
[August 1936]

Dear Sir:
. . . During the war, the United States Government promised to place stations in every town, following the war, to be used as permanent protection for the masses of people in the U.S. who would likely be attacked in case of gas attacks in case gas air raids were launched at the U.S. If the gas ever attacks from other countries, not only our soldiers, but our women and children would be found dead, blind, maimed, and with burned bodies. It would be "good-night" to the U.S.A. My advice to you, as the President of the United States, would be to see that these gas dugouts, or chambers, be built, equipped with gas masks, and placed throughout the country, first on our coasts, then one thousand miles inland, after that scattered all over, in strategic places, available to the general public. . . . We read daily in our newspapers where large numbers of the Russian people are wearing gas masks, likewise the Japanese, while the United States is standing still with reference to this matter. Admittedly, we need good roads and modern improvements, but I believe the people's lives are at stake without adequate gas protection. We hear continuously, over the radio, the cry of "safety first" on our highways, but never "safety first" from the dangers of possible air raids. . . .

A. H., New London, OH[45]

Secretary of War
February 23, 1935

Dear Sir:
Recently I read a magazine article in which the writer depicted the terrible effects of gas bombs dropped upon our cities. This writer stated that the women and children would be the first to suffer and would suffer the most in these attacks,

because it would be practically impossible to equip them with gas masks etc. I am presenting to you an idea that would protect all the people of a city during a gas attack. This idea that I submit for your consideration is the forcing of fresh air under pressure by means of pipes into every house and building in the city. This unpolluted air could be obtained by means of stand pipes attached to the sky scrapers of the city extending if necessary many feet above the building. These pipes could be equipped with either exhaust or force fans or with both force and exhaust fans. . . . The air from these pipes could be carried to air compressors that would force the air into cylinders or tanks that would be strong enough to stand 100 lbs per sq. inch pressure. Then the air in these tanks could be piped under pressure to every building in the city in the same manner as water is piped to buildings at the present time, then by turning valves fresh air could be brought to every house immediately. Of course the pressure in the pipes entering the buildings would be reduced to one pound per sq. inch or less. One pound pressure would flood a building with fresh air instantly and at the same time prevent the gas from entering. All this would cost a lot of money but at the same time it would be the means of giving our idle men work. . . .

Most Sincerely Yours,
I. H., St. Xavier, MT[46]

This letter proposed air-raid defenses designed to preserve the core of American civilization:

President Franklin D. Roosevelt
June 3, 1936

My dear Mr. Roosevelt,
You have constructed in Washington a wonderfully beautiful home for the archives of the nation and its library, in which to store their treasures. The Alexandrian Library in Egypt once contained similar treasures of ancient civilization. But that library was destroyed in war and with it perished its arts, knowledge, and civilization. And men had to start all over again. We are not free from the risk of war. We are less protected against it than ever before. Foreign aeroplanes in mass formation have penetrated as far west as Chicago. Bombs are more potent than artillery. If war occurred—and how can we hope forever to escape it—what is to prevent aeroplanes from penetrating to Washington, bombing the city, and burning that library? . . . It has been said and repeatedly that the next great war would wipe out civilization. If it destroyed the libraries, why might it not wipe out our civilization, as the destruction of the Alexandrian Library wiped out Egyptian civilization? Can our libraries be protected? Bombs can penetrate to a depth of

perhaps 25 or possibly 50 feet. If in time of war we could store our libraries in vaults 75 feet below surface, why would not this protect them against bombings? Obviously, vaults would protect. If from the hundreds of millions to be raised and spent the coming year (one and a half billions) but four millions are appropriated to vault construction (one under each library site) Washington's libraries would be protected at an expenditure of say $1,000,000 on the archive home, $1,000,000 on the Smithsonian Institution, $1,000,000 on the Congressional Library, and $1,000,000 on the Patent Office. Why would not that moderate expenditure of but $4,000,000 protect those irreplaceable treasures and meet with universal approval? And if, following that example, other libraries did the same why would not our civilization itself be protected? . . .

Yours very truly,
J. M., Yonkers, NY[47]

This writer believed U.S. cities should have active as well as passive defenses against raids:

Honorable Marvin Jones, Congressman from Texas
January 9, 1939

Dear Friend:
I have already sent you a telegram stating that we favored our President's plan to improve our national defense. Here is a suggestion that I offer for what it is worth: Encourage large cities, especially on our sea coast, to maintain anti-aircraft guns and gunners as a part of their regular municipal police system. It might be that the federal government could sell modern anti-aircraft guns and equipment to the cities at cost or even less than cost. The federal government could provide one technician, at regular army officer's pay, to each city so cooperating. . . . [I]t seems to me that any city subject to attack from the air would be glad to meet the expense of maintaining adequate anti-aircraft defense in peace times as one of the surest means of discouraging attack on their city. . . . All of our great cities, it seems to me, could with practically no increase in personnel expense maintain during peace times, a nucleus anti-aircraft defense. Certainly if I were a large property owner in any of our coast cities or such inland cities as Denver, Kansas City, Oklahoma City and Chicago, I would be more than glad to help defray the expense of maintaining a permanent anti-aircraft defense as a means of assuring the protection of property and lives where I have immediate interest. With best personal regards and hoping that our national defense program will go through without a hitch,

I am Sincerely, your friend,
J. P., Borger, TX[48]

Antiaircraft guns formed the core of a city's air defenses, but they could never stop a determined attack. Tethered balloons offered another option: the British had suspended large wire nets around London during World War I to snare nocturnal raiders. The next writer suggested a fitting balloon defense against gas bombers:

> To the Honorable Franklin Roosevelt
> October 8, 1935
>
> Please excuse me as I come with my short message of preparedness. So our country is preparing for war. I wish to add my bit for your consideration. I am opposed to war but in favor of defense provided it is forced upon us. My plan: Make plenty of small balloons and bombs filled with poisonous gas, attach bombs to balloons as shown in plot, attach fuse to a cap fixed to each bomb. Cut fuse to such length as will explode each bomb at such distance apart as would be necessary to fill air with blinding gas. When planes are coming in send up balloons just ahead of planes so when pilot comes in contact with stifling gas he will lose control of his plane. Arrange stations in line far enough out and close enough to each other to meet all requirements. . . .
>
> As ever,
> O. H., Midlothian, TX[49]

As the 1930s ended, Americans apprehensively watched European political conflicts once again degenerate into war. Although the onset of hostilities in 1939 resembled the affairs of 1914, America's role had profoundly changed. Many Americans remained disillusioned with the failed efforts to create something better out of the chaos of World War I, and no longer believed that idealism could somehow replace the realpolitik practiced overseas. Few, however, thought that the United States could successfully insulate itself from events abroad. For better or worse, the nation had become an integral part of the world military equation.

CHAPTER 7

Balancing Act:
The Era of Semibelligerency

Although Americans supported France and Britain against Germany, popular sentiment ran strongly against involvement in another European war. President Roosevelt had no choice but to observe neutrality laws while providing modest amounts of aid to the Allies. After Germany overran Poland, the two sides settled down behind their defenses. This pause spurred speculation that the "Phony War" would end without a World War I–style bloodbath. *Scientific American* predicted that the failure of interwar disarmament treaties would reduce violence:

> [T]he very deadliness and enormity of modern armaments have done more than all the cries of horror by the pacifists during the past decades, if not to stop war, at least to limit rigidly the bloodshed of a modern war between powerful nations. While the burden of armaments is a heavy load for populations to bear in peace times, it seems to us that this war may yet prove that it is the armaments themselves which have more effect than common disarmament which renders a country defenseless. It may follow from this that all peoples may see the utter futility of armed warfare, between equals and devote their energies solely toward the sort of economic warfare which is being waged today.[1]

America's muted reaction to the war reflected the sense of security provided by the vast ocean separating the New World from the Old. The Royal Navy had insulated America from previous European conflicts, and most expected it to do so again. Some argued that America could no longer count on the British, and that it needed a "two-ocean navy" capable of simultaneously defending both coasts. Pacifists accused Navy boosters of using scare tactics to push for more ships. The *New York Times* weighed in with this disparaging comment:

Congress should dismiss as fantasy the idea so frequently advanced in committee rooms and on the floor—the idea that the combined navies of the so-called totalitarian states, Germany, Italy and Japan, might attack this country, sink our fleet, and by blockade or invasion defeat the United States. The prospect is patently absurd. Even the total combined fleets of those nations are probably inferior in fighting power to our own navy; and moreover, one cannot imagine the circumstances under which that combined strength could be applied against the American Navy. Even were Japan, Germany, and Italy able and willing to strip their own coasts of all protection, an overseas expedition thousands of miles from bases would leave the attacking fleets of these, or any other Powers, at a definite disadvantage—one so great that it would insure their almost certain defeat.[2]

The dramatic events of 1940 undercut these comfortable assumptions. As France collapsed and England braced for invasion, even the worst-case prewar scenarios seemed plausible. America might soon face the combined Axis fleets, powerfully augmented by captured French and British ships. British leaders used the specter of Germany seizing the Royal Navy to extract more aid from America. London's ambassador announced that, if Hitler captured the British fleet, "there would be no superior armed power to prevent Hitler and his friends from thundering at your doorstep."[3] The *Washington Post* put its warning like this:

> If Germany wins, what becomes of the British Navy? Some say it would flee—to Canada, to Singapore. If it did flee it would be brought back for surrender to Germany. Hitler would say to Britain, "Bring back that navy and deliver it, or I will raze England as I have razed Poland." Some say the British would scuttle their navy. But that too, Hitler would probably prevent by intimidation. . . . As quickly as Germany with her newly acquired navy, could cross the sea, she would seize, as a recognized right of conquest, every British island on this side of the Atlantic. She would seize Newfoundland, and every British island in the West Indies, and every French one and Dutch one.[4]

Two months later, the *Post* added this:

> Nothing else will serve now than a comprehensive and carefully worked out deal with the British government relating to our security and their defense. In such a deal we would need, in the first place, an understanding that in the event that the British isles were forced to ask Germany for an armistice, the British navy, other than an agreed proportion required for Singapore and Indian Ocean, would be withdrawn to Canada. Secondly, we would need a provision that it would thenceforth function as a joint Canadian and American force.[5]

This letter proposed a trade to keep Allied ships out of German hands:

Chief of Staff, U.S. Navy
June 14, 1940

. . . It is a safe bet that with our entire fleet concentrated over in the Pacific to keep
the Japs from getting too hostile or ambitious,—and with both the British and
French fleets concentrated in the North Atlantic, that the United States would
not likely be attacked by either the Japs on the one side, and certainly not yet
by Hitler and/or Mussolini on the other side, or both of them, if and when they
came here. With two navies in one ocean (Atlantic), and with our entire navy in
the Pacific—the United States stands a fair chance of living in peace for some time
to come. . . . If we had both Allied fleets in the Atlantic, with their naval flying
squadrons, and with our fleet in the Pacific, could we not then, with great safety,
immediately turn over to France 90% of our air equipment, our tank equipment,
our military trucks, our machine guns and Garand rifles, in the thought that by
the time we needed them we would have plenty of replacements? We could make
a deal with France and England (even democracies move sort of fast these days),
that if in the final analysis they were beaten into submission, that before the final
surrender, both these fleets could be sailed into American harbors to be turned over
to us in payment for war equipment advances and war debts long owed. . . .

Humbly subscribed,
Mr. Nebraska, Mr. New York [sic][6]

Many doubted whether agreements reached with nations in peril would be
honored after their collapse. Winston Churchill warned Roosevelt that, while his
own government would never surrender, any successor seeking favorable terms
would have little to bargain with but possession of the Royal Navy.[7]

This writer suggested giving British sailors another incentive to continue the
fight:

Secretary of the Navy
August 20, 1940

Dear Sir:
Considering the fact that Germany has so far succeeded in what she attempted to
conquer, I believe we should make sure that she should not use the families of the
officials of England or of the navy as hostages to secure the British Navy. Could
the families of the officers of our navy entertain those of the English fleet—Or

could some such strategy be worked out with Canada to insure that Hitler could not get the fleet by means of hostages and threats of torture of navy families, in the event he should conquer England. In the present emergency, some such strategy as suggested, to get the English fleet on this side of the Atlantic in case of England's fall, would do us more good than all the billions of dollars we could spend for defense later. If Mr. Roosevelt is not already working at defense from this angle, will you please call it to his attention.

[Respectfully],
J. G., Kearneysville, WV[8]

If the British were to surrender, direct action to seize the Royal Navy might become necessary:

Adjutant General's Office
[ca. May 1940]

Dear Sir:
In the event of a German victory and realizing what to expect from Hitler and his underlings with their thrust for world domination and their ruthless unprincipled methods or efforts to obtain it, I have a suggestion to offer. Namely, so as to insure the certainty of us having sufficient time in which to prepare ourselves for any aggression. That the U.S. beat the Nazis to the punch, so to speak. And should the circumstances arise that the Allies should find themselves forced to hand in their fleets we should step in with ours or part of ours and take possession. Caution of course would have to be used so that a repetition of the Scapa Flow scuttlings would not take place and sufficient extra oil supplies to refuel them would have to be at hand. This should be done without a declaration of war as that appears to be the procedure followed by the Nazis and would of course be continued with us were they convinced we were unprepared. Should any objection be raised as to its unfairness etc. it could then be explained to be done towards part payment towards unpaid war debts. Surely the British would have no cause to object as they would be losing their ships anyway. But however aware of the uncertainties of human nature perhaps it is as well that they (the British) are not notified in advance. . . .

Very truly yours,
J. P., Oakland, CA[9]

British military fortunes would ultimately determine who possessed the Royal Navy. Many Americans wondered how England could possibly hold out. Perhaps the best chance lay in acknowledging a new order in Europe:

[Secretary of the Navy]
September 19, 1940

My Dear Mr. Secretary:
. . . It is proposed that the United States of America take the following steps to bring the present hostilities in Europe to an end and to insure its own security in the future: 1. The United States shall offer to enter into a permanent treaty of federation with Great Britain and the self-governing dominions of the Empire, which treaty shall include at least these three provisions: a. Complete free trade among all members of the federation; b. A single general staff and high command for all military and naval forces; c. Some central body which shall have sole power on behalf of all members of the federation to declare war and to negotiate treaties. To do its part in providing for the common defense of the federation, the United States shall agree to complete the rearmament and military training program already commenced. 2. In consideration of the entry of the United States into this Anglo American federation, all British possessions in the western hemisphere shall be transferred outright to the United States, and the several provinces of Canada and Newfoundland shall be admitted into the Union as states. 3. Before the treaty of federation shall become binding on any party thereto, Great Britain and the Dominions must first offer terms of peace to Germany and Italy, providing that Germany and Italy shall not interfere with the British Empire or with any territory in the western hemisphere and that the Anglo American federation shall not interfere with any settlement which German and Italy may make with the other countries of continental Europe. . . . The implicit corollaries of these proposals by the United States would be that if the proposals were accepted by Great Britain but refused by Germany, the United States would forthwith enter the war upon the side of Great Britain. On the other hand, if the proposals were declined by Great Britain, the United States would then feel free to revert to complete and even-handed neutrality. . . .

G. J., Asst. Dean, University of Chicago Law School
Chicago, IL[10]

Some officials and reporters warned that Axis forces would next seek to infiltrate South America. *Reader's Digest* downplayed this threat:

Hitler would first have to acquire bases in this hemisphere. Those bases would have to be much closer to the United States than is Germany, otherwise there would be no sense in bases. Brazil is the South American base to which the President is fond of referring. This is because Hitler could take over West Africa and concentrate his forces at Dakar, which is only 1600 miles from Pernambuco in Brazil. Hitler will be able to cross over the Atlantic at this narrow stretch to Brazil, and, as Senator Claude Pepper has described it, roll on through Venezuela, Colombia, Central America and Mexico to the Rio Grande. This proposal is so grotesque that it hardly calls for an answer. Before he started from Germany he would be 3300 miles from the United States. After traveling 5000 miles to Brazil he would be farther away from the United States than when he started. And he would have to march a million men with all their supplies through tropical jungles and over rugged mountains![11]

To defend the Americas, the United States would need help from its Latin neighbors. The *New York Times* noted that the South American nations "are not only unprepared to defend themselves against any possible invasion but that they are not even equipped to cooperate efficiently in any joint inter-American defense plans. In a crisis the ten South American republics could mobilize only five battleships, three modern cruisers, twenty-four destroyers and fourteen submarines for the defense of more than 13,000 miles of coastline on three oceans."[12] These two writers suggested uses for Latin American naval units:

Secretary of the Navy
December 20, 1940

Dear Mr. Knox:
Not to criticize, but to suggest a plan of progress I am writing to you as follows. It has occurred to me as a feasible plan, and not only one of expediency but one of sound policy for the American nations, to form an all American naval patrol, to patrol the recently designated neutrality zone. Such patrol to be formed of existent naval units from each of the seaboard nations of the Americas and to be maintained financed and governed by them. This patrol by exercising the authority of each participating nation and the force of their navies could guarantee safety from attack to all merchantmen bound to or from any American port while such craft were in this zone. . . . Thus European powers getting supplies from the Americas could withdraw naval units now engaged in patrol of thousands of miles of American coastal waters and adjacent seas, and use such units to augment convoys and other uses. Nothing new or novel is claimed for this plan it is simply a suggestion to use all the force of the western hemisphere to back up the Monroe Doctrine. Should this letter get past your first line of defense and come to your attention I would appreciate a reply.

Yours truly,
D. W., St. Maries, ID[13]

[Navy Department]
June 22, 1940

Dear Sir:

. . . The naval construction of the past few years plus the large number of destroyers from the last war will provide sufficient (although not as many as is desirable) auxiliary warships for two fleets—but this country does not now have enough battleships for such a step. However, in the navies of the South American nations there are five battleships. These ships, in groups of one and two, can not defend the nations now owning them against an attack by an aggressive enemy. However, these nations would not be in danger of attack if the main United States battle fleet could be moved to the Atlantic Ocean without fear of an attack on the West Coast by Japan. The five battleships owned by the South American nations (two by Argentina, two by Brazil, and one by Chile), the present Atlantic squadron of three battleships, and a remilitarized Wyoming could provide a fleet of nine battleships for defense in the Pacific. Admittedly these ships are relatively small and old, but, unless the naval authorities are wrong as to the preponderance of force necessary to attack across 3,000 miles of ocean, they should be sufficient to make an attack on Hawaii or the West Coast so hazardous that Japan would not dare try it. With such a fleet for protection in the Pacific the main United States battle fleet could then be moved to the Atlantic. Although the South American nations might be willing to cooperate in such a plan for the defense of the Americas, it is neither necessary nor desirable that the battleships be obtained by a system of alliances. The alliances would not provide the centralized control necessary for such a program to be effective, and it would expose the South American nations to the possibility of a war with Japan which they neither desire or are prepared for. A much simpler procedure would be to use a method similar to that by which airplanes built for the Army and Navy of this country are now being shipped to the Allies. That is, let the South American nations owning battleships turn them in on account for new and more powerful warships to be constructed in the United States, for designs and materials for building warships in their own country (such as Brazil is now doing), or for aeroplanes or any other defensive weapons that these nations might desire. Such a program would not only provide the U.S. immediately with a two-ocean navy, but it would allow the nations with the old battleships to augment and modernize their navies and defenses. . . .

D. G., New Haven, CT[14]

With the Axis powers threatening to seize bases in Latin America and the Caribbean, the Panama Canal seemed more vulnerable than ever. This famous writer proposed a more secure route for moving ships between the Atlantic and Pacific oceans:

[Early 1941]

Panama Canal means sailing too far south. Too easily destroyed, not only by bombing aeroplane, but also by sabotage—a few spies each with a stick of dynamite. Ship Railway from Galveston to San Diego. Rises to high altitude, but can be without defiles and passes, and escape all large-city traffic. The multiple tracks—8, 12, 16 or more parallel standard tracks enable as large a load as desired to be carried. . . . This railway should cut one-third the time of transfer of the fleet from one ocean to the other—but always the largest argument is that while any portion of it that might be bombed can be quickly repaired, without holding up the entire system, the Panama Canal could easily be blocked entirely. The cost would be huge—but not much more than a new canal, and to safe-guard it, there is no need of acquiring such island bases as the country is now taking over. Should America be attacked through Mexico, this would be a better Maginot Line, with moveable fortresses, with large guns, meeting an emergency anywhere. Unlike the Maginot Line, these moveable units could not be turned into traps. With this line, we could build ships anywhere in Texas, Arizona, New Mexico, along the line, and not just at easily reached and bombed ports on the seashore—always so few and so vulnerable. The railway would lessen the maintenance cost that would result if we have to build two big navies.

Sinclair Lewis[15]

If Britain collapsed and the Nazis established positions in the Americas, an attack on the United States could soon follow. German forces invading America presumably would employ advanced technology and Blitz tactics that had proven devastating in Europe. *Life* explained it this way: "What Nazi Germany knows, and what the Allies do not yet seem to know, it that war has undergone a great change since Nov. 11, 1918. It is today a huge coordinated operation of modern machines—airplanes, armored cars, tanks, tractors, trucks, motorized guns. The importance of manpower has gone down as the importance of mechanized materiel has gone up."[16]

One novel aspect of Blitz warfare involved the use of German paratroops to seize vital airfields, destroy forts, and sow confusion behind enemy lines. *Life* reported that paratroops aimed "to immobilize, destroy, annoy. They are saboteurs, who attack communications, prevent defenders from using their bridges and railways, and divert reserves from the front line. In the Lowlands their mission was to come down behind forts and flooded fields and wage miniature blitzkriegs everywhere. Never before in history was there such a blizzard from the sky."[17] Americans reasoned that Nazi paratroops would spearhead any attack on the United States. A group of New York women formed an antiparatroop rifle corps. Their leader stated "that if the housewives of Europe had been armed and trained, the story might have been a very different one there. As it was, she said, the men, all at the front, were not in a position to cope with such aerial attacks."[18]

The next two writers suggested schemes to deal with an airborne Blitz:

President of the United States
May 10, 1940

Dear President Roosevelt:
. . . The real might of air power has not yet been demonstrated, but it soon will be. Mr. President we must hurry, America is like the British yet, asleep. We must hurry, the airplane is so fast, so swift, so deadly. We must establish small arsenals with latest type machine guns in every town. Parachute troops must be exterminated before they land; each town must have its own little arsenal and be drilled like the Swiss; we must hurry. The government can arouse the people to their danger; they must be aroused before they will act. They must be trained in this new kind of warfare to meet troops landed by planes behind the lines in their midst. Mr. President this country must be awakened to the danger that confronts all democracies. Millions of men will die because the other nations slept while Hitler armed. They will pay in blood for it now; we have time, but we must hurry.

Yours very truly,
W. I., Vineland, NJ[19]

General [Adm.] H. R. Stark, Chief of Operations, U.S. Army [Navy]
May 21, 1940

Dear Sir:
. . . Upon invading a country the German air force did not wait for the defenders to get out of their beds, dress, and get their planes into the air. The invaders simply landed at the enemy airfields and set up their guns before the defenders could reach their own guns. The same thing could perhaps happen here. Attempts were apparently made in Europe to prevent this by parking automobiles on the landing fields. This of course proved to be of little success because it was only a temporary measure, and the planes of the defenders could not use the fields. Permit me to suggest a method which might prove worthy of trial. Assume an early morning surprise attack. The enemy planes, including transports loaded with soldiers, swarm

over the defender's airfield. The soldiers stationed at the field are asleep. The sentry on duty immediately closes a switch. The landing field becomes a mass of flame. Obviously the attacking planes dare not land in such an inferno. . . . Thus the attacking force has been repulsed. This was accomplished by previously running large gas lines underground to gas jets sunk slightly below the surface of the landing fields, the jets being spaced at intervals across the landing field's surface. When the sentry closed the switch the gas was released and ignited electrically at each jet. . . .

Respectfully,
M. B., Washington, DC[20]

Along with paratroops, Hitler employed fast-moving mechanized forces to exploit breakthroughs and encircle enemy units. With its vast auto industry, America could reap the advantages of mechanization by creating a motorized militia:

Secretary of the Navy
May 26, 1940

Honorable Sir:
In as much as ours is the most mobile country and has the best road system known and in view of what is happening abroad, naturally everyone has their thoughts. Some right, some wrong. However, the following is a thought and is forwarded to your hand for whatever use you may see fit to consign it. To counteract rapid progress of a hostile group coastwise and overland: (1) Form a corps of selected men and women on a five year basis. (2) Furnish a vehicle similar to a station wagon that can be used for regular domestic uses to each group or squad of eight, but that can be quickly converted into an armored car, constructed absolutely standard throughout, for the purpose of mounting arms, two-way radio, and other equipment. (3) Arms, radio and equipment to be kept in headquarters units, under constant control, where alarm could be sounded. (4) The Corps to be selected by the Department of Justice and their agents and membership to be free or at a fee of not over one dollar per month. (5) Drills to occur weekly, and to cover a period of two days and the intervening night, gunnery to be held at least every month. (6) Employers to cooperate by establishing one "Defense Day" a week (with pay) for all employees belonging to the Corps. Thus the employer would finance one day and the member would furnish his services for the other day that would normally be his day off. (7) Speedboat Corps for inland and coastwise to be similar except for vehicle. Details to be worked out by government and the manufacturers. Promising full cooperation in any defense action taken, I am,

Sincerely,
W. D., Avenel, NJ[21]

The Germans used dive bombers (Sturzkampfflugzeug, known as Stukas), extensively on pinpoint bombing missions. Stukas ultimately proved extremely vulnerable, but for a time these ungainly aircraft acquired a reputation that was little short of mythical. *Scientific American* noted that this aircraft, "popularly known and feared as 'Stuka'—wreaked havoc in Spain, grounded the ill-fated Polish Air Force in just three days, helped make central Norway untenable for the Allies, and was a prime factor in bringing about the capitulation of France."[22] These two writers proposed methods to counter Stukas:

War Department
June 18, 1940

Dear Sir:
As the result of study of the German "diving bombers" and other military tactics as broadcast by various war correspondents accompanying the German armies in the field, I acquired a new idea which I think might have possibilities and which idea, if useful in National defense, I am willing to offer to the Government without charge. This idea consists of a new anti-aircraft gun on the order of a huge shotgun, using a bore of from 8 or 10 to 12 inches and shooting either lead or cast iron balls of from 2 to 3 inches in diameter and having a range of from 1,000 to 2,000 yards. . . . It seems to me that the effectiveness of such a gun might well be illustrated by a common illustration. As I see it, an airplane—undoubtedly the most delicate of all engines of war—is, in the last analysis, but an artificial bird. Being an artificial bird, it is easily put out of commission by a slow moving projectile of great shocking force. It seems to me that "grape shot" shot from such a gun would provide this shocking power, especially where a plane flying at such tremendous speed toward the gun would increase the shocking power of such projectile, as I doubt if any airplane, armored or otherwise, could possibly withstand such a burst. It appears to me that an airplane under such circumstances is comparable to a duck. If you went duck hunting, would you use a rifle or a shotgun? So far as I know or have been able to ascertain, so far as the diving bombers are concerned, the Allies have been duck hunting with a rifle and not a shotgun. If the French and British had had such a gun during their recent battle in France, there is a strong possibility, if not a probability, that the result might have been different. . . .

Very Respectfully Yours,
A. G., San Francisco, CA[23]

Acting Secretary of War
December 22, 1939

Sir:

I have been very reluctant to write you regarding a plan for the protection of land forces and boats against machine gunning and bombing now being done, particularly in the European war by the dive bombers. . . . As I understand it, the dive bomber approaches the objective, whether ground forces or a ship, with terrific speed and unloads his bombs at very close range. By having a series of trench mortars of slightly longer range than the ones used by us in the war, such dive bombing and strafing of troops could be to a large extent eliminated. Attached to the end of each projectile would be a steel cable of approximately 1/4 inch diameter. This coiled cable would be 600 or 700 feet long, and the other end would be firmly attached to the truck, the ground, or possibly to the ship. When the plane began its dive the gun would be trained in the air directly in line with the oncoming ship. When he was approximately 1/2 mile away the gun would be fired. It would carry high into the air the steel cable. Should he dive directly at the objective, the pilot could not avoid having the ship come into contact with this cable which, of course, would immediately wreck the plane. Should he attempt to dodge he would miss his objective. The cable would be in the air for some 15 seconds, or the approximate time it would take the ship to travel one mile. He could of course release his bombs at a higher altitude, but the effectiveness should be materially reduced. I am told by a naval officer that the planes bombing the English merchantmen are approaching very close to their objective before releasing their bombs. This would be impossible if each ship were equipped with a series of these small guns and a coil of cable. After a shot was fired the cable would be drawn in and would be ready for the next attacker. . . .

Yours truly,
E. R., Bakersfield, CA[24]

The British actually developed a device like that described above, using rockets to propel the cable skyward. Upon snagging the plane, parachutes attached to either end of the cable would open and the sudden drag they created would cause the victim to lose control and crash.[25] Remarkably, on at least one occasion this contraption succeeded in bringing down a low-flying German bomber (although not a Stuka) during an attack on England.[26]

These two letters involved means for spoiling the Stuka pilot's aim:

Commandant, Ninth Naval District
May 21, 1940

. . . Incorporated in this letter is the exposition of the possibilities of using a Gamma ray projector against dive bombing attacks the feature of which is impairment of eyesight of the airplane pilot making the attack. It is a well known fact to those who have had any experience with the electric arc that certain emanations of the Gamma division are extremely injurious to the unprotected eye. In practical arc welding a colored shield is used for eye protection by the welder. It is this injurious effect on the eye that I suggest could be made practical use of in training a highly specialized Gamma ray projector directly upon an approaching airplane in its dive. While I have no military knowledge of the exact tactics that are used by dive pilots. The information I received through magazines and newspapers seems to me that they hit off at an angle directly at the target and when at about an altitude of 100 yards over the target, the bomb would be released. The entire idea is predicated upon the close approach of the bomber to its target upon which this projector would be mounted. It would be impossible, I believe, for a pilot to use any type of shield against Gamma rays and still have sufficient visibility of the target. . . .

I. W., Bowling Green, KY[27]

National Inventors Council
January 20, 1941

Gentlemen:
. . . I want to make a suggestion which might be of service in combating dive bombers, particularly in the Mediterranean. My thought is, to work out mirrors and reflectors of such power, using sun rays in the day time, which could be directed on the plane cockpit and would blind the pilot temporarily as he made his dive, thereby causing him to miss the target and even possibly crashing.

Very truly yours,
H. B., New York, NY[28]

As Britain continued to defy Hitler, American leaders tried to provide significant aid while remaining neutral. Although America produced enormous quantities of military equipment, getting this materiel to England posed a problem. German U-boats had nearly strangled Britain in World War I, and all parties expected they would try again. Britain therefore asked for American destroyers left over from

World War I to escort convoys. In the summer of 1940 Roosevelt agreed to trade fifty old destroyers to Britain for island bases in the western hemisphere. *Time* claimed that the bases were worth far more than the old destroyers: "[T]heir real value is to complete a U.S. defensive ring around the Caribbean and provide real outposts against attack from the Atlantic. But the biggest overall value is preventive: however useful the bases are to the U.S. they would be even more useful to any enemy who got them first."[29] The destroyers-for-bases agreement enjoyed wide popular support. This writer excoriated isolationists for delaying the deal:

Senators Wheeler, Holt, Vandenberg, Clark, Norris, Taft, Lundeen and Nye
August 18, 1940

Gentlemen:
If there is anything in your veins except water you would do well to banish excuses and red tape and extend help to England in this crisis. Hitler, by his written word in *Mein Kampf* and by invading America with "Fifth Columnists" and spies, has long ago declared war on the United States. Hamstrung by such men as you, Lindberg, Ford, Father Coughlin, and religious fanatics, the United States is playing the part of a vicious slacker in this world drama. With all of our luxury, and with all of the gold of the world in our vaults we quarrel and quibble over turning fifty antiquated destroyers to our neighbor in her hour of need. In your utter ignorance and stubbornness you refuse yet to see and admit that England, led by the great patriot Churchill, is fighting our war. If we continue to cringe and cower and let England go down, this nation must fall likewise. We do not deserve to continue to exist. Would to God that you and all your kind could be compelled to crawl on your hands and knees over the dead bodies of the women and children of Europe during the coming winter. Out of that might possibly come an awakening. . . .

Yours truly,
F. F., Klamath Falls, OR[30]

This letter suggested a private venture to overcome the legal and political hurdles involved:

Secretary of the Navy
August 22, 1940

Dear Sir:
I am handing you a souvenir—one of over eighteen hundred (1,800) bonds of the German nation, which were defaulted by the nation on both interest and

principal. The value of these bonds is somewhat over 180,000 marks. I am desirous of collecting the bonds, or of enforcing payment. So much in explanation of the purpose of this letter to you, and my proposition, following: Pending collection or settlement of the bonds, I propose to deposit all of them into your hands to hold as security for final payment of the price as may be agreed upon for the purchase by myself of as many as one hundred (100) of the U.S. Navy destroyers, or more, same to be delivered to me or my designated agents as soon as arrangements can be completed. In event of your acceptance of [this] offer and security, I propose to lease all of the destroyers sold to me to the British government, for its services to me in collecting all of my bonds of the German government now past due, the payment of which the German government refused to make, and continues to refuse. The consideration to be paid by me for the one hundred destroyers and the condition of delivery can be worked out in a conference, after you have considered the matter and have advised me of your favorable conclusions on my offer herein. I shall be glad to hear from you in this matter. Very respectfully,

S. H., Richmond, VA[31]

Opponents complained about the deal's effects on American neutrality, as well as on the incongruity of giving away warships when the country was engaged in its own naval buildup:

[Navy Department]
[ca. September 1940]

I see where we are going to lease or loan war equipment to Great Britain. What if Germany wins this war. Certainly they are not losing at the present time. If they win, possibly they will not care to go to war with us, but suppose they lease or loan their navy to Japan? We certainly would have no kick whatsoever, because we are the ones that are originating this scheme. Are we prepared to fight Japan and Germany alone? Give away another 50 war ships and where will we be? You fellows know what is going on on the other side, but to just an ordinary heel on the outside it looks to me like Roosevelt's outstanding boner of his career, and there certainly are many boners. We on the outside know that the U.S. is committing a war act against a neutral country, no matter how it is covered up and tried to be covered.[32]

Unsigned

By sending ships and supplies to England, Roosevelt stretched the limits of neutrality as far as he dared. After winning a third term in November 1940, however, he was willing to take greater risks. Roosevelt faced increasing pressure to let the U.S. Navy escort convoys to Britain. As the *New York Times* put it, "In Britain the major problem is one of supply. If she cannot maintain a bridge of ships across the Atlantic, she dies."[33] This writer argued that only the U.S. Navy could ensure that aid reached Britain:

> To the Editor of the *New York Times:*
> . . . This great navy is lying practically dormant in face of the greatest need and opportunity in its history. Here are the alternatives—and our choice may determine whether our children, their children, and possibly generations to come, will bless or despise us: 1. Prompt and complete cooperation of our naval power, supported to the utmost by our industrial resources, to insure that Britain and China shall defeat aggression at its sources—and thus perpetuate our "American way of life" free of all acts and all threats of aggression, or, 2. Suffer the defeat of Britain and China and assimilation by victors of their resources, while we endeavor, so far as time permits, to convert our country into a garrisoned fortress, somewhat like England today, but with little offensive power and infinitely greater coast lines and areas for perpetual isolated defense—at best, an intolerable existence destructive of all that makes our lives worth living. . . .
>
> A. G., New York[34]

Escorting British convoys with U.S. warships would almost inevitably lead to war with Germany, so Roosevelt sought less provocative alternatives.[35] The *New Republic* suggested one option:

> Are German ships operating inside the "neutrality zone"? If so, we ought to know about it. Indeed, there would be no harm in finding out where the Nazis are and what they are doing as far out to sea as we can efficiently use our available forces in locating them. There could be no valid objection if information so obtained were relayed to such ships as might be in danger. Indeed, even the most squeamish would hardly protest if an American warship which sighted a German raider or submarine were to flash the news to the wide air, for whomever it might concern. Such a drag-hunt would be good practice, in addition.[36]

The president ordered expanded Atlantic "neutrality" patrols, but these had little effect on U-boat operations.[37] The *Washington Post* explained, "[N]o one should be deceived into thinking the patrol system anything but a makeshift compromise in defense of which competent naval authorities can offer only a feeble, conventional murmur of hope. The theory of the patrol system is that American ships and planes will spot German planes and submarines for the British, warning convoys away and summoning the British navy and air force. This is merely an extension out into the Atlantic of the old neutrality patrol in hemisphere waters."[38] These two writers proposed actions that would not technically involve escorting convoys:

Hon. Frank Knox [Secretary of the Navy]
November 27, 1940

Dear Sir:
Would the consent of Congress, or anybody else, be needed to have a few good swift American cruisers make a "good will" trip to points in the Indian Ocean or thereabouts and if they "happened" to see a German raider chasing a freighter kind of get in the way, or just hang around to see the fun anyway? According to the press an English freighter was sunk there a few days ago. It might do the navy boys good to cruise around in that part of the world and get acquainted. Also that neutrality patrol—if some destroyers were watching the 300 mile, or whatever the limit is, would it not be a good time to survey it about the same time a convoy leaves a Canadian port. The fact that Britain only had one armed merchantman (the "Jarvis Bay") with a 38 ship convoy does not look good to me. We are in the war anyway and the quicker we do something the better for us.

Respectfully,
V. B., Chicago, IL[39]

Commander-in-Chief, United States Navy
November 11, 1940

Sir:
No one has yet determined the comparative efficiency of a dozen different fluid fuels for U.S. naval units of various types on a great-circle cruise New York to Ireland. If Spain and Russia can help the Axis without any involvement (not to mention Japan blasting one of our warships), why can't we be a little impudent, too? These test cruises would call for squadrons of perhaps twelve warships—cruisers, submarines, whatever suited the test needs. If food ships from Canada happened to sail just as our squadron was off St. Johns and chose to take position between our two lines of test-ships, if they could keep up to whatever speed we kept down to, what affair would it be of ours? We needn't speak to them. Incidental target

practice along the route at irregular intervals would make this testing route of ours unhealthy for submarines or pocket battleships of any nation, and these could be discerned with the assistance of the aircraft carriers which would need the fuel test just as much as the other units. Why not?

Respectfully,
R. L., Nutley, NJ[40]

American aircraft were a key element of aid to Britain. Larger models flew directly overseas, but smaller types had to travel by ship. This writer suggested a way to deliver planes while avoiding U-boats:

The President
March 14, 1941

Sir:
I think that the following suggestion is well in line with American sentiment as expressed in the passage of the Lease-Lend Bill. Today's papers carry a story about the Navy's new Curtiss dive bombers which have a range of 1,200 miles. As we will undoubtedly send a large quantity of these to the British we should give some thought to a method which would insure prompt and safe delivery. I believe that we should station one of our large aircraft carriers about 1,000 miles out in the Atlantic. The planes could be ferried by civilian pilots who would refuel on our carrier and make delivery to the British at one of their aircraft carriers which would be stationed still another 1,000 miles nearer England. Once aboard the English carrier the planes could be refueled, the bomb racks loaded and British pilots could take over for the last lap. In this connection, the route of the final lap could be so laid out that the British would have a one-way patrol of the area that is now considered the most dangerous for their convoys. These planes would probably be more than a match for the German planes that are now attacking convoys.

Respectfully,
E. R., New York, NY[41]

After Germany overran Denmark, the *Christian Science Monitor* warned that Axis forces might seize the Danish possession of Greenland: "Greenland, so far from being a barrier, is now a gateway to the Americas; any air-base established there would be within striking distance—for purposes of war or peace—of Canada and the United States."[42] American forces occupied Greenland first, but foul weather made the island unsuitable for naval and air operations.[43] This writer proposed solving this problem:

President of the U.S.A.
April 28, 1941

Dear Mr. President:
The writer, taking in consideration that the consensus of opinion seems to be
that Greenland is not suitable for a year-round base, respectfully suggests that a
dam be built off Cape Hatteras, so as to divert the Gulf Stream from her present
[northeasterly] direction to a more northerly direction, thereby forcing the Stream
to flow closer to Greenland. This would change the climate of the southern part
of Greenland and hence a year-around base would be feasible. The building of
such a dam off Hatteras could be done in very little time and the cost would not
be prohibitive. The writer appreciates that the diversion of the Gulf Stream would
materially affect the climate in such places as Wales, Ireland, and Scotland, etc., but
that would only be for the duration of the present war, after which said dam could
easily be blasted away with dynamite.

Respectfully submitted,
T. H., New York, NY[44]

After American troops relieved the British garrison in Iceland, Roosevelt authorized
U.S. warships to escort vessels to and from that island.[45] This brought America to
the brink of war in the Atlantic, but Hitler, focused on the Russian campaign,
ordered his U-boats not to attack U.S. Navy ships. Roosevelt's carefully calibrated
escalation of American involvement successfully avoided war for the time being,
but less than three months later the attack on Pearl Harbor made such nuances
irrelevant.

As European colonial powers crumbled before the Blitz, Japanese leaders
saw unprecedented opportunities for expansion. The oil-rich Dutch East Indies,
French Indochina, and British-controlled Malaya and Burma all seemed ripe for
conquest. Japan signed a mutual defense treaty with Germany and Italy, then pressured Vichy France into allowing Japanese troops to occupy parts of Indochina.
Roosevelt moved the Pacific fleet from the West Coast to Pearl Harbor to deter
Japan, setting the stage for the "day of infamy."[46] The *New York Times* concluded
that Japan dared not attack America:

The recent treaty between Germany, Italy and Japan is the greatest international
bluff of all time. All three agree to go to war against us if we "attack" any one of
them. The treaty was designed to influence our relations with Japan. It is a bluff
because there is not one single thing the Germans or Italians can do to perform
their promise of assistance. The thought was that we could be scared out of taking
the steps with reference to Japan which our national interests demand that we

take. We should recognize the silly bluff for what it is and ignore it. Looking at it dispassionately, we can come to one conclusion: The bluff is a confession of fear and weakness, an admission of helpless vulnerability to the things we can do.[47]

Some Americans, like this writer, favored confronting Japan immediately while Hitler was still preoccupied with Britain:

Secretary of the Navy
October 5, 1940

Dear Sir:
Among approved age-old axioms is one appropriate to present war-threatening conditions: "Thrice-armed is he whose cause is just," and this was amended by that noted humorist-philosopher Josh Billings to read: "and FOUR times, he who gets his lick in fust." . . . It was hinted, in that secret way in which our newspapers keep all military secrets, that Admiral Richardson told the President that his fleet could have destroyed the Japan outfit within two hours, with his own fleet left in shape to bombard Japanese ports out of existence and isolate the Jap army in China to be eaten up by the Chinese. Assuming this situation correctly reported, let's do that very thing! Send our fleet to Singapore, if necessary to first establish a base, or preferably, seek out the Jap fleet (without any form of notice) attack and destroy it completely; then bombard all ports that guns can reach and teach Japan a lesson that will always be remembered—China taking care of the land forces in Asia. Even if we lose a large proportion of our fleet (unlikely), we will still be stronger than with Japan's in existence and ours unscarred. Our fleet can return to the Atlantic and not worry about the west coast. . . . Of course this step would have to be taken without a band or parade; but the result would please all America, and solidify democracy better than anything else. Please try it.

Sincerely yours,
D. O., Childersburg, AL[48]

Others warned that war with Japan would only interfere with U.S. aid to Britain, who faced the most dangerous Axis power. The *New Republic* explained it like this:

[If] Japan took up the challenge and America, in the decisive naval engagement, destroyed the Japanese fleet, it would not serve to keep Japan out of the Netherlands Indies and Singapore unless Great Britain won in Europe. If Germany won, America would of course have to recall its fleet to the Atlantic. If America were to lose the decisive naval engagement—and it must be remembered that the American fleet would go into action against the handicap of fighting thousands of miles from its base—then quite literally the American continent would be at the mercy of any powerful opponent on either ocean. And if Germany should win in Europe, the most melodramatic imaginings of those who now seem hysterical might become real.[49]

This writer agreed:

Secretary of the Navy
October 5th, 1940

Headlines in papers—"U.S. set to fight Japan—Knox," "Conflict near, warns Knox." Do you mean we are going to swallow Hitler's bait, planned at Brenner Pass to have Japan exasperate the U.S. to weaken our aid to England. Has Hitler gotten us "buffaloed." Better broadcast some more embargoes to counteract effect of headlines.

R. S., Oakland, CA[50]

Amateur strategists expected that war with Japan would quickly culminate in a decisive sea battle for control of the Pacific. Military planners realized, however, that a war would involve seizing bases and whittling down the enemy. They estimated that the U.S. Navy would need years to defeat Japan.[51] The United States would enjoy a crucial advantage in any long war due to Japan's near-total dependence on imported oil. The *Christian Science Monitor* claimed this dependence made war more likely: "Approximately two thirds of Japan's oil requirements are supplied by the United States, and the remainder comes from the Netherlands East Indies. An embargo on oil from the United States would have the immediate effect of increasing Japan's demands on the Dutch oil fields, which now divert to Japan only an estimated 10 percent of their output. Any reluctance on the part of the Dutch authorities in complying with such demands invites invasion, because Japan must have oil."[52] This writer advocated preempting Japanese access to East Indies oil:

Hon. Gifford Pinchot
December 21, 1940

Dear Gifford:
In accordance with your request I attach herewith a plan that I believe is practical and necessary for the safe entry of the United States in the war on the side of Great Britain. . . . In order to free our fleet for the Atlantic the danger from Japan's naval power must be eliminated. This can be done in only two ways—one is war

with Japan in the Orient, the outcome of which is doubtful. . . . The second, and cheaper, quicker and surer means of accomplishing this end would be the immediate destruction of the oil wells in the East Indies. . . . [I]f Japan were cut off from ten out of every eleven barrels of oil of her minimum economic and naval requirements, her internal economy would be utterly disrupted and her fleet immobilized. Presently, it would be hopeless to defend the East Indies against a determined attack by Japan, and as these islands produce 182,000 barrels daily of good oil, and have a refining capacity of 180,000 barrels, their conquest by Japan would leave her permanently predominant in Eastern Asia. . . . It must be a "fait accompli" from which action we cannot retract, with no oil physically available to the Japanese except from California or through the Panama Canal. They must know that their fleet is immobilized, as would be their merchant marine, and therefore their internal economy ruined and their war machine out of action. Japan could not carry on a campaign of over three months duration and have fuel to get her fleet home. . . .

Sincerely yours,
J. L., Tulsa, OK[53]

While U.S. leaders tried to keep the Axis at bay through deterrence and foreign aid, America began mobilizing for war. This head start proved invaluable, but many opposed the loss of personal freedoms that accompanied mobilization. A proposed government-mandated exercise program struck one writer as too similar to the group calisthenics portrayed in Nazi newsreels:

Hon. Frank Knox, Secretary of War [Navy]
October 4, 1940

Dear Mr. Knox:
It is very discouraging to one who, in spite of a Mid-western Republican background and active Republican sympathies, nevertheless wrote his Congressman in support to the compulsory military training program, and hoped for all possible material aid to the cause of Britain, to hear of the proposal made under your apparent blessing, to conscript the national physique through some inane form of mass, compulsory calisthenics. Please bear in mind before you lend material aid to the cause of totalitarian exercise that while the people of the United States have a right to expect that such of their number as are necessary and available should have experience and knowledge concerning the business of defending our liberties, they do not have a right that every citizen not engaged in receiving that experience

and knowledge should be able to jump through a flaming hoop over a barrier of up-ended swords in the manner of all fascists. If, when the citizen is not engaged in actual military training his muscles are not as taut as bow-strings, his back sags and his belly protrudes, and he smokes too many cigarettes it is strictly his business and not that of the people of the United States as represented by their duly elected or appointed and unduly frightened officials, at least not to the extent of compelling him to jump about in his undershirt in depressing imitation of Nazi exhibitionism. Next we will be told to go out and have some illegitimate children by the biggest woman we can find. . . . [I]f that physical education program goes through on a compulsory basis my present reaction is to go to jail rather than leap-frog my way with the rest to dictatorship, for that circumstance would stand as a milestone toward the end of my opportunity to live and attain within the limits of my capabilities.

Sincerely,

E. S., Champaign, IL[54]

As in 1917 America's isolation delayed but could not prevent her entry into a struggle for world dominion. Although some complained that the United States had played only a minor role in the first two years of war, the time had not been wholly misspent. Economically, militarily, and perhaps most important psycho-logically, the nation was far more prepared for war in 1941 than it ever could have been in 1939. Fortunately, America's key allies had survived the enemy's initial assaults, and stood ready for U.S. power to tip the scales decisively against the Axis.

Dangerous Minds: Fear and Fanaticism in Total War

W orld War II's unprecedented scope, and the novel technologies and practices it unleashed, gave Americans an opportunity to ponder a dizzying array of war-related problems. In this emergency, national leaders could not afford to overlook any source of potential ideas. More than ever before, officials sought citizens' help in solving military problems. In 1940 the government created the National Inventors Council to screen inventive military ideas. *Reader's Digest* reported that by early 1942 citizens had sent in "45,000 separate inventions and ideas. All have been examined with respectful attention; hundreds are being tested; scores have actually been put to work. . . . In this basket there may be an idea that will win the war."[1] Such publicity encouraged others. By mid-1944 the Council had screened nearly two hundred thousand submissions.[2]

In the dark days following Pearl Harbor, defeatist "loose talk" threatened civilian morale. *Reader's Digest* claimed, "The most heroic act of patriotism that some of us can perform, in a time like this, is to shut up. If I can't do anything else for my country, I can refuse to act as a delivery boy for rumors."[3] The government urged citizens not to spread rumors, and several cities set up "rumor clinics" where individuals could report stories they had heard and obtain an official refutation or correction.[4] This writer proffered an ambitious antirumor system:

J. Edgar Hoover
February 10, 1942

Dear Sir:
At the risk of wasting your time, I offer for what it is worth, the following idea for
1) stopping the spread of rumors and 2) tracking down those responsible therefore.
It works somewhat as follows: Z, the father of a rumor, tells it to A. A phones
x-1000 and answers the following questions: a. My name is A (Optional to answer

this question), b. My address is (" "), c. I heard one rumor, to wit; d. I heard it from (Z or his description), e. at 1) place 2) time, f. How many others 1) present and 2) heard same, g. Identity of others. . . . A publicity campaign could then be designed to include civilian population in "intelligence services" by making it individual duty to report all rumors and to keep silent thereafter for 48 hours. Duty is self policed because it is also duty of those who hear it to ask "Have you reported it?". . .

Sincerely Yours,
D. G., Butler, PA[5]

Idle talk could do more than depress morale. A government campaign symbolized by the alliterative slogan "loose lips sink ships" warned against inadvertently revealing military secrets. The *Christian Science Monitor* suggested a possible ban on one substance known to enhance loquaciousness: "Lips loosened by drink were seen here today as a dangerous channel for leakages of military and production information currently plaguing officials. Seriousness of the situation is partly reflected by the efforts now being made by liquor interests themselves to caution drinkers against lowering censorship on their talk while in the verbose atmosphere of a tavern, tap, or cocktail lounge. The situation, highlighted by several unfortunate incidents of recent date, may focus—from an altogether different angle— public demand for wartime prohibition."[6]

This writer submitted a scheme for securing American communications:

Secretary of the Navy
February 19, 1942

Dear Mr. Knox:
I have been thinking about our American Indian here in the state. I doubt if there is a Jap or German that can interpret their language and I was just wondering if it would not be a good idea to recruit a lot of these educated Indians and use them in short wave broadcasting. In so doing it would appear that a lot of information could be handled by radio that you would not want to risk in other languages.

Yours truly,
W. W., Weatherford, OK[7]

Pearl Harbor came as a terrifying shock to most Americans. For the first time in memory the country and its allies were clearly on the defensive. That disaster, followed closely by defeats in the Pacific, raised fears that Axis forces might reach

America's shores. Coastal cities seemed especially vulnerable, and Americans looked skyward with trepidation. These two writers proposed defenses against nocturnal Japanese bombing raids:

Commanding Officer, Second Interceptor Command
December 30, 1941

Sir:
. . . The "blackout" experiences as we have seen them displayed in the city of Seattle have been quite creditable, as evidencing the willingness of the community to cooperate in the efforts of the military authorities to preserve their safety. It so happens that Mrs. A. and myself live on the top of a high building from which we are able to see the entire circuit of the city over an arc of about three hundred degrees. On these successive blackouts we have watched with interest the elimination of the lights and have been able to note from our point of view many windows where lights are not properly blacked out, and in several instances where lights were either innocently or deliberately displayed. It is quite reasonable to suppose that in the event of an actual invasion of our locality from the air, "fifth columnists" active here would attempt to assist the enemy fliers by light signals or other displays of the kind. It has occurred to the writer that if panorama photographs would be taken from the top of the Smith Tower, the Northern Life Tower, and from other points of vantage after the blackout is supposed to be complete, there would be disclosed from these photographs as taken indisputable evidence of violation of the military requirements. It might be said in that connection that photographs taken from two angles, if the cameras were set with the accuracy of surveying instruments, would disclose the exact house and even the exact floor and window from which and out of which a light was displayed. . . .

C. A., Seattle, WA[8]

Commander Western Interceptor Command
December 9, 1941

Dear Sir:
Since yesterday evening all radio broadcasting stations along the California coast have been shut down, for the reason that they might serve as direction-finding beacons for Japanese raiding planes. In this connection, may I suggest the following idea (military ruse) which may possibly be of some value in the present situation.

The idea is, in brief, to install temporary radio-broadcasting transmitters (using portable signal corps sets of the U.S. Army) well back from the coastline in the inland desert and mountain areas. These hidden and secret radio transmitters would carry the regular broadcasting programs, network features, and so on, and would use the call letters of the appropriate stations on the coast (such as KNX Los Angeles), the real transmitters in the coastal cities remaining silent as at present. It is believed that this stratagem, if carried out with due secrecy and efficiency, would not only protect our coastal cities from air raids as well as the present total silence, scheme, but might decoy Japanese raiding planes far inland where they could be definitely located and destroyed by our interceptor-fighters. Respectfully,

W. W., Santa Barbara, CA[9]

To confuse bombers, officials camouflaged America's vital aircraft factories. Workers painted roads and houses on their roofs and erected "Potemkin villages," complete with fake shrubbery. There remained a glaring weakness in the factory camouflage program, however:

National Inventors Council
January 11, 1943

Gentlemen:
In the March 1942 issue of the *Reader's Digest*, I came across an article entitled "Second Call for Inventions" by Stuart Chase. I have had the opportunity of visiting several large scale war plants most of which have been ingeniously camouflaged against air reconnaissance or air attacks. And yet all this care and camouflaging is rendered null and void because the war plants are surrounded with thousands of automobiles which gleam and glitter in the sunlight and in the moonlight. They act as a signpost, or guide and even though the war plant is completely hidden, the air raider can put two and two together. If they are told that their objective is in this vicinity, though they do not see it, they do see a concentration of automobiles. The war plant must be near them. By bombing within that area, they are sure to hit their target. If the war plants are so effectively camouflaged, surely the automobiles that are parked about them should be so. I have invented an inexpensive automobile surface coat which can be easily applied. Though it is waterproof, it can be readily removed. Leaving the original finish unharmed. However, when applied, it leaves the car surface dull and drab colored, and in perfect harmony with camouflaged surroundings. I believe as a precautionary measure, this surface coat should be applied to all cars which spend time in parking places adjacent to war plants. . . .

Yours truly,
D. L., Stony Brook, NY[10]

This writer submitted a drastic scheme for neutralizing incendiary bombs:

January 3, 1942

Sir:

The utter stupidity of using anti-aircraft artillery as employed to date for the defense of cities is clear. London painted the sky with shell bursts at night, while the enemy painted London with blood. . . . Some time ago, a naive communique from London mentioned with childish glee that "the Nazis have stopped using high explosives over London since this puts out the fires caused by their incendiaries." The astounding thing about this is that neither the British nor the Nazis took the cue from this to quickly bring under control serious fires in their own cities. I suppose this is because it is difficult to get the old brain working on anything radically new. A section of our bombardment group could save us millions of dollars in property damage and countless lives by bombing the centers of severe fires, bringing them under almost instant control. . . .

Respectfully,
J. B., New York, NY[11]

Allied successes in 1942 ended any threat of invasion, but the *Saturday Evening Post* warned against complacency: "American strategists know that Allied naval power precludes the occupation of any part of the North American continent. They know that Germany has neither the transport tonnage nor the war vessels with which to protect an armada of the magnitude needed for such an operation. But this would not rule out sacrifice invasion raids designed to disrupt vital areas along the coast, and calculated to create an irresistible demand in the United States for defense rather than for the attacks that alone will win the war."[12]

This writer proposed a system to detect seaborne raiders:

Commandant, United States Coast Guard
July 28, 1942

Dear Sir:

. . . In connection with attempted landings on our shores by saboteurs, spies, etc., an idea occurred to me, which, I believe, might be of interest to the Navy, F.B.I. and particularly the Coast Guard. I am assuming that the most appropriate time for such landings is at night, or during hazy and foggy weather. On isolated stretches of our shores where such attempts to land might be made, it seems to me that a system of short posts (probably iron pipe), equipped with photo-electric cells, set back far enough on the beach or shore to be above the point of highest tide, and spaced 200 feet apart, more or less, as the circumstances will permit, would prove to be an effective alarm system. These posts might be made to appear as possible anchorage for barbed wire entanglements to be installed later, or any other appropriate disguise. Each post, after allowing sufficient length for setting in the sand or ground, should have two small openings or eyes to project infra-red ray beams to the adjacent posts containing photo-electric cells. One hole or eye could be located a foot or so above the beach level and the other, two-and-a-half or three feet above the beach level. In such a set-up, dogs, other small animals and birds would not break both beams simultaneously. Any alarm so received, via buried cable to the Coast Guard Station covering that sector, might be discounted. If, however, both beams for a given sector registered a "blackout," the central station could immediately check that sector. . . .

Respectfully yours,
L. C., Elizabeth, NY[13]

These two letters described possible volunteers for ad hoc shore patrols:

War Department
May 30, 1942

With the continued curtailment of civilian transportation, practically the only vehicles which will be left on our highways soon will be the common carrier truck and bus, neither of which has as yet been materially restricted in its operations. This situation will mean that there will be many thousands of miles of American highway which will be deserted after dark, except for the above-mentioned vehicles. As there is some possibility of commando type raids on our shores in the future, any extra watchfulness on the part of our civilians may be of great value. It is my thought that the truck and bus drivers who are regularly operating on the highways paralleling our coastal areas should be organized into a special counter-espionage group. For the purpose of systematically observing and reporting any suspicious activities on highways near our coast lines. If the drivers of the trucks and busses were properly organized, they would know what to report and would know where to report. As it is now, if the driver of a truck sees something unusual, he would probably hesitate to report it for fear of exposing himself to possible ridicule. Or he might not know exactly where to make a report. Under the arrangement I contemplate, a selected group of drivers would be so organized that any information they pick up would be instantly transmitted to the proper authorities. . . .

J. S., Kansas City, KS[14]

Federal Bureau of Investigation
August 4, 1942

Gentlemen:

... I neglected to state to you in my former letter my suggestion that it might be advisable for the government to require the registration of amateur astronomical telescopes. . . . The advantage of such instruments for coastal patrol would likewise seem apparent. There is a great army of these instruments to be found in the hands of amateur astronomers over the United States and, I think, in Canada too. . . . For some time I have considered the matter of taking my instrument up the coast, at least on Sundays, and placing it along some barren portion of coastline and searching for submarines, the landing of enemy agents etc. on a voluntary basis but this hardly seemed the thing to do until owners so using their instruments could be assured of some kind of identification or license that would insure that their motives were entirely patriotic if they ran across the paths of our own coast guardsmen. . . .

Yours very truly,
G. L., Los Angeles, CA[15]

This writer warned of an unconventional Japanese threat to the West Coast:

Federal Bureau of Investigation
July 18, 1942

Dear Mr. Hoover:

... Can't you see how an Oriental imagination could play with the idea of one day tossing a lot of high explosive into the Japanese Stream as a war measure against Canada and the U.S.A.? Just as we on the west coast would undoubtedly select a point off the Aleutian Islands to divert the warm stream by the aforesaid means. Anyone in Pacific Grove, California, or in other West Coast towns will tell you how occasionally large glass globes used to wash in to the beaches. I was bathing with my family one Sunday at Pacific Grove, when the first of these that I ever saw came in. I was told that the Japs used them as floats for their nets in lieu of cork. . . . Think of what would happen to the Bremerton yards, to Boeing Aircraft Works, to any vital project on the West Coast, if sub-Arctic weather were to be loosed upon them. Glance at your map, and you will see that Seattle is on the same latitude parallel as the mouth of the Saint Lawrence River on the East Coast. Now, even the Saint Lawrence's severe winter is softened considerably by the influence of the not-distant Gulf Stream. Try to imagine Seattle's winter, were the full influence of the Japanese Stream diverted from the West Coast waters! Hence, if your agents ever report to you that unexplained explosions are taking place in the vicinity of the Aleutians, the fat will have already been in the fire. In fact, I'll dread the above danger far more than I will the possibility of the Japs building up a good air base for intercepting our future aircraft-transfer to Siberia. One thing you may rest assured of, and that is those glass globes of the Japs have timed the flow of the Japanese Current to a second. With all good wishes to you in your great work, I am,

Sincerely Yours,
E. C., Mobile, AL[16]

J. Edgar Hoover's "G-men" played a well-publicized role in the campaign against spies and fifth columnists. These two letters include proposals to help secure the home front:

Federal Bureau of Investigation
March 13, 1942

Dear Sirs:
Further to my suggestions which I believe from our last letter is on file at your office. There is a considerable number of photo finishers throughout the U.S.A. that have snapshots pass through their hands without giving them a second look as to valuable information for an enemy. I myself in this business have taken it upon myself to destroy any part or all of any snapshot film that I consider would be of information to an enemy. Might I suggest that a letter of instructions to this effect be sent to every photo finisher in the country with specific instructions to report any such work revealing positive definition of naval or military, or war manufacturing information, to their local office immediately before the customer claims the work so that the person may be questioned when they come to receive their work. Also that the photo finisher have a specific identification mark on each print so that it can be traced for neglect of such orders from headquarters.

Yours very respectfully,
R.W., Miami, FL[17]

War Department
March 9, 1942

Dear Sir:
. . . It is stated that on a flight from New York to Washington on January 12, 1942, oil storage tanks were clearly visible from the plane which departed from New York at 7:30 A.M. On the return flight leaving Washington at 11:00 P.M., that night the informant said that the location of at least three anti-aircraft batteries was clearly

definable in Maryland, Pennsylvania and New Jersey, when the search lights picked up and followed the plane. . . . [V]ital definite information can be easily obtained by unauthorized persons riding the airlines and observing. He states the opinion that it would be easy for an enemy agent to take pictures unobserved by passengers on the plane or stewardess particularly if such person occupied the rear seat. The informant has suggested that in his opinion an effective, quick and cheap remedy is the frosting of the outside of the two window panes by means of a spray. He feels that the airlines would not be subjected to passengers objecting to blacked out windows. The informant further states that the frosting could be quickly removed with some chemical in the event non-commercial use of the planes was desired.

Very truly yours,
J. Edgar Hoover
Washington, DC[18]

While the feared attacks on America never materialized, U-boats operating off the Atlantic Coast threatened to disrupt the entire war effort. A handful of submarines created havoc in sight of public beaches and busy harbors, sinking scores of ships in 1942. Rumors soon spread that the enemy had secret bases on this side of the Atlantic. *Newsweek* reported, "No official will confirm them, but stories continually crop up that American wrapped breads, U.S. theater-ticket stubs, and similar evidence that crews have been ashore have been found aboard Axis subs captured off the coast."[19] *The Nation* theorized that "[t]here are quite possibly secret bases maintained by Axis sympathizers in Gulf or Caribbean waters and these are doubly important in that they may both furnish a resting place for submarine crews and give information of ship sailings."[20] If the rumors were true, victory might depend on finding clandestine U-boat bases:

U.S. Navy Intelligence Department
January 31, 1942

Please pardon this second letter. If you do not know just how these German subs operating off our coast get their gas, I suggest you require all persons having floating markers over one mile from the mainland remove them at once. They could be taken in by the owners in roughly four hours. I know fishermen along the island off the Maine coast set their lobster traps in water a hundred and fifty feet deep and their buoys might locate oil tanks as well as lobster pots or other fishing gear. It is obvious these subs do not go to Germany for their gas, and may get it any place from East Port to Key West. Wanting to help, I am

A. A., Warrenville, IL[21]

Naval Intelligence
February 26, 1942

Gentlemen:
It may be obvious—but if overlooked, it might be serious: Any small private
motor "fishing" boat any where on our vast coast line might easily bootleg fuel
oil to enemy submarines simply by attaching a fuel oil tank to the keel of the
small "fishing" craft and meet Axis subs anywhere offshore. Inspection of motor
boats could easily be made by passing under the keel, from bow to stern, a slender
blade-like rod removably attached [sic] to U.S. naval craft. This might answer the
question: How do Axis submarines keep in service on our side of the Atlantic and/
or Pacific?

Respectfully,
D. S., York, PA[22]

If U-boats refueled offshore, perhaps their methods could be used against them
through subterfuges like these:

Inventors Council
March 11, 1942

Dear Sirs:
The following idea is offered for combating Nazi submarines along the seaboard.
It has been reported in the papers that a submarine hijacked a fishing boat for its
fuel oil. It may, therefore, be worth while for the Navy to provide reliable, selected
fishing boats with a supply of appropriately prepared oil which could damage the
enemy power plant when used. It should be possible to add to the oil a soluble
explosive (possibly nitroglycerine) or a substance that would corrode the engines.
Offhand I should guess that the introduction of a soluble explosive would provide
the most effective action.

Sincerely yours,
B. C., Johns Hopkins School of Medicine, Baltimore, MD[23]

National Inventors Council
January 22, 1943

Dear Sirs:
Pictures of American soldiers pulling oil barrels ashore in the Pacific islands, and a news item stating that Japanese ships had dumped supplies near some of the Pacific islands in the hope that the surf would wash them ashore to supply Japanese soldiers on land; these suggest to me that we could make mines that float, yet resemble oil barrels in every particular almost. The case would be identical, and the lettering too, except for one little key letter or mark that the Navy insiders would be tipped off to, so that our men will not be injured by them. These could be dumped overboard perhaps amidst the floating wreckage near where submarines operate, and would likely be picked up by enemy submarines. These floating mines, inside of alleged oil barrels, when opened or lifted or set up on end would explode. If one of these was brought to the side of the submarine and was lifted up, it would blow up the submarine before they would have a chance to use the radio to explain their fate to headquarters.

Sincerely yours,
C. R., Schenectady, NY[24]

U-boats seemed to know just where to find vulnerable merchantmen. Possibly enemy agents had tipped off submarines about shipping schedules:

Bureau of Naval Intelligence
[ca. May 1942]

Gentlemen:
Experts may overlook a seemingly unimportant matter, an electric razor is a miniature broadcasting station. An enemy agent aboard a merchant ship could easily and innocently appearing, communicate with a sub lying on the surface with prearranged signals by switching on and off his razor and escape detection in the harmless act of shaving. Such a person might use a coil of some sort to boost the wavelength. This is in all probability old stuff to you and still it may have been overlooked.

Very truly yours,
B. V., Minneapolis, MN[25]

Naval Intelligence
[ca. March 1942]

Dear Sirs:
I am just an American citizen with a little imagination. Please watch carrier pigeons,
it is possible they give information to enemy subs.

J. F., New York, NY[26]

This writer described a possible communication scheme used by seagoing
U-boats:

Chief of Naval Intelligence
[ca. January 1942]

Dear Sir:
So obvious are, and have been, the German gun shelling of the Dover (English
Channel) coast, it appears to me (pardon the phrase) as dumb as the past British
military and naval leaders have proven themselves to be, they would understand the
signaling significance of that repeated shelling. Can the repeated shelling be other
than a series of signals to the hidden submarine commanders; i.e. "Converge upon
such and such longitude and meridian—ships leaving the U.S.—ships leaving
Mediterranean bound for—ships leaving English ports, etc." German strategists
know that following every shelling of the Dover coast the report of such shelling,
via radio, etc. will be known to the world shortly after. Submarine officers listening
in at sea and hidden ports hear the same news. Immediately they start to stalk their
prey. German strategists also know that while the guns are streaming shells across
the channel there will be no surface craft about and not any planes in the air. What
better opportunity for home based submarines to slip through the channel to sea? I
base this conjecture upon the following: just as soon as I hear the radio report that
Dover has been shelled, I mark the time upon my calendar. Invariably after four
days there are a series of submarine sinkings all the way from the Irish coast to the
beaches of this country, the Mediterranean and other spots, but they do not occur
until days after the shellings. . . .

Respectfully yours,
N. W., Oklahoma State Penitentiary, McAlester, OK[27]

Fuel tankers remained a favorite U-boat target. When torpedoed, their volatile
cargoes often added to the carnage. News accounts stressed the horrible fate

awaiting sailors abandoning sinking tankers. The *New York Times* described how "the tanker and the sea turned into a 'burning hell' immediately after the torpedo from the enemy submarine hit the ship. . . . Red Cross boats were rushed to the scene. They arrived quickly, but they were unable to get close because of the flames and intense heat."[28] This writer proposed a device to help tanker crewmen avoid immolation:

National Inventors Council
June 27, 1944

Gentlemen:
. . . For some time I have been thinking of an arrangement which would save lives when a ship is sinking or burning and the water around the ship is ablaze with burning oil or gasoline. My idea would be to develop a combination miniature balloon and life raft. This could be so designed that it could be inflated with helium or some other lighter than air gas from a tank aboard ship. . . . Suppose a ship is on fire or sinking and there is burning oil or gasoline on the water all around the ship. The order is given to abandon ship so each one aboard fits a life vest around himself and inflates it with gas. The amount of gas to be measured so as to be just enough to lift him skyward far enough to get away from the licking flames and smoke. The winds will carry him away from the burning oil or gasoline to a point where he feels safe in descending into the ocean which he could do by regulating a valve provided in the unit. He would only release enough gas to descend into the water and retain enough of it to keep him afloat. . . .

Yours very truly,
H. R., Kent, OH[29]

To an unprecedented degree, World War II pitted American ideas against those of the enemy. U.S. propaganda benefitted from the enemy's predilection for publicizing their racial theories and then practicing them in barbarous ways. This allowed America to portray itself as a champion of freedom, perhaps even using the promise of liberation to win over the people of one continent:

Bernard Baruch
December 29, 1941

. . . Today, the Anglo-Saxon powers are fighting for their very existence and for their future. At the moment their military strength, though growing, is still far from being superior to that of the Axis. They must, therefore, not leave one stone unturned, they must use all the means at their disposal even if they seem monstrous at first sight, or even dangerous to timid souls. One of these means is the plan proposed here: Great Britain and the US issue a Declaration of Emancipation of all colored peoples of Africa, and solemnly promise to these peoples complete sovereignty and the end of every form of colonial rule or dependence of any other sort once this war is over, providing these peoples take an active part in the destruction of the Nazi war machine. Such a Declaration of Emancipation for Africa by the Anglo Saxons would be a strategy a la Napoleon. It would be the first great spiritual counter-blow against Berlin and Tokyo's war of propaganda. The effects of such an act would be noticeable in the whole world, especially amongst the 50 million Negroes, Mulattoes and Indoes [*sic*] in Latin America. All colored nations would tie their fate to that of the Anglo Saxons and would be a tremendous help in the struggle, extremely valuable fanatical fighters. We would also be in a position to launch a terrific propaganda campaign based on the enslavement plans which the Nazis have in store for the colored nations throughout the world. . . .

T. T.[30]

In Axis-occupied countries, reading Allied leaflets or listening to broadcasts could bring brutal punishment. This writer proposed cloaking propaganda in a form that civilians under Axis rule could read safely:

National Inventors Council
March 1, 1943

Re: Counter-Propaganda
It is suggested that we get a copy of one of the official Nazi newspapers such as "Beobachter" or the "Sturmer" and thoroughly duplicate it in size, type, style and paper so as to make it impossible to tell the difference between the imitation and the real thing. Then insert such counter-propaganda as will do the most good and drop copies over German cities and villages as our planes are returning from their mission. The enslaved people of Germany are afraid to touch obvious Allied propaganda. But papers, which look like their own newspaper they will read and will pass them on to neighbors.

B. J., Fort Myers, FL[31]

Beginning in 1943 the Allies began to capture large numbers of German soldiers. This writer suggested these might be manipulated to encourage additional Axis troops to surrender:

National Inventors Council
June 15, 1943

Gentlemen:
The purpose of this idea is to demoralize and render the German soldiers easy to
capture. The procedure is to select from each group of prisoners one or two of
the most intelligent-looking and send them to a special prison camp. Here they
are to stay from one to three months, receiving excellent treatment and insidious
propaganda; after which they will be exchanged or forced to escape back into
Germany, where no doubt they will whisper to all their friends that being captured
by the Americans was a lucky break. The reason for selecting a few from each group
is to give the merits of our prison camps the widest possible publicity. The method
of handling these prisoners will require some skill. Their good treatment must be
sincere enough to keep them from realizing that they are being propagandized or
indoctrinated. . . . About the time they got to throughly liking their new prison
home and about the time their disillusionment about us and their enthusiasm for
us reached a peak they would be exchanged, or if there were no opportunity for
that, they would be forced to escape into Germany in as many ways as we could
devise. . . .

Yours very truly,
A. Y., Compton, CA[32]

One group of enemy soldiers remained immune to surrender appeals: almost all
Japanese soldiers preferred death to capture. Tales of Japanese fanaticism and mass
suicide added to the widespread belief that this enemy possessed truly alien characteristics. Japanese psychology also had a significant effect on their susceptibility
to Allied propaganda. *Science Digest* reported that they "possess something of the
nature of the bee, which, when detached from the hive, is as helpless as a piece of
flesh torn from the body of a living animal. Mediocre as individuals, they have a
capacity for collective effort which is truly remarkable. . . . [T]his group conscious-
ness has meant that the Japanese are ideal totalitarian citizens."[33]

Social scientists tried to explain Japanese behavior, attributing their rituals,
religion, and aggressive foreign policy to such diverse factors as overly strict toilet
training, a massive inferiority complex, or arrested emotional development.[34] Such
conclusions reinforced perceptions that Japanese motives might elude comprehen-
sion by Western minds, creating both problems and possibilities for psychological
warfare. *The Nation* published the following opinion:

From the point of view of our experts on psychological warfare General Hideki Tojo's empire is by far the hardest nut to crack of all the Axis countries. The Japanese people are almost completely isolated from the outside world, both physically and psychologically. . . . Appeals to a pro-democratic minority in Japan will be useless for some time to come because no real tradition of democracy as we know it exists in Japan. Propaganda emphasizing the hardships of war will be equally ineffective, for the Japanese are used to hardships and find them challenging rather than discouraging. On the other hand, Japan's superstitions and its characteristic fear of ridicule may be used to good advantage if our propagandists understand the Japanese mind well enough.[35]

Perhaps Japanese superstitions could be used against them. The *New York Times* described one such superstition: "The belt of a thousand stitches found on a Japanese pilot shot down during the Dec. 7 attack on Pearl Harbor was a sennin-bari, and a similar belt is worn by most Japanese soldiers. It is in the nature of a charm which it is believed will protect the wearer from bullets or other danger. . . . It is just another of the many superstitions that play so large a part in the daily life of the Japanese masses."[36] This letter proposed using captured belts to undermine enemy morale:

Chairman, Associated Defense Committee [of Chicago]
July 7, 1943

Dear Sir:
The Japanese people have been making "thousand stitch belts" which are supposed to make the soldier wearing them invulnerable to bullets. Undoubtedly many users of these belts have been killed by our men and probably many of those belts could be gathered up. If our fliers were to drop some of those—torn and bloody—over Japan, it might shake their faith in their so-called spiritual protection, a part of their superstitious religion.

Yours very truly,
L. L., Burlingame, CA[37]

The *Chicago Tribune* noted that Japanese beliefs regarding certain numbers might create a unique vulnerability:

[T]he average Japanese is hounded from the age 1—the age at which he is born—to the grave by a coteries of five superstitions, the violation of any one of which means death. The numeral 4 is the most common, probably because you can't count without it. The Japs find the word most deplorable because in the native tongue it is pronounced, altho not written, the same way as the word for death, *shi*. . . . Take any island, take even the coast of Japan proper, and have our boys come riding in standing on boats covered with the numeral 4. They will come from the northeast in the middle of a driving tropical rain and will yell *shi, shi, shi*, as they come.[38]

The Japanese fear of "four" might be particularly acute on a particular date:

Secretary of the Navy
February 21, 1944

Sir:
I wonder whether it has occurred to any of our experts on enemy morale that we are approaching a date, which, according to Japanese superstition, is of more ominous significance than any other day in a century. I am referring to the fourth day of the fourth month of this year: 4-4-1944. The Japanese word for "four" is "shi," which is also their word for "death." Hence, 4 is an unlucky number. This superstition is so deep-rooted that, for instance, in Tokyo, where people select and buy their own telephone number, only an inexperienced foreigner would choose a number containing the figure 4, only to find that his personnel would refuse to use the telephone. The above-mentioned date contains 4 fours—this only occurs once in a century. It is of course for your experts to figure out how best to exploit this superstition, both in the timing of tactics, and in broadcasts to the enemy. I am not advocating the adjustment of our major strategy to this consideration, but I do believe that any attacks that would be normally planned for the first week of April will be greatly facilitated, if our men in the Pacific area are informed of the significance of this date for the Japanese, and are advised to make the best of it by focusing their main effort on this day.

Yours very respectfully,
H. Z., Chicago, IL[39]

Another Japanese concept foreign to Western thought concerned the importance of "saving face." Press reports suggested that Japanese could act in irrational, self-defeating ways if threatened with the loss of face:

Chairman, Associated Defense Committee [of Chicago]
June 24, 1943

Dear Sir:
In the Japanese belief regarding "face" one of the worst things that can happen to a man is to allow another to blacken his face. It would probably annoy and infuriate

the Japanese if we spread pictures of their Emperor with a blackened face over their territory from planes, but as the picture of their Emperor is sacred, and as they would undoubtedly pick up any pictures of him they found lying on the ground (it being against the law for anyone to look down on the Emperor), if we were to make up a leaflet with the Emperor's picture on it and a picture of General Tojo (or anyone else we would deem suitable) with a blackened face on the same leaflet (but lower down), it would probably be picked up if spread over Japan and would cause much loss of faith in the man with the blackened face.

Yours very truly,

L. L., Burlingame, CA[40]

The emperor's place in Japanese religion puzzled most Americans. Crude portrayals of Shintoism implied that the Japanese revered their emperor and ancestors just as Western monotheists worshiped Jehovah or Jesus. These two writers proposed exploiting Japanese emperor and ancestor worship:

Naval Combat Intelligence Division
May 10, 1945

Dear Sirs:

. . . Ancestor worship is the basis of the Japanese philosophy of living, as well as dying. With our vast Hollywood resources of artists, actors, methods of camouflage, and other artistic means of deception would it not be possible to stage upon the Japs a terrifying return of their most noble ancestors. Perhaps it could be done by plane, in such staggering numbers, that it would throw them into complete pandemonium. This would possibly be particularly effective with isolated, remote, pockets of Japs. Or the messages from their ancestors might drop from the heavens upon them. These might bear considerable weight, if accurate names of deceased relatives could be obtained. If the above plan is not feasible, could the radio be utilized? Why not consult Orson Welles. Perhaps he would be as successful in terrifying the Japs, as an entire nation, as he was in causing this nation to believe that the end of the world had come. . . .

Sincerely,

W. H., Portland, OR[41]

Commandant, U.S. Marine Corps
November 9, 1942

Dear General Holcomb:
. . . After reading Lieutenant Colonel Warren J. Clear's article in the *Reader's Digest*
of November, 1942 on "Close-Up of the Jap Fighting Man," my mother-in-law
was struck with the idea of Marines, and tanks and planes being equipped with
likenesses of Hirohito. Since the Jap is trained from the age of six and taught that
the Emperor is the Supreme Being, and that to look upon "Him" is sacrilegious,
or even upon his likeness, and since hundreds have lost their lives trying to save
his portrait from burning buildings; well, to see some Marines charging him,
plastered with his ugly likeness, or some tanks covered with "His" picture come
barreling down on him, would at least confuse him. And if the Jap would bow low
with shame at the sight of the Emperor, what a decided advantage that would be!
Airplanes could drop leaflets with his picture in the streets of Tokyo for the populace
to trample on. That would be confusing and demoralizing. This suggestion may be
worth consideration because of the veneration of the Japanese for their Emperor.

Yours very truly,
Senator C. Wayland Brooks
Washington, DC[42]

U.S. policy makers remained divided over how to treat the emperor. Many saw
him as a tool of Japan's militarists, though others disagreed. The *Christian Science
Monitor* reported that some officials felt "Japanese Emperor-worship might well be
an asset, that Shintoism which involved Emperor-worship (which many Americans
have felt was the root of all evil in Japan) could become an asset once the Emperor
was freed from domination by the military clique. . . . This government repeats that
Emperor worship is not necessarily an evil that must be wiped out. And it therefore
takes the position that if Emperor worship, which has been used as a unifying
force for militarism, could be developed for peaceful purposes it might well be a
good thing to keep."[43] The argument often boiled down to whether U.S. planes
should bomb the emperor's palace. The *New York Times* reasoned, "[P]reparation
for the postwar modernization of Japan's political structure can be carried out most
dramatically and effectively by bombing the Mikado's palace and by flooding the
nation with leaflets in which the purpose of this attack upon the imperial institution is make abundantly clear. . . . [T]he purpose of such bombing is to dramatize
for the Japanese people the approaching end of their antiquated Emperor cult."[44]
This writer suggested that bombing the Palace could decimate Japan's leadership:

Secretary of War and Chief of Staff
[ca. June 1942]

. . . The Palace must be pulverized. On the next trip, our men must bomb the
Palace as viciously as the Sumida River arsenals or the Yokohama chemical,
rubber, tank, and auto plants. The Grand Shrine at Ise is the burial place for
Japanese ancestors of the Imperial Family. If the Palace is bombed, and the Shrine
demolished, a wholesale hara-kiri will follow, and the entire government will be
overthrown. Imperial household authorities must commit suicide. The head of the
Metropolitan police force would kill himself. Premier General Hideki Tojo and his
Nazi trained staff would resign. The minister of War and the head of the Imperial
Western Defense Command would be put to shame. The Board of Shinto would
be tossed out. Hysteria would prevail. . . . To bomb the Imperial Palace on the next
trip will hasten an end of the war, and, by suicide, many of Tokyo's leaders will die
ahead of the day of an Axis hanging.

J. Y., New York, NY[45]

The most extreme expression of Japanese fanaticism took the form of kamikaze
attacks by waves of pilots who attempted to crash their planes into American ships.
Coming just ahead of the expected invasion of Japan, news of these suicidal pilots
had a strong impact on American public opinion. The *Christian Science Monitor*
explained, "Japan's employment of suicide planes against the American fleet off
Okinawa may be the tactics of desperation. But this should not obscure the fact
that these planes have proved dangerous. . . . The fact that the Navy has suffered
over 4,000 casualties off Okinawa alone suggests what is has meant to stay on the
job in the face of Japan's V-weapons."[46] Kamikazes so worried the Navy that it
established a special task force to develop new defensive methods, but could find
no magic bullet for stopping pilots determined to die with their victims.[47]

This writer proposed a protective antikamikaze system for American ships:

Construction and Engineering Department, U.S. Navy
April 27, 1945

Gentlemen:
Have just listened to a broadcast by Walter Winchell, re. a Jap suicide plane attacked
a U.S. hospital ship. Perhaps this idea of a dumb squeegee pusher (window washer)
may help remedy the situation. Let's try to raise four balloons by cable in each
corner of ship. Place trained bazookas in each balloon so their total fire will cover
entire surface above ship. Set electric eye in each balloon so that when its ray is

broken, it immediately sets off bazooka gun. Now let's say the balloons are 100 or 150 feet above surface of ships and there would be a rubber net tied to the balloons, the net couldn't stop a Jap suicide plane, but it could break its fall, thereby making the impact less deadly, besides give the men a chance to scamper to safety. I do hope, gentlemen, you will consider this, because if an electric eye could open garage doors, it surely could be made to fire guns, even better than any sound instrument, because light travels faster than sound.

Respectfully yours,
H. G., Los Angeles, CA[48]

To Americans, mass suicide seemed part of an utterly foreign belief system. *Popular Science* provided lurid details of the rituals involved:

> After their graduation from cadet school, these Kamikaze pilots get a six-month special training course, and then a great feast. The feast may last for several days. It includes plenty of sake and the finest foods. The prettiest geisha girls entertain these death-dedicated airmen. The pilots paint their faces white, simulating death's pallor. . . . They dress in ceremonial robes of black. During the final days of their leave, before their fatal mission, they walk through the streets with hands folded across their chests. They never smile. People meeting them bow and get out of their way.[49]

Religion played a part in the kamikazes' fervor. Commanders assured them that their deaths would make them gods, fit to join the guardian spirits of the nation at Yasukuni Shrine. This holy place, dedicated to the souls of all Japanese killed in war, served as the guardian shrine for the entire nation. If religion motivated the kamikazes, were religious shrines legitimate military targets? The *New York Times* suggested they were:

> [We should be] directing our airmen to call upon the imperial ancestors who are enshrined at the Grand Shrines of Ise at Yamada. . . . Some may object to such procedure on the ground that these places are not military objectives and therefore such bombing violates the international rules of warfare. But the real fact is that these national symbols of imperial power may well be called the fountainhead of Japanese militarism, the sources from which military leaders draw their authority and gain the prestige necessary to make the people bow to their will.[50]

This writer suggested a propaganda tactic with a similar aim:

Rep. Frank W. Boykin
June 4, 1945

Dear Frank:
An article in tonight's press states "Every Jap naval pilot ordered into suicide corps to save Japan. If this tactic is successful, the broadcast said, victory is assured for Japan. If otherwise, the Navy will have many heroes for our shrines." The thought occurred to me that the main reason the Japs want to die in a suicide squad is to perpetuate their future as a "hero in a shrine." This being the case, it seems to me that in order to kill the ardor of the Japs and discourage them, we should announce over the radio and through millions of leaflets distributed in Japan that when we win the war, we will not allow any shrines in Japan. That should have the effect of making the Japs stop such tactics and discourage all the Japanese people. Of course I do not know how this would react in the Japanese mind or how this would work in Japan, but it may be that it is a very potent thing to do. The reason I think it would be worth trying out is that if it doesn't work, no harm has been done, and if it does work, it will be worth while, if the Japanese people will understand that no shrines will be permitted after we win the victory. If they do not have "shrines" they do not have any incentive to die. . . .

J. D., Fort Worth, TX[51]

If, as Japanese propaganda claimed, every man, woman, and child preferred death to surrender, the prospects for ending the war without a massive bloodbath looked poor. The *Los Angeles Times* observed, "Suicide as a weapon is now standard equipment of the Japanese. . . . This enemy across the Pacific is giving signs that he will not collapse as easily as the Nazis. From the highest to the lowest, the Japanese army appears determined to fight it out to the finish."[52] By 1945 America dominated the air and seas around Japan, threatening to cut off the islands entirely. The *Washington Post* reported, "[T]he bombing offensive goes on and the blockade gets tighter and tighter so that Japan is now confronted with the possibility of being cut off from Korean sources of rice and Manchurian production of soya beans. To be sure, given Japan's minimum production of staple food products, Japan cannot be wholly starved out. But her people are increasingly hungry, and that hunger is likely to prove in the course of time a very material factor in the final outcome of the war."[53] In addition to imports, much of Japan's food supply came from fishing:

National Inventors Council
January 26, 1943

Dear Dr Blake:
It is known that sea-fish constitute a major part of Japanese national proteinic [*sic*] food supply. In years of unsuccessful fishing Japan experiences partial proteinic [*sic*] famine with consequent development of specific diseases due to the lack of protein in the nutritious diet. I believe that not less than 15%, or maybe as much as 20%, of all fish used in Japan for food is represented by several varieties of salmon (dog-salmon, humpback salmon, and blue-back salmon) which is caught in Kamchatka Sea, the sea of Okhotosk, and at certain parts of the Kurile chain. It is also known that from year to year the school of salmon follow the same route during the migration period, unless their migration is perturbed either by seismic or serious weather disturbances. The geographical positions of salmon runs are definitely known. Therefore, I consider it worthy of investigation whether we could produce artificial disturbances on salmon routes of spawning migration thus averting the fish from the Japanese fishing installations. In my opinion, several thousands of very slightly leaking barrels of tar submerged on the way of salmon shoals will turn the fish aside of their usual route, and thus will make fish to be lost to the Japanese fishery.

A. S., Washington, DC[54]

Blockade offered a possible alternative to a bloody showdown in the home islands. The *New Republic* reported as follows:

[Fears of suicidal resistance] have already succeeded, to some extent, in dividing Allied leaders. While there are still some who believe that Japan must be completely destroyed by being made into a battlefield, so that all her people can see with their own eyes the ruin brought upon them by their militaristic leaders, there are others who think that a satisfactory ending to the war against Japan would be the so-called unconditional surrender which might come without invasion of the home islands. They believe that Japan can be brought to the point of surrender by the current blockade (now being extended to the Straits of Korea and the Sea of Japan) and by the B-29 offensive under the command of Major General LeMay.[55]

This writer proposed total isolation of the islands in perpetuity:

Secretary of the Navy
September 26, 1944

Sir:

I have learned that about one quarter or one half of the civilian inhabitants committed hari-kari on the capture of Saipan. Further, one of the Jap officer stated that if we conquered Japan we would be forced to kill 80 million Japs. Now if the above is true, once we conquer Japan and defeat the Japs on the mainland, we will lose a lot of men policing the damned Japs—if it is done in whole or in part on foot, by assassination. . . . Since the Japs are fanatics—men, women and children, and will probably run amok when they get a good chance to knife our men in the back—I respectfully suggest that you consider the method of patrolling Japan by air and by the use of the navy say from Formosa, the Philippines, and from China, thereby permitting the swine to die on the vine, a la Truk [Lagoon]. The above method would save us the loss of soldiers and sailors and if they decided to kill they could kill each other and not a bad idea either. Further the above solution would give us a chance to keep the navy, army, etc. in trim by a constant patrol in the years following the war out there.

Respectfully,
L. H., Orlando, FL[56]

The *Washington Post* questioned whether blockade and bombardment would sway Japan's leaders: "Whether these methods would compel the Japanese to surrender is in the last analysis a political question. A fanatical government that could not be overthrown internally might never surrender, even if all the Japanese industry were destroyed and half the population of the home islands were killed or starved."[57]

This letter suggested procuring substitutes for U.S. troops:

Representative Pete Jarman
March 21, 1945

Dear Peterson:

A number of your constituents, including myself, believe it would be a wanton sacrifice of American lives to place U.S. land troops in China and Japan. We have practically driven Japan off the seas, and so long as we keep Japan off the seas she can do the U.S. no damage. Why should the U.S. place land troops in China, and lose thousands, perhaps one or more million American lives during the land fighting for China? China has a population of four hundred millions, and ample man power to build up an army sufficiently large to crush Japan if we furnish the equipment. The U.S. no doubt will soon be able to establish landings in S. E. China, and furnish this equipment rapidly, and in ample volume. It seems to us that the logical policy of our government should be: Arm the Chinese, Filipinos and Koreans and let them do the land fighting to throw off the yoke of Japan, the U.S. aiding in the air and on the sea, no matter how many years it may take. . . .

Yours sincerely,
W. M., Livingston, AL[58]

Eventually neither an invasion nor mass starvation proved necessary. Two atomic bombs and a Soviet declaration of war convinced Japan's leaders that mass suicide could not stave off defeat. Japan's surrender ended the fighting, but the problem of occupation remained:

Senator Ed Johnson
September 14, 1945

Dear Mr. Johnson:
. . . May I suggest as follows: That Chinese veterans after 8 years of fighting, suffering and near starvation, the wanton slaughter of their families, are not and will not be soft toward the Japanese for many years to come—absolutely a fact! For us to send young recruits to Japan to replace those who are justly entitled to return after their suffering and privations would in my opinion be folly, for Japanese hypocrisy and cunning would work serious undermining of our victory over that race. . . . Chinese troops close at hand, at least as interested in holding down the Japs, would cost much less to transport. They are already trained; would cost less than half as much to maintain as Americans. . . .

Sincerely,
M. S., Canon City, CO[59]

Despite such misgivings about Shintoist fanaticism, the Japanese proved compliant in defeat. American forces employed the emperor's (now mostly moral) authority to control the islands with a minimum of force. In short order, the formerly incomprehensible foes turned their attention and legendary industry away from military conquest and toward the development of a modern consumer-oriented economy. In the great Pacific war of civilizations, there were no losers—only converts.

CHAPTER 9

Bombs Away! America Rules the Skies

An unequaled industrial base, ample fuel supplies, and wide-open training areas allowed the United States to fully exploit the promise of military aviation during World War II. America's war began and ended with devastating air raids: one at Pearl Harbor and one at Nagasaki. The contrasting results illustrated the changing global balance of air power. By war's end, U.S. flyers had gained near-total ascendancy over the battle fronts. Air superiority became a staple of American military operations, and formed a major foundation of national power through the Cold War and beyond.

From the beginning, U.S. leaders aimed to use air power to destroy the enemy's war-making capacity. The air war plan drawn up shortly before the attack at Pearl Harbor called for a massive campaign against economic targets throughout Nazi-occupied Europe. War planners argued that bombing enemy industries would prevent a Great War–type stalemate, and promised to achieve pinpoint accuracy to avoid civilian casualties that might make such operations politically unpalatable.[1] In response, aviation companies geared up to mass-produce long-range bombers to carry tons of bombs deep into enemy territory.

Early defeats and the relative weakness of U.S. land and naval forces made long-range bombing appealing to the public. For a time, heavy bombers seemed to be the sole means of striking back. They could deliver crippling blows even as America remained inferior on the ground and at sea. Strategic bombing both satisfied the desire for speedy retaliation and provided the promise of eventual victory. *Popular Mechanics* published the following prediction:

> By 1943 American factories will be producing hundreds of four-motored bombers each month, and these mighty air battleships may well be the deciding factor of the war. Two and one-half years of aerial warfare in Europe and several months fighting in the Pacific have indicated that the nations which first acquire a fleet of

long-range, hard-hitting planes will win final victory. . . . With land armies locked in static combat and with the world's navies checkmating one another on the high seas, the big bomber appears the best weapon in the arsenal of democracy with which to get at the Germans, Italians and Japanese. It will carry the war right up to their ports, their factories, their railroads and their cities.[2]

Military leaders believed that bombing would weaken enemy defenses prior to the Allied counterattack. *Fortune* likened strategic bombing to "an internal siege that prevents the supply flow from inside sources to the fighting fronts. The possibilities of this internal blockade are no less real and apparent that are those of an encircling blockade which eventually so weakens an enemy that his circumference of defense is unable to put up effective resistance against frontal assault."[3] Others hoped that bombing could substitute for a bloody ground campaign. *Reader's Digest* argued the point in this way:

Compared to the losses we should suffer in any great surface offensive, an all-out air attack would be cheap. . . . A six months' air campaign to bring about the end of German resistance would cost a maximum of only 30,000 men even if every man were killed in every bomber lost. . . . "We face an invasion of Europe which will involve casualties such as this nation has never endured." But do we have to resign ourselves to the heartaches of great land offensives? There is an alternative, and 1942 has proved it sound.[4]

Once committed to strategic bombing, U.S. air commanders tried to identify targets whose destruction would disrupt the Nazi war effort. The public read news reports of strikes on aircraft engine plants, U-boat building yards, and other facilities. Some offered suggestions on which industries to target:

William B. Ziff
October 11, 1942

Dear Sir:
I write you this letter because your book proves you to be the outstanding expert for all questions of the coming air battle of Germany. For 3 years of war (I lived in England during the first 10 months of war) I am wondering why I never saw a report about an air attack against one of the weakest and at the time most important links of the German war industry. I talked already in England about it, but apparently not to the right people. To cut a long story short: I happen to know a little bit about the German ball-bearing industry, which already in 1938 developed a severe bottleneck, as no car, no tank, no airplane can operate without ball-bearings and

as there were certain difficulties to increase production sufficiently. . . . The point I want to make is as follows: The German ball-bearing industry is concentrated in a relatively small town: Schweinfurt. The two biggest producer-concerns (Fichtl & Sachs and Kugel-lager Fischer) have their main factories there. They cannot be missed, as practically no other important industries are located there. Destruction of ball-bearing factories and equipment will have the most severe consequences, as ball-bearings are irreplaceable. . . . I cannot think of any other single item which is as vulnerable and as important and as concentrated on one known spot just now in Germany. So it would be most probably of tremendous influence for the German war industries, if the Schweinfurt production could be smashed in one night beyond repair or removal. . . .

Very sincerely and respectfully yours,
F. G., Beverly Hills, CA[5]

Germany depended heavily on electricity for war production. The German power grid could prove vulnerable to an unconventional weapon:

General H. H. Arnold
March 7, 1944

A friend has sent me the following suggestion concerning the bombing of Germany:

"I think you might know whom to contact in your department to learn if this idea of mine is helpful to the Army. Clip a couple of iron conduits or pipes to the underside of a plane which, when on a drive over Germany, could drop the pipes over primary high voltage electric distribution lines and short circuit the system so all light and power would be shut off the areas being passed over. If the distribution systems cover large regions, like our Niagra Falls lines do in New York State, it will affect large areas. I suggest the pipes be fastened together at sixty or ninety degree angles to each other and small parachutes be attached at each pipe end so they will drop in a horizontal position to reach to more wires. . . . Between England and Berlin a great amount of damage to lines might be done by simply dropping metal while enroute."

There may be no merit to this suggestion. I am merely passing it on for what it is worth.

Robert Patterson, Undersecretary of War
Washington, DC[6]

The Germans built fortified U-boat bases along the French Atlantic coast, with reinforced concrete bunkers that proved impervious to Allied bombs.[7] *Time* reported, "The home pens along the coasts of Europe have taken pounding after pounding from the air, yet the submarines still use them."[8] Citizens suggested alternative means of attacking these shelters:

Bureau of Naval Intelligence
March 31, 1943

Sir:
After viewing the News Reel pictures of the submarine base at Lorient and the following air attack on it, may I suggest the following: As this base is constructed with a thickness of over thirty feet of concrete and steel as protection of great strength against air attack, the side towards the sea is open of necessity to allow the subs to enter. My thought is that this open side could be attacked by torpedo planes or by skip bombing. If the supports were hit, it might be possible of causing the whole structure to cave in. If they were missed, the torpedoes would continue on and with luck, sink any subs inside as they are not in a position to move out of the way. The above may not be possible, but there are times when a civilian comes out with a "bright idea" that might work. Anyway, I've got it off my mind.

With respect,
R. F., Newark, NJ[9]

Army officials noted, "[T]hese bases are defended by torpedo nets as well as by heavy anti-aircraft gun installations and for this reason it may be difficult to use torpedoes effectively."[10] These two writers proposed dropping substances to penetrate the defensive nets:

National Inventors Council
February 24, 1943

Gentlemen:
I wish to offer, for what it may be worth, a suggestion for attacking the submarines sheltered in the "garages" at Lorient, St. Nazaire, and other points on the French coast. . . . I suggest that in the future, a large proportion of the bombs dropped on these objectives be replaced with containers full of concentrated sulphuric acid: and that particular attention be given to placing as many as possible of such containers in the waters immediately adjacent to the shelters, and in the channels leading to them, rather than upon the structures themselves. A number of tons of this acid dropped into the approaches to the garages just after the turn of the tide from ebb

to flood would surround all the vessels within the garages with an actively corrosive medium which would immediately be taken into all the circulatory systems of the submarines, and perhaps, even into the ballast bunkers. This would result in seriously crippling the boats through failure of tubing, pumps, valves, and metallic packing, would deeply pit piston rods, cylinder walls and any working surfaces with which it might come into contact. . . . Those containers of acid which failed to fall into the water approaches to these garages, but which fell on the structures themselves, would by no means be wasted. Previous bombings must have created thousands of cracks reaching to greater or less depths into the reinforced concrete of which the shelters are built. Seepage of concentrated acid into these cracks would first attack the cement, and when diluted by the highly prevalent natural moisture of that region, or by attempts to wash it away, would soon destroy the reinforcing steel. Thus the structures would become much more susceptible to future demolition bombings.

Yours truly,

A. M., San Antonio, TX[11]

Senator A. H. Vandenberg
[ca. 1942–43]

Dear Sir:
As the submarine base in one of the harbors in France is so well built, 11 ft. concrete roof reinforced, that bombs do not materially damage it. . . . If instead of dropping bombs on such structure it was daily bombed with from 25 to 100 tons of plain undistilled petroleum, all wooden docks as well as buildings would become saturated with an inflammable, disagreeable gas producing element that will float upon the water, creep behind the piling, underneath the building, saturate same and if fire started with a good strong westerly breeze, it would be nearly impossible to put out the fire. Until a fire starts there is nothing that makes a place so disagreeable as to be saturated with plain petroleum. It sticks to the feet, gets into and over everything and becomes subject to inflammation here and there. I do not know that we could drop the petroleum from our Flying Fortresses with sufficient accuracy to cover the base completely, but it seems to me that it is worth trying for if it is successful it would eliminate one of our major disadvantages. . . . At least if this does not destroy the base it will make it a terrible place to work in as the water will carry the oil into, onto, and against every place where water flows.

Yours very truly,

J. M., Detroit, MI[12]

This writer proposed weakening the bunkers' roofs so that Allied bombs could penetrate:

Inventor's War Council
January 22, 1943

Dear Sirs:
I am a student mechanical engineer currently working as a shipfitter at the local shipyard building Liberty ships. Recently, I witnessed a large-scale thermite weld: the welding together of two halves of a cast-steel stern casting. About 150 lbs. of molten steel was used in this weld. I was greatly impressed by this practical demonstration of the intense heat (about 5,000 F) generated in a matter of seconds. It is well known that concrete absorbs great quantities of water during the process of hardening. This water is retained as water of crystallization. Molten metal—such as iron—coming into contact with concrete converts this water into steam of sufficient pressure to shatter the concrete violently. If such mission has not already been sufficiently well accomplished, how about such a raid on the concrete submarine canopies at Lorient as this: A wave of several hundred bombers dropping 100 lb or 150 lb incendiary bombs containing only thermite with suitable igniters. These should shatter and weaken the concrete sufficiently to permit penetration by high explosive demolition bombs of the standard type dropped by a second wave of bombers following three to five minutes later.

Respectfully submitted,
R. S., Portland, ME[13]

Special forms of bombing might trap the U-boats in their lairs:

Assistant Secretary of the Navy for Air
February 25, 1943

Dear Di:
In discussing the air war against the subs and the great sheds at Lorient and elsewhere that defy the heaviest bombs, Mr. Stuart Crandall, the President of the concern I am working for, suggested dropping bombs of underwater cement to gum the gates, etc. You may not know it, but whereas ordinary cement would wash away if dropped in a strategic position, or could be jet pumped away, underwater cement is so adhesive and holds the position in which it is placed so well, that a lump can be placed by hand on the lip of a flowing dam and it will harden right there. Let me know if you want any more dope about this.

As ever,
R. L., Cambridge, MA[14]

National Inventors Council
March 4, 1943

Gentlemen:
The following suggestion may be pretty crazy, but, on the possibility that it might have some potential value, I must take a chance on wasting your valuable time. Years ago, if memory serves me correctly, someone was sure to bring out, on one of the national holidays, a small cone of material which was set upon its base on a plate. The tip or point of the cone was then lighted with a match. The burning was slow. As the material burned, it expanded, pushing out across the plate, snakelike in shape and motion. I believe they were called "snakes" or "serpents," or some similar name. . . . The size of the "snake" indicated quite a lot of expansion had taken place in the process of burning. It has occurred to me that our Chemical Warfare engineers could develop this substance into one which would burn under water, and perhaps have even greater expansion and be of better consistency when the burning had stopped. A large amount of such a material in bombs with time or contact fuses, dropped from planes or planted by boats, expanding in the harbor or harbor entrances of the enemy, particularly submarine bases, while not destroying the bases or rendering them permanently ineffective, would certainly produce a large quantity of material which would have to be removed and would impair the usefulness of the bases until the material had been cleaned out. A constant dumping of such material in the harbors might prove highly effective. . . .

Yours very truly,
H. M., Montville, NJ[15]

As Allied bomber fleets grew, some commentators argued that destroying entire cities, or at least threatening to do so, was a legitimate tactic. The *Saturday Evening Post* predicted, "Early next year the world may witness an astounding thing. Our air supremacy may by then be so well established, some believe, that it will actually be possible for Messrs. Churchill and Roosevelt to warn the Germans over the radio, a day or so in advance, just which of their cities is next going to be obliterated. . . . Fifty-two big cities account for more than 90 percent of Germany's production. The theory is that as these disappear the enemy will suffer internal hemorrhages which will prove fatal."[16] Although city bombing did not wreck German morale, their Italian allies were less enthusiastic:

National Inventors Council
November 16, 1942

Dear Johnny:
. . . The idea behind this suggestion is to secure ports on the European side of the Mediterranean with as low a cost as possible, by the use of psychological warfare. The idea is to deal with the individual city as though it were a medieval city separated from the rest of the country and to create fear and panic in the city and divide the civilian population against the military population. The method is to drop pamphlets over the city, for example, the city of Naples, which will inform the public that from bases in Africa the city will be bombed heavily with the complete destruction of the city within twenty-four hours unless the following takes place: (1) the civilian population leave the city by the roads in every direction, thereby jamming the roads with civilians in an outgoing direction. (2) The military defenders of the city are to assemble at a designated beach on which they are to surrender their weapons, tanks, and small arms. This beach should be one which is accessible to naval gunfire in case of treachery. . . . The above actions would be somewhat similar to the action of fortified cities in the Middle Ages surrendering to an invader. Let us assume that this is done. The following might happen: (1) A panic seize the city and the civilian population take to the road. The military and police authorities would try to stop this. A conflict would result—in some instances the soldiery would refuse to fire on their own population. To such extent as people streamed out of the city the roads would be blocked. This much alone would be valuable in case a naval assault were to be made following up an aerial bombardment, the purpose of the aerial assault being to soften up the coast defenses.[17]

Unsigned

Rome, filled with ancient treasures and home to one of the world's great religions, posed a delicate political problem for Allied air commanders. This writer suggested that the Allies could resolve the religious issue by using specially selected pilots in raids on the Eternal City:

Chief of Staff, U.S. Army
July 19, 1943

Dear Sir:
Would it be feasible to have the future bombing of Rome carried out by volunteer American and British Roman Catholic air crews? If it were possible to do this and

the United Nations could advertise the fact to the Italian People and the rest of Europe I believe it would have a tremendous effect on our enemy's morale.

Respectfully yours,
W. B. (Roman Catholic), Yonkers, NY[18]

This writer proposed bombing Germany's rural transportation links:

Chief, Army Air Forces
October 25, 1943

Dear General Arnold:
It seems to me that there is a possibility of paralyzing Germany by the sole means of air attacks of a very one-sided nature, using bombs perhaps as light as 50 pounds.... 2000 simultaneous cuts of railroad lines between towns, railroad centers and railroad junctions would paralyze the whole railroad system of Germany for the time between bombing and repair. Approximately weekly repeat bombing would sustain complete paralyzation and thus destroy Germany in several weeks. . . . To bomb a railroad center looks more enticing than a simple track between woods and fields, because the quantitative destruction in the case of centers exceeds that of remote tracks, by far. If we compare a few bent rails in the woods with a heap of twisted and broken structure in a smoking "center," we may have difficulties in divorcing our calculations from the violence of the visual picture. It is even more difficult since the emotional reaction can be supported by one viewpoint: A great amount of destruction requires more man-hours of repair work than a small amount of destruction. However, the point is not "How many man-hours are needed," but "However many man-hours are needed, how can they be applied to the job and what is the situation while the job is being done?" In the case of a "center," the repair work can start right after the bombs are dropped, and the great number of tracks and switches often permit substitute connections while the damaged ones are being repaired. In the case of bombs dropped on a remote track, the repair of point B can be started only after point A is repaired and permits point B to be reached. In other words scattered track bombing puts the repair work in a vicious circle: Repair needs transportation and transportation needs repair. During the Germans' struggle in this vicious circle the total traffic is paralyzed.

A. P., New York, NY[19]

These two writers suggested targeting certain natural terrain features:

Major General Thomas Handy, General Staff Operations Division
[ca. October 1942]

Dear Major General:
Page 73, of *Time* October 19 mentions you, so I am taking this opportunity to write you about an idea, which I have had for some time. It involves the bombing of volcanoes, with the idea of getting them into action. I have wondered if bombs exploded within them would cause them to erupt? If such were the case, this method might prove effective against Japan. They have plenty [of] volcanos to work on. For a trial shot, possibly a couple dropped into Mt. Vesuvius might have telling effects on Italy. If my idea works, you can readily see the terror, destruction and damage which might ensue. This method might even produce earthquakes and roll a few Jap islands into the sea. Since I know nothing about volcanos, I am passing this idea along to you. My hope is that it has merit and if so, I know it will be used and help us end this war as quickly as possible. I will appreciate having your opinion on this matter.

Very truly yours,
P. B., Minneapolis, MN[20]

Secretary of War
October 3, 1944

Honorable Sir:
I have a war suggestion to offer you. Enclosed you will find a relief panorama of the Rhine River in Germany. I came across it the other evening in my library. If you can use it, you are welcome to it with my best wishes. Here is my suggestion. At a point, marked by red pencil, at the Loreley, you will note a high rock formation on one side of the river. Across from it there is also a high rolling stretch of land. The channel at this point is narrow. I suggest that the rock formation be bombed with block busters, sending the rock into the channel of the Rhine River, thus cutting off from the East to the West. If the map cannot serve war purposes, kindly return it to me.

Sincerely yours,
F. K., St. Louis, MO[21]

Selecting targets was one thing—actually bombing them in the face of a determined enemy proved quite another. Daylight strategic bombing relied on the defensive powers of American bombers because Allied fighters lacked the range to protect them over the targets. British experience had demonstrated the vulnerability of unescorted bombers, but U.S. commanders argued that American models could fight their way through the defenses. The name of the most publicized heavy bomber, "Flying Fortress," suggested a level of protection distinctly at odds with reality. News accounts of early missions reinforced popular faith in the bombers' capabilities by repeating wildly exaggerated claims of enemy fighters destroyed. *Popular Mechanics* proclaimed, "Our big bombers are now in the real battlewagon class. Flying Fortresses and Liberators have been bombing Europe night and day, their gunners knocking down 20 German fighters for every bomber lost."[22]

As U.S. raids began to penetrate deeper over Germany, however, losses rose dramatically. *Newsweek* laid out the dismaying statistics: "As a result of German concentration on defenses, in the past few weeks more Allied planes than ever before have fallen over Germany. Last week's figures were typical: 44 down over Krefeld, 20 over Huls and Antwerp, 35 over Mulheim, 33 over Wuppertal, 30 over Bochum-Gelsenkirchen. And in a raid over unstated objectives where clouds prevented accurate bombing, 17 more American planes were lost. In seven days and nights 184 Allied bombers fell, and nearly 1,500 highly trained airmen went to their deaths or to prison camps."[23] Even manufacturers' advertisements, which previously had boasted of the Flying Fortress' striking power, reflected the change. Boeing ran photos of battle-mangled Fortresses that had somehow managed to limp home, noting, "[even] with the vertical or horizontal tail surfaces partially destroyed in battle, or with one or more engines shot away, a Fortress can still be flown successfully."[24] Astute readers could conclude that American bombers were regularly being badly shot up. The fate of crew members in these flying sieves was best left to the imagination. *Time* argued that greater force would solve the problem:

The Flying Fortresses can take on the enemy 3-to-1 and come through with light losses or no losses at all; but when the ratio goes up to 7-, 8- or even 10-to-1, even their concentrated fire cannot always break down the Nazi attack. . . . One answer is to increase the number of bombers in each raid, thus reducing the proportion of enemy fighters to each bomber. . . . [W]ith 500 Flying Fortresses, for instance, the U.S. might lose no more or even fewer than a flight of 100, because of the concentrated fire and the lowered odds of the German fighters.[25]

This writer proposed adding more firepower to protect bomber formations:

General Henry H. Arnold
July 9, 1943

Dear General:

I am taking the liberty of writing you of an idea that maybe feasible in the air service that perhaps could be the means of destroying more German fighters with less loss to our forces, viz: Heavily armor a number of bombers, the same to not carry any bombs. The armor weight to be in lieu of the bomb weight. The bombers to be armored as much as possible to take a beating and also to hand it out. The armored bombers to fly same as any other bombers in formation and pretend to be hurt or crippled thus luring the German fighters on, as I read they gang up on the cripples. Meanwhile the bomber's defensive fire power could be increased as well as the armor to strengthen the bomber to take a mauling as well as dish it out to the extent of the weight of the bombs that it formerly carried.

Very truly yours,
C. F., Long Beach, CA[26]

U.S. air commanders tried the escort-bomber concept. Specially modified bombers, with extra guns and ammunition instead of bombs, flew along on raids to improve the group's defensive power. The project failed to stem losses because these bomber-fighters lacked the maneuverability to protect damaged planes that fell behind.[27] News of these up-gunned hybrids reached the public, prompting suggestions for their optimum employment:

Lieutenant General Arnold
October 15, 1943

My Dear General:

I trust you will accept my suggestion in the spirit in which it is written, a little American like millions of others whose full desire is to win the war with the lowest cost in lives of our finest young men, nothing else matters. I enclose herewith an idea came to me after hearing about the way you armed some of our B-17 as escort fighters for the B-17 carrying bomb loads. . . . In addition to all other plans made so far, set aside say 1000 B-17 for a special task force. Arm 500 of them with all the fire power possible, but no bombs pick out the most important target in Germany, send over 500 B-17 that are armed with all the guns possible, as the German planes will expect only a few to be so armed, the result, destruction of all or practically all planes in that area, later send over the other 500 B-17 mostly all loaded with the greatest amount of bombs they can carry. A clear target, a great destruction.

F. D.[28]

After a series of particularly costly missions, *Newsweek* published the following admission:

> The ideal of the Eighth Air Force was to strike deeper and deeper into Germany with accurate precision bombing by day. . . . [T]his advance received a setback at Schweinfurt. There, on the Main River in the Central Reich, the Eighth struck a crippling blow at the German ball bearing industry. But it took a heavy blow in return; 60 bombers were shot down and many others limped home, fatally damaged. . . . [N]o more deep penetrations have been made since Schweinfurt. It is a reasonable supposition that the cost mounted too high and that deep penetrations without fighter escort have been abandoned.[29]

The Allies desperately needed to increase the range of their escort fighters:

> Headquarters of the Army Air Forces
> December 11, 1943
>
> Dear Sir:
> The inference is that after their heavy losses on the Regensberg and Schweinfurt missions, coincident with the enemy's large-scale use of rocket gun fighters, the Eighth Bomber Command decided to discontinue, at least for the time being, further large scale deep penetrations by our heavy bombers, beyond escort range. The problem demanding quick solution would therefore appear to be: How best to improvise increased escorting fighter range with existing fighter types? I am taking the liberty, therefore, in writing you to suggest a possible answer. Suppose the heavies go out on a [deep penetration] escorted not simply by P-38s or P-47s with extra tanks as at present, but by P-38s so remodified as to have a jettisonable fuel capacity well in excess of this, where their ability successfully to take off and fly without combat maneuver is only just retained. This united formation of heavies and overloaded P-38s must be escorted out by, say, P-47s up to the latter's limits of range. At this juncture the P-38s must be light enough to function as escort in the normal manner. It might even prove advisable to triple-tier the heavies' escort: super-ranged P-38s, escorted by belly-tank P-47s, in turn escorted at first by Spitfires up to their own range. . . .
>
> Very sincerely,
> J. F., Santa Barbara, CA[30]

Mr. Vanden Berg:

I have an idea that may help win the war, and I don't know who to send it to. I hope you will forward it to the proper authorities. Here is my idea. So far no one has made a good long-range fighter plane. Our bombers need fighter plane protection on long-distance raids. My idea is to tow fighters behind bombers the same way they tow gliders. When enemy planes are spotted, the fighters could be unhooked and could engage the enemy planes so that our bombers could carry out their mission unmolested. After the fight the fighters could either fly home or some device could be used which would enable them to hook on to the tow line again. Take-offs, which are a problem in glider towing, could be eliminated by having the fighter use its motor until the planes are at the altitude at which they are to fly. In considering the possibilities of this idea I had in mind two planes which I think would work very well. They are the Boeing Flying Fortress and the Lockheed Lightning. The tow hook could be fastened to the nose of the Lightning very easily and not get caught in the propellers. This may not be at all practical or possible but in case it is, I am sending it to you to forward. Thank you.

Sincerely,

C. V., Saginaw, MI[31]

The next two letters proposed screening the bombers from enemy defenses:

General H. H. Arnold
October 21, 1943

Sir:

Please do not consider this a crack-brained idea, but it might help in the protection of our bombers when on long missions with so much enemy fighter resistance. . . . On a mission to targets involving several hundred bombers, the "Dragon" now escorting same and which have fire power and armor could carry the necessary elements to form the smoke screen or cloud at a point where interception takes place on the way to the target and return. With suitable long-range fighter escort for the "Dragons" they could be protected to a great extent from interference in laying the smoke screen. At high altitudes with minimum air turbulence (except as localized by the many props of the screened bombers) the screen would remain constant for many miles behind the formation. At the point of target the bombers can pass through and ahead of the screening "Dragons" or the underside of screen can be discontinued to permit visibility for bombardiers, run the target and return to the escorting screen to return to base. Anti-aircraft would have the screen to fire on but with considerable inaccuracy, as each formation of bombers could be distributed within the screen at intervals that would make it practically impossible to concentrate fire on any one group of bombers. . . .

Respectfully submitted,
P. G., Jacksonville, FL[32]

October 13, 1943

I assume that the menace of enemy fighter planes is great when a large bomber force attacks an enemy air field. Suppose one or more special bomber planes, a little in advance of the flight, at a great height, released a huge number of special fragmentation bombs in the form of a pattern for a given area about the attacked air field or objective. Each of these fragmentation bombs would be suspended by a long steel cable from its own parachute. The parachutes might be disproportionately large so that the fragmentation bombs would float down at the slowest rate possible. The result would be a ceiling of floating bombs. These bombs should be so manufactured that a strong tug or yank resulting from a blow on the bomb or any part of the steel cable or parachute will explode it. Exactly timed, our raiding party would come in above the ceiling of parachutes, do their work, and depart. Enemy fighter planes in rising from the air field might dodge one parachute only to run head long into some part of another. . . .

L. G., New Haven, CT[33]

By early 1944 the Allies had finally developed a fighter, the P-51 Mustang, with enough range to escort bombers all the way to their targets. As losses of Axis interceptors grew, the death of so many experienced pilots gutted Germany's defensive strength. Still, German pilots enjoyed the advantage of fighting over friendly territory. If they escaped their crippled planes uninjured, they could quickly return to action:

Chief, Air Corps U.S. Army
June 24, 1943

Dear General Arnold:
I have a suggestion to make which I believe may result in more German fighter pilots being killed rather than shot down. It is simply that all gunners be instructed to keep shooting at an enemy ship after it has been hit as long as the ship is within

range. By doing this many a pilot will be killed or wounded so that he never has a chance to bail out. The above is simply the procedure my father and I have used in duck hunting in the South where most of our shooting is in old abandoned rice fields. Almost any duck that falls wounded in the grass gets away. This seems simple but if you do not force yourself to keep shooting at the crippled bird as long as he is in the air, you may knock down two or more birds and get (pick up) none. If a person is not an experienced hunter, he could well make the same mistake: hit and shoot down a plane while the pilot escapes. As so many fights are happening over German held territory, I thought that the above might result in more of their pilots being killed outright.

Sincerely yours,
J. C., Boston, MA[34]

Although friendly escorts blunted Axis fighter attacks, American bombers still faced deadly fire from antiaircraft guns concentrated at targets throughout Germany:

National Inventors Council
November 6, 1944

For the purpose of weakening the effectiveness of enemy anti-aircraft fire, in so far as it may yet be dependent on visual detection, I submit for your consideration the following described simple device. . . . Unlike a smoke screen, the visual obstruction to ground observers will constitute no bar [sic] of flyers' view of the ground. What I propose is: 1) A multiplicity of small (e.g. 3 to 6 inch span) paper mache or any other suitable press-formable sheet material, gliders (plan view replicas of our various aircraft) cheaply press-formed in one operation by the tens of thousands, so they stack together like ice cream cones. . . . The "shells" or cartons being shot ahead of bombers or merely dropped from one or more advance scouts flying at high altitude. . . . By the time the bombers approach a few minutes later, the 50,000 gliders constitute a blanket about 1,000 feet thick confusing visual detection or triangulation of the bombers by any ground station in a 16 square mile area. Thus to a [ground] observer, a 4 inch glider at 147 feet above ground subtends the same angular dimension as a 60 foot span fighter at an altitude of 26,400 feet; and what appears to be a 150 foot bomber at three miles up, is a 6 inch model 53 feet above ground. . . . To complete the illusory effect, the gliders can be semi-transparent, perhaps irregularly edged, and so colored that their appearance at short distances duplicates that usual hazy outline and hue of real aircraft at high altitudes. . . .

Yours respectfully,
H. I., Dayton, OH[35]

Despite heavy losses in daylight missions, the U.S. pilots eschewed night bombing as practiced by the British. Only late in the war, over Japan, did America resort to nocturnal raids on enemy cities. Darkness offered bombers some protection against defenses, though at the cost of reduced accuracy. These two letters proposed methods for protecting night bombers:

Air Corps, United States Army
[ca. March 1942]

It is a clear night and the bombers are coming over very high. A thin moon and some clouds only partially conceal the naval base. No bombs yet. Searchlight crews searching the sky and anti-aircraft gunners presetting their aim from spotter and detector information wait tensely. Almost within range now. Pursuit planes are working their way up, but almost too late. All eyes are straining upward into the night to the 30,000 foot level. In the bombers, three warning clicks come over the radiophones. Crews close their eyes, cover them with their hands, turn toward the inside of the planes. Almost immediately the black sky bursts into one blinding sheet of light. Time fused flash bombs, each of 500,000 candlepower, have exploded simultaneously at half a dozen (or more) different altitudes above the guns and the interceptors. Blinded and paralyzed, the ground and air defenses are momentarily useless. Men see suns, stars, rainbows and skyrockets, everything but enemy planes. Aloft, bombardiers change course, commence their bombing runs, knowing that for one or two minutes, at least, they can work unhampered.[36]

Unsigned

[National Inventors Council]
June 3, 1943

The position of our night bombers is often given away to the enemy fighter planes by the glow from the exhausts. To eliminate this annoying situation, I suggest that we create a similar one astern of the bomber. Let the bomber trail a five hundred foot or longer length of pianoforte wire rope astern of her, the trailing end of which is made to emit sparks (if tubular) or to glow with a dim light, or some other object covered with luminous paint. The enemy fighting plane will naturally concentrate his guns on the glow that is closest to him, viz., the end of the wire. Well, that would be to the bomber's benefit, and the enemy line of fire would not hurt the bomber because the end of the wire rope is bound to be on a lower level than the bomber itself.

T. R., Santa Monica, CA[37]

Defenders sometimes relied on sound to detect night raiders, a tactic that created opportunities to achieve deception and surprise:

National Inventors Council
April 27, 1942

Gentlemen:
I beg to refer to the article in the March issue of the *Reader's Digest* where you invite the submitting of ideas suitable for war purposes. May I take the liberty to outline the following. It is a well known fact that air bombarding, besides the destruction of industries, etc. has a very detrimental effect on the whole population of a bombarded area, because people cannot work, or if they have to take to air raid shelters will be robbed of their sleep and unfit for work the next day. I have imagined a kind of siren imitating the noise of an airplane motor. Such a siren should be driven by compressed air from a steel cylinder which would be attached to a suitable parachute, big enough to keep the whole apparatus for a very long time high in the air. Now a flight of airplanes going to attack Berlin, for instance would drop on their way over there, over suitable areas (not to be bombed that night) a couple of the above outlined apparatus, which when launched, would start to put the siren in movement. From the ground, it would appear as if airplanes were going to attack and of course air alarms would be given and the whole machinery of air defense put in movement, for the price of a rather cheap apparatus floating through the air, while the airplanes which launched these apparatus would be already far away. I suppose that with a slight charge of explosives, exploding when the compressed air is all used up, the apparatus could be destroyed still in the air, in order not to leave any trace of it. Kindly excuse my very bad English, which I hope has notwithstanding allowed to make me sufficiently clear. I beg to remain, Gentlemen, very faithfully yours,

E. K., São Paulo, Brazil[38]

National Inventors Council
September 11, 1942

Dear Sirs:
I submit for the consideration of the council the following idea in connection with air raids over urban districts at night. It is almost a universal policy among cities that upon hearing the alert, lights are extinguished, and, when the all clear sounds, lights go on again. Also, for more or less obvious reasons, the all clear

signal is a siren sound, of a given type, distinguishable from say, the alert signal. I propose that when a given city is to be bombed at night, at a predetermined time prior to the actual arrival of the bombing planes over the target area, a scouting plane, drop, by parachute, over the general target area, a siren giving the all clear signal, which will then settle to the ground and continue to give the all clear signal, until manually stopped, or until the power supply gives out. It is reasonable to assume that, particularly in those cities where radios are not permitted or otherwise not normally in service generally, many people will be deceived, and a more or less widespread return of the illumination to the city can be anticipated. It is also reasonable to assume that confusion among the populace and the military personnel can safely be anticipated and expected. It is also clear that the personnel manning anti-aircraft batteries will similarly be confused, and desirable seconds before the delusion is recognized can be used to advantage. . . .

Very truly yours,
A. C., New York, NY[39]

This writer suggested mounting a daytime raid under cover of celestially produced darkness:

War Inventions Board
July 4, 1942

Gentlemen:
As an appropriate thought for the 4th of July I would like to suggest a night bombing in the daytime for the Japanese base of Sapporo and various fortifications around the Japanese north island of Hokkaido in the mid-morning darkness of February 4/5, 1943 (if we are still in a position to do so at that time). I think it would have a surprising psychological effect on the superstitious inhabitants of that enemy country, and would be a lot of fun, a "first," in fact. If you will look at pages 220 and 221 of the new American Nautical Almanac for the year 1943, you will see that there is a total eclipse of the sun there at the time. A total eclipse bombing would be a new thing, certainly—the Americans put out the sun and then bomb h—l out of them. But look out for similar deviltry from the Japs in the afternoon at Kodiak, Alaska during the same eclipse (The Date Line makes different dates). If this has already been investigated, please disregard.

Respectfully yours,
E. W.[40]

Given the inevitable cost in blood and treasure, Americans wanted bombing missions to inflict the maximum possible damage. Bombed factories often resumed production in just a few days, forcing pilots to hit them repeatedly in an attempt to wreck them completely. These two letters suggested means to achieve complete devastation in a single blow:

General H. H. Arnold, USAAF
June 24, 1943

Present bombing procedure does not fully utilize the potential destructive power of aircraft bombs, due principally to the present lack of coordinated detonation. . . . Procedure—In place of making a run directly over the selected target, the planes would lay their bombs in a circle or circles around the target. The size of the circles depending upon the pre-determined target to be obliterated and the number of planes to be used. . . . The key to successful obliteration of the target under this method lies in the fact that all bombs so dropped would be time bombs, so timed that they would all be exploded simultaneously and after our planes had flown safely beyond range. With a ring of bombs thus laid and exploding as one bomb, the explosive force created through the exerted pressure of expanding or compressed air from the bomb or bombs from any sector of the arc meeting a like pressure from any other sector would set up such destructive forces that it is doubtful that within the target circle human life could withstand the concentrated concussion and material damage would in like measure be enormous. . . . This needs no special equipment, no secret weapons, no elaborate training program. The element of surprise would be there for with so many apparently dud bombs falling the enemy would be confused.

Respectfully submitted and with a keen appreciation of the work you and the A.A.F. are doing.
C. H., Monterey Park, CA[41]

U.S. Senator Wayland Brooks
November 11, 1943

Dear Comrade:
. . . Briefly the aim is to employ multiple, vertically connected bombs, spaced so as to produce selected time intervals between the individual bomb impacts to produce a harmonic, horizontal motion in the rock substrata; in effect a local earthquake of increasing intensity and of the required duration to disturb industrial smokestacks,

chimneys, submarines or ships in dry dock or on ways, non-reinforced concrete or brick structures, turbo-generators and underground or mining operations. . . . By having the bombs strike thus, each successive bomb will penetrate into a deeper and deeper crater. The deepening explosive reactions will strike [with] increasing effectiveness to set up horizontal periodic movement of bedrock strata on which industrial buildings rest, and thus induce destructive critical shocks. . . .

Sincerely yours,
J. M., La Grange, IL[42]

Poor accuracy also limited the effectiveness of raids. *Reader's Digest* boasted that American bombers used "the tremendously accurate secret Norden bombsight, which virtually guarantees precision bombing from great heights. . . . [T]here is probably every justification for the boasts of American bombardiers that they can drop a bomb in a barrel from 20,000 feet."[43] Such accuracy existed only in theory. In real attacks, most bombs completely missed the target. As the *Chicago Tribune* explained, "When a bomb is released from a plane four or five miles up a factory covering a few acres is a tiny target. The smallest error on the part of the bombardier means wasted effort. The presence of enemy fighters and anti-aircraft fire do not promote accuracy."[44] These two writers submitted ideas to help bombs find their targets:

Chief of the Bombers
May 31, 1942

There is one point that is not generally known (which is probably all the better), and that I have never yet seen mentioned in connection with the dropping of bombs. I think that it is important that for accuracy in bomb dropping, the airplane should be traveling due east or due west at the instant the bomb is released. The reason is that an object dropping any considerable distance does not drop in a perpendicular line. It always strikes east of the perpendicular. Distance east depends on height from which it was dropped and direction in which plane is moving. I see mentioned a great many "near misses" and am wondering how many of the "near misses" strike east of the target. Probably most if not all of them do. This momentum that carries the bomb east of perpendicular is caused by the centrifugal rotation of the earth. It is greatest at the Equator and nil at the poles. And of course varying with the latitude. . . . You should have this all figured out and tables constructed according to different heights of plane and difference in latitude. If you have not already such data, it will pay you to look into the matter and have them prepared. I am taking chances on giving you a pointer that you may already have, because I consider it a very important point and not to be overlooked for accuracy, and that is what counts.

Respectfully,
E. A., Marshall, IL[45]

Associated Defense Committees [of Chicago]
[ca. 1944]

Dear Sir:
If the content of this letter does not come within the jurisdiction of your organization, will you please refer it to the proper committee. I am writing regarding a proposal by means of which it may be possible to eliminate or damage some enemy steelmaking capacity. While there are obvious limitations to the idea, there may be sufficient merit in it to justify further consideration. Scrap iron and steel are used almost universally in certain steelmaking processes. In countries hard pressed for sources of iron there probably is a continuous flow of scrap from battlefields and from bomb-wrecked structures to the steel mills. To utilize any appreciable tonnage of this material, it must be recharged into the smelting furnaces with only superficial inspection. I would propose, therefore, that together with the bomb loads released for the purposes of wrecking steel bearing structures, certain selected pieces of broken scrap should be unloaded. The type of scrap should correspond to that which would be produced in the demolition. These selected sections of scrap could be drilled and the proper high explosive charge inserted. The hollow section could be resealed, so that the charge could not be recognized. The explosive should be selected so that it would not discharge on falling to the ground but would explode at high temperatures. It would be expected that such scrap would be gathered up and distributed to steelmaking furnaces. The high temperatures needed to melt the scrap would cause the charge to explode. If the explosion were effective the steelmaking unit might be demolished. . . .

Very truly yours,
M. T., East Chicago, IN[46]

Both sides developed electronic guidance systems for bombs and rockets, but the most obvious way to make "smart" bombs was to put something intelligent inside the weapon itself. The twentieth century's preeminent behavioral psychologist suggested using animals:

National Inventors Council
March 17, 1941

Gentlemen:
. . . When the Nazis invaded the lowlands last spring, I began to think seriously about the old suggestion of training animals to direct marine, land, and aerial torpedoes, bombs, and so on. . . . The simplest case, it seemed to me, was that of a falling bomb. Here the animal has no need to control the acceleration and has only a minor amount of steering to do. (A moving picture taken by the Germans from a dive bomber has recently convinced me of the simplicity of this case.) It also seemed that the simplest animal for purpose was a bird. The vision of birds excels that of man in this kind of work, and they easily adjust to such changes in acceleration as would be involved. The problem, then, was this: Can a bird be taught to steer an apparatus in such a way that if the apparatus moves toward a field, it will strike a target placed in that field? . . . I succeeded in finding several means by which the bird could be taught to steer, both up and down and from side to side. I had no difficulty in training pigeons to operate this device and to hit the target consistently. . . . I see no difficulty at all in the construction of suitable bombs. I daresay the necessary steering mechanisms are already available. The bird would, of course, activate merely a set of small relays, and the actual steering would be carried out by some other source of energy. The bird could be installed before the flight in a small glass nose. . . .

Sincerely yours,
B. F. Skinner
Minneapolis, MN[47]

The next two writers proposed air-dropping animals to carry ordnance or to attack the enemy directly:

National Inventors Council
May 17, 1942

Gentlemen:
I wish to submit an idea for improving the effectiveness of incendiary bomb raids, particularly on Japan. I understand that only about 6% of the bombs dropped in the average raid actually start fires, also that if preparations are made to combat fires this percentage can be reduced still more, as was done in London after the first great fire raid. My scheme would I believe make a wider distribution of the bombs possible as well as the placing of each one in [or] under a building, lumber pile or other material where it would be much more effective than one dropped directly

from a plane. It would be in effect sort of a remote control for the bomb that would be provided in a very simple manner. The incendiary used should be small, such as the ones that were about the size of a fountain pen and used by German agents in the last war to secrete in the cargoes of ships to start fires at sea. The timing was accomplished in these by an acid that ate through a wall in approximately a desired number of hours. One or more of these bombs would be attached to the back or sides of a common rat with an inflammable fastening so that it would release itself as soon as the device ignited if it had not already been chewed off by the rat. These armed rats would be dropped by parachute just slow enough [so they will land] conscious. This would require a very simple parachute which could be made of cellophane to decrease visibility or of strong paper that would disintegrate after landing the rat. The rat would be attached to the parachute in such a manner that he would be released on landing so that he would be able to run for shelter encumbered only by the incendiary. He would immediately seek a hiding place under a building and probably start gnawing at his burden. If this could be made to release readily the rats would deposit the incendiaries in many inaccessible places that would usually be under inflammable material and give the fires a good start before they were discovered. . . .

Yours very truly,
F. T., La Crosse, WI[48]

Commander, Drew Field

My dear Colonel:
My friend, Mr. J. M. Lassiter of 107 East Park Avenue, one of the best informed men to my knowledge in the United States on honey bees, their culture, and habits, told me that he had an idea that several hundred bees encased in breakable containers dropped from an airplane would be more effective against an enemy squadron than a bomb because each bee would be a fighting instrument in itself to attack the individuals of the fighting squad. . . . Mr. Lassiter states that he can procure the bees and encase them either in crockery, glass jars, or paper if the latter will be weighted so as to drop quickly when thrown out of an airplane. . . . [Y]ou can appreciate the fact that a bee will be pretty damn mad after being thrown from an airplane and dropped through the air from quite a height. When he hits the ground, he will attack anything coming under his vision. Please give this due consideration and let me have your reaction at your earliest convenience.

Regards and best wishes,
J. W., Tampa, FL[49]

The next two letters proposed modifying bombs to increase their effectiveness:

[National Inventors Council]
[ca. April 1943]

Published accounts of the maneuvering performed by U.S. ships in order to dodge falling bombs make clear that the success of such dodging is in no small way dependent on the visibility of the falling bombs. It is the purpose of this note to propose that the crews of U.S. bombers attacking Jap ships should be supplied with "bomb envelopes" colored sky blue if the bombs are to be dropped under a blue sky, but colored soft gray-white if the bombs are to be dropped from an overcast sky. Suitable tests should be made to determine the sort of fabric surface and the precise colors which together will minimize the visibility of falling bombs as seen projected against various backgrounds. How effective change of surface texture and color is in decreasing visibility can be ascertained by anyone who watches a handful of squares of equal size cut from tinfoil, white paper and soft sky blue paper fluttering down from high up in the blue sky. Of course, the absolute minimum of visibility would be attained by using bomb cases of transparent plastic filled with a transparent liquid explosive, but no doubt this is impracticable. . . .

L. L., Columbus, OH[50]

[National Inventors Council]
June 29, 1942

Dear Sirs:
It seems to me that it would be very simple and practical to put headlights on bombs which would not only illuminate the targets that were being bombed at night, but would also allow the aviators to take pictures of the actual striking of the bomb. Here's the idea. Take the headlights, generators, and fans off all the old junk cars in America and attach them to the bombs. Attach the fan to the generator shaft so that the air pressure caused by the falling of the bomb would cause it to revolve, generating current to light the old headlight attached to the nose of the bomb. Can you imagine how the Jerries would feel with hundreds of search lights zooming at them from the sky. If it didn't do much good I believe it would have a bad morale effect on them. . . .

Respectfully yours,
H. T.
Los Angeles, CA[51]

This writer advocated gumming up enemy equipment:

Chief of Staff, War Department
June 2, 1943

Dear Sir:
May I suggest using a substance in bombs that will fuse onto railroad rails and
necessitate grinding them smooth before they could be used again. Believe such a
material is now used to spray on metal and wood surfaces at present. Such a bomb
would splatter its contents over quite an area and should be very economical to
make and do untold damage that would be much more effective than blowing
holes in roadbeds that can be quickly filled up and the few damaged rails replaced.
Would think that a small plane load of these bombs scattered at proper intervals
along the right of way would immediately put miles of rails out of commission—
very definitely—for a long period of time. Also such bombs would play hob
with the machinery in plants being bombed, as it would ruin finished surfaces
permanently. . . .

Respectfully submitted,
G. O., Philadelphia, PA[52]

This writer suggested a special bomb to hinder enemy troop movements:

National Inventors Council
July 19, 1944

Dear Sir:
I am writing to suggest a small whistling bomb, for use against the enemy in the
following manner. Consider a column of troops proceeding along a road. If one
of our bombing planes flies over, the enemy troops take cover and thereby lose a
certain amount of time. This loss of time is itself a costly matter to the enemy, and
the delay of a column might result in the loss of a battle in which the troops are
needed. Statistically, the enemy loses a certain number of personnel if he fails to
take cover, or loses a certain amount of time for the whole column if he does take
cover, and he will accordingly adjust his actions in such a way as to balance the
losses due to these two types of procedure, taking into account such factors as the
proximity of our airplane, whether it appears to be actually dropping bombs, etc.
Suppose now that in addition to dropping the regular fragmentation bomb we drop
a considerable number of small decoy whistling bombs which simulate the sound
of a fragmentation bomb in falling. A whistle could be designed which would give
a good imitation of the sound of a falling fragmentation bomb so that the enemy

would find it difficult or impossible to distinguish them. Such bombs might weigh only about 1/20 as much as the regular fragmentation bomb, and accordingly our aircraft could carry a very large number of them. The enemy column would be subjected to bombing, especially at night, by a mixture of fragmentation bombs and decoy bombs almost continuously. Every five or ten minutes or so the enemy troops would hear a bomb approaching, and not knowing which type it was, they would have to incur the loss of time due to taking cover or the statistical loss of personnel due to remaining out in the hope that the bomb they hear is of the decoy type. . . .

Very truly yours,
A. B., Washington, DC[53]

Pilots often had difficulty distinguishing friend from foe, prompting ideas for preventing fratricidal air attacks:

National Inventors Council
September 7, 1943

Gentlemen:
. . . I again explain my process of Improved means or methods of signaling the identification of ground troops to friendly airplanes and vice versa. My method is a secret signaling system which only can be deciphered by troops or planes having the decipherer, some kind of specific light filter. Helmets or other devices such as tanks, vehicles, cannons are to be painted in spectrally different colors which looks for the plain eye the same color as usually painted helmets. The aviator looking through the specific light filter will see the helmets in a different color. By means of this device troops in columns are able to identify themselves or to give signals to the aviator. In the latter case only a certain number of helmets are to be painted in a spectrally different paint. By arranging groups of different painted men the aviator will see dark and light or dark and colored spots giving him some kind of a morse-like signal. . . .

Yours very truly,
G. B., New York, NY[54]

The final year of war witnessed the introduction of revolutionary aerial weapons, including guided missiles. The *Saturday Evening Post* envisioned their future:

We can expect automatic flying bombs to have great range in the next war. They will be capable of coming from Europe to America, and will have a 5000-mile range, but no one would know where they would land because of the inability to compute variable winds. . . . Those best qualified to evaluate the buzz bomb say that its possibilities are unlimited. . . . They visualize as a reality a war in which gunners sitting at the keyboards of instruments resembling church organs will be able to fire salvos of buzz bombs from great batteries for thousand of miles. In short, they think that in the matter of H. G. Wells–Buck Rogers warfare the world is still in its infancy.[55]

This writer proposed using robot missiles against Japan:

Chief of Naval Operations
July 19, 1944

In the light of the recent developments of the jet propelled flying bomb and the practical uses which it has been put to as evidenced by the various reports from the European front, it has occurred to the undersigned that the flying bomb has not been fully exploited and that perhaps the Navy could make greater use of it especially when attacking an island empire. It is believed by the undersigned to be entirely feasible and not beyond the realm of engineering possibilities to build both surface and sub-surface rocket launching crafts. The size and shape of these launching crafts would naturally have to be commensurate with the military characteristics desired based on the tactics developed for such crafts. The missions of a rocket launching craft would be to position itself at some advantageous predetermined position some 100 to 200 miles from the enemy coast line where the craft could launch its cargo of jet propelled flying bombs onto any enemy large city for a complete and saturation raid of destruction. . . .

Maj. N. C., Ordnance Dept., Washinton, DC[56]

Few anticipated the most revolutionary development in strategic bombing, a weapon so destructive as to change the calculations upon which all previous plans relied. The atomic bomb precipitated the end of the war, and discussion of its implications took place against a very different military and political background. By the time Japan surrendered, strategic bombing had become synonymous with the American way of war. Whether adherence to the principles of air power would prove practical, or even sane, in a nuclear world, remained to be seen.

CHAPTER 10

Hit The Beach! Invasion and Liberation

B y late 1942 the Allies had blunted Axis attacks across the globe and begun to take the offensive. America would play a major role in liberating Axis-controlled areas, and U.S. commanders faced tough choices on when and where to strike. Allied leaders had already decided to focus on defeating Germany first, reasoning that Hitler's forces posed the most serious threat. As *The Nation* explained, "The Japanese would never have begun this war if Hitler had not won such signal successes in Europe; their only hope of averting a disastrous finish depends on the defeat by Germany of Britain and Russia. And contrariwise, if we lick the hell out of Japan but allow Britain to fall, we shall have merely exchanged a Japanese threat to our security for a much more serious German one."[1]

Just as in 1917, much depended on keeping Russia in the war. *Time* noted, "Russia must not be allowed to fall if U.S. aid can prevent it. Russia's fall would turn loose on Asia and Africa a terrific Nazi army, an army of millions of men, thousands of planes and thousands of tanks, an army big enough to fight on a 2,000-mile front—as it is now doing. . . . Hitler has to destroy the Russian army in 1942 or lose the war. And the U.S. has to keep Russia fighting or face a war that will be immeasurably longer and tougher."[2] Britain and America supplied war materiel and bombed Germany, but only a major offensive in Europe could divert Hitler's forces into a two-front war. The second front thus became the major topic of discussion regarding U.S. strategy.

The Nation, which for ideological reasons advocated aiding Russia at all hazards, proposed sending American forces to the Russian front: "An A.E.F. large enough to tip the scales of destiny should be conveyed to Siberia, there to effect at last a junction, in body and soul, with the armies of Russia. . . . [A]n expeditionary force, even as large as half a million men with the full equipment of mechanized warfare, can be conveyed to Alaska and from Alaska to Asia if our will grasps the

means."[3] This writer emphasized the psychological impact of sending U.S. troops
to Russia:

Chief of Air Corps
June 23, 1943

Dear Sir:
. . . May I say a few words about invasion? As I listen and read the news, I think
Germany is far more afraid of Russian vengeance than of the English or the
American variety. I think the collapse will come when Germany can feel and see
Russian vengeance pressing relentlessly nearer. This would terrorize women and
children as well as the men who love them. Allied troops and supplies could be
landed in a Russian port without the enormous cost of invading enemy territory.
Our supply lines would be long, but so would Germany's. We could thicken things
up by invading Italy at the same time action begins in Russia. It is Germany I'd like
to see invaded—not France or Belgium. Isn't the least costly way for us through a
Russian port?

Sincerely Yours,
E. W., Logan, UT[4]

Most Americans accepted that the Allies could best aid Russia by striking somewhere in Western Europe, and the media freely offered advice on where the landings should occur. In 1942 the Allies lacked the strength for an all-out attack.
Any invasion that year would have to hit a peripheral area. *The Nation* claimed
that Scandinavia offered the best target for a limited offensive: "Since our forces
should, by preference, operate near those of Russia and as far as possible from
the main center of German power, Norway is clearly the battlefield indicated.
Norway, moreover, offers numerous possible landing places distributed through
an area where scattered German garrisons are handicapped by poor transportation. A successful Norwegian campaign would also cut off much Kiruna ore from
Germany and strengthen Allied supply lines to Russia. It is, in fact, in Norway
that according to our 1941 plan we should strike our first blow."[5] A Scandinavian
campaign would also forestall an Axis connection across the top of the world:

To the President
[ca. April] 1942

Navigation will open in Spitzbergen in less than six weeks. If we get there first we
can drive the Germans out of northern Norway. If we don't put a stopper there, the

German bombers will cross the Arctic and join the Jap fighters in Alaska. . . . Lund and Navy bombers can be delivered Los Angeles–Prince George–Fairbanks (or Dawson), Akalavik, Elsmere, Greenland–Spitsberget to Murmansk. . . .

Sincerely,
E. S., Washington, DC[6]

The Nation added that the northern strategy could have diplomatic advantages:

Talk in London about a possible invasion of the European continent "on a limited scale" is making the Swedes extremely uneasy. Nowhere is there any real prospect of this kind of limited second front except in northern Norway. But an attack there, the Swedes fear, would be likely to put an end to their cherished neutrality and pitch them into the war. . . . [I]f Germany chooses to defend northern Norway it will have to make use of the Swedish railroad. That is why Sweden fears that if the United Nations choose this locale for their second front it will be confronted by a German ultimatum within a few hours. What will Sweden do in such circumstances? Considering the feeling that has developed among the people since the occupation of Norway, it is an excellent guess that Sweden will fight. . . . Thus the opening of a second front in Norway might well make Sweden a belligerent on the side of the United Nations.[7]

Another northern nation might also join the Allied camp:

President of the United States
March 25, 1942

Mr. President:
In connection with the second front in Europe I would like to express some ideas, which as I think, could be of some value to our honorable common cause. The purpose of the second front is to assist the Russian armies. Its importance especially emphasized in anticipation of great German drive against Russia in the spring. . . . [W]e cannot have more major setbacks now and in the near future. Psychologically and politically any major setback would be almost disastrous. Our crying need is success. Therefore we must have a plan of lesser magnitude but with better chance to put it through. I call it a military-diplomatic plan. It consists of the military and diplomatic moves in the northern Scandinavia. The first part of the plan incorporates a well known proposition to invade Norway. I agree with the idea that the northern territory of Norway should be invaded. Simultaneously a large and only American expeditionary force must be sent to Russia in order to replace

the Russian armies from the Ribachii Peninsula down to the south and to the Lake Ladoga, Gulf of Finland, and Leningrad. . . . If the American forces will occupy the front along all the Russo-Finnish frontier it is reasonable to expect that the Finns will quit fighting. They are fighting the Soviet[s] and became instrumental for Germany only because they feared for their independence. They are afraid of the fates of Latvia, Estonia and Lithuania. The presence of a large American armed force would eliminate this fear and the head of Finnish fighting armies Marshal Mannerheim would no more be able to persuade his soldiers to fight. Moreover, I feel that no single Finnish soldier would fire a shot at any American soldier. . . .

Very truly yours,
A. D., Beechhurst, NY[8]

Further strategic possibilities beckoned in southwest Europe. Spain and Portugal remained neutral, but the Axis had demonstrated that neutrality provided no shield against invasion. Iberia might offer a lightly defended "back door" into the heart of Europe. The *Christian Science Monitor* speculated that diplomacy could lead to a bloodless invasion:

There has been some talk lately to the effect that Portugal, which has a military alliance with Britain, might abandon its present policy of neutrality and invite the British onto the Continent via Lisbon. This long way round would have the advantage of offering a fairly safe landing out of reach of all but a few long-range Nazi bombers. The whole project would depend, however, on the attitude of Spain. Unless the Spanish also were prepared to throw in their lot with the Allies there would be no point to the scheme, and so far there is no reason to believe that Gen. Francisco Franco has changed his fundamentally pro-Axis views.[9]

This letter claimed the Spanish people would aid a southern expedition:

May 18, 1942

The demand for the opening of a second front in Western Europe in order to relieve the anticipated pressure upon Russia has already made a tremendously popular appeal in Great Britain and, to a lesser extent, in the United States. . . . It is the argument of this paper that if such relieving action becomes necessary the United Nations should open a new front by an attack through Spain. . . . The country as a whole is ready for revolt. A British, or more particularly an American, expeditionary force, landing suddenly at Bilbao for the purpose of opening a new front against Hitler along the line of the Pyrennees and, incidentally, of supporting a revolt against Franco, would be received with enthusiasm by a great majority of the people of Spain. . . . [T]he occupation of Spain would have the negative virtues of blocking an Axis move in the same direction. Gibralter would be secured, Portugal would be made a certain ally instead of becoming a possible base for enemy operations; German plans for the utilization of French Africa would be destroyed. One of the real advantages of an attack through Spain is the fact that it could never result in another Dunkirk. If the Allied forces find themselves too hard pressed in the fighting in the western reaches of France they can retire into the passes of the Pyrennes where they can resist indefinitely. Thence they can again sally out into the French plains whenever the German pressure shows signs of relaxing. The real point is, of course, that if the Germans detach enough troops from the Eastern Front to force an allied withdrawal into Spain, that in itself will be proof of the validity of the proposed strategic adventure. For Hitler would not detach enough troops and equipment to drive the Allies out of France without giving up all hope of defeating Russia.[10]

Unsigned

Although possible Iberian and Scandinavian campaigns prompted the most speculation, other potential targets merited discussion:

Department of National Defense
August 3, 1942

I just read an article in Sunday's *Arizona Republic* to the effect that the German war lords were in fear of U.S. and Great Britain opening a second front. That's the kink. To date Hitler has been able to check mate us in every move and with the help of the little yellow Jap has robbed the U.S. of 50 thousand of the finest men who ever lived in any country at any time. . . . Since our Government has already declared war on the unfortunate satellite victims of the Nazi fiends what is there to prevent Britain and U.S. from using Bulgaria as an entrance for the much talked of second front? That is the only spot in all of Europe where we would be close to Germany and have the added help of Turkey's two million bayonets. It burns me up to think that as soon as Hitler knocks Russia out he can hurl his whole force onto our one and last remaining ally and ground forever these precious weapons. Rumania and Hungary are right next door to Bulgaria and they have suffered so severely from the vile Germans in the last hundred years that they would gladly help us. Just look at the map and see how wonderful a place Bulgaria really is for a second front. . . .

[Anonymous]
Phoenix, AZ[11]

In November 1942 invasion speculation ended as Allied troops descended on Algeria and Morocco. After a six-month campaign cleared North Africa, questions mounted over where and when to strike next. Fascist dictator Benito Mussolini's weak regime seemed the logical target, but some believed an Italian campaign would lead to a strategic dead end. *The Nation* argued both sides. One article held that Italy offered an opportunity to engage German forces without undue risk:

> In the north any major Allied offensive, whenever attempted, would run into a continuous block of enemy territory stretching from the Pyrenees to Norway, an area served by a most highly developed system of roads, railways, and waterways, permitting the enemy to concentrate greatly superior forces at any threatened point in a minimum time. In the Mediterranean area, on the other hand, communications between the various sectors of the enemy's front line are severely limited, owing in part to the deeply indented coastline and in part to the paucity of means of transportation. Conditions are favorable for the isolation and capture of a large number of important Axis positions—Sardinia, Sicily, the Peloponnesus, Crete—by the judicious exploitation of Allied naval and aerial superiority. From the vantage-points thus gained it should prove not too difficult to extend the offensive to sections of the mainland and thus, step by step, to force the enemy back in a series of strictly limitable operations, without committing the outcome to a single, irretrievable action as would inevitably be the case in the north.[12]

Another *Nation* article reasoned that these same factors precluded the possibility of a decisive Allied victory:

> [Therefore] even a highly successful invasion would be inconclusive. For the Italian peninsula, which presents few serious obstacles of terrain to an invader marching up from the south, terminates in one of the most effective natural barriers to be found anywhere in the world. Germany could hold the Alpine passes with a small fraction of the number of men that would be needed to break through them. Thus an Italian campaign, valuable in its contribution to ultimate victory, is a strategic blind alley so far as getting directly at Germany is concerned.[13]

Allied leaders chose the Mediterranean option for 1943, but most commentators agreed these offensives were no substitute for a landing in France. Both dictator Joseph Stalin and the editors at *The Nation* remained dissatisfied. Both warned that delaying a full-bore attack risked serious consequences:

> The building of a large-scale American army started fully three years ago. For half that time we have maintained troops in Britain. Yet not more than half a dozen

American divisions were engaged in either the Tunisian or the Sicilian campaign, despite the fact that our High Command has deliberately chosen to make Europe the site of its greatest efforts. This is a miserable showing for a nation of our power and resources. . . . The policy of making cautious attacks around the periphery of Hitler's European conquests was wise at an earlier period of the war, but if continued today, when our growing military might makes more direct blows feasible, it will result simply in continued bad relations with our main ally, Russia, an unnecessary prolongation of the war, and disagreement at the peace table.[14]

As preparations for the second front accelerated, the New York Times reminded readers of the stakes: "Invasion of western Europe will be the consummation of years of planning and months of effort; it will shape the course, duration and outcome of the war; it will justify—or negate—all the strategy, all the planning, all the fighting that has gone before."[15] Newsweek added that a successful landing would all but guarantee victory: "The sole possible great victory that Germany could gain is the smashing of the much-advertised second front. All would now seem to depend on this operation. Should it be successful Germany's number is up and Russia, I imagine, will push on at top speed. . . . But should it prove a temporary failure—which is possible—then for the time being at least the Germans will once again be facing a single front."[16]

Until late 1943 commentary about the invasion of "Fortress Europe" centered around the strategic implications of particular landing areas. The actual process of getting ashore did not seem unduly hazardous. At Guadalcanal and Attu, at Oran and Sicily, amphibious landings met minimal resistance on the beaches. Then in November 1943 the Marines attacked Tarawa atoll, where for the first time the enemy attempted to defeat an amphibious attack at the water's edge.[17] Fighting behind fortifications, Japanese defenders took a terrific toll of the Marines struggling ashore through chest-deep water. The Marines lost a thousand dead to seize a nondescript chunk of sand and coral covering less than three hundred acres. News of these losses shocked the American public, as photos and newsreels showed bodies floating in the surf alongside wrecked landing craft.[18]

Newsweek lamented, "To take that fragment of coral, only a square mile in area, cost the Marines 1,026 killed and 2,557 wounded. In 76 hours the Marines had thus suffered 72 more deaths than in all their four months on Guadalcanal. The dead on Tarawa were only 429 fewer than the 1,455 Army men killed in the 38-day campaign for Sicily, big as Massachusetts."[19] The Tarawa slaughter cast a pall over preparations for the second front. Even The Nation admitted, "Landing on a heavily fortified enemy coast is one of the hardest of all military problems, and we must expect bad losses. Sea and air superiority give an enormous advantage; indeed, without them such an operation would be impossible. But as other actions have shown, they are not enough. The decisive step must be taken the hard way by individual infantrymen who, braving heavy casualties, overcome enemy defenses and hold off attack until artillery and tanks can be landed and can then spread out."[20] Casualty estimates in the press were enough to give even fervent second front enthusiasts pause. The *Chicago Tribune* noted, "[T]he war in Europe and the Pacific has moved into zones which the enemy must defend bitterly and which can be taken only by frontal assault. One well-qualified estimate is that it may cost 1,000,000 lives to breach the Nazi defenses and establish a bridgehead in western Europe."[21] *Colliers* explained that the landings in France would face even greater risks than the Tarawa force: "We landed about 5,000 men at Dieppe. Our casualties: 3,350. Our casualties at Tarawa (a comparatively small operation) were 3,500. It is an axiom of amphibious warfare that casualties increase relatively to the number of troops landed. If we land 200,000 men on our initial assault, we must expect well over fifty per cent casualties. If we land a million men, the percentage of casualties will rise sharply."[22]

News articles included detailed descriptions of German coastal defenses, known as the Atlantic Wall. *Fortune* reported as follows:

> [These fortifications,] built by the fabulous Todt organization, seem to have little resemblance to lines à la Maginot. There are no marvels of underground cities, and only few long-stretched interlocked construction of concrete and steel. The emphasis is on massed surface fire power. Concrete pillboxes (sometimes made of dug-in obsolete tanks) and dugouts are placed in strategic locations to provide safety for gunners during expected air-artillery bombing by invaders. Guns as big as fifteen-inchers guard vital ports; eight-inchers are installed at beachheads. Behind points of likely invasion, artillery is ready to bring massed fire on the beach. Every stretch of beach from Brittany to the Netherlands, say the Germans, can be swept by fire.[23]

Fears of massive losses prompted some to second guess invasion plans. The *Washington Post* quoted a senator who predicted the attack would produce "Another Tarawa on a huge and tragic scale," and "declared that, in his mind, an attempt to bomb Germany out of the war was still worth trying."[24] This letter warned of the strategic risks involved:

President of the United States
March 29, 1944

Before permitting possible tragic mistakes through land invasion of Europe I urge your immediate reconsideration of entire strategy upon which European invasion plans are based. Urge your particular consideration of the possible traps which could defeat our cause regardless of success, failure or stalemate of invasion itself. For your aid in such considerations I submit the following questions and facts: 1. Would not a large scale invasion of Europe now enable Russia to pull out of the war as in 1917 and leave America and England to face the full burden of German attack? In such case, will we face the possibility of our vast invasion army being held immobile as at Anzio and Cassino or pinned against the sea as at Dunkirk? 2. In case immobilization or disaster should befall our European invasion armies at this time, would not this enable both Russia and Germany to proceed with their current organization of Europe without participation by either America or England? . . .

J. R., Berkeley, CA[25]

Despite the misgivings percolating up from the public, Allied leaders remained committed to the invasion. Losses could be tolerated if, as at Tarawa, the attack succeeded. Preliminary bombardments would precede the landings, but at Tarawa the enemy's camouflaged fortifications survived the barrage intact. The *New York Times* warned against too much reliance on firepower: "The impression has grown up here at least that Allied bombers will be able to 'blast a path' through the defenses along which invading tanks and infantry will move without much interference in view of past Allied air efforts against shallower or less complete fortifications. This appears to be a dangerous overestimate of air power's effect and an exaggeration of its role in the coming combined operation, an exaggeration that the air generals deplore."[26]

German troops had camouflaged their coastal forts to escape bombardment, prompting this idea to pinpoint enemy defenses:

May 1, 1944

Gentlemen:
Here is one you may have considered before. If not it may be worth something. Why not take about 200 small craft, steered by radio, and start them across the Channel about 4 A. M. Let them go right on to the shore. The Heines [Germans] will not know it is a phoney and all their guns will come out. Your planes can

spot and attend to these and it will take some time to replace them. You may have landed and take them over before they are repaired.

An Oklahoma Country Boy, Oklahoma City, OK[27]

Newsweek published the following assertion:

[T]he use of gas would have enabled us to capture Tarawa almost without a casualty. If the tons of bombs dropped on Tarawa from the air had been heavy gas, of the mustard type, the island would have been so thoroughly drenched that in all probability not a defender would have survived. After four or five days, giving time for the gas to evaporate, the Marines could have walked ashore without opposition. In the end, every Jap on Tarawa was killed or committed suicide anyway, except a handful of laborers and a few soldiers captured while unconscious from wounds. But the victory cost us, in dead and wounded, several thousand of our most valiant youth. . . . To our enemies this is a war of survival or extermination, or was so long as they had a prospect of victory. Are we fighting it as such? Or are we, by an anachronistic devotion to the code of the duel, committing thousands of our bravest youth to avoidable death?[28]

The preparatory barrage could also include nontoxic gas:

Lieutenant General H. H. Arnold
December 22, 1943

Dear General Arnold:
The recent experiences of our fighting men at Tarawa and in Italy lead me to make the following suggestion for softening up such a situation. The so called "Liquified Petroleum Gases," propane, butane, and pentane are liquids or gases at atmospheric pressure depending upon their temperature. They are familiar to most persons as the "Bottled Gas" used by householders who live beyond the public service gas lines. One of the characteristics of these hydrocarbons is that their vapors are heavier than air. The Fire Underwriters require that a bottled gas installation must be located not less than ten feet from the nearest cellar opening, because if a leak should develop the vapor will flow down into the cellar like water. . . . It is my thought that if the landing at Tarawa had been preceded by a cessation of the bombardment during which time drums of butane were dropped on that flat terrain from the heights which would burst the containers when they struck the ground, the resulting vapors would have collected in the foxholes and pill boxes of the enemy. After some time, say an hour, bombardment with incendiaries could be resumed, if the flashes from enemy guns, lighted cigarettes, or other means had not

already ignited the vapor and driven their occupants out of their pill boxes so they could be dealt with by the various means which the fighting forces have available for that purpose. . . .

Yours very truly,
R. C., Boston, MA[29]

Any invasion force would have access to an unlimited supply of seawater, possibly useful as a landing weapon:

[National Inventors Council]
December 27, 1943

High pressure water systems should have several uses when applied to landing craft. Several craft . . . running roughly abreast, should screen themselves & following invasion craft from enemy observation and fire. Each invasion force should have enough of these craft to provide cover for each wave of landing craft. On reaching shore the high pressure jets could be used to uncover mines, excavate trenches in the beach for landing troops, demolish enemy trenches, uncover enemy pill boxes buried in sand, wash out & tear down foliage concealing enemy positions, blind enemy blockhouses, flood fox holes, disclose snipers hiding in trees, etc. . . .

J. H., Bridgewater, VA[30]

This letter advocated flooding enemy dugouts by amplifying a natural seaside phenomenon:

National Inventors Council
December 28, 1943

Dear Sirs:
. . . The proposal relates to invasion of coastal areas where the land is low and level and the command of the sea and air is complete. Such areas as are to be found on parts of the French coast, in Belgium, Holland, and some islands of the Pacific. It is proposed to lay a considerable number of lines of small depth charges parallel to the shore or in parallel curves with a common focal point not far inland. By exploding these, beginning with the outer and following with the others in carefully calculated sequence a wave can be built up of sufficient size to serve one or more of the following purposes. First: Destruction of enemy in pill-boxes if they exist near the normal shore line. Second: Floating landing boats over bars or reefs. By riding the crest to the most advantage boats might be left high on solid ground

by the receding wave. Third: Waves of sufficient height might in some cases be used to explode land mines if they were known to be planted very near the water.

Sincerely yours,
J. W., Lawrence, KS[31]

This writer suggested employing another seaside natural resource to screen an attack:

Representative Edith Rodgers
January 24, 1944

Dear Mrs. Rodgers:
First of all I want to thank you for your prompt reply as what I have for an idea has got to get under way right away. I have gotten up this idea for the purpose of making beachheads and am certain it will work most efficiently and will be the means of saving the lives of thousands of our boys. I am going to send you a drawing that I have made showing just about the effect it will have in action. It may seem like some wild dream but don't let anyone side-track [this] idea just because they think it is fantastic. This plan is to use some of our amphibian tanks and with a propellor on the top of the tank turning in reverse thus blowing sand, dust, dirt, smoke screens and gas if it comes to that in the face of our enemy. The idea is, of course, to temporarily blind them. The main use would be to make landings but it could be used to do many a big job. The men operating these devices would quickly discover its advantages. The tank would be equipped with everything to use going into combat including a rear platform to carry men to be ready as soon as it got ashore to shoot the bewildered enemy as the tanks advance, as you will see in the drawing. After one has had his face filled with smoke and nearly blinded for half a minute they have not got just what it takes to come out shooting, but our men will be ready the minute they appear in sight. . . .

Sincerely yours,
J. S., Georges Mills, NH[32]

No matter how fierce the bombardment, the defenders would soon target troops coming ashore. The invaders were most vulnerable as they left their boats and waded in through the surf. A patriotic advertisement captured the ordeal of the Tarawa attack:

We took the beach-head at dawn. Our destroyers stood out to sea and threw in the shells and our planes pounded hell out of their pill boxes, and then we came in . . . but the wind and the tide tricked us. The landing boats grounded off shore and we jumped over the sides and stood in the warm, shallow water and stared at the faraway beach and then at each other . . . and our eyes and our mouths were wide with fear as we waded in . . . and we fell under their guns like wheat to the blade of the reaper [ellipses in original].[33]

This writer suggested a method to clear underwater obstructions:

Commander in Chief, U.S. Fleet
September 10, 1944

The writer has seen a number of Pacific islands surrounded by off-shore coral barrier reefs where he thought it might be quite feasible to blast channels for landing craft through the coral heads and narrow sections of such outlying reefs by the use of ordinary naval torpedoes set to run at shallow depths and discharged from aircraft or torpedo boats. Coral is generally quite soft and friable. It seems possible that a considerable section of such reefs would be pulverized by an ordinary war head or that a special type explosive head could be developed that would give better penetration in the axial direction. . . . As envisaged in tactical use, the torpedoes would be delivered by a squadron of torpedo boats, destroyers, or planes, immediately in advance of the landing forces, with smoke from WP [white phosphorous] shells or from aircraft screening the shore batteries. Two or more torpedoes would be laid down in the same track where obstacles in depth are expected. Dye similar to that used in aviators' life jackets would be ejected from the exhaust of the torpedo or from torch pots to give a persistent wake for landing craft to follow and to mark permanently swept channels. . . .

Commander J. B., USN, USS *West Virginia*[34]

These two writers offered schemes to decrease the troops' vulnerability to enemy fire:

National Inventors Council
June 20, 1943

Dear Sirs:
. . . At present time, invasion troops are landed by invasion barges in which many troops are closely packed. This offers a beautiful, concentrated target for enemy artillery. I believe a more efficient method would be to have powerful out-board motor boats equipped with outboard riggers to which the proper number of tow lines are attached; these lines would have holding loops attached and be spaced at [a] proper distance. Troopers would put these holding loops about their shoulders and be towed thru the water by the out-board motor boat. The boat could be

armored and run right up upon the beach and serve as a protection barricade. The soldiers would be lightly equipped with a sack of grenades and sub-machine guns. As many as 200 could be towed by one boat. While in the water, they would offer only a dispersed target. Their steel helmets would protect their heads. . . .

Yours truly,
H. S., San Pedro, CA[35]

National Inventors Council
December 8, 1943

Gentlemen:
Having read the accounts of the invasion of Gilbert Islands and realizing that there will be many more islands to be invaded in the same manner, I propose the following sea camouflage: While the troops are disembarking from the boats, the time when soldiers make such an easy target from the shore, it is proposed to float from rapidly moving boats all along the invasion coast thousands of camouflage colored balloons the size and color of helmets. The balloons will be a temporary hiding and the decoys that will help to blend soldiers' heads with the surroundings and would thus help to avert concentrations of enemy fire on real targets. There is also a psychological advantage.

Very truly yours,
W. S., New Orleans, LA[36]

Land mines posed a further threat to the landings, turning beaches into potential death traps. Articles on the Atlantic Wall stressed the huge numbers of mines. *Popular Science* reported, "The beach itself is sown with land mines—the deadly Tellers to blast tanks and the terrible S mines which leap from the sand at the slightest touch and spray shrapnel at belly height. Literally millions of mines have been planted along hundreds of miles of beaches."[37] *Fortune* described a veritable universe of mines: "There are mines: mines offshore, mines on the beaches, mines beyond the beaches. There are belts of them miles long in front of defense lines, strong points, and fortified cities. Their function is to slow the invader, hamper the use of armored vehicles, and though only incidentally, to inflict casualties. Fire from other defenses sweeps over them."[38]

The Allies had mine-clearing methods, but these dangerously slowed operations. This writer proposed clearing mines with aerial bombardments of wooden blocks:

A Suggestion for Breaking Through Mine Fields
[ca. July 1944]

Light planes fitted with dusting tanks under wings or fuselage fly low over mine field[s], one behind the other, releasing white chalk or lime dust, marking the course of the projected break through. When the dust is exhausted in the lead plane's hopper tanks, the next plane begins to release its dust, etc. The marker planes are closely followed by cargo and transport planes, whose crew are rapidly tossing out large hardwood blocks with well rounded corners, along the marking trail. These blocks are about 15 inches square and have a saw finish, so as to retain a yellow chalk dust with which they are covered. These blocks leave a yellow marking where they hit and roll, indicating to following sappers that the spots covered by yellow dust are safe to walk in, while probing areas in the trail that have not been hit by falling or rolling blocks. Bombs have been used for this purpose, but it seems that the above described blocks would be cheaper and more effective. They could also be used over and over.

Respectfully,
C. M., Venice, CA[39]

These two writers proposed using aircraft to sweep mines or neutralize antitank obstacles:

National Inventors Council
December 14, 1942

Gentlemen:
The purpose of this letter is not to describe a new invention, but to suggest a new use for a weapon we already have. The weapon is the blimp. The new function is the clearing of mine fields. The idea is to have the blimp fly high enough to be safe from mine explosions, but low enough to be in contact with a ground crew. From the blimp hangs a strong steel cable which is attached, on the ground, to a special, heavily built harrow. The ground crew consists of (1) anti-aircraft men to protect the blimp from air attack, and (2) service men to repair and replace harrows. The blimp, of course, drags the harrow along the ground, exploding all mines in the path of the latter and opening a safe way for troops to follow. It seems to me that

this method of clearing mine fields is safer and faster than the present method. You, of course, are in a better position than I am to determine the merits of this new approach to a problem which will become more and more difficult with each new offensive of the United Nations.

Yours very truly,
A. S., Gabriels, NY[40]
Chief of Army Air Command
April 30, 1944

Dear Sir:
Obstacles constructed with millions of hours of labor can be nullified in a few hours by the Air Force, without bombing. The Command knows just where those obstructions exist, and knows just where those tanks and other war vehicles wish to cross. The [photos] show these obstructions to be less than five feet high, and a total cross section to be less than 100 feet wide, of course they will stop or hinder tanks. But the Air Force can make a fill at any spot desired by the tank command up to 500 feet wide in a few hours. Transport planes some ten or more have been equipped with dump door[s] in their bottoms, such as [a] gondola or dump or other type of coal cars. These are filled with brick bats, rubble, gravel from pits, and ordinary clay and sand, and are dumped at a desired spot ahead of the tanks, to a thickness and width that when tanks arrive they drive right over these obstructions. . . . After a beach head is established, the wreckage of wrecked buildings can be used for this purpose but before landing a supply should be established somewhere in England and loading facilities taken care of. Submitted without expectation of reward, I want to help in some way to save lives of our men.

Respectfully yours,
J. G., Washington, DC[41]

In a pinch, armies cleared mine fields by moving living creatures (animals, or even enemy prisoners) through them to set off the explosives. This letter proposed a more humane solution:

War Department
December 21, 1942

Gentlemen:
When I read this week about the difficulties which the German mine fields caused in Africa to the Eighth Army an idea flashed through my mind which I submit to you for examination. I think that it would be easy to build relatively small size self-propelling cars on tractors. The bodies could be filled with sand to give them

weight. The cost of these cars should be, in my estimate, not more than $50.00 each. The cars should be directed either by radio or else furnished with robot drivers. . . . The loss of large quantities of these cars which would be blown up in mine fields would be compensated sufficiently if these would eliminate the loss of lives and time. If you think this idea is of no value I am very sorry to have taken up your time.

Very truly yours,
A. J., New York, NY[42]

This writer proposed using animals to clear mined beaches on D-Day:

National Inventors Council
January 26, 1944

Gentlemen:
If this idea is any good it might save thousands of lives when our troops start the European invasion. It is conceded that the beachheads are almost impregnable with mines. Our experienced engineers can't remove them in front of our invasion forces and our troops will be exposed with lots of casualties. Let's turn loose thousands or a million hogs that are now jamming our packing houses onto the beachhead just prior to the invasion landings. These porkers will start rooting and fanning out into every nook and cranny setting off mine triggers by the thousands. The enemy will think the invasion has begun and cut loose with everything they have. They will waste lots of valuable ammunition and the reserves will start moving in—our planes can smash them while our troops are following the hogs a night or so later. These hogs can be landed with shallow barges and if necessary strap some kind of floater on them and let the tide help carry them on to shore. . . . Let's start the invasion with American swine and make it swine against swine. . . .

Yours very truly,
C. Q., Lookout Mountain, TN[43]

A human-animal team might avoid minefields that would stop ordinary troops:

Chief of U.S. Air Force
August 8, 1943

Your Excellency:
In the present war the greatest loss in time and casualties is taken in passing through the mine fields in front of the enemy's position. Now, as in all wars, the elements of speed and surprise are the most important. We already have the infantry of the

air—the paratroops, and I think it is time to experiment and develop a new branch of service—the air or glider cavalry. My idea is that a lightweight horse attached to a glider with a suspensory harness (similar to those used to load horses on board a ship) could provide the starting power for the glider. The cavalryman armed with an automatic rifle or tommy gun and hand grenades could traverse by horse-glider the five to ten miles of mine fields, land in the enemy's position or behind it, leave the glider, and take the position on horseback. This would also enable cavalry to jump over the enemy's front line for scouting and to return the same way. Both cavalrymen and horses should be selected of light weight. The horse shall be covered with light armor from below. It is not questioned that after preliminary training and exercise the horse will be able to land with the glider; the ability of trained horses to jump down is the best illustration of that. . . .

Respectfully yours,
B. L., Winchester, NH[44]

This writer believed animals could help locate hidden enemy positions:

National Inventors Council
April 10, 1944

Dear Colonel Lent:
After reading your article in *Liberty*, an idea came to me that is crazier than most, but might be worth your time reading anyway. One hazard of advancing troops, according to war articles, is locating enemy snipers, machine guns, etc. before they ambush our men from having the advantage of being quiet while our men are moving, thus seeing our movements before we see the blaze of their guns. . . . [S]tart a campaign to gather up all the unwanted alley cats and unclaimed dogs in dog pounds, or at least a sizeable contingent as a trial, and save American useful birds and sheep and young cattle, while making use of the cats and dogs to carry small charges of explosives towards suspected enemy locations, or perhaps a derringer shooting blanks, after a certain time, which would lead the enemy to think Americans were crawling towards them in the dark, and so snipe, or machine gun towards the cats or dogs, and thus give away their own locations to our men, so we would have the advantage. And anyone who says "that's inhumane, it would be better to have American boys shot down than the stray cats and dogs" would be un-American, and probably an enemy sympathizer.

J. C., Ottawa, KS[45]

Dogs participated in the war on all fronts. This letter proposed all-dog military units for the invasion:

[National Inventors Council]
[ca. May 1943]

May I suggest that, an organization on the part of the Army, of a battalion of German police dogs to be used in conjunction with our parachute troops. . . . Offensively, the dogs could be parachuted to earth prior to the troops and attack the enemy's ground troops, thus confusing them. In this manner they would be invaluable in a surprise attack in that they would be able to stealthily seize and hold artillery, anti-tank, or anti-aircraft guns until our troops landed. Using dogs in this manner would have its advantage in that it would reduce the loss of human life among the soldiers, because dogs present a smaller target; it would limit the number of men necessary to protect or seize an objective; it would harass the enemy while our troops picked them off, it would speed defense in that dogs are more easily transported, can move faster over rough terrain and are more economically kept.

Respectfully submitted,
T. B., Vestal, NY[46]

Perhaps the invaders could somehow bypass the beach defenses, as *The Nation* noted:

[T]he greatest advantage of helicopters, if we had them at the moment, might be in connection with an invasion of the Continent from England. . . . Even at their present stage of development helicopters could be landed at points one or two hundred miles in from the French coast, beyond the elaborate shoreline protections. Men could land from them, plant their time bombs or dynamite precisely where they could do the most good, gather information directly or from the native population, supply subject populations with bombs and arms, take back recruits, seize German prisoners from among the occupying forces. If the invaders found themselves outnumbered, they could leave quickly at a hundred miles an hour. And the invaders could come in great numbers. Helicopters with relatively small horse-power motors could be turned out with the speed of automobiles.[47]

The Atlantic Wall was too long to be strong everywhere, so secrecy and an intelligent choice of landing sites were crucial. This writer proposed landing on an unsuitable—and therefore unguarded—stretch of coast:

To Colonel Lent
May 5, 1944

It was suggested to me that certain points on the "invasion coast" might be considered by the enemy as most unlikely to be points of attack because they have a narrow beach with high precipitous cliffs. These cliffs are, however, of chalk like the cliffs of Dover. Due to the character of the chalk, suitable bombardment by Navy guns could be made to cause a collapse of the whole cliff—turning what was an effective barrier to invasion into a ramp up which tanks or amphibious equipment could drive. Incidentally, the resulting landslide would effectively bury any mines that might have been laid along the beach.

M. V., Washington, DC[48]

One group of Allied soldiers would bypass the beach defenses during the initial assault. Thousands of paratroopers were to drop inland to disrupt enemy movements. The *New York Times* observed that the invasion would involve paratroops "on a more massive scale than anything ever before attempted by any army. Air-borne troops—parachutists and transport-glider infantry—will constitute not just a menace to enemy communications, but a means of establishing a front behind the enemy's Atlantic Wall."[49] This letter described a weapon to give paratroops a ready-made fighting position:

National Inventors Council
August 19, 1942

Dear Sirs:
Some protection for parachute troops would be provided if each man carried a small crater-forming bomb—this bomb to be dropped from a certain height (to avoid injury from explosion) while [the] trooper is floating to earth. The shelter of a bomb crater might prove advantageous.

Very truly yours,
R. C., Lowell, MA.[50]

This letter proposed a ruse similar to one the Allies actually used to create confusion during the paratroop landings:

U.S. Army Air Forces
April 13, 1944

The writer submits plan which he believes would be of help to our armed forces. Purpose of plan: To draw a percentage of the enemy gun fire away from our landing forces at invasion time and to confuse the enemy. Plan: 1. At the time designated for our landing forces to invade enemy territory our bombers or troop carrying planes should fly over enemy territory. 2. At zero hour parachutes bearing dummies should be released in large quantities from an altitude high enough to take "X" minutes before enemy forces can recognize that the forms are not human bodies. 3. It is expected that the enemy seeing these para-dummies would think they are paratroops and would direct gun fire at these dummies. 4. Para-dummies to be released inland as well as near coastal guns. This may unnerve coastal gun crews and cause them to fire at dummies. 5. Surprise is most important element. . . .

Respectfully yours,
A. S., Brooklyn, NY[51]

The second front promised liberation for millions of Europeans under Nazi occupation. In return, the Allies expected these oppressed masses to actively aid the invasion. Press articles assured Americans that the resistance was active in the expected invasion zones. *Newsweek* reported, "From the northern tip of Norway to the southern tip of Greece, a vast international army of guerillas, saboteurs, and anti-Axis fifth columnists was in action, hampering production, wrecking trains, and blasting buildings."[52] Presumably the landings would spur the underground to mount an all-out effort at the critical time. Even the threat of an uprising would hamper the Germans' ability to meet the attack. This letter suggested a ploy to lay the psychological groundwork for an insurrection:

Director, Federal Bureau of Investigation
January 29, 1942

Dear Mr. Hoover:
. . . Broadcast to all the peoples of Europe, Germany as well as the conquered, that a day will be set on which all these peoples are to revolt in one grand concerted movement. Let us say that no such day ever will be set, that it is all a solemn bluff. Consider the moral effect on all the garrison armies of Germany of this sword of Damocles hanging over their heads, and on the German high command, even if it believes it to be a bluff. To put it very mildly, it would be at least a strong deterrent to withdrawing garrison troops from those countries for front line service. For even if

the [high command] is sure it is a bluff and counters by broadcasting to that effect, it knows damned well that some large proportion of the peoples involved will not take it as a bluff. And still back of this is the cold fact that a general and concerted revolt is the only kind they need hold in much fear. There is also to be considered the inspiriting etc. effect on the subject peoples. And here again the encouraging idea or dream of united and concerted action by all of them together as contrasted with the practical hopelessness of a detached or isolated national revolt. In short, it spreads and builds up, in both the conquered and the Germans, the idea of the one thing in this field that the Germans have most cause to dread. Which is a handy thing to have in operation even if it never gets beyond the idea stage. . . . But it is entirely conceivable that at some stage in the future such a day could be set with a warranting prospect of success. If things go well with us it becomes at least a very real possibility. Consider what this bluff will have done in preparing the way for that day. Instead of coming up before the peoples as a comparatively eleventh-hour proposition it will have been something they have been definitely thinking about, planning for and preparing for for months or years. . . .

A. H., Carmel, NY[53]

The partisans would need arms in order to help liberate their homelands. *Popular Science* predicted that by D-Day the Allies would have sent them millions of submachine guns: "When the signal is given, the enslaved peoples of Europe will spring to action everywhere. The compact, fast-firing, easy-to-operate Sten gun will kill many Nazis behind the lines while the Allied armies fight on the newly opened fronts. . . . Parachutes will drop the cheaply built Stens to the people's armies, along with the bullets to fire in them."[54]

Weapons for the resistance could only arrive by air, but the Allied Air Forces were tied up in the bombing campaign. *The Nation* suggested a special force of air-smugglers:

The conquered peoples of Europe constitute a vast untapped reservoir of military power. Ways and means of sustaining their hopes, of arming them, and of employing them in direct military operations when the state of Allied preparedness and Axis exhaustion permits an invasion of the continent of Europe should be one of the prime concerns of Allied grand strategy. . . . The airplane must be used to distribute most of the weapons, although the ability shown by the British commando parties to land at various points on the coast of Europe may suggest other ways of handling the problem. The places where arms are to be landed can be worked out with the advice of the governments-in-exile, which know the sentiments of the population. Since their distribution must not be allowed to weaken the military air power of the main Allied movement to which the whole plan is ancillary, non-military or obsolete aircraft and civilian pilots must be employed. There were some 17,000 certified private planes and 63,000 licensed civilian pilots in the United States on January 1, 1941. The number has increased since that time, and a civilian air corps of 20,000 pilots is in process of formation. This pool of non-military pilots should be able to provide the men required to fly ten thousand weapon-carrying planes into the occupied areas of Europe when the time for the invasion arrives. If each plane carried five submachine guns and from twenty to twenty-five hand grenades, the transportation problem would be solved.[55]

Firearms, no matter how numerous, do not make soldiers out of shopkeepers and secretaries. The next two letters contained plans for adding trained soldiers to the ranks of the underground in Western Europe and Asia:

Chief of Staff, War Department
December 7, 1942

. . . [N]ow [that] the American and other Allied forces are in Africa before the drive on France is made from this base, if it is possible, through confidential and undercover efforts be made to induce Marshall Petain to suggest to the Germans [that] the million prisoners (French) be freed together with other French soldiers in France armed by the Germans to apparently fight the Allies when they do enter France. When the Allies have landed in France, through underground sources, have the French turn against the Germans by secret command of Marshall Petain, who of course might be shot by the Germans but from what I know of the Marshall he would be willing to sacrifice his life, if necessary, for the cause of France. If the above suggestion was carried out the million prisoners now held in Germany would not be sacrificed. . . .

Respectfully submitted,
M. J., Rumson, NJ[56]

Commandant, U.S. Marine Corps
April 5, 1943

Dear Sir:
I know I'm no military expert and you will probably ignore this letter. I've heard how General MacArthur wants to retake the Philippines and I know every loyal American wants to see the heroic defenders of Bataan and Corregidor free. I know

the Marine Raiders can do nearly anything. So why couldn't they be sneaked ashore at night maybe free some of the captured Americans and form huge [guerrilla] bands in the mountains and jungles. The natives of the islands would join them and give them all possible aid. A band like this could do much damage and make it easier for MacArthur later. . . .

Respectfully yours,
T. T., North Arlington, NJ[57]

The Normandy landings marked the beginning of the end for Germany, but Allied victory did come quickly or cheaply. Six months of fighting brought their armies only to the German border, while casualties steadily mounted. As the advance ground to a halt, *The Nation* issued a somber warning:

> It must be stated flatly that what the Allied armies in the West are now fighting is a war of attrition, similar in its general outlines to the last war; and in a war of attrition one accepts heavy casualties with the understanding that the enemy's casualties are heavier and that he is less able to bear them. . . . Undoubtedly the Germans are less able to bear casualties than are the Americans—and here it must also be stated that it is indeed the Americans, not the Allies, who are bearing the brunt of the casualties; we have the manpower that England, France, and the smaller United Nations of the West so sorely lack. They stood their casualties earlier in the war, and we Americans must realize that it is now our own sons, husbands, brothers, and lovers who are proving that the Germans will fall first in a war of attrition. This is a hard realization to face.[58]

Growing battle losses and the demands of a two-front war stretched America's manpower supply. War plants required millions of men, and Americans wondered whether the country could provide enough for both front and factories. These two letters proposed utilizing untapped manpower sources:

Senator R. Alexander Smith
March 1, 1945

My Dear Senator Smith:
. . . It is my understanding that the Army is in need of several hundred thousand additional men between the ages of 18 and 30. . . . I know how seriously the drafting of these few hundred thousand men is going to cripple not only production in my own industry but in other industries on which we are dependent for materials and equipment. It is hardly necessary to state that the less abundant are our war

equipment and supplies, the more American lives there will be lost. That point has been made time and again by our military commanders. On the other hand, it is my understanding that the French have 800,000 men, some of whom have been trained and who have a keen desire to fight, but have not the weapons necessary to take an active part in the fighting. I am told that the reason for not furnishing them these weapons is that we would not then have enough for our own troops. In this regard, may I ask why wouldn't it be possible to furnish these men with arms and munitions first and our own men later if necessary? Couldn't the Americans wait in reserve while the French do some of the fighting as well as vice versa? Certainly it is their fight as much as ours. They can storm the Siegfried Line as well as Americans. Also we have a much better chance of supplying both armies if production is maintained at a high rate and not curtailed as will be the case if these relatively few men between the ages of 18 and 30 are drafted. . . .

Sincerely yours,
M. F., Bloomfield, NJ[59]

National Inventors Council
May 3, 1945

Gentlemen:
According to an article by Kaempffert in last Sunday's science section of the *New York Times*, one of the devices needed by the Army is something "which will enable a man to see at night without the aid of visible reflected light." I am writing to inform you that an arrangement for accomplishing this result can readily be made, for the use of certain specially selected personnel. There are many persons (unfortunately, chiefly in the higher age categories) who because of cataract, or sometimes trauma, have had the lens removed from one or both eyes. . . . Persons without a lens of their own but provided with spectacles made of quartz, fluorite, or other material transparent to the ultraviolet, are just about as sensitive to light in the near ultraviolet as they are to ordinary yellow light. . . . All that is needed, therefore, is to pick out persons who have had cataracts for the special scouting or other work required to be carried on in the dark, provide them with suitable spectacles and a lamp, flashlight or searchlight giving a beam rich in ultraviolet and which has the visible light filtered our of its beam by the appropriate type of "glass." . . .

Yours very truly,
H. M., Professor of Biology, Amherst, MA[60]

Beset from both east and west, bombed day and night, Germany eventually collapsed. When the end came, the Anglo Americans found they had liberated most of Western Europe. The second front had succeeded, and its success laid the foundation of U.S. strategy for the next forty years. What had been freed at such a price would be protected, even at the risk of nuclear annihilation. The troops would stay, and America's new military frontier ran through the heart of a divided continent.

CHAPTER 11

Red Hordes and Radiation: The Cold War Begins

Many Americans hoped that victory over the Axis would usher in an era of peaceful relations between the victorious Allies. Such hopes quickly faded as disagreements over spheres of influence unraveled the Soviet-American alliance. Doubts about the Russians soon hardened into an official view that Soviet communism threatened world peace and the United States. Thus, just as hostilities ended, fears grew of another ruthless power that espoused a worldview antithetical to American values, and which single-mindedly focused on global domination.

Even after demobilization, America retained its enormous industrial base, the world's largest navy, a reservoir of trained manpower, and most important, sole possession of the atomic bomb. Rather than match Stalin's huge armies, U.S. leaders relied on their ability to obliterate Russian cities if war came. This advantage would last only until the Soviets unlocked the bomb's secrets. The *Washington Post* predicted, "The chances are that as from August 1945, it will be at least five years before any nation other than England, which already has a good start, can be ready to make military use of atomic weapons."[1] From that point forward, however, America would face mortal danger. The *Los Angeles Times* quoted one expert who told Congress that "within 20 to 30 years a man might press a button in Russia and kill everybody in the United States."[2]

In an effort to maintain an atomic monopoly, U.S. leaders proposed the Baruch Plan, setting international restrictions on nuclear research. America would give up its atomic bombs only after the United Nations established a regime of inspections and controls. Predictably, the proposal went nowhere.[3] As *Time* noted, "Some plans to control the atom were good, some bad. None would work in the world of 1946. This dreadful fact was illuminated last week when the U.S. presented to the U.N. a proposal so reasonable, so technically sound that controversy over details subsided, leaving a dull, sickening realization that the best was not good enough. International atomic control was a right and necessary objective, but it meant possession of the atom by the great, illimitably sovereign nations which were divided into two camps, each distrusting and opposing the other."[4]

American leaders now faced a choice. Act quickly to maintain the monopoly by force, or acquiesce in the development of atom bombs by the Soviets. Some Americans supported using nuclear weapons to prevent a future Armageddon. Unbeknownst to the public, America's nuclear arsenal could never have supported such a plan. In 1946 the United States had only nine atom bombs, and only thirteen by 1947.[5]

Chief of Staff, U.S. Army
January 10, 1946

Dear Sir:

. . . General, it astounds me that we have not already taken positive action to control completely the atomic menace while we yet have the opportunity. The time is now far too short for further procrastination via world round table conferences, et cetera, et cetera. We must act now for the good of the world or lose everything. . . . On D-Day [the date plan will be put in action] announce to the world, after appropriate explanation of the then present status of atomic control that the United States has, as of that instant, assumed complete responsibility for atomic warfare throughout the world—that an ultimatum is issued to all nations that immediate action is directed to commence complete disarmament. That a time limit of two (2) hours be set for a reply of acceptance of such ultimatum from all major powers or, in lieu of such reply, the U.S. will direct immediate and positive actions by our Air Forces stationed throughout the world to bomb atomically that nation's major city or cities without further warning. If no reply is received one hour after such initial bombing, all major cities of that nation will be destroyed forthwith for noncompliance. That U.S. commissions be prepared for dispatch to all major countries to supervise complete disarmament to include the termination of all manufacture of any and all equipment pertinent to warfare. . . . The above plan is definitely not a plan that can be put before the people, or for that matter, before our national law makers. The plan calls for instantaneous action and the utmost secrecy. I feel so confident of its success, that once it is placed in operation, it will be consummated before public reaction sets in. By that time the operation will have been completed and the world will go to its knees in gratitude for the foresight exercised by the greatest country in the world, the United States of America . . . .

Respectfully,
Col. W. H., U.S. Army[6]

The United States might preserve its monopoly by controlling the key ingredient at its source:

Secretary of the Navy
June 20, 1947

. . . In the present state of the art of producing atomic weapons, uranium is essential. Thorium can also be used along with the essential uranium. For the foreseeable future it looks as though such weapons could not be produced without uranium. It follows that, as far as we now know, whoever controls the mines where uranium and thorium ores can be practically mined, can control at the source the materials needed for the manufacture of atomic weapons. If the United States commissions controlled these mines, then the United States, together with its friends and allies, could exert an absolute control over the manufacture of atomic weapons, and could thereby save the world from otherwise certain warfare in which these weapons would be used by all major contestants. . . . The diplomatic and military task of the United States in the immediate future therefore requires devotion to the task of getting the essential strategic allies so as to be able to bring overwhelming force to bear, where required to prevent or overcome resistance, in order to establish a control of the uranium and thorium mines of the world. . . .

H. H., Armonk, NY[7]

Although nuclear weapons threatened global devastation, some viewed the bomb as a tool in humanity's struggle to control the environment. The *New York Times* proposed these uses of atomic weapons:

Explosives are important in peacetime. They blast the foundations for city skyscrapers, they loosen the coal and ore in our mines, they make it possible to tunnel through mountains, to dig canals which join oceans and irrigate deserts. If one small atomic bomb could flatten a city, what about using atomic explosives to blast the long-sought sea-level canal across Panama, or to improve the climate of the Sahara Desert by letting in the waters of the Mediterranean Sea?[8]

These two letters proposed other peaceful uses for A-bombs:

Navy Department
March 4, 1946

Respectfully suggest you consider changing locale of pending atomic bomb tests from Bikini Atoll to Greenland where, in my estimation, bombings opening up mountainous copper deposits would be of tremendous practical value to our country. These mountains of copper discovered by my friend, Captain J. G. Bernier, years ago still await development. Use of atomic bomb to plumb rich mineral deposits in icecaps would be valuable peacetime application of atomic energy. Happy to discuss further and provide detailed data.

Sincerely,

J. H., New York, NY[9]

March 14, 1946

Dear Mr. President:

Items in the current news such as the proposed atom bomb tests on 90 ships and the recent airplane crash against a mountain peak prompt me to write this suggestion. Instead of wasting bombs on ships from the salvaging of which many tons of steel could be saved, why not use some bombs on those dangerous mountain peaks throughout the country that are in the path of the airliners. It would save many lives in the future and perhaps allow some of the Pacific coast rains to fall inland where the desert area is now. I have the honor to remain,

Respectfully Yours,

C. R., Chicago, IL[10]

This writer proposed using nuclear blasts to protect the Gulf Coast from hurricanes:

National Inventors Council
October 19, 1945

. . . [T]here should be carried out research to determine whether it is possible to prevent such an accumulation of energy over the Gulf of Mexico (and adjacent waters) by initiating upward air currents of the Gulf, and especially in a belt of the order of 200 miles along the coast. If such a belt could be given a "land type" stratification of the atmosphere by bleeding the energy in the lower atmosphere during the hurricane season, from late July to the end of September, then the tropical hurricanes would blow themselves out harmlessly over this strip of water just at they now blow themselves out over land with destructive effects on the coast regions. The "bleeding" could take the form of a large number of small, manmade cyclones, initiated by the release of atomic energy (heat) at suitable levels of altitude. Probably a number of explosions staggered vertically would be the most effective. . . . [I]f the militarists in a potential totalitarian aggressor nation realize that their own engineers and physicists need between 5 and 6 years to solve the same problems which U.S. engineers and physicists master in 2 or 3 years, then they may well postpone their plans of aggression.

Very truly yours,
F. V., Houston, TX[11]

While the United States sought to control nuclear know-how, it conducted bomb tests at Bikini Atoll to gauge the effects of this new weapon. *Newsweek* reported one Yale professor "feared that the underwater bomb would blast a crack in the ocean floor. Water rushing into the crevasse might come in contact with molten rock, he wrote, setting off explosions that would create waves a mile or more high moving at high speeds. [Prof. H. S.] Uhler further warned that the explosions might upset the gyroscopic balance of the world, setting off earthquakes and catastrophic shudderings of this sorely stricken human carousel."[12] This letter warned that an underwater test might set off an uncontrollable chain reaction:

Secretary of the Navy
July 11, 1946

Dear Jim:
Supplementing my recent letter to you, I now learn that Professor Kistiakowsky of Harvard thinks that if there is any danger of a chain reaction from the next experiment in connection with the atom bomb, it would be just as bad even in a small lake as it would be in the ocean, and he believes that if the proposed test is made, it should be carried out in nothing bigger than a tank containing at the most ten or twenty tons. . . . The more I think about it, the more I am convinced that the experiment should not be held until there has been a safe test. With best personal regards,

Very sincerely yours,
C. W., New York, NY[13]

The Bikini tests measured the bomb's effects on military units exposed to the blast. *Time* commented on the tests:

[T]he ships in Bikini Lagoon will be manned by "guinea pig" crews: 200 goats, 200 pigs, 4,000 white rats. They will wait their fate in the same positions which a human crew would occupy in battle stations: rats in the turrets, on deck, in engine rooms, gun-tubs and bridges. The goats will be tethered among them. . . . After the blast, the goats, pigs and rats will be collected and rushed to the U.S.S. *Burleson*, a transport equipped to house them. There, medics will study the effect upon them of the deadly gamma rays.[14]

This writer suggested a plan to measure the secondary effects of nuclear radiation:

Assistant Secretary of War
January 31, 1946

Dear Sir:
Believing the War Department does not wish to overlook one single thing of value during the proposed atom bomb experiment, the writer ventures to make the following suggestion which could be overlooked and which should be of great interest. Have live animals such as goats and rabbits placed in bomb range and feed them to dogs after the bombing—canning some for later tests—to see what effect such food will have upon any animal consuming such food. Collect fish killed in the test and feed to cats—canning some for later tests. The idea, of course, is to ascertain whether animals or fish suitable for human consumption could be so utilized after an atomic bombing. The idea of canning (or preserving) such food for later consumption is, of course, to ascertain whether a delayed consumption of such food would change its food value. Various kinds of preserved foods in tins and glass containers might also be tested. The idea of such tests is obvious.

Respectfully submitted by
A. P., El Paso, TX[15]

In 1949 two events radically changed the strategic balance. Communist forces overran China, and the Soviets exploded an atomic bomb.[16] The next year troops from North Korea (the Democratic People's Republic of Korea) invaded South Korea (the Republic of Korea), and America intervened. When the war began the Soviets had about two dozen A-bombs, and the United States more than two hundred. Both sides restrained themselves to prevent an atomic exchange.[17] Fortunately for the world, though not for the Koreans, the peninsula provided the perfect setting for a limited war. Open on the south to the U.S. Navy and bordered on the north by China, Korea became an arena where, by observing some simple rules, the opponents could pummel each other unmercifully without setting off a nuclear holocaust.

American troops had difficulty distinguishing between North Koreans and South Koreans, while enemy soldiers often mingled with crowds of refugees. These two letters proposed ideas for identifying disguised enemies:

Secretary of Defense
August 3, 1950

Dear Sir:
The tactic used by the North Koreans (and by the Germans in the Battle of the Bulge) of wearing American uniforms to confuse our forces leads me to suggest the following method of defeating it. Place concealed loudspeakers a distance in front of our lines to be determined by experienced tacticians. Let orders in the language of the enemy be given over these speakers when soldiers in American uniform approach. If they are actually the enemy, their reactions will give them away. For example, a shout of "Heil Hitler" given over such a system in the Battle of the Bulge would have uncovered the Nazis masquerading in American uniforms. When we counter attack, loudspeakers carried on tanks or other vehicles could be used to give the enemy confusing orders. Let us fight deceit with deceit. I'm sure your tacticians and technicians can amplify and apply this idea better than I can. I trust that the foregoing will help our cause.

Sincerely yours,
H. E., New York, NY[18]

[The President]
July 31, 1950

Why couldn't we put [on] some kind of tattoo mark that the North Koreans couldn't copy. Then if you see someone that's suspicious you could look at them and see if they had the mark on them. You may have tried that already but I'm just trying to help. . . .

Yours truly,
B. B., Rye, NY[19]

After a few months a U.S. counterattack smashed the North Korean army and opened the entire peninsula to conquest. Another American triumph seemed at hand. The *Los Angeles Times* predicted, "Whether the Korean war, now vigorously and victoriously prosecuted in the immediate vicinity south of the Communist capital of Pyongyang, will soon enter the final stage or will degenerate into a longer and tedious guerrilla warfare, the prevailing impression among observers of the Far Eastern picture is that Soviet, as well as Chinese Communists, have obviously written off the whole business as an unfortunate gamble."[20] A month later swarms of Chinese "volunteers" swept down from Manchuria. American troops now faced an enemy with limitless manpower reserves. Headlines spoke of "Hordes of Chinese" rolling south, or of a "Million Reds on Heels of UN Retreat."[21] Chinese armies took enormous losses without faltering. The *New York Times* made this argument:

> [M]ounds of dead and seas of blood have far less effect upon Oriental psychology and Chinese Communist determination to achieve an objective than upon our own; the enemy tactics are based upon the "human sea" or mass assault and heavy casualties are an anticipated part of the price of victory. . . . An army built around such tactics "keeps coming"; heavy casualties are no deterrent to its drive. When it stops it may stop because it has run out of supplies, or ammunition or weapons, or temporarily of men. But men, we should always remember, are the cheapest commodity of the Orient.[22]

The *Chicago Tribune* noted, "Mao is the only military leader who can afford such losses. He has more than 5,000,000 men under arms. They cannot be demobilized because there is nothing for them to do in overcrowded China. The loss of one or two million such men actually would improve China's economic position by conserving its scanty food resources."[23] These two writers proposed special weapons to break Chinese human waves:

The President
March 1, 1951

Your Excellency:
As my former commander-in-Chief (I am an honorably discharged captain Reserve Corps of Military Police) am taking the liberty of imparting to you directly an idea for psychological as well as effective exterminating power against Chinese Commies. Since bayonet fighting by our boys has been so effective against our enemies and from their fear of cold steel, my idea is to have long extended revolving steel blades on the front of our tanks. I believe our engineers and ordnance experts can arrange to have them revolving in synchronized fashion such as propellers in planes with the machine gun bullets firing between the blades. Also equip the tanks with terribly screeching sirens. These would be very effective in their mass suicide

attacks and put the fear of God as well as our power in them. Respectfully and may God give you the power to carry on. Admiringly,

C. S., Newark, NJ[24]

President Truman
January 3, 1951

Dear President Truman:

. . . With the tremendous amount of Chinese being thrown against our troops, even with the toll we are taking they still keep coming and we are outnumbered not by just 10-1 but by about 40-1, knowing how staggered our defense lines are set up. Please sir, consider this plea! For the men at the front—can't we put into rapid production "flame throwers." When we used them on Okinawa it really sizzled things up to almost a hundred feet away. For those hundreds of Chinese rushing our boys with no regard for their lives we could annihilate thousands more than we are now and we could also hold our lines until they expend hundreds of thousands and give us our chance to see what "Uncle Joe's" boys are going to do. . . .

Thank You,
W. B., Zanesville, OH[25]

Eventually U.N. forces held, as U.S. planes provided vital battlefield support and hindered Chinese efforts to move troops and supplies south from the border. American firepower counterbalanced enemy manpower, while the massed Chinese provided lucrative targets, as these two letters suggested:

President of the United States
December 5, 1950

Dear Sir:

. . . I believe we can kill or wound every Red in Korea in a month or so with my plan. I sure hope and pray that you will use my plan so we can save our boys in Korea. My plan is: Take 100 flying box cars or C-97s that carry large loads. My plan is to dump crushed rock on them, not larger than a pound each. When the enemy gets hit with a rock falling half a mile or 2,000 ft. it has a lot of killing power. The enemy won't have much fight left with broken arms, legs, bruised back or fractured skull. You see a ton of rock has 2,000 pound pieces just think 100 planes with 2,000 pieces each what a destruction that would be, and if they are sowed like hailstones over the enemy at night they can't dodge them. . . . You see the thicker the enemy bunches up the more killing power you have, that is just what you want them to do when they try to go through your lines. . . .

Sincerely yours,
H. W., Seattle, WA[26]

Army Chief of Staff
December 7, 1950

Dear Sir:
Please permit me a suggestion. I don't know whether this has been submitted previously, or whether it is feasible. In this emergency, if we have enough bombs, why don't we use what we have. Suspend commercial air line flights temporarily, and send the planes to Japan and Korea. Let them be used to drop bombs on the enemy. With such hordes in the field, the bombs would be sure to find a mark, even without pin-pointing. Round-the-clock bombing could make them lose the will to continue fighting. Don't mean to presume, but as I thought about the above, it seemed to make sense in this situation.

Respectfully,
M. A., New York, NY[27]

To counter U.S. air power, Communist commanders emphasized nocturnal operations. *Time* explained, "Probably no soldiers on earth really prefer fighting at night, but the Chinese and North Koreans have good and obvious reasons for avoiding daylight assaults. The U.N. artillery, close air support and air observation function best by day. At night it takes about 20 minutes for star shells or a flare plane to illuminate a combat area, and this time is valuable to the furtive Reds."[28] This writer proposed a means to target the enemy after dark.

Secretary of Defense
April 30, 1951

Dear General Marshall:
It seems most of the fighting in these days is being done at night. I suggest that proper thought and research should be given for the use of luminous spray on men and equipment of the enemy.

Respectfully,
J. B., Chicago, IL[29]

Korean rivers played a significant role as military obstacles. They often formed the only clear demarcation lines in a countryside filled with nondescript hills and valleys. Red forces attempted to conceal their bridges from U.S. aircraft. The *Christian Science Monitor* published this report:

> This maneuver was effected through the employment of a typical Soviet engineering device known as the underwater invisible bridge. . . . [This is] a crude but effective suspension type made of logs one foot in diameter lashed together with steel cable. Under cover of night sometime last week, one end of the bridge was secured to the west bank of the Naktong while the other end was taken across and secured to the American-held side. Weighted down with heavy stones, the bridge traverses the river roughly a foot underneath the surface. Infantry, tanks, and self-propelled artillery already have crossed over the bridge which cannot be seen from the air because of the muddy Naktong River water.[30]

This letter proposed a method to locate sunken bridges:

> War Department
> August 16, 1950
>
> Ought to be comparatively easy to design floating flags that would snag on underwater bridges to mark location of same for benefit of bombers. Calculating flow of river same could be dropped by plane and timed to arrive as bombers are overhead.
>
> L. C., San Francisco, CA[31]

During the winter, frozen rivers aided Communist attacks. The *Los Angeles Times* revealed, "[T]he Yalu River has frozen solid, permitting untold numbers of Chinese reserves to cross over the ice."[32] These two letters contain suggestions for preventing such crossings:

> Army Chief of Staff
> January 4, 1951
>
> Dear General Collins:
> From accounts in the news I understand that the Chinese in Korea are able to employ or exploit their numbers so effectively because of the frozen rivers over which they are able to cross at any point. One way in which what rivers remain in our hands might be rendered unfit for their use should it be necessary for us to

retreat behind them is through the use of lamp black. This black substance spread upon the ice at all places our forces could not guard would melt the ice because of its heat absorbing properties. Sunlight, of course, would be required for it to act. This method of melting ice has been seriously considered in recent years as one method of getting a few more weeks of navigation in the Great Lakes.

Very truly yours,
C. B., Ypsilanti, MI[33]

Army Chief of Staff
December 2, 1950

Dear General:
If study has not been given to the suggestion I make below, I respectfully suggest that such a study be hurriedly made. It seems that our troops will be south of the Chongchon river by the time that action could be taken in keeping with this suggestion. Therefore, all troops crossing the Chongchon at night can militarily be assumed to be Red, and we should like to destroy as many as possible, and to keep the others from reaching the southern bank. Small cans, possibly holding 5 gallons each of oil or gasoline, and other holding napalm are dropped from planes about the middle of the stream. These are dropped one to each 50 yards. Such spacing would mean only 35 to the mile, or 350 to each 10 miles of river. . . . Some results that seem to a layman to be quite sure: a. Red troops would be greatly disconcerted in an attempted crossing; organized systems for crossing would be demoralized. b. The river itself and to some extent both banks would be illuminated. Fighter planes and bombing planes flying overhead could follow the course of the river more easily and their firing and bombing would be more accurate.

Sincerely,
P. M., Sardis, MS[34]

As Red armies pushed south, their supply lines stretched hundreds of miles from China to the front. The Air Force tried to disrupt movement along these supply routes, but the *New York Times* reported, "The Communists have thousands of trucks and utilize them chiefly at night, when air power's limitations still are major and our attacks relatively ineffective."[35] The *Christian Science Monitor* noted an innovative tactic:

The Fifth Air Force has unveiled "Operation Tack." Pretty sharp idea, too. Planes range along the roads behind Communist lines and drop nails. Millions of nails—

stubby, flat-headed, one and one half inches long. The kind you use to lay asphalt roofing. The purpose is to flatten Communist tires, especially the tires of supply trucks that move in the night. . . . The trucks run over the nails and the nails puncture their tires. That halts the convoy. The only way they can keep going is to get out and pick up all those nails.[36]

The Chinese quickly responded, affixing large brooms to their trucks to sweep the roads clear of nails.[37] This writer proposed a variation on the nail-dropping plan:

[Secretary of Defense]
August 25, 1950

Dear Mr. Johnson:
I am an old oil monkey 75 years of age with an idea to end or seriously block the war in Korea. My plan is as follows. Fill 5 gallon cans with heavy oil from which the gasoline content has been removed by refining. These cans to be dropped by airplanes on the highways in Korea every 300 feet. Traction will be affected—all cars and tanks will come to a stop. The drivers' shoes will become saturated with oil as well as their hands and it would be impossible to operate a machine under these conditions, I know. The operation would be inexpensive and almost as good as the atomic bomb, and anything but cruel. I have not mentioned my idea to anyone. Don't think me presumptive in writing you.

Very sincerely,
C. T., Long Beach, CA[38]

During the 1940s the government had studied methods for producing rain. The Los Angeles Times noted, "[F]ighting forces may achieve victory by commanding the weather. . . . So if a general has absolute control over weather he should be able to bring defeat on his enemy by blinding him, by grounding his aircraft, by halting troop movements with washed-out bridges and impassable roads."[39] This writer suggested enlisting the Korean weather as an ally:

Army Chief of Staff
December 8, 1950

Dear Sir:
. . . We have suggested to General Wedemeyer, and wish to pass on to you the suggestion of further consideration of use of modern technique for the making and control of rain to hamper and delay and disrupt enemy supply and transportation. We know this technique has been highly developed in the last few years in a very

effective degree. . . . With enemy transportation operating over rather primitive highways and railroad facilities and over long stretches of country in both northern Korea and Manchuria, and with cloud conditions as reported there, it would seem that this technique of rain-making with resulting floods and snow packs could be used to create overwhelming obstacles at reasonably safe distances from our own areas of operation. The operation could be undertaken with a minimum of supplies which could be flown from this country to the combat area in a matter of hours. We believe this operation could be undertaken over Manchuria and Red China without the general alarm or criticism which would follow any attempt to bomb strategic points, and we strongly urge the careful consideration of this move over enemy territory, including Red China territory.

Yours very truly,
L. B., Oakland, CA[40]

By early 1951, the two sides had reached a stalemate. Each powerful alliance could throw enough forces into the narrow peninsula to prevent the other from breaking through. For the first time in more than a century, Americans would have to settle for something less than victory. The *Washington Post* published this lament:

It is sad but true that no good solution is now possible in Korea. The high objectives which the General Assembly proclaimed in the resolution of October 7—namely, "the establishment of a unified, independent and democratic government of Korea"—are not attainable. The best that can be had now is an armistice at the old frontier of South and North Korea, at the thirty-eighth parallel. It is also the least that the United Nations can accept. An armistice in the middle of Korea would amount to a recognition by both sides that Korea cannot be unified in a limited war.[41]

U.S. News and World Report noted that the change in U.S. military objectives meant the following:

[T]he strategy unfolding in Korea is one of attrition. It is not to put in big new forces and try to conquer hordes of Chinese. Instead, the idea is to use present U.N. strength in Korea to whittle down Communist forces committed there. Enemy losses compared with U.N. losses have been in a ratio of nearly 10 to 1 thus far. That, over a period of time, could be a high price for Communist forces to pay. It will force the Chinese to use up weapons and equipment that must be in limited supply. It will force a sacrifice of masses of skilled soldiers from Red China's best divisions. Replacements for wrecked equipment then would take weapons from Russia's war arsenal, while replacements for Chinese casualties could lower the enthusiasm of Chinese forces for fighting the West."[42]

Many Americans questioned the wisdom of engaging in a war of attrition with China. The *Wall Street Journal* put it like this:

Let us suppose that we attain General MacArthur's objective and kill countless thousands of Chinese at the cost of only a few tens of thousand of Americans. What have we gained thereby? . . . Quite apart from morality, to kill Chinese is not an objective worth the price of the Americans who must also be killed. And until the questions are answered as to what lies beyond there will be the grave suspicion that there is no objective beyond. This would be a blunder worse than a crime. For thus we will fall into the trap in which Asia has engulfed so many peoples of the past, the trap of sheer mass which the killing of plagues, disasters and wars all combined have not sufficed to dissolve.[43]

With victory impossible, perhaps a withdrawal made sense:

President Harry S. Truman
May 21, 1951

My dear President Truman:
Because of the cost in lives and material of the Korean Invasion, I have offered the idea to the Honorable Howard W. Smith, representative in the House, for the withdrawal of our troops. As that country is impoverished, I offer the idea of transporting the entire population to America, and rehabilitating them here. There is enough unclaimed land and resources in America to take care of people who will volunteer to be removed from that Communistic zone. This could be done at far less cost to our Government than the prosecution of the war. Thanking you for any consideration shown to the above purpose.

Most respectfully yours,
J. B., Catlett, VA[44]

Once Americans realized that conventional weapons could not break the stalemate, arguments supporting the nuclear option began to surface. During the Chinese offensive, President Truman created a political storm when he publicly refused to rule out using atomic weapons. The crisis prompted this writer to propose revamping the national command system:

December 27, 1950

Dear Mr. President:
I am enclosing a copy of a letter just written to 26 of my friends in the Senate and 19 in the House. I do not know whether or not my suggestion will receive consideration or deserves any. I do want you to know, however, that the spirit in making it is one intended to be helpful to you rather than to in any way embarrass you. As I have indicated in my letter to the Senators and Congressmen, I doubt that any one man—past, present or future—can be expected to carry single-handed the responsibilities of the present times. . . . I suggest: 1. That the 82nd Congress enact a law early in the session which will create a bi-partisan National Emergency Council for a twelve month or longer period, composed of the President of the United States and ten others nominated by the President and subject to the confirmation of the Senate. 2. That all presidential war powers, including use of the atomic bomb, be the province of the Council, with the President obligated to follow the determination of the majority. 3. That the members of the Council give such service their prime attention for the duration of the emergency (or as long as Congress continues the Council). 4. That failure on the part of the President to completely utilize the Council, as provided by Congress, would be construed as neglect of duty and make him subject to impeachment. . . .

Earnestly yours,
F. B., Seattle, WA[45]

This letter from the father of a future vice president proposed a nuclear scorched earth policy:

President Truman
April 14, 1951

My dear Mr. President:
. . . Korea has become a meat grinder of American manhood. Military authorities, including Gen. Ridgeway, have said that under present policies a conclusive military victory is impossible. We must recognize that under present policies our Communist foes have the capacity, what with geographic and human preponderances in their favor, to continue this meat grinder operation indefinitely. . . . Something cataclysmic, it seems to me, is called for. We have it. Please consider using it. . . . After removing all Koreans therefrom, dehumanize a belt across the Korean Peninsula by surface radiological contamination. Just before this is accomplished, broadcast the fact to the enemy, with ample and particular notice that entrance into the belt would mean certain death or slow deformity to all foot soldiers; that

all vehicles, weapons, food, apparel entering the belt would become poisoned with radioactivity, and further, that the belt would be regularly re-contaminated until such time as a satisfactory solution to the whole Korean problem shall have been reached. This would differ from use of the atomic bomb in several ways and would be, I believe, morally justifiable under the circumstances. . . .

Respectfully submitted,
Albert Gore, M. C., Washington, DC[46]

Rather than evacuate or irradiate Korea, American troops settled in for a prolonged conflict. The trench lines resembled World War I's Western Front, and the steady toll of U.S. casualties continued with no end in sight. Some Americans suggested using Asian proxies—as Stalin appeared to use the Chinese—to limit U.S. losses. America had available its own Chinese army, and *The Nation* published this suggestion:

What can be done with the Nationalist troops? Some say they should be sent against China's mainland, only a hundred miles across the Formosan Straits. Or part of them could be shipped to Korea. A third possibility is to use them to reinforce the French in Indo-China. American and even Chinese Nationalist military men admit that the nationalists are now wholly incapable of seizing a beachhead on China's mainland and holding it. . . . There remains the alternative of sending these forces to Korea. It is a tempting plan. Militarily, it has the advantage that supply lines are already operating in Korea.[47]

This writer proposed letting the Chinese fight each other in Korea:

[Secretary of Defense]
August 3, 1952

Gentlemen:
In view of the stalemate in Korea, and the apparent lack of an "out" from the situation, how about replacing most of our ground troops with Nationalist Chinese ground troops who have been training on Formosa? It is really more their battle than ours, and Chiang [Kai-shek] has been waiting to get into the fight for some time now. He is supposed to have a half-million highly trained Chinese infantrymen now, on the island of Formosa. What possible objection could there be to the substitution of these troops to save the lives of our own American boys? This would be giving Russia a taste of their own medicine. Not one Russian soldier will die in battle while they have "satellite" troops to take their place. They are saving Russian troops for the defense of Russia, or for some major move. Why in

hell don't we get smart too, and save our American soldiers for either the defense of America, or for some major crisis? . . .

Respectfully yours,
L. W., Columbus, OH[48]

These two writers proposed raising anticommunist armies abroad:

Senator Ed. Johnson
November 2, 1950

Dear Senator Johnson:
. . . The war in Korea looks bad for the United States at this time. Why wouldn't it be a good plan to give the Japanese the right to have their own government and take our soldiers out of Japan and let the Japs help drive the Chinese Reds out of Korea. They licked the Chinese alone years ago. They don't like the Chinese now, neither do they like Russia. They are close to Korea and could put in enough men to drive the Chinese Reds out of Korea in a short time.

F. T., Denver, CO[49]

[ca. April 1951]

Since the United States of America is to lead the way, furnish much of the goods and material, augment the manpower, and in many fashions foot a good deal of the bill and arms in a project just some little short of all out war, could we not formulate a sort of Allied strategy, and well afford to consider some plan which would 1. Offer opportunity to men of enlistment and service, in some form of European or world force for democracy, to consist of 2. Hand picked, screened, processed and examined personnel, to serve for some specified term? This under the Supreme Command as is presently worked out, in whatever theater should be necessary or expedient, 3. to be offered under American standard of pay, rations, clothing, shoes, medical care, arms, supplies, etc., and possibly some sort of assurance of opportunity for men to participate in a program for promotion and advancement. 4. This under some form of civil rights declaration, to build up and maintain a Nations United For Freedom Armed Force, which would, could, and was set up to offer more to men of any nation, than just induction and conscription to fight for more of what they already have, and already fear and hate. 5. To prove to them and convince their loved ones that they can do better than bow to or lean toward the Communistic line of reasoning for freedom. 6. If not too wild or far-fetched—offer the opportunity of earning a visa or passport of entry to an Allied state or country of their choice, upon having earned an honorable discharge from service in such force. 7. Such visa to grant under examination and acceptance by proper authorities the opportunity for the holder to earn under specified rules and examinations, citizenship papers in another land of their choice. . . .

E. D., Albany, OR[50]

Both sides used propaganda to sway the undecided masses of humanity for or against communism. These two writers suggested making America more attractive to a global audience:

President of the United States
May 19, 1951

Dear Mr. President:
As an old constituent of yours from Joplin, Mo. I would like to be permitted the liberty of making a suggestion designed to smother the communist propaganda based on what they choose to call Capitalism. Capitalism as we understand it here and which is based truly upon free enterprise has been turned by Joe and his breed into a nasty word which seems to be effective when used to rouse sentiment against this country. Why not call it something else and while choosing a name, make it mean something that will carry weight in our cause? For such a word, I would like to suggest LIBERTISM, for under our system of government we are at liberty to say, and often do, anything we wish. We can work and live anywhere we wish, so our mode of life and expression could very well fly its flag under a coined word such as the one I suggest. If given a start by you, such a word would rapidly catch hold to the defeat of the nasty sounding epithet Capitalists. Wishing you well sir, with providential guidance during these difficult times.

Yours most sincerely,
H. W., Hazelton, PA[51]

Major General Harry H. Vaughn, Presidential Aide
September 28, 1950

My Dear General:
. . . What I want to do is set out a means of selling democracy throughout the world that will far more than offset Russia's bid to put over communism. The Voice of America is dedicated to that but as far as I'm concerned it is [a] feeble

voice crying in the wilderness no matter how much money or intelligence is put into it. For the simple reason it can only reach adult minds and that's like bouncing rubber balls off granite. The ones to reach if we are to sell democracy and America is the kids. The best way to read kids is thru play. Therefore our best channel is thru athletics, particularly baseball. Now it so happens that baseball lends itself perfectly to the dual purpose of spreading democracy and spying. Or rather it could by an extension of the now regularly used system of the major leagues to scout and discover new players and to sponsor new teams and leagues for the development of players. Suppose for instance that one or two of the major league owners announced that they are not getting sufficient high class talent in the USA and are going to sponsor leagues in other countries. There are lots of ex big-leaguers of sufficient intelligence to assimilate training in gathering information who could be utilized as league heads and organizers as well as managers of teams and spies. If there were leagues organized in Britain, So. Africa, Turkey, Siam, So. America etc. and the kids taught baseball and with it a knowledge of America and democracy they would flock to play the game. The equipment and pay of course would ostensibly come from the Big League owners but should be provided by the USA. Baseball is infectious. Play it close to the Russian border and give the youngsters a chance to earn big money; to advance to other higher leagues; and for trips to the USA and you have set up a disease that will certainly spread across the border. But in addition to selling democracy, it would set up the greatest network for gathering information ever devised. And no intelligence Office on Earth could ever break the code for secret information would go forth to baseball headquarters as only hits runs and errors. . . .

Respectfully,
P. B., Midway City, CA[52]

Korean peace talks began in 1951 and dragged on interminably as the negotiators wrangled over a host of issues. Neither side had anticipated the most contentious item: more than half of the captured communist soldiers refused to return home, as *Time* reported:

> The U.N. did not ask the prisoners where they wanted to go; it asked them whether they would "forcibly resist" repatriation. If a man said yes, he was asked seven further questions (content not revealed) to make sure he was sincere. If he passed this test, he was deemed unwilling to be repatriated. The results were startling. These said they would "forcibly resist repatriation": 44,000 out of 96,000 North Korean soldiers, 15,600 out of 20,700 Chinese soldiers. . . . Almost against its will, the U.N. had uncovered a wonderful political and psychological asset in Asia— 100,000 living witnesses against the hatefulness and tyranny of Communism. It was unfortunate that this great asset stood in the way of a truce.[53]

Red negotiators demanded the return of these prisoners, the Americans refused, and the repatriation issue remained the major stumbling block to peace. The *Los Angeles Times* explained, "[O]ur side has in a manner become the prisoner of its own prisoners. . . . Most of the 132,000 prisoners that we hold were captured in the great push to the north in the autumn of 1950. Many of these and others captured since were induced to surrender by our propaganda which had been carried over the lines in various ways. Thus, we have a moral obligation not to send these people back where they would no doubt be killed for their lack of loyalty to Communism."[54] This letter argued that protection of these prisoners could prove crucial in any future war:

President of the United States
April 5, 1952

Mr. President:
. . . If anticommunist and voluntary prisoners are returned to the Communists, and if such prisoners are put to death or in concentration camps to a slow death, it will be one of the greatest defeats for the free world. . . . Unless the free world would want to surrender voluntarily to the Communists, sooner or later a war must come. There is no compromise between cancer and a human body. In case of war, one of the main hopes of the free world is to convince masses of communist soldiers [to] surrender to the free world forces. But by sending back now anti-communists and voluntary surrendered prisoners, and the Communists setting an example in China and North Korea by killings and deportations in concentration camps and hard labor and slow death, there would be no more surrenders in future war with the Communists. And this alone will be one of the main causes of defeat of the free world, taking in consideration of the enormous manpower reserve of the Communist world. . . .

Very respectfully yours,
A. R.[55]

Despite such arguments, some Americans questioned why U.S. troops were dying to uphold the rights of enemy soldiers. This writer proposed a formula for returning the prisoners:

President of the United States
October 12, 1952

Dear Mr. President:
Having read that you, as Commander in Chief of the armed forces, call upon General MacArthur, or anyone else to submit their plan for peace, I as a private

citizen respectfully submit the following: Let the United Nations obtain from the enemy in Korea a positive guarantee that all returned prisoners would be fully reinstated as citizens of their respective countries without penalties or punitive or other discrimination whatsoever. That would be a "face-saver" for both Communists and [the] United Nations. Acting in good faith, the prisoners would be returned, and the war ended. Should the enemy fail to live up to the guarantee (and we have no prima facie reason for really believing that they would not) then the onus of guilt would be upon them, not upon the United Nations. And our boys could come home!

Yours respectfully,
A. B., New York, NY[56]

This writer argued that treating prisoners as refugees would overburden America:

President-Elect Eisenhower
December 25, 1952

. . . The first mistake for us to confess is the astounding offer of refuge which we now learn was made in order to get individual Chinese to give themselves up to our troops. What in the world did our officers have in mind? With our immigration laws, where did they think they would put those who didn't want to go back to their homes? Where would we put them if the Chinese government gave in tomorrow and told us to keep them? Why, if we continue to fight aggressors all over the world, and to offer them refuge if they will surrender, we could have the whole world falling into our arms and moving in on us. Of course it was a bright idea for General Washington to offer land to British soldiers and mercenaries who would desert. We had plenty of it. But under present conditions I think we might very well admit to the world that we made a stupid blunder; let the Chinese laugh at our embarrassing dilemma and leave us with the prisoners on our hands. . . .

J. T., Middleton, WI[57]

These two writers proposed solving the impasse without breaking America's word to would-be defectors:

Department of Defense
August 16, 1952

Gentlemen:
. . . It is evident that the exchange of prisoners is the main issue. Why not tell them that we will give them all the prisoners we have whether they sign an agreement or not and that we are going to start by returning the prisoners that do not want to go

back and that we will give them back in bunches of 1,000 or 10,000 and that they will be just as we received them and that is fully armed and backed by U.N. troops to see that they get there and also protected by our bombers. I honestly believe that when the Red peace negotiators realize what it would be like to have bunches of fierce Chinese Reds (who hated them) suddenly thrust upon them [they would give in]? Well this is as far as I can take it, so please think it over and perhaps an idea may form that would help some. Of course the idea could be only a bluff but they would not know it. . . .

J. B., Cincinnati, OH[58]

Secretary of Defense
August 11, 1952

Dear Mr. Lovett:
As it appears to be openly admitted that there is no prospect of a peaceful settlement of the Korean War, and as the question is frankly asked how can the conflict be ended, if that is the wisest possible course to pursue, I would like to offer a suggestion. The last remaining obstacle to peace seems to depend on the number of prisoners to be exchanged. Why not make an offer to ransom those who refuse to be returned? It would be a comparatively small sum considering the daily cost of the war, the lives that would be saved, and the U.N. prisoners held by the Chinese that would be returned. Yet it might be large enough to tempt the Chinese. They would "save face" and the U.N. would have kept their word. Historical precedents have shown that in dealing with barbarians there has always been something tangible to close the bargain.

Very sincerely yours,
A. M., Winchester, VA[59]

The *New York Times* noted that accounting for American prisoners created another problem because "[t]he enemy has listed as prisoners only a fraction of the United States and United Nations troops carried on our rosters as missing."[60] This writer offered an idea for documenting captured American soldiers:

Secretary of Defense
June 11, 1952

Dear Sir:
In regard to our American and or U.N. prisoners of war in Korea, may I make this suggestion. Knowing that in the future as in the past the Communists will never

make an accurate accounting to U.S. of the names and numbers of our men held, why not issue to each of our soldiers [a] medallion about the size a little larger than our half dollars, with an eagle on it and with the soldier's serial numbers with code letters by states. Then advise our soldiers to carry it loose in his pocket. When and if he should be taken prisoner he should be instructed to drop this medallion unobserved on the road. Several of our soldiers could drop them at the same time about five yards apart so that later our followup troops would find them or the civilian population would find them and turn them in to our Army headquarters. We could even give the civilians 25 cents for each one found. This would give us a sort of spot check on our P.O.W.s.

Respectfully yours,
P. F., Culver City, CA[61]

After three years of fighting, the Communists relented on the prisoner issue and the war ended with the border roughly where it had begun. After a string of successful wars, the outcome in Korea disappointed many Americans. Although not a victory, the war confirmed U.S. leaders' belief that military power could at least contain, if perhaps not roll back, Communist expansion. For the time being, however, the other side seemed content to use less provocative means to achieve its goals. With both sides chastened by Korea's costs, Americans began enjoying a decade of a sometimes terrifying, but essentially bloodless, "Cold War."

CHAPTER 12

Conclusion: TV Wars, Tonkin, and Beyond

After Korea, U.S. and Soviet bloc forces continued their standoff, their ever-growing nuclear stockpiles helping to keep the peace by making the prospect of war so horrible. The Cuban missile crisis in October 1962 provided a terrifying demonstration of this effect. Ordinary citizens followed news of the confrontation as television brought the action directly into American homes. By the early 1960s both sides implicitly accepted that another limited war was under way in Vietnam, fought entirely by local proxies. In light of the Korean and Cuban experiences, this seemed a safer, less-provocative way to struggle for global supremacy.

The Tonkin Gulf incident of August 1964 brought the United States and North Vietnam into open conflict. From the start, America's war effort faltered on both the military and political fronts. U.S. units struggled to locate an elusive foe hiding in mountainous jungles and among an apathetic or even hostile population. Finding the Vietcong became a major American preoccupation. The *New York Times* published the following:

> [Army scientists] are anxious to dispatch battalions of bedbugs to Vietnam to help in the fight against the elusive Vietcong. . . . [T]he bedbug would be used to sound the alarm when guerrilla forces bent on ambush moved into position along a jungle trail. Since bedbugs let out a "Yow!" of excitement when they sense the nearness of human flesh, scientists at the Army's Limited War Laboratory in Aberdeen, Md. are working to perfect a sound amplification system that will make the insect's cries audible to human ears. The combat bedbug, a particularly large and noisy specimen about the size of a man's thumbnail, is carried in a special capsule that allows him to smell out a man about two blocks to the front or side but not the trooper carrying him. A small scouting party could, theoretically at least, precede a large body of troops along a jungle path and smell out any attempts at ambush.[1]

The public pitched in with ideas on how to root out the hidden enemy. Forty to fifty such letters were sent every week to the office of the Secretary of Defense. Others went directly to the armed services. The ideas ranged from dropping rattlesnakes in likely Vietcong hiding spots to attacking enemy tunnels with explosive-laden rats or with suffocating soapsuds.[2] These two writers proposed plans for providing the enemy with items that would reveal their position:

Special Assistant to the President
January 19, 1965

Dear Mr. Valenti:
If you can spare a few minutes from your busy schedule to listen to some armchair strategy on South Vietnam, it could prove useful to our country. . . . The Vietcong has largely succeeded by these tactics: 1. Ambush. 2. Direct military confrontation only when they have superiority of position, men, and firepower. 3. Otherwise, withdraw and hide—to strike in stealth another day. . . . Let me suggest a few new approaches to this problem: A. Free Soap—At first glance this may appear outlandish—but it has its possibilities. As a gift from America to the Vietnamese villagers (especially in Vietcong territory), we pass out or air drop a large number of small gift packages of soap and candy (the latter is pure decoy to misdirect attention away from the soap). The Vietcong will no doubt laugh hysterically at our stupid generosity—but what they will not know is that the soap contains flourescent dye—invisible under ordinary light—but brilliantly visible under ultra-violet light. It could make the Cong sitting ducks for air attacks, night or day—at least, until the concept is understood. Preferably the dye should be long lasting. . . .

Sincerely,
L. P.[3]

Presidential Aide
November 13, 1965

Hon. Pres. Aide Valenti:
I feel that an organization composed of military intelligence and booby trap experts, etc. would be very effective in our war in Vietnam. The following are some examples of the weird ideas I feel might help our cause. A captured enemy may be allowed to escape with some sort of material planted on his person so that he might be traced to his hiding place and other enemy troops. Pets allowed to get into enemy hands that have been operated on and implanted with a listening

device that may be traced to territory hiding the enemy. . . . I trust the ideas herein may have some merit.

Respectfully yours,
W. C., Philadelphia, PA[4]

As the war ground on, America devoted great efforts to winning the "hearts and minds" of ordinary Vietnamese. The *Los Angeles Times* published this report:

> We are spending more than $700 million this year on what the President has called "the other war"—programs of nation-building—in an effort to make the Saigon government in particular, and democracy in general, so attractive that communism and the Viet Cong will hold no appeal for the peasant masses. . . . This is a scheme under which farmers are given three small Yorkshire or Berkshire pigs, eight bags of cement for building a sty and some U.S.-grown surplus corn. The pigs are fattened and one is sold to cover costs. The other two are kept for breeding. But the hog population may be rising faster than morale.[5]

This letter included a plan to win over Vietnamese farmers:

The President
January 3, 1969

Johnson left you a mess, and also a political booby trap. He is casting the South Vietnamese as villains, obstructing a peaceful settlement in Paris. I hope you don't buy this one. For in my opinion, no permanent honorable settlement can be achieved in Paris. It must be done out in Vietnam, and it may take two years of skillful planning and some fighting. . . . [We need to win] the support of the peasants. They are 70% of the country. The great mass of them are still uncommitted. Democracy and Communism are only meaningless foreign words. How to get their loyalty for Saigon? Recently we have been introducing into South Vietnam a variety of rice developed out in that Philippine Institute, now called "Honda" rice because, using this new seed, you can raise enough rice to buy a Honda. The trouble is that the VC [Vietcong] have stolen enough of this seed to begin raising and distributing it in areas they control, so any advantage to us will soon be lost. Now for my gimmick: fertilizer, distributed at cost but only in villages we control. If you read my book on Asia, you will find that I go thoroughly into this subject of fertilizer and what it does for crops, from India up to Japan. And this fertilizer we can control. Honda rice makes possible two crops a year. This means two doses of fertilizer. And the peasants, who already know what fertilizer can do,

will then fight to keep the VC out of their villages, so that we will sell them more
fertilizer for the next crop. . . . Fertilizer could get you out of a completely pacified
Vietnam in less than two years, particularly if you stir free elections in with the
fertilizer. Because then what would there be left to fight about?

Respectfully Submitted,
W. W., Emporia, KS[6]

Televised images of the carnage affected American perceptions of Vietnam, contrib-
uting to an erosion of public support for the war. These two writers addressed this
phenomenon. One suggested keeping war images off the air, the second proposed
using a telethon to help end the war:

The President
October 13, 1965

Dear Mr. President:
. . . The purpose of this letter, however, it to protest the exhibition of television
pictures of actual warfare in the wilds of Vietnam where our boys were being picked
off by snipers and actually showing the dead and wounded of the boys. . . . I hang
my grey haired head in shame this morning that I together with perhaps ten million
or more other viewers were carried back to prehistoric days, where we sat beside a
cave man and watched with him the killing, maiming and torturing of our fellow
creatures in actual warfare, and where we could almost hear the photographers
saying "We are sorry we can't show the blood flowing from the wounds of your
sons and brothers, but maybe we can do that the next time." I am sorry that you are
confined in the hospital but maybe you can pass the word to the proper authority
to have such brutal and realistic war pictures banned from exhibition to civilized
viewers.

Thanking you, I am yours very respectfully,
W. P., Pittsburgh, PA[7]

Joseph Califano
December 8, 1967

Dear Mr. Califano:
This is with reference to another proposal of which you no doubt have many, for
open diplomacy with North Vietnam. From my experience, there is no doubt

that overt and clandestine efforts are being made throughout the world. However, it does seem strange to me that by utilizing mass methods of communication "a clown" can raise millions of dollars for muscular dystrophy and we do not seem to be able to mobilize public opinion for the cause of peace! Therefore my proposal is to use several conceivable methods of communication for a twenty-four hour period; a peace "telethon" if you like, which will be beamed directly to the citizens in Vietnam. The objective is obvious. Means will be grasped by men of goodwill as well as by the lunatic fringe and once and for all, the latter will be transparently obvious to everyone.

Sincerely yours,
W. L., Stamford, CT[8]

With morale at home and in the front lines ebbing, the administration began to look for a graceful exit. Once again American diplomats haggled with Communist negotiators, while their captured fellow citizens languished in Red prison camps. This writer described a plan to bring American prisoners home without depriving the North Vietnamese of their bargaining chips:

Deputy Assistant to the President
March 24, 1972

Dear Al:
A suggestion has just recently come to my attention from a wartime officer in my command in Korea, who has left the service but still is a most dedicated American. He is prepared to overtly or covertly arrange for volunteers (including himself) to go to North Vietnam—one for each prisoner to be released. He suggests that those volunteering could be obtained with various skills, if such was desired by Hanoi. He and his associates feel very, very strongly about this matter and it may surface, whether or not it has Government backing, shortly. In view of the situation, I felt it should immediately be brought to your attention for any suggestions or advice you have in this matter. . . .

Sincerely,
A. T., Chevy Chase, MD[9]

As U.S. troops left Indochina, the president brokered a peace deal that, like the peace deal in Korea, left the combatants in place.[10] The pact bought America's client state only a brief reprieve: the Communists overran South Vietnam just two years later. That disaster proved strategically inconsequential. Fifteen years after losing

Vietnam, the United States "won" the Cold War. Flaws in Russian Communism ultimately proved more important than success in limited wars. Through the process of elimination, America had achieved global military predominance.

Predictably, the post–Cold War status quo proved unstable. New crises and conflicts arose, and Americans learned that unequaled military might provided no absolute defense against attack or even a guaranteed victory in war. In this new struggle, the public again offered its ideas, from stampeding herds of swine through the streets of Baghdad to air-dropping grizzly bears at the mouths of Afghanistan's mountain caves. Proving that wealth and presidential ambitions are no substitute for originality, one magazine editor advocated thwarting attacks by hijacked airliners by resurrecting the practice of surrounding vital structures with balloon-borne nets.[11]

Just as every war is different from the last, so are the public conceptions about the war, and so are the sources from which the public draws its ideas. If the conflict in Vietnam was the first televised war, it may be that the first Internet war has arrived. The status of the armchair warrior has changed as well. The Cold War left as one of its legacies a growing industry of professional thinkers who exist to "analyze" military problems, large and small. Ensconced in think tanks and foundations, they form an institutionalized, structured version of the independent, concerned citizen brainstorming to solve vital military problems. Might the full-time pondering of these quasibureaucrats eventually supplant individual strategists as the professional Army did away with the Minuteman? Perhaps someday, but for the foreseeable future the armchair warrior is alive and well.

Notes

The notes include reference to items that are currently available only in person. Some of these items are on microfilm, others are hard copies in file boxes arranged by various filing systems according to the source (which is usually a government agency). For instance, to see the citation "RG 38, ONI Administrative 1942–46, A13-7, Box 343," the reader would go to the National Archives and speak to an archivist, and ask for that specific box.

Abbreviations in Notes

AAF	Army Air Forces
AAG	Army Adjutant General
AWC	Army War College
CNO	Chief of Naval Operations
HSTL	Harry S. Truman Presidential Library
LBJL	Lyndon B. Johnson Presidential Library
NBCR	Navy Bureau of Construction and Repair
NIC	National Inventors Council
ONI	Office of Naval Intelligence
OPD	Operations Division, U.S. Army
RG	Record Group, National Archives
SecNav	Secretary of the Navy
WHCF	White House Central Files

Introduction

1. Richard Henry Lee to Washington, August 1, 1775, in *The Papers of George Washington*, Revolutionary War Series, vol. 1 (Charlottesville: University of Virginia Press, 1985), 209–10.

2. Jack McLaughlin, *To His Excellency Thomas Jefferson; Letters to a President* (New York: W. W. Norton & Company, 1991), 237–39.
3. Harold Holzer, *Dear Mr. Lincoln: Letters to the President* (Reading, MA: Addison-Wesley, 1993), 47–68.

Chapter 1. To the World Stage: The Spanish War and the Philippine Insurrection

1. Allan Keller, *The Spanish-American War: A Compact History* (New York: Hawthorn Books, 1969), 18–19.
2. Tim McNeese, *Remember the Maine! The Spanish-American War Begins* (Greensboro, NC: Morgan Reynolds, 2002), 82–83.
3. John Grenville, "American Naval Preparations for War with Spain, 1896–1898," *Journal of American Studies* 2, no. 1 (April 1968): 33–47 (33–38).
4. "Joint Attack on Havana," *New York Times*, April 14, 1898, 6.
5. RG 80, SecNav 1897–1915, File 8153, Box 314.
6. "Spain's Naval Strength," *Harper's Weekly*, XLII, April 16, 1898, 370.
7. Frank Anderson, "Torpedoes, Ancient and Modern," *New York Times Magazine*, April 3, 1898, 12.
8. "Navies of Spain and the United States," *Harper's Weekly*, XLII, April 30, 1898, 426–27.
9. RG 80, SecNav 1897–1915, File 8153, Box 314.
10. RG 80, SecNav 1897–1915, File 8153, Box 314.
11. RG 80, SecNav 1897–1915, File 8153, Box 314.
12. G.J.A. O'Toole, *The Spanish War: An American Epic—1898* (New York: W. W. Norton & Company, 1984), 173.
13. "Reinforce Dewey at Once," *Chicago Daily Tribune*, May 21, 1898, 12.
14. "To Southern Ports the Army Is Moving," *Atlanta Constitution*, May 11, 1898, 1.
15. RG 80, SecNav 1897–1915, File 8153, Box 314.
16. Editorial, *New York Times*, May 14, 1898, 6.
17. RG 80, SecNav 1897–1915, File 8153, Box 314.
18. "For the Canaries?" *Washington Post*, June 17, 1898, 1.
19. RG 80, SecNav 1897–1915, File 8153, Box 314.
20. RG 94, AAG 1890–1917, File 72283, Box 520.
21. RG 80, SecNav 1897–1915, File 8153, Box 314.
22. RG 80, SecNav 1897–1915, File 8153, Box 314.
23. RG 94, AAG 1890–1917, File 94239, Box 678.
24. "Spanish Battleships Approaching Northern Ports with Loaded Guns," *Atlanta Consititution*, April 28, 1898, 1.
25. RG 80, SecNav 1897–1915, File 8153, Box 314.
26. "The Strategy of Spain," *New York Times*, May 19, 1898, 8.

27. RG 80, SecNav 1897–1915, File 8153, Box 314.

28. "Effect of Steam Navies," *Chicago Daily Tribune*, May 1, 1898, 32.

29. "Spain's Trick Forestalled," *Los Angeles Times*, April 19, 1898, 3.

30. RG 80, SecNav 1897–1915, File 8153, Box 314.

31. "Give Sampson a Chance," *Chicago Daily Tribune*, May 4, 1898, 6.

32. Ivan Musicant, *Empire by Default: The Spanish-American War and the Dawn of the American Century* (New York: Henry Holt and Company, 1998), 277.

33. "Real Fighting May Begin in a Week, if not Sooner," *Los Angeles Times*, April 27, 1898, 1.

34. RG 80, SecNav 1897–1915, File 8153, Box 314.

35. RG 80, SecNav1897–1915, File 8153, Box 314.

36. "Santiago Bay—A Bottle with a Narrow Neck," *Chicago Daily Tribune*, May 21, 1898.

37. David Trask, *The War with Spain in 1898* (Lincoln: University of Nebraska Press, 1996), 307.

38. "Cevera Is There," *Washington Post*, May 29, 1898, 1.

39. Frank Freidel, *The Splendid Little War* (Boston: Little, Brown, 1958), 52–54.

40. Caspar Whitney, "Army Ready to Fight," *Harper's Weekly*, XLII, June 4, 1898, 550–51.

41. "Southern States Make a Mistake," *Chicago Daily Tribune*, May 26, 1898, 6.

42. RG 94, AAG 1890–1917, File 75490, Box 548.

43. "Only a Small Army Ready," *New York Times*, April 15, 1898, 3.

44. RG 94, AAG 1890–1917, File 83049, Box 612.

45. RG 94, AAG 1890–1917, File 81668, Box 605.

46. RG 80, SecNav 1897–1915, File 8153, Box 314.

47. RG 94, AAG 1890–1917, File 81726, Box 605.

48. Trask, *The War with Spain*, 362–64.

49. RG 80, SecNav 1897–1915, File 8153, Box 314.

50. "Gen. Emilio Aguinaldo, the Big Man of the Philippines," *Los Angeles Times*, May 11, 1898, 4.

51. Musicant, *Empire by Default*, 547–49.

52. Louis Halle, *The United States Acquires the Philippines: Consensus vs. Reality* (Lanham, MD: University Press of America, 1985), 34–36.

53. Brian Damiani, *Advocates of Empire: William McKinley, the Senate and American Expansion 1898–1899* (New York: Garland Publishing, 1987), 124–25.

54. Stanley Karnow, *In Our Image: America's Empire in the Philippines* (New York: Random House, 1989), 129–30.

55. "Aguinaldo as a Ruler," *New York Times*, January 23, 1899, 6.

56. Karnow, *In Our Image*, 138–40.

57. RG 94, AAG 1890–1917, File 209158, Box 1312.

58. RG 94, AAG 1890–1917, File 266894, Box 1768.

59. "Future of the Philippines," *New York Times*, April 26, 1899, 1.
60. "To Live in the Philippines," *New York Times*, March 13, 1899, 1.
61. "The Philippine Problem," *Harper's Weekly*, March 16, 1901, 297.
62. RG 94, AAG 1890–1917, File 467313, Box 3281.
63. Franklin Mallory and Ludwig Olson, *The Krag Rifle Story* (Silver Spring, MD: Springfield Research Service, 1979), 55.
64. Philip Shockley, *The Krag-Jørgensen Rifle in the Service* (Aledo, IL: World Wide Gun Report, 1960), 35–37.
65. "Better Arms for Troops," *New York Times*, March 9, 1899, 1.
66. RG 94, AAG 1890–1917, File 228078, Box 1447.
67. "Adjutant General to Rep. B. F. Marsh," April 8, 1899; RG 94, AAG 1890–1917, File 228078, Box 1447.
68. "Lethal Slugs of Lead," *Washington Post*, June 12, 1898, 26.
69. "Hurrah for Our Side!" *Chicago Daily Tribune*, April 29, 1899, 12.
70. RG 94, AAG 1890–1917, File 224859, Box 1420.
71. John Gates, *Schoolbooks and Krags: The United States Army in the Philippines, 1898–1902* (Westport, CT: Greenwood Press, 1973), 110–12.
72. "The Situation in Luzon," *New York Times*, December 13, 1899, 1.
73. "The Filipino and His Future," *Los Angeles Times*, December 2, 1899, 8.
74. Laurence Berkove, ed., *Skepticism and Dissent: Selected Journalism 1898–1901 by Ambrose Bierce* (Ann Arbor, MI: UMI Research Press, 1986), 175.
75. RG 94, AAG 1890–1917, File 285051, Box 1909.
76. RG 94, AAG 1890–1917, File 353154, Box 2373.
77. "Filipinos Resort to Guerilla War," *San Francisco Chronicle*, December 13, 1899, 1.
78. "Corralling the Insurgents," *New York Times*, December 1, 1899, 1.
79. RG 94, AAG 1890–1917, File 287759, Box 1926.
80. "Must Be Crushed," *Washington Post*, April 3, 1900, 6.
81. Gates, *Schoolbooks and Krags*, 205–9.
82. Karnow, *In Our Image*, 194.

Chapter 2. Gun Bases, Pancho Villa, and Hyphenated Americans: Prelude to Armageddon

1. Mark Ellis and Panikos Panayi, "German Minorities in World War I: A Comparative Study of Britain and the USA," *Ethnic and Racial Studies* 17, no. 2 (April 1994): 238–59 (239).
2. Ronald Fernandez, "Getting Germans to Fight Germans: The Americanizers of World War I," *Journal of Ethnic Studies* 9, no. 2 (Summer 1981): 53–68 (56–57).
3. "Code Change Aids Street Musicians," *New York Times*, August 11, 1915, 5.
4. RG 165, Entry 296, War College Correspondence 1907–19, Box 262, 8123.

5. RG 94, AAG 1890–1917, Box 7607, 2549255, filed in 2197337.

6. Christopher Duffy, "The Liege Forts," in *The Marshall Cavendish Illustrated Encyclopedia of World War I*, vol. 1 (New York: Marshall Cavendish, 1984), 132–38.

7. Norman Draper, "Krupp's and the Siege Guns," *Collier's*, October 31, 1914, 20.

8. "Mobile Siege Guns in the Present War," *Scientific American*, October 3, 1914, 266.

9. "German Gun Bases Were Long Prepared," *New York Times*, October 20, 1914, 4.

10. "Germans Here Safe if They Obey Law," *New York Times*, March 27, 1917, 1.

11. "High-Explosive Bombs, Suspected Gun Base Found; Volunteers Called," *Los Angeles Times*, March 29, 1917, II-1.

12. RG 94, AAG 1890–1917, Box 7607, 2366598, filed in 2197337.

13. RG 94, AAG 1890–1917, Box 7607, 2321115, filed in 2197337.

14. "Former U.S. Arsenal Worker Held for Plot—Naturalized German Accused of Ruining Shells Being Manufactured for Government," "Fire Destroys Cherry Street Pier Building; Suspect Enemy Aliens," "German Woman Charged with Spitting on Flag," *Philadelphia Inquirer*, December 7, 1917, 1, 7, 9.

15. "The Kaiser's Secret Army Here," *Literary Digest*, December 1, 1917, 15.

16. RG 80, SecNav 1916–26, Box 2512, 28517-398.

17. RG 80, SecNav 1916–26, Box 2512, 28517-410.

18. Graham Metson, ed., *The Halifax Explosion December 6, 1917* (Toronto: McGraw-Hill, 1978), 12–14.

19. RG 80, SecNav 1916–26, Box 2513, 28517-464.

20. RG 94, AAG 1890–1917, Box 7607, 2336970, filed in 2197337.

21. RG 80, SecNav 1916–26, Box 2512, 28517-405.

22. RG 94, AAG 1890–1917, Box 7607, 2324906, filed in 2197337.

23. RG 80, SecNav 1916–26, Box 2511, 28517-261.

24. W. Watts Biggers, "The Germans Are Coming! The Germans Are Coming!" *U.S. Naval Institute Proceedings* 111, no. 6 (June 1985): 38–43.

25. William Clark, *When the U-Boats Came to America* (Boston: Little, Brown, and Company, 1929), 34–35.

26. J. Muller, "The Invasion of America," *Boston Globe*, April 18, 1915, SM9.

27. RG 80, SecNav 1916–26, Box 2513, 28517-522.

28. Robert Browning, *Two If By Sea: The Development of American Coastal Defense Policy* (Westport, CT: Greenwood Press, 1983), 170–73.

29. Emanuel Lewis, *Seacoast Fortifications of the United States: An Introductory History* (Annapolis, MD: Leeward Publications, 1970), 100–101.

30. "Fears for New York in Attack by Sea," *New York Times*, March 24, 1916, 6.

31. RG 94, AAG 1890–1917, Box 7795, 2267945.

32. RG 80, SecNav 1916–26, Box 2513, 28517-551.

33. RG 80, SecNav 1916–26, Box 2513, 28517-544.

34. "Predicts Air Raids on American Cities," *New York Times*, October 22, 1917, 9.

35. "Can the Germans Bomb New York from the Air?" *American Review of Reviews*, May 1918, 492–96.

36. RG 80, SecNav 1916–26, Box 2512, 28517-369.

37. "City Lights Out in Air Raid Test," *New York Times*, June 5, 1918, 1.

38. RG 94, AAG 1890–1917, Box 8864, 2564363.

39. John Eisenhower, *Intervention! The United States and the Mexican Revolution, 1913–1917* (New York: W. W. Norton, 1993), 166.

40. Joseph Stout, *Border Conflict: Villistas, Carrancistas, and the Punitive Expedition, 1915–1920* (Fort Worth, TX: Christian University Press, 1999), 17–18.

41. "One Excitement at a Time," *Boston Globe*, March 15, 1916, 12.

42. Arthur Henning, "Wilson Orders 5,000 Soldiers to Catch Villa," *Chicago Daily Tribune*, March 11, 1916, 1.

43. "Says US May Buy Part of Mexico—President Has Plan, Editor Hears," *Boston Globe*, March 12, 1916, 24.

44. RG 94, AAG 1890–1917, Box 8133, 2390550.

45. "Somebody's Loony," *Chicago Tribune*, May 1, 1916, 8.

46. "The Greater United States," *Washington Post*, May 21, 1916, MT 4.

47. RG 94, AAG 1890–1917, Box 8133, 2390550.

48. "American Army 'Most Pathetic'; Would Take Years to Conquer Mexico, Says Col. Glen, U.S.A.," *Washington Post*, March 15, 1916, 3.

49. "Obregon Threat Finds U.S. Unprepared for Real War," *Chicago Tribune*, May 3, 1916, 4.

50. RG 94, AAG 1890–1917, Box 8133, 2390550.

51. RG 94, AAG 1890–1917, Box 8133, 2390550.

52. "Mexico: Its Political Situation, Its Resources, and Its Military Strength," *Scientific American*, April 29, 1916, 450–51.

53. RG 94, AAG 1890–1917, Box 8133, 2390550.

54. RG 94, AAG 1890–1917, Box 8133, 2390550.

55. "Congress Moves to Fill All Army Gaps," *Washington Post*, March 15, 1916, 1.

56. RG 94, AAG 1890–1917, Box 8133, 2390550.

57. RG 94, AAG 1890–1917, Box 8133, 2390550.

58. RG 94, AAG 1890–1917, Box 8133, 2390550.

59. RG 94, AAG 1890–1917, Box 8133, 2390550.

60. "Aeroplanes in Mexico," *Atlanta Journal*, March 16, 1916, 6.

61. Grady McCright, "Pershing's Airwar in Mexico," *Aviation Quarterly* 5, no. 4 (1979): 350–56.

62. Michael Tate, "Pershing's Pets: Apache Scouts in the Mexican Punitive Expedition of 1916," *New Mexico Historical Review* 66 (January 1991): 59–65.

63. RG 94, AAG 1890–1917, Box 8133, 2390550.

64. RG 94, AAG 1890–1917, Box 8133, 2390550.

65. RG 94, AAG 1890–1917, Box 8133, 2390550.

66. "Mexican Uprising in Border States Threatened," *Chicago Tribune*, May 10, 1916, 1.

67. RG 94, AAG 1890–1917, Box 8133, 2390550.

68. RG 94, AAG 1890–1917, Box 8133, 2390550.

69. "May Call 500,000 Men: Huge Volunteer Force Under Consideration, It Is Said," *Washington Post*, June 21, 1916, 1.

70. "Carranza and Uncle Sam," *Los Angeles Times*, June 20, 1916, II-4.

Chapter 3. A New Type of Pirate: World War I at Sea

1. William Sims, *The Victory at Sea* (1920; repr. Annapolis, MD: Naval Institute Press, 1984), 10–11.

2. William Willoughby, *Government Organization in War Time and After* (New York: Appleton and Company, 1919), 31.

3. Inside cover, *Scientific American*, June 2, 1917, 541.

4. C. H. Claudy, "Ideas That Will Not Work," *Scientific American*, September 29, 1917, 226.

5. Richard Compton-Hall, *Submarines and the War at Sea, 1914–1918* (London: Macmillan, 1991), 98–99.

6. RG 80, SecNav 1916–26, 27219, Box 2161.

7. Carson Ritchie, *Q-Ships* (Suffolk, UK: Terence Dalton Limited, 1985), 39–41.

8. Clark, *When the U-Boats Came to America*, 294–95.

9. RG 80, SecNav 1916–26, 27219-575, Box 2161.

10. RG 80, SecNav 1916–26, 27219-536, Box 2161.

11. RG 80, SecNav 1916–26, 28517-301, Box 2512.

12. RG 80, SecNav 1916–26, 27219-569, Box 2161.

13. RG 80, SecNav 1916–26, 27219-470, Box 2160.

14. RG 80, SecNav 1916–26, 27219-477, Box 2160.

15. RG 80, SecNav 1916–26, 27219-596, Box 2161.

16. "The Submarine Problem—VI," *Scientific American*, July 7, 1917, 10.

17. Dwight Messimer, *Find and Destroy: Antisubmarine Warfare in World War I* (Annapolis, MD: Naval Institute Press, 2001), 113–14.

18. Dwight Messimer, *Verschollen: World War I U-boat Losses* (Annapolis, MD: Naval Institute Press, 2002).

19. "The Submarine Problem—XVII," *Scientific American*, October 13, 1917, 268.

20. RG 80, SecNav 1916–26, 27219-661, Box 2162.

21. RG 80, SecNav 1916–26, 27219-611, Box 2162.

22. Messimer, *Find and Destroy*, 130.

23. "The Submarine Problem—XV," *Scientific American*, September 23, 1917, 208.

24. RG 80, SecNav 1916–26, 27219-630, Box 2162.

25. "Mortars to Fight the Submarine," *Scientific American*, December 29, 1917, 495.
26. "Finding the Submarine," *Scientific American*, February 2, 1918, 105.
27. RG 80, SecNav 1916–26, 27219-673, Box 2162.
28. T. Gilbert Pearson, "Training Sea Gulls for National Defense," *Art World*, January 1918, 364.
29. RG 80, SecNav 1916–26, 27219-712, Box 2162.
30. RG 80, SecNav 1916–26, 27219, Box 2160.
31. RG 80, SecNav 1916–26, 27219-560, Box 2161.
32. RG 80, SecNav 1916–26, 28517-224, Box 2510.
33. "The Submarine Problem—III," *Scientific American*, June 16, 1917, 596.
34. C. H. Claudy, "I Can End the War," *Illustrated World* 28, no. 1 (September 1917): 8.
35. "Submersible Freighter Versus the Submarine," *Scientific American*, May 26, 1917, 518.
36. RG 80, SecNav 1916–26, 27219-391, Box 2159.
37. "Submersible the Ultimate Answer to the Submarine," *Scientific American*, June 2, 1917, 552.
38. RG 80, SecNav 1916–26, 28517-262, Box 2511.
39. "Beating Germany via the Air," *Scientific American*, July 28, 1917, 59.
40. RG 80, SecNav 1916–26, 27219-592, Box 2161.
41. Compton-Hall, *Submarines and the War at Sea*, 82–83.
42. J. Bernard Walker, "Closing the North Sea with a Bomb-Curtain," *Scientific American*, June 23, 1917, 616–17.
43. RG 80, SecNav 1916–26, 28517-448, Box 2513.
44. RG 80, SecNav 1916–26, 27219-608, Box 2162.
45. J. S. Cowie, *Mines, Minelayers, and Minelaying* (London: Oxford University Press, 1949), 66.
46. Tamara Melia, *"Damn the Torpedoes": A Short History of U.S. Naval Mine Countermeasures, 1777–1991* (Washington, DC: Department of the Navy, 1991), 33.
47. Edwyn Gray, *The Killing Time: The U-boat War, 1914–1918* (London: Seeley, Service & Co. 1972), 176.
48. RG 80, SecNav 1916–26, 28517-289, Box 2511.
49. RG 80, SecNav 1916–26, 28517-616, Box 2513.
50. RG 80, SecNav 1916–26, 27219-694, Box 2162.
51. RG 80, SecNav 1916–26, 28517, Box 2510.
52. Thomas Frothingham, *The Naval History of the Great War: The Stress of Sea Power 1915–1916* (Cambridge: Harvard University Press, 1925), 122–23.
53. "A Naval Offensive," *Scientific American*, October 13, 1917, 266.
54. "How Kiel Can Be Penetrated," *The Forum*, March 1918, 280–90.
55. RG 80, SecNav 1916–26, 28517-380, Box 2512.

56. RG 80, SecNav 1916–26, 28517-416, Box 2513.

57. RG 80, SecNav 1916–26, 27219-631, Box 2162.

58. RG 80, SecNav 1916–26, 28517-441, Box 2513.

59. RG 80, SecNav 1916–26, 27219-652, Box 2162.

60. RG 80, SecNav 1916–26, 27219-586, Box 2161.

61. RG 80, SecNav 1916–26, 27219-537, Box 2161.

62. RG 80, SecNav1916–26, 27219, Box 2161.

63. John Keegan, *The First World War* (New York: Alfred Knopf, 1999), 416–17.

Chapter 4. Over There: The Campaign in Europe

1. "Hints for the Amateur Strategist," *Independent* 94 (April 27, 1918): 155–56.

2. "Russia, the Ultimate Decisive Factor in the War," *Scientific American*, June 17, 1916, 634.

3. "Slav Army Unlimited," *Washington Post*, September 3, 1916, ES 1.

4. RG 165, Entry 296, AWC 1903–19, 8123-246, Box 262.

5. RG 165, Entry 296, AWC 1903–19, 8123-284, Box 262.

6. "America Should Help Russia," *Washington Post*, May 16, 1918, 6.

7. RG 165, Entry 296, AWC 1903–19, 8123-328, Box 262.

8. James Morgan, "The Fortunes of the World at Stake in Italy," *Boston Globe*, November 4, 1917, 46.

9. RG 165, Microfilm M-1023, Reel 22, 8123-474.

10. Emile Mayer, "The Strategy That Will Win the War," *Yale Review* 7, no. 3 (April 1918): 449–63.

11. "Strike Down Hapsburg," *Washington Post*, May 11, 1918, 6.

12. RG 165, Entry 296, AWC 1903–19, 8123, Box 262.

13. RG 165, Entry 296, AWC 1903–19, 8123-378, Box 263.

14. Gordon Gordon-Smith, "War in Watertight Compartments," *Washington Post*, July 22, 1917, 11.

15. RG 165, Entry 296, AWC 1903–19, 8123-394, Box 263.

16. "The Impending Attack," *Washington Post*, December 12, 1917, 6.

17. RG 165, Microfilm M-1023, Reel 22, 8123-434.

18. James Morgan, "Can the War Be Ended and Victory Won in the Air?" *Boston Globe*, July 7, 1918, 40.

19. "How the German Line Can Be Broken," *Scientific American*, June 23, 1917, 614.

20. RG 165, Microfilm M-1023, Reel 22, 8123-476.

21. RG 80, SecNav 1916–26, 26983, Box 2117.

22. RG 165, Entry 296, AWC 1903–19, 8123-762, Box 263.

23. C. Grey, "To Carry the War by Air into Heart of Germany," *Boston Globe*, July 29, 1917, 44.

24. RG 165, Entry 296, AWC 1903–19, 8123-305, Box 262.

25. Memo "Acting Director War Plans Division to Chief of Staff," April 12, 1918, Subject: "Introduction of insect pests into Germany"; RG 165, Entry 296, AWC 1903–19, 8123-378, Box 263.

26. RG 165, Entry 296, AWC 1903–19, 8123-262, Box 262.

27. RG 80, SecNav 1916–26, 28517-308, Box 2512.

28. RG 165, Entry 517, Board of Ordnance & Fortifications 1917–18, Inventions, Box 2.

29. RG 94, AAG 1890–1917, 2623298, Box 9040.

30. RG 165, Microfilm M-1023, Reel 22, 8123-505.

31. George Rothwell Brown, "Plan to Smash Huns: U.S. Staff for Frontal Attacks, Like Pickett at Gettysburg," *Washington Post*, November 11, 1917, 1.

32. "Why Not Revive Chain Shot?" *Scientific American*, March 24, 1917, 305.

33. RG 165, Microfilm M-1023, Reel 22, 8123-436.

34. "Torpedoing the Enemy's Trenches as a Preliminary to Infantry Attack," *Scientific American*, May 12, 1917, 463.

35. RG 165, Entry 517, Board of Ordnance & Fortifications 1917–18, Inventions, Box 1.

36. RG 165, Microfilm M-1023, Reel 22, 8123-451.

37. RG 165, Microfilm M-1023, Reel 22, 8123-413.

38. RG 165, Entry 296, AWC 1903–19, 8123-351, Box 263.

39. RG 165, Entry 517, Board of Ordnance & Fortifications 1917–18, Inventions, Box 2.

40. RG 165, Microfilm M-1023, Reel 22, 8123-420.

41. "Trench Knives for U.S. Soldiers," *Atlanta Constitution*, September 24, 1917, 26.

42. C. Cory, Jr., "Masked Terrors of No Man's Land," *Illustrated World* 28, no. 6 (February 1918): 826–29.

43. Anthony Saunders, *Weapons of the Trench War, 1914–1918* (Stroud, UK: Sutton Publishing, 1999), 52–62.

44. RG 165, Entry 517, Board of Ordnance & Fortifications 1917–18, Inventions, Box 1.

45. RG 165, Entry 296, AWC 1903–19, 8123-333, Box 262.

46. RG 165, Entry 296, AWC 1903–19, 8123-339, Box 262.

47. RG 165, Entry 296, AWC 1903–19, 8123-368, Box 263.

48. RG 165, Entry 517, Board of Ordnance & Fortifications 1917–18, Inventions, Box 2.

49. "Armored Tractors in the European War," *Scientific American*, October 7, 1916, 322.

50. René Bache, "Our Forts on Wheels," *Illustrated World* 27, no. 4 (June 1917): 512.

51. Uncle Dudley, "Tactics and Tanks," *Boston Globe*, August 15, 1918, 6.

52. RG 80, SecNav 1916–26, 28517-456, Box 2513.

53. RG 165, Entry 517, Board of Ordnance & Fortifications 1917–18, Inventions, Box 1.

54. RG 165, Entry 517, Board of Ordnance & Fortifications 1917–18, Inventions, Box 2.

Chapter 5. Disarmament and Depression: The Great War's Aftermath

1. Christopher Hall, *Britain America and Arms Control, 1921–1937* (New York: St. Martin's Press, 1987), 13–14.

2. J. Bernard Walker, "Naval Strength of United States, Great Britain and Japan: How Age of Ships Will Affect Relative Fighting Efficiency by 1924," *Scientific American*, November 1921, 11–13.

3. Malcolm Murfett, "Look Back in Anger: The Western Powers and the Washington Conference of 1921–1922," in *Arms Limitation and Disarmament, Restraints on War, 1899–1939*, ed. B.J.C. McKercher (Westport, CT: Praeger Publishers, 1992), 86–87.

4. "How to Disarm," *The New Republic*, January 12, 1921, 184–85.

5. RG 80, SecNav 1916–26, File 3809, Box 9.

6. RG 80, SecNav 1916–26, File 3809, Box 11.

7. RG 80, SecNav 1916–26, File 3809, Box 9.

8. Bruce Berkowitz, *Calculated Risks: A Century of Arms Control, Why It Has Failed, and How It Can Be Made to Work* (New York: Simon and Chuster, 1987), 41–43.

9. Emily Goldman, *Sunken Treaties: Naval Arms Control between the Wars* (University Park: Pennsylvania State University Press, 1994), 281–85.

10. "Battle Cruisers as Ocean Liners,"*Scientific American*, February 1922, 99.

11. RG 80, SecNav 1916–26, File 3809, Box 9.

12. RG 80, SecNav 1916–26, File 3809, Box 9.

13. "A Use for Uncle Sam's Scrapped Ships," *Illustrated World* 37 (May 1922): 403–5.

14. "Would Sink Ships to Make New England Winters Milder," *Washington Post*, April 9, 1922, 64.

15. RG 80, SecNav 1916–26, File 3809, Box 9.

16. RG 80, SecNav 1916–26, File 3809, Box 9.

17. "Outlaw the Submarines," *New York Times*, November 17, 1921, 16.

18. RG 80, SecNav 1916–26, File 3809, Box 9.

19. RG 80, SecNav 1916–26, File 3809, Box 9.

20. RG 80, SecNav 1916–26, File 3809, Box 9.

21. RG 80, SecNav 1916–26, File 3809, Box 9.

22. "The Fleet in the Air," *New York Times,* August 22, 1921, 12.

23. Commander E.G. Allen, USN, "Weapons at Sea: The Place of Aircraft and the Battleship," *Scientific American*, July 9, 1921, 25 etc.

24. RG 80, SecNav 1916–26, File 3809, Box 9.

25. RG 80, SecNav 1916–26, File 27219, Box 2160.

26. "Bombing the Battleship: Smoke Screens and Phosphorous Bombs Enable the Airman to Make Close-Up Attacks," *Scientific American*, April 1924, 252, 296.

27. RG 19, NBCR 1925–40, File A13-7, Box 99.

28. Miles Martindale, "Two Years of Disarmament," *American Mercury* 1, no. 1 (January 1924): 62–68.

29. "A Land Armament Basis," *Washington Star*, February 19, 1922-22.

30. "New Weapons of War," *New York Times*, November 27, 1921, XX-10.

31. "Japanese Naval Construction," *New York Times*, June 29, 1922, 14.

32. "Outranged by British," *Los Angeles Times*, December 21, 1922, 12.

33. Hall, *Britain, America and Arms Control*, 52–54.

34. "Mr. Hoover and Naval Disarmament," *The New Republic*, November 28, 1928, 28–29.

35. RG 80, SecNav 1926–40, File A13-7, Box 541.

36. H. N. Brailsford, "Abolish the Battleship," *The New Republic*, December 25, 1929, 132–34.

37. Robert Kaufman, *Arms Control during the Pre-Nuclear Era* (New York: Columbia University Press, 1990), 135–38.

38. "Disarming Disarmament," *Christian Science Monitor*, November 25, 1930, 20.

39. "Aggressive Weapons," *Washington Post*, April 13, 1932, 6.

40. O. W. Riegel, "Will We Stay Out of the Next War? III: The Propaganda Balance Sheet," *The New Republic*, August 14, 1935, 11–13.

41. Advertisement, *Literary Digest*, November 27, 1937, inside front cover.

42. Paul Koistinen, *Planning War, Pursuing Peace: The Political Economy of American Warfare, 1920–1939* (Lawrence: University Press of Kansas, 1998), 262–65.

43. RG 407, AAG 1926–39, 381 National Defense, Box 2310.

44. RG 407, AAG 1926–39, 381 National Defense, Box 2310.

45. RG 407, AAG 1926–39, 381 National Defense, Box 2314.

46. Harry Carr, "The Lancer," *Los Angeles Times*, April 12, 1935, A1.

47. RG 407, AAG 1926–39, 381 National Defense, Box 2312.

48. RG 407, AAG 1926–39, 381 National Defense, Box 2314.

49. RG 80, SecNav 1926–40, File A13-7, Box 541.

50. RG 407, AAG 1926–39, 381 National Defense, Box 2313.

51. RG 407, AAG 1926–39, 381 National Defense, Box 2310.

Chapter 6. Vulnerable Giant: Defending the Homeland

1. Walter Eddington, "Japan Wants Sea Power to Enforce Supremacy in Asia," *Washington Post*, January 26, 1936, B9.

2. Hanson Baldwin, "Powerful Forces Are Pushing Japan Forward," *New York Times*, August 1, 1937, E3.

3. RG 38, ONI Administrative 1942–46, A13-7, Box 343.

4. Hanson Baldwin, "The Pacific Game Goes Grimly On," *New York Times*, March 13, 1938, 8-1.

5. Waldo Drake, "Why Naval Ratios Can't Halt Japan," *Los Angeles Times*, December 30, 1934, J8.

6. "National Defense," *New York Times*, April 19, 1936, E9.

7. RG 38, CNO Division of Naval Intelligence, 1929–42, File A16-1, Box 236.

8. RG 407, AAG 1926–39, Decimal 381 National Defense, Box 2311.

9. RG 407, AAG 1926–39, Decimal 381 National Defense, Box 2311.

10. "How Japan Could Attack America," *San Francisco Examiner*, November 7, 1937.

11. RG 407, AAG 1926–39, Decimal 381 National Defense, Box 2308.

12. Vernon Nash, "The Japanese-American War Myth," *The Nation*, December 11, 1935, 671–72.

13. Lewis, *Seacoast Fortifications of the United States*, 115–16.

14. RG 407, AAG 1926–39, Decimal 381 National Defense, Box 2310.

15. RG 407, AAG 1926–39, Decimal 381 National Defense, Box 2307.

16. RG 407, AAG 1926–39, Decimal 381 National Defense, Box 2311.

17. RG 407, AAG 1926–39, Decimal 381 National Defense, Box 2313.

18. RG 407, AAG 1926–39, Decimal 381 National Defense, Box 2307.

19. Letter to Chief of Staff to Rep. Overton Brooks, January 10, 1938.

20. RG 407, AAG 1926–39, Decimal 381 National Defense, Box 2312.

21. RG 38, CNO Division of Naval Intelligence, 1929–42, File A16-1, Box 237.

22. RG 38, CNO Division of Naval Intelligence, 1929–42, File A16-1, Box 236.

23. RG 407, AAG 1926–39, Decimal 381 National Defense, Box 2305.

24. Toshio Yatsushiro, *Politics and Cultural Values: The World War II Japanese Relocation Centers and the United States Government* (New York: Arno Press, 1978), 182–83.

25. "Air Defense Bases, to Authorize the Selection, Construction, Installation and Modification of Permanent Stations and Depots for the Army Air Corps, and Frontier Air-Defense Generally," Hearings Before the Committee on Military Affairs, House of Reps, 74th Cong. 1st Sess., February 11–13, 1935, 136–37.

26. Myron Goldsmith, "Can Our West Coast Be Invaded?" *Liberty Magazine*, May 6, 1933, 5–9.

27. RG 407, AAG 1926–39, Decimal 381 National Defense, Box 2311.

28. RG 407, AAG 1926–39, Decimal 381 National Defense, Box 2311.

29. RG 38, CNO Division of Naval Intelligence, 1929–42, File A16-1, Box 236.

30. RG 38, ONI Administrative 1942–46, A13-7, Box 343.

31. RG 407, AAG 1926–39, Decimal 381 National Defense, Box 2309.

32. RG 38, ONI Administrative 1942–46, A13-7, Box 344.

33. Nicholas Roosevelt, "U.S. Must Be Ready to Defend Panama Canal, Our Most Vital—and Most Vulnerable Spot," *Washington Post*, January 29, 1939, B 6.

34. R. S. Fendrick, "One Lone Enemy Could Destroy Panama Canal," *Boston Herald*, May 27, 1934, B5.

35. "Two Baskets or One?" *Los Angeles Times*, August 5, 1939, A4.

36. "A Sea Level Canal," *New York Times*, December 11, 1938, E9.

37. RG 407, AAG 1926–39, Decimal 381 National Defense, Box 2309.

38. RG 407, AAG 1926–39, Decimal 381 National Defense, Box 2312.

39. Stuart Chase, "The Two-Hour War," *The New Republic*, May 8, 1929, 325–27.

40. "Experts Depict Helpless Cities during Air War," *Chicago Tribune*, October 20, 1934, 4.

41. William Gilman, "Planes Will Drop Death, Terror and Pestilence from Skies in Next War," *Washington Post*, March 3, 1935, F4.

42. "Bogey of Aerial Bombardment," *Scientific American*, June 1923, 374.

43. H. G. Bishop, "Terror from the Sky: Reality or Bogy?" *New York Times,* March 25, 1934, SM4.

44. "Bombing U.S. City with Gas Is Urged at Chemist's Meet," *Washington Post*, July 7, 1927, 3.

45. RG 407, AAG 1926–39, Decimal 381 National Defense, Box 2309.

46. RG 407, AAG 1926–39, Decimal 381 National Defense, Box 2311.

47. RG 407, AAG 1926–39, Decimal 381 National Defense, Box 2309.

48. RG 407, AAG 1926–39, Decimal 381 National Defense, Box 2306.

49. RG 407, AAG 1926–39, Decimal 381 National Defense, Box 2310.

Chapter 7. Balancing Act: The Era of Semibelligerency

1. "Arms Against War," *Scientific American*, April 1940, 203.

2. "Amateur Strategists," *New York Times*, May 1, 1938, E8.

3. "Lothian Says Nazis Want British Navy," *New York Times*, June 5, 1940, 7.

4. Mark Sullivan, "Lindbergh Errs," *Washington Post*, May 21, 1940, 9.

5. Livingston Hartley, "Atlantic Defense, a Deal with Britain," *Washington Post*, July 28, 1940, B7.

6. RG 38, ONI Administrative 1942–46, A13-7, Box 343.

7. James Leutze, *Bargaining for Supremacy: Anglo-American Naval Collaboration, 1937–1941* (Chapel Hill: University of North Carolina Press, 1977), 75–85.

8. RG 38, CNO Division of Naval Intelligence 1929–42, A16-1, Box 237.

9. RG 407, AAG 1926–39, Decimal 385, Box 2326.

10. RG 38, ONI Administrative 1942–46, A13-7, Box 343.

11. John Flynn, "Can Hitler Invade America?" *Reader's Digest*, April 1941, 1–6.

12. John White, "South America's Arms Weak," *New York Times*, June 2, 1940, 70.

13. RG 38, CNO Division of Naval Intelligence 1929–42, A16-1, Box 239.

14. RG 38, CNO Division of Naval Intelligence 1929–42, A16-1, Box 237.

15. RG 71, Bureau of Yards and Docks 1925–42, File A13-7, Box 103.

16. "Blitzkrieg Machines Give Germans Victory over Allies in Norway," *Life*, May 13, 1940, 25.

17. "Parachute Troops Rain Down behind Dutch-Belgian Lines," *Life*, May 20, 1940, 29.

18. "Women's Rifle Corps Formed for Defense," *New York Times*, May 23, 1940, 18.

19. RG 38, CNO Division of Naval Intelligence 1929–42, A16-1, Box 237.

20. RG 71, Bureau of Yards and Docks 1925–42, File A13-7, Box 103.

21. RG 38, CNO Division of Naval Intelligence 1929–42, A16-1, Box 237.

22. James Peck, "Helldivers," *Scientific American*, October 1940, 186–88.

23. RG 74, Navy Bureau of Ordnance Restricted January 1940–April 1942, A13-7, Box 86.

24. RG 407, AAG 1926–39, Decimal 381 National Defense, Box 2305.

25. Ian Hogg, *Anti-Aircraft: A History of Air Defense* (London: Macdonald and Jane's, 1978), 107.

26. Alfred Price, *Sky Battles! Dramatic Air Warfare Actions* (London: Arms & Armor Press, 1993), 40–41.

27. RG 38, ONI Administrative 1942–46, A13-7, Box 346.

28. RG 167, NIC, 1940–46, Box 126.

29. "What the Bases Mean," *Time*, September 16, 1940, 18.

30. RG 38, CNO Division of Naval Intelligence 1929–42, A16-1, Box 238.

31. RG 38, CNO Division of Naval Intelligence 1929–42, A16-1, Box 237.

32. RG 38, CNO Division of Naval Intelligence 1929–42, A16-1, Box 239.

33. Hanson Baldwin, "Bridge of Ships to Britain a Vital Factor in War," *New York Times*, March 23, 1941, E3.

34. "Move for Defense," *New York Times*, November 10, 1940, E9.

35. Robert Devine, *The Reluctant Belligerent: American Entry into World War II* (New York: Wiley & Sons, 1965), 111–13.

36. "The Atlantic Sea Lane," *The New Republic*, March 31, 1941, 423.

37. Patrick Abbazia, *Mr. Roosevelt's Navy: The Private War of the U.S. Atlantic Fleet, 1939–1942* (Annapolis, MD: Naval Institute Press, 1975), 174–75.

38. Joseph Alsop and Robert Kintner, "Weakness of the Patrol System," *Washington Post*, May 1, 1941, 15.

39. RG 38, CNO Division of Naval Intelligence 1929–42, A16-1, Box 239.

40. RG 38, CNO Division of Naval Intelligence 1929–42, A16-1, Box 239.

41. RG 38, ONI Administrative 1942–46, A13-7, Box 343.

42. Earl Hanson, "Should Uncle Sam Adopt Greenland?" *Christian Science Monitor Weekly Magazine*, May 18, 1940, 8–9.

43. Dan van der Vat, *The Atlantic Campaign: World War II's Great Struggle at Sea* (New York: Harper & Row, 1988), 181–82.

44. RG 71, File Bureau of Yards and Docks 1925–42, A13-7, Box 103.

45. Terry Hughes and John Costello, *The Battle of the Atlantic* (New York: Dial Press, 1977), 176–77.

46. Allen Millett and Peter Maslowski, *For the Common Defense: A Military History of the United States* (New York: The Free Press, 1984), 197.

47. "Action in the Pacific Is Regarded as Road to Peace," *New York Times*, November 24, 1940, E10.

48. RG 38, CNO Division of Naval Intelligence 1929–42, A16-1, Box 238.

49. "Singapore and the English Channel," *The New Republic*, December 16, 1940, 827.

50. RG 38, CNO Division of Naval Intelligence 1929–42, A16-1, Box 238.

51. Ian Cowman, *Dominion or Decline: Anglo-American Naval Relations on the Pacific, 1937–1941* (Oxford: Berg, 1996), 179–80.

52. Frederick Oliver, "Why the Fleet Should Go to Singapore, a Naval View," *Christian Science Monitor Weekly Magazine*, November 2, 1940, 3.

53. RG 407, AAG Classified 1940–42, Decimal 381 National Defense, Box 667.

54. RG 38, CNO Division of Naval Intelligence 1929–42, A16-1, Box 238.

Chapter 8. Dangerous Minds: Fear and Fanaticism in Total War

1. Stuart Chase, "Second Call for Inventions!" *Reader's Digest*, March 1942, 29.

2. Office of War Information, "Wanted: Inventive Ideas," ca. 1944, RG 38, Navy Commander-in-Chief Restricted 1944, File A13-7, Box 774.

3. Lloyd Douglas, "Mental Armament for Civilians," *Reader's Digest*, February 1942, 5.

4. "Citizens Receive Corrective Facts in Rumor Clinic," *Christian Science Monitor*, December 26, 1942, 7.

5. RG 38, ONI 1942–46, File A13-7QQ, Box 343.

6. Robert Mullen, "Liquor-Loose Lips Spur Call for Prohibition," *Christian Science Monitor*, February 20, 1942, 1.

7. RG 72, Navy Bureau of Aeronautics 1925–42, File A13-7, vol. 5, Box 794.

8. RG 38, ONI 1942–46, File A13-7QQ, Box 344.

9. RG 407, AAG Classified 1943–45, Decimal 385, Box 2453.

10. RG 167, NIC, 1940–46, Box 190.

11. RG 18, AAF 1939–42, Decimal 400.111, Box 601.

12. Roscoe Drummond and Glen Perry, "How Our Forces Will Meet Invasion," *Saturday Evening Post*, August 29, 1942, 9–10 etc.

13. RG 80, SecNav/CNO Confidential 1942, File A13-7, Box 398.

14. RG 165, OPD 1942–45, File 095, case 198, Box 386.

15. RG 38, ONI 1942–46, File A13-7QQ, Box 345.

16. RG 165, OPD 1942–45, Decimal 095, case 44, Box 385.

17. RG 38, ONI 1942–46, File A13-7QQ, Box 344.

18. RG 38, ONI 1942–46, File A13-7QQ, Box 343.

19. "Capital Straws," *Newsweek*, June 15, 1942, 11.

20. Donald Mitchell, "Shipyards and U-Boats," *Nation*, August 22, 1942, 148–50.

21. RG 38, ONI 1942–46, File A13-7, Box 341.

22. RG 38, ONI 1942–46, File A13-7, Box 343.

23. RG 167, NIC, 1940–46, Box 116.

24. RG 167, NIC, 1940–46, Box 46.

25. RG 38, ONI 1942–46, File A13-7, Box 344.

26. RG 38, ONI 1942–46, File A13-7, Box 343.

27. RG 38, ONI 1942–46, File A13-7, Box 345.

28. "39 Die on Tanker Fired off Curacao," *New York Times*, February 22, 1942, 19.

29. RG 167, NIC, 1940–46, Box 117.

30. RG 407, Classified AAG 1943–45, Decimal 385, Box 2453.

31. RG 167, NIC, 1940–46, Box 158.

32. RG 167, NIC, 1940–46, Box 3.

33. Jan Morrison, "New Light on the Japanese," *Science Digest*, March 1944, 54–56.

34. John Dower, *War Without Mercy: Race and Power in the Pacific War* (New York: Pantheon Books, 1986), 123–33.

35. Selden Menefee, "How to Speak to Japan," *The Nation* 156, January 2, 1943, 17–18.

36. "Good-Luck Belts," *New York Times*, January 11, 1942, SM26.

37. RG 167, NIC, 1940–46, Box 3.

38. Marcia Wynn, "How to Win the War," *Chicago Tribune*, January 22, 1944, 12.

39. RG 38, ONI 1942–46, File A13-7QQ, Box 343.

40. RG 167, NIC 1940–46, Box 3.

41. RG 319, Army G-2 1941–48, Decimal 385, Box 958.

42. RG 127, Marine Corps Commandant 1939–50, File 2515-15, Box 2194.

43. Neal Stanford, "Should U.S. Bomb or 'Use' the Emperor?" *Christian Science Monitor*, December 11, 1944, 1, 9.

44. Jesse Steiner, "Shall We Bomb Hirohito's Palace?" *New York Times*, March 11, 1945, SM5.

45. RG 18, AAF 1939–42, Decimal 385, Box 597.

46. "Japan's V-Weapon," *Christian Science Monitor*, June 1, 1945, 18.

47. Edwin Hoyt, *The Kamikazes* (New York: Arbor House, 1983), 283.

48. RG 72, Navy Bureau of Aeronautics 1943–45, File A13-7, Box 459.

49. Allen Raymond, "The Rising Sun Pins Its Hopes on Jap Suicide Killers," *Popular Science*, June 1945, 65–67.

50. Jesse Steiner, "Shall We Bomb Hirohito's Palace?" *New York Times*, March 11, 1945, SM8, 45–46.

51. HSTL, WHCF, File 197, Box 685.

52. Polyzoides, "Chiefs' Suicides Spur to Fanaticism of Japs," *Los Angeles Times*, June 29, 1945, 4.

53. Barnet Nover, "Hungry Japan: The Blockade and the Food Supply," *Washington Post*, July 14, 1945, 4.

54. RG 167, NIC, 1940–46, Box 2.

55. "Military Review," *The New Republic*, July 9, 1945, 37–38.

56. RG 38, Navy Commander-in-Chief Restricted 1944, File A13-7, Box 774.

57. Ernest Lindley, "Real Victory Not Assured by Blockade," *Washington Post*, June 3, 1945, B5.

58. RG 165, OPD 1942–45, Entry 418, Decimal 385, Box 1319.

59. RG 165, OPD 1942–45, Entry 418, Decimal 385, Box 1319.

Chapter 9. Bombs Away! America Rules the Skies

1. Michael Sherry, *The Rise of American Air Power: The Creation of Armageddon* (New Haven, CT: Yale University Press, 1987), 50–53.

2. Wellwood Beall, "Flying Battleships Will Win the War," *Popular Mechanics*, July 1942, 42–45 etc.

3. "Festung Europa," *Fortune* 128 (August 1943): 109–11 etc.

4. Francis Drake, "Why Don't We Really Try to Bomb Germany Out of the War?" *Reader's Digest*, May 1943, 35–39.

5. RG 165, OPD 1942–45, Decimal 385, Box 1318.

6. RG 18, AAF 1942–44, Decimal 400.111, Box 996.

7. Robin Neillands, *The Bomber War: The Allied Air Offensive against Nazi Germany* (New York: The Overlook Press, 2001), 184, 198.

8. "The Subs Are Still Coming," *Time*, January 11, 1943, 25.

9. RG 38, ONI 1942–46, File A13-7, Box 343.

10. RG 18, AAF 1942–44, Decimal 400.111, Box 1003.

11. RG 167, NIC 1940–46, Box 3.

12. RG 18, AAF 1942–44, Decimal 400.111, Box 1002.

13. RG 167, NIC 1940–46, Box 44.

14. RG 18, AAF 1942–44, Decimal 400.111, Box 1002.

15. RG 167, NIC 1940–46, Box 3.

16. Edgar Snow, "This War Will Be Won from the Sky? The Results Are Impressive," *Saturday Evening Post*, November 13, 1943, 21, 109–10.

17. RG 167, NIC 1940–46, Box 2.

18. RG 18, AAF 1942–44, Decimal 400.111, Box 997.

19. RG 18, AAF 1942–44, Decimal 400.111, Box 1003.

20. RG 165, OPD 1942–45, Decimal 095, Box 385.

21. RG 165, OPD 1942–45, Decimal 385, Box 1319.

22. "Flying Battlewagons," *Popular Mechanics,* May 1943, 8–12.

23. "Unhappy Valley," *Newsweek,* July 5, 1943, 25–27.

24. Boeing Ad; "How Can They Come Back?" *Newsweek*, March 6, 1944, 5.

25. "New Lessons Learned," *Time,* May 17, 1943, 28.

26. RG 18, AAF 1942–44, Decimal 400.111, Box 999.

27. Martin Bowman, *Castles in the Air* (Washington, DC: Brassey's, 2000), 63.

28. RG 18, AAF 1942–44, Decimal 400.111, Box 999.

29. "Air War of 1943 Set Great Record, but Failed in Knocking Out Reich," *Newsweek,* January 10, 1944, 25.

30. RG 18, AAF 1942–44, Decimal 400.111, Box 999.

31. RG 18, AAF 1942–44, Decimal 400.111, Box 1005.

32. RG 18, AAF 1942–44, Decimal 400.111, Box 1000.

33. RG 18, AAF 1942–44, Decimal 400.111, Box 1000.

34. RG 18, AAF 1942–44, Decimal 400.111, Box 998.

35. RG 167, NIC 1940–46, Box 188.

36. RG 18, AAF 1939–42, Decimal 400.111, Box 599.

37. RG 167, NIC 1940–46, Box 190.

38. RG 167, NIC 1940–46, Box 190.

39. RG 167, NIC 1940–46, Box 192.

40. RG 167, NIC 1940–46, Box 3.

41. RG 18, AAF 1942–44, Decimal 400.111, Box 1000.

42. RG 18, AAF 1942–44, Decimal 400.111, Box 1002.

43. Alan Michie, "What's Holding Up the Air Offensive against Germany?" *Reader's Digest,* February 1943, 21–28.

44. "The Balance Sheet of Bombing," *Chicago Tribune,* January 31, 1943, 16.

45. RG 72, Navy Bureau of Aeronautics 1925–42, File A13-7, Box 794.

46. RG 167, NIC 1940–46, Box 2.

47. RG 167, NIC 1940–46, Box 88.

48. RG 167, NIC 1940–46, Box 88.

49. RG 18, AAF 1942–44, Decimal 400.111, Box 1006.

50. RG 167, NIC 1940–46, Box 44.

51. RG 167, NIC 1940–46, Box 44.

52. RG 18, AAF 1942–44, Decimal 400.111, Box 1003.

53. RG 167, NIC 1940–46, Box 43.

54. RG 167, NIC 1940–46, Box 189.

55. Martin Sommers, "The Buzz Bomb Will Revolutionize Warfare," *Saturday Evening Post,* September 23, 1944, 15 etc.

56. RG 38, Navy Commander-in-Chief Restricted 1944, File A13-7, Box 774.

Chapter 10. Hit The Beach! Invasion and Liberation

1. "Our Grand Strategy," *The Nation* 153, December 13, 1941, 600–601.
2. "Tough Baby from Moscow," *Time*, May 11, 1942, 17.
3. G. A. Borgese, "A.E.F. to Siberia," *The Nation* 154, April 11, 1942, 417–18.
4. RG 18, AAF 1942–44, Decimal 400.111, Box 1006.
5. Donald Mitchell, "Strategies for Spring," *The Nation* 154, March 28, 1942, 361–62.
6. RG 38, Navy Commander-in-Chief Restricted 1942, File A13-7, Box 34.
7. Gunnar Leistikow, "Invasion via Norway," *The Nation* 155, August 1, 1942, 93–94.
8. RG 165, OPD 1942–45, Decimal 385, Box 1318.
9. Mallory Brown, "Allies Pressed to Occupy Madagascar," *Christian Science Monitor*, March 18, 1942, 7.
10. RG 165, OPD 1942–45, Decimal 385, Box 1318.
11. RG 319, Army G-2 1941–48, Decimal 385, Box 956.
12. Herbert Rosinski, "How Africa Changed the War," *The Nation* 155, December 5, 1942, 612–14.
13. Donald Mitchell, "The Coming Battle of Italy," *The Nation* 156, June 12, 1943, 832–33.
14. Donald Mitchell, "The Red Army's Offensive," *The Nation* 157, September 4, 1943, 255–66.
15. Hanson Baldwin, "Invasion: The Five Great Problems," *New York Times*, May 14, 1944, SM5–7, etc.
16. J. F. C. Fuller, "Tactics and Politics on the Russian Front," *Newsweek*, May 1, 1944, 25.
17. Samuel Morrison, *History of United States Naval Operations in World War II, Volume VII: Aleutians, Gilberts and Marshalls, June 1942–April 1944* (Boston: Little, Brown & Company, 1962), 182.
18. Ronald Spector, *Eagle Against the Sun: The American War with Japan* (New York: The Free Press, 1985), 266.
19. "Global War Promises U.S. Much More Blood and Tears," *Newsweek*, December 13, 1943, 42–44.
20. Donald Mitchell, "Germany at Bay," *The Nation* 158, Feburary 5, 1944, 151–53.
21. "More 'Tarawas' Must Be Faced, General Warns," *Chicago Tribune*, December 18, 1943, 2.
22. Quentin Reynolds, "Invasion," *Collier's*, April 8, 1944, 16–17, 53, etc.
23. "Festung Europa," *Fortune* 28, no. 2 (August 1943): 109–111, etc.
24. "Senator Chandler Sees Invasion as 'Huge and Tragic Tarawa' hair," *Washington Post*, December 26, 1943, M2.
25. RG 165, OPD 1942–45, Decimal 385, Box 1319.
26. Drew Middleton, "Bombers' Invasion Role Important, but Limited," *New York Times*, May 14, 1944, E5.

27. RG 165, OPD 1942–45, Decimal 385, Box 1393.
28. Ernest Lindley, "Thoughts on the Use of Gas in Warfare," *Newsweek,* December 20, 1943, 24.
29. RG 18, AAF 1942–44, Decimal 400.111, Box 998.
30. RG 167, NIC 1940–46, Box 116.
31. RG 167, NIC 1940–46, Box 2.
32. RG 167, NIC 1940–46, Box 3.
33. Advertisement, *Time,* February 7, 1944, inside front cover.
34. RG 38, Navy Commander-in-Chief Restricted 1944, File A13-7, Box 744.
35. RG 167, NIC 1940–46, Box 3.
36. RG 127, Marine Corps Commandant 1939–50, File 2515-20, Box 2195.
37. Hal Borland, "How Strong Is Germany's Fortress Europe?" *Popular Science,* January 1944, 49–53, etc.
38. "Invasion Tactics: A D-Day View of What an Invader Faces and How He Plans to Win," *Fortune* 29, no. 3 (March 1944): 124–31.
39. RG 167, NIC 1940–46, Box 49.
40. RG 167, NIC 1940–46, Box 49.
41. RG 18, AAF 1942–44, Decimal 400.111, Box 1000.
42. RG 167, NIC 1940–46, Box 49.
43. RG 167, NIC 1940–46, Box 49.
44. RG 18, AAF 1942–44, Decimal 400.111, Box 1002.
45. RG 167, NIC 1940–46, Box 3.
46. RG 167, NIC 1940–46, Box 2.
47. Henry Hazlitt, "Helicopters for Victory," *The Nation* 155, August 15, 1942, 129–31.
48. RG 167, NIC 1940–46, Box 2.
49. "Air-Borne Troops Will Establish Invasion 'Front' Behind Beaches," *New York Times,* April 25, 1944, 1.
50. RG 167, NIC 1940–46, Box 3.
51. RG 18, AAF 1942–44, Decimal 400.111, Box 1004.
52. "Ailing Europe's Nazi Doctors Plagued by Symptoms of Unrest," *Newsweek,* May 25, 1942, 36–38.
53. RG 38, ONI 1942–46, File A13-7, Box 343.
54. "Sten Gun to Be Forerunner of Invasion," *Popular Science,* September 1943, 54–55.
55. H. A. DeWeerd, "Guns for Europe's Guerrillas," *The Nation* 154, February 21, 1942, 217–18.
56. RG 407, AAG Classified, 1940–42, File 385, Box 677.
57. RG 127, US Marine Corps Commandant, 1939–50, File 2515-20, Box 2195.
58. "Hard Winter Coming," *The Nation* 159, December 23, 1944, 760–61.
59. RG 165, OPD 1942–45, Entry 418, Decimal 385, Box 1319.
60. RG 167, NIC 1940–46, Box 110.

Chapter 11. Red Hordes and Radiation: The Cold War Begins

1. Arthur Compton, "Atom Is Force to Destroy—or Humanize Man," *Washington Post*, October 28, 1945, B1.
2. "Atomic Bomb Stirs Thinking," *Los Angeles Times*, October 10, 1945, A4.
3. Daniel Yergin, *Shattered Peace: The Origins of the Cold War* (New York: Penguin Books, 1977), 238–40.
4. "Beyond the Bomb," *Time*, June 24, 1946, 25.
5. Lawrence Freedman, "The First Two Generations of Nuclear Strategists," in *Makers of Modern Strategy*, ed. Peter Paret (Princeton, NJ: Princeton University Press, 1986), 737.
6. RG 319, Army Plans and OPD 1946–48, Decimal 385, Box 404.
7. RG 80, SecNav Forrestal Correspondence 1940–47, Box 72.
8. Harry Davis, "When Can the Atom Be Put to Work?" *New York Times*, December 9, 1945, 90.
9. RG 80, SecNav Forrestal Correspondence 1940–47, Box 72.
10. HSTL, WHCF, File 692A, Box 1528.
11. RG 167, NIC 1940–46, Box 192.
12. "Bikini: Breath-Holding before a Blast—Could It Split the Earth?" *Newsweek*, July 1, 1946, 20.
13. RG 80, SecNav Forrestal Correspondence, 1940–47, Box 72.
14. "Model T at Crossroads," *Time*, March 11, 1946, 52–56.
15. RG 319, Army Plans and OPD 1946–48, Decimal 385, Box 404.
16. Walter LaFeber, *America, Russia, and the Cold War, 1945–1971* (New York: John Wiley & Sons, 1972), 79–85.
17. Stanley Weintraub, *MacArthur's War: Korea and the Undoing of an American Hero* (New York: The Free Press, 2000), 250.
18. RG 330, Office of Secretary of Defense July–December 1950, File 381 National Defense, Box 596.
19. HSTL, WHCF, File 471B, Box 1306.
20. Polyzoides, "Reds Write Korea Off as Bad Gamble," *Los Angeles Times*, October 16, 1950, 4.
21. "Withdraw from Pyongyang Line and Manchuria Border," *Chicago Tribune*, December 3, 1950, 1; "Million Reds on Heels of U.N. Retreat," *Los Angeles Times*, December 5, 1950, 1.
22. Hanson Baldwin, "Basic Facts in Korea," *New York Times*, May 23, 1951, 6.
23. Walter Simmons, "Expect Chinese to Pour 'Human Sea' at Yanks," *Chicago Tribune*, November 6, 1950, 9.
24. RG 407, AAG 1951–52, Decimal 385, Box 677.
25. RG 407, AAG 1951–52, Decimal 385, Box 677.
26. RG 341, Air Force Deputy Chief of Staff—Plans 1942–54, File 095, Box 36.
27. RG 319, Army Chief of Staff 1950, Decimal 095, Box 562.

28. "Battle of Korea," *Time*, January 5, 1951, 15.
29. RG 407, AAG 1951–52, Decimal 385, Box 677.
30. "Korean Reds Mass for Attack; GOP Charges Truman Failure," *Christian Science Monitor*, August 14, 1950, 1.
31. RG 341, Air Force Deputy Chief of Staff—Plans 1942–54, File 095, Box 32.
32. "Chinese Hordes Widen Wedge in U.N. Defense," *Los Angeles Times*, November 29, 1950, 1.
33. RG 319, Army Chief of Staff 1951–52, Decimal 095, Box 647.
34. RG 319, Army Chief of Staff 1950, Decimal 095, Box 563.
35. Hanson Baldwin, "Air Power in Korea—III," *New York Times*, November 29, 1951, 6.
36. "War in Korea Takes New Tack; Strew Nails to Pierce Tires," *Christian Science Monitor*, February 7, 1951, 7.
37. Max Hastings, *The Korean War* (New York: Simon and Schuster, 1987), 172.
38. RG 341, Air Force Deputy Chief of Staff—Plans 1942–54, File 095, Box 36.
39. "Mud for the Foe," *Los Angeles Times*, February 18, 1951, B4.
40. RG 407, AAG 1949–50, Decimal 385, Box 710.
41. Walter Lippman, "Limited War," *Washington Post*, April 17, 1951, 15.
42. "Korea Can Be Held by U.N.: Strategy Geared to Long Fight," *U.S. News and World Report*, January 12, 1951, 11–12.
43. "Killing," *Wall Street Journal*, February 15, 1951, 8.
44. HSTL, WHCF, File 471B, Box 1307.
45. HSTL, WHCF, File 471B, Box 1307.
46. HSTL, WHCF, File 692A, Box 1528.
47. "Chiang's Troops to Korea?" *The Nation* 176, January 17, 1953, 41–43.
48. RG 407, AAG 1951–52, Decimal 385, Box 677.
49. RG 407, AAG 1949–50, Decimal 385, Box 710.
50. RG 407, AAG 1951–52, Decimal 385, Box 677.
51. HSTL, WHCF, File 427, Box 1285.
52. HSTL, WHCF, File 427, Box 1285.
53. "The Prisoners Speak," *Time*, May 5, 1952, 30–31.
54. Raymond Moley, "We Are Held Prisoner by Our Own Prisoners," *Los Angeles Times*, August 16, 1952, A4.
55. HSTL, WHCF, File 471B, Box 1351.
56. HSTL, WHCF, File 471B, Box 1307.
57. HSTL, WHCF, File 471B, Box 1306.
58. RG 407, AAG 1951–52, Decimal 385, Box 677.
59. RG 407, AAG 1951–52, Decimal 385, Box 677.
60. Hanson Baldwin, "Two Complex Disputes Hold Up Korea Truce," *New York Times*, March 30, 1952, E5.
61. RG 407, AAG 1951–52, Decimal 385, Box 677.

Chapter 12. Conclusion: TV Wars, Tonkin, and Beyond

1. William Beecher, "Bedbug May Help to Hunt Vietcong," *New York Times*, June 6, 1966, 11.
2. Fred Hoffman, "Ideas Come by the Score on How to Win Viet War," *New York Times*, October 11, 1965, C2.
3. LBJL, WHCF, File ND19/C0312, Box 234.
4. LBJL, WHCF, File ND19/C0312, Box 250.
5. Carl Rowan, "U.S. Moves Ahead in War to Win Vietnam's Heart, Mind," *Los Angeles Times*, September 4, 1966, B7.
6. Richard M. Nixon Papers, WHCF, File CO-165, Box 85.
7. LBJL, WHCF, File ND19/C0312, Box 248.
8. LBJL, WHCF, File ND19/C0312, Box 282.
9. Richard M. Nixon Papers, WHCF, File ND18-3/CO-165, Box 10.
10. Stanley Karnow, *Vietnam: A History* (New York: The Viking Press, 1983), 653–55.
11. Steve Forbes, "Spider Webs in the Sky," *Forbes*, November 26, 2001, 33.

Bibliography

Abbazia, Patrick. *Mr. Roosevelt's Navy: The Private War of the U.S. Atlantic Fleet, 1939–1942.* Annapolis, MD: Naval Institute Press, 1975.

Berkove, Laurence, ed. *Skepticism and Dissent: Selected Journalism 1898–1901 by Ambrose Bierce.* Ann Arbor, MI: UMI Research Press, 1986.

Berkowitz, Bruce. *Calculated Risks: A Century of Arms Control, Why It Has Failed, and How It Can Be Made to Work.* New York: Simon and Schuster, 1987.

Biggers, W. Watts. "The Germans Are Coming! The Germans Are Coming!" *U.S. Naval Institute Proceedings* 111, no. 6 (June 1985): 38–43.

Bowman, Martin. *Castles in the Air.* Washington, DC: Brassey's, 2000.

Browning, Robert. *Two If By Sea: The Development of American Coastal Defense Policy.* Westport, CT: Greenwood Press, 1983.

Clark, William. *When the U-Boats Came to America.* Boston: Little, Brown, and Company, 1929.

Compton-Hall, Richard. *Submarines and the War at Sea, 1914–1918.* London: Macmillan London, 1991.

Cowie, J. S. Mines, *Minelayers, and Minelaying.* London: Oxford University Press, 1949.

Cowman, Ian. *Dominion or Decline: Anglo-American Naval Relations on the Pacific, 1937–1941.* Oxford: Berg, 1996.

Damiani, Brian. *Advocates of Empire: William McKinley, the Senate and American Expansion 1898–1899.* New York: Garland Publishing, 1987.

Devine, Robert. *The Reluctant Belligerent: American Entry into World War II.* New York: Wiley & Sons, 1965.

Dower, John. *War Without Mercy: Race and Power in the Pacific War.* New York: Pantheon Books, 1986.

Duffy, Christopher. "The Liege Forts." In *The Marshall Cavendish Illustrated Encyclopedia of World War I*, vol. 1. New York: Marshall Cavendish, 1984.

Eisenhower, John. *Intervention! The United States and the Mexican Revolution, 1913–1917.* New York: W. W. Norton & Company, 1993.

Ellis, Mark, and Panikos Panayi. "German Minorities in World War I: A Comparative Study of Britain and the USA." *Ethnic and Racial Studies* 17, no. 2 (April 1994): 238–59.

Fernandez, Ronald. "Getting Germans to Fight Germans: The Americanizers of World War I." *Journal of Ethnic Studies* 9, no. 2 (Summer 1981): 53–68.

Freedman, Lawrence. "The First Two Generations of Nuclear Strategists." In *Makers of Modern Strategy*, edited by Peter Paret. Princeton, NJ: Princeton University Press, 1986.

Freidel, Frank. *The Splendid Little War*. Boston: Little, Brown, 1958.

Frothingham, Thomas. *The Naval History of the Great War: The Stress of Sea Power 1915– 1916*. Cambridge: Harvard University Press, 1925.

Gates, John. *Schoolbooks and Krags: The United States Army in the Philippines, 1898–1902*. Westport, CT: Greenwood Press, 1973.

Goldman, Emily. *Sunken Treaties: Naval Arms Control between the Wars*. University Park, PA: Pennsylvania State University Press, 1994.

Gray, Edwyn. *The Killing Time: The U-boat War, 1914–1918*. London: Seeley, Service & Co., 1972.

Grenville, John. "American Naval Preparations for War with Spain, 1896–1898," *Journal of American Studies* 2, no. 1 (April 1968): 33–47.

Hall, Christopher. *Britain, America, and Arms Control, 1921–37*. New York: St. Martin's Press, 1987.

Halle, Louis. *The United States Acquires the Philippines: Consensus vs. Reality*. Lanham, MD: University Press of America, 1985.

Hastings, Max. *The Korean War*. New York: Simon and Schuster, 1987.

Hogg, Ian. *Anti-Aircraft: A History of Air Defense*. London: Macdonald and Jane's, 1978.

Holzer, Harold. *Dear Mr. Lincoln: Letters to the President*. Reading, MA: Addison-Wesley, 1993.

Hoyt, Edwin. *The Kamikazes*. New York: Arbor House, 1983.

Hughes, Terry, and John Costello. *The Battle of the Atlantic*. New York: Dial Press, 1977.

Karnow, Stanley. *In Our Image: America's Empire in the Philippines*. New York: Random House, 1989. ———. *Vietnam: A History*. New York: The Viking Press, 1983.

Kaufman, Robert. *Arms Control during the Pre-Nuclear Era*. New York: Columbia University Press, 1990.

Keegan, John. *The First World War*. New York: Alfred Knopf, 1999.

Keller, Allan. *The Spanish-American War: A Compact History*. New York: Hawthorn Books, 1969.

Koistinen, Paul. *Planning War, Pursuing Peace: The Political Economy of American Warfare, 1920–1939*. Lawrence: University Press of Kansas, 1998.

LaFeber, Walter. *America, Russia, and the Cold War, 1945–1971*. New York: John Wiley & Sons, 1972.

Lewis, Emanuel. *Seacoast Fortifications of the United States: An Introductory History* Annapolis, MD: Leeward Publications, 1970.

Mallory, Franklin and Ludwig Olson. *The Krag Rifle Story*. Silver Spring, MD: Springfield Research Service, 1979.

McCright, Grady. "Pershing's Airwar in Mexico." *Aviation Quarterly* 5, no. 4 (1979).

McLaughlin, Jack. *To His Excellency Thomas Jefferson: Letters to a President*. New York: W. W. Norton & Company, 1991.

McNeese, Tim. *Remember the Maine! The Spanish-American War Begins*. Greensboro, NC: Morgan Reynolds, 2002.

Melia, Tamara. *"Damn the Torpedoes": A Short History of U.S. Naval Mine Countermeasures, 1777–1991*. Washington, DC: Department of the Navy, 1991.

Messimer, Dwight. *Find and Destroy: Antisubmarine Warfare in World War I*. Annapolis, MD: Naval Institute Press, 2001.

———. *Verschollen: World War I U-boat Losses*. Annapolis, MD: Naval Institute Press, 2002.

Metson, Graham, ed. *The Halifax Explosion December 6, 1917*. Toronto: McGraw-Hill, 1978.

Millett, Allen, and Peter Maslowski. *For the Common Defense: A Military History of the United States*. New York: The Free Press, 1984.

Morrison, Samuel. *History of United States Naval Operations in World War II, Volume VII: Aleutians, Gilberts and Marshalls, June 1942–April 1944*. Boston: Little, Brown & Company, 1962.

Murfett, Malcolm. "Look Back in Anger: The Western Powers and the Washington Conference of 1921–1922." In *Arms Limitation and Disarmament, Restraints on War, 1899–1939*, edited by B.J.C. McKercher. Westport, CT: Praeger Publishers, 1992.

Musicant, Ivan. *Empire by Default: The Spanish-American War and the Dawn of the American Century*. New York: Henry Holt and Company, 1998.

Neillands, Robin. *The Bomber War: The Allied Air Offensive against Nazi Germany*. New York: Overlook Press, 2001.

O'Toole, G.J.A. *The Spanish War: An American Epic—1898*. New York: W. W. Norton & Company, 1984.

Price, Alfred. *Sky Battles! Dramatic Air Warfare Actions*. London: Arms & Armor Press, 1993.

Ritchie, Carson. *Q-Ships*. Suffolk, UK: Terence Dalton Limited, 1985.

Saunders, Anthony. *Weapons of the Trench War, 1914–1918.* Stroud, UK: Sutton Publishing, 1999.

Sherry, Michael. *The Rise of American Air Power: The Creation of Armageddon.* New Haven, CT: Yale University Press, 1987.

Shockley, Philip. *The Krag–Jørgensen Rifle in the Service.* Aledo, IL: World-Wide Gun Report, 1960.

Sims, William. *The Victory at Sea.* New York: Doubleday, Page & Company. Reprint, Annapolis, MD: Naval Institute Press, 1984.

Spector, Ronald. *Eagle against the Sun: The American War with Japan.* New York: The Free Press, 1985.

Stout, Joseph. *Border Conflict: Villistas, Carrancistas, and the Punitive Expedition, 1915–1920.* Fort Worth: Texas Christian University Press, 1999.

Tate, Michael. "Pershing's Pets: Apache Scouts in the Mexican Punitive Expedition of 1916." *New Mexico Historical Review* 66 (January 1991): 59–65.

Trask, David. *The War With Spain in 1898.* Lincoln: University of Nebraska Press, 1996.

van der Vat, Dan. *The Atlantic Campaign: World War II's Great Struggle at Sea.* New York: Harper & Row, 1988.

Washington, George. *The Papers of George Washington.* Revolutionary War Series, vol. 1. Charlottesville: University of Virginia Press, 1985.

Weintraub, Stanley. *MacArthur's War: Korea and the Undoing of an American Hero.* New York: The Free Press, 2000.

Willoughby, William. *Government Organization in War Time and After.* New York: Appleton and Company, 1919.

Yatsushiro, Toshio. *Politics and Cultural Values: The World War II Japanese Relocation Centers and the United States Government.* New York: Arno Press, 1978.

Yergin, Daniel. *Shattered Peace: The Origins of the Cold War.* New York: Penguin Books, 1977.

Index

About the Author

Joel R. Davidson is an attorney in the Washington, D.C., area and a graduate of Yale Law School. He earned a PhD in history from Duke University in 1992. He is the author of *The Unsinkable Fleet: The Politics of U.S. Navy Expansion in World War II* (Naval Institute Press, 1996).